Praise for *The History of Bones*

"A picaresque roller coaster of a story ———————————————— d drugs and the perpetual quest to ret———————

—*The New York Times*

"He is, like it or not, a voice of his generation—a man, with or without a saxophone, who was king in the days before New York was taken over by people without joy in their hearts."

—*The New York Review of Books*

"There is a purity to John Lurie's writing that feels almost spiritual—the stories unspool from him, seemingly effortlessly, with the fluidity of a great jazz player. Lurie has lived many lives—'More than once I have witnessed the inexplicable,' he tells us—and this book moves us through them all."

—NICK FLYNN, author of *Another Bullshit Night in Suck City*

"[*The History of Bones* is] like a post-beat period *Portrait of the Artist as a Young Man*, written from the perspective of a Montaigne, taking stock of a life lived up to this point, figuring out where there was meaning, where there wasn't, and if there is some greater truth to be gleaned that can apply to everyone."

—*Cleveland Review of Books*

"The book is a worthy read if for nothing else than to get a glimpse of lower eastside Manhattan in the dire and dynamic late 1970s and early '80s."

—*California Review of Books*

"No other human's strange struggles and triumphs are like this. I was transfixed reading Lurie's yearning to make sense of it all, slamming his fist through the precious veneer of the early eighties New York art/music scene. Yeeeooooow."

—FLEA, author of *Acid for the Children*

"Lurie weaves a gloriously gritty, informative and entertaining portrait of Downtown NYC in the 1980s."

—*NYS Music*

"He just wanted to make beautiful music. That sounds naive, but John Lurie is and was truly unpretentious. The music he made with the Lounge Lizards and after that in film scores and under a pseudonym Marvin Pontiac is beautiful. It certainly deserves to be re-examined in a new light."

—*All About Jazz*

"Look behind John Lurie's adventure so far and see how it flows from epiphanies: their arrival, their loss, the very possibility of them. Epiphanies consign an artist to life as a hunter-mystic, in a world where the impeccable and the tawdry are equally sacred—a hell of a place, and it's from here that Lurie's candor throws us epiphanies to take away. This is not a book headed for bookshelves; it's coming to crash on your couch."

—DBC PIERRE, author of *Vernon God Little,* winner of the Booker Prize

"Lurie is a master storyteller, a raconteur of the first order. His storytelling weaves its way through everything he does—whether it's his voice over the telephone, a riff or a run on his alto sax, a movie score, a scene-stealing performance, or an explosion of color from his paint brush. Lurie's stories are filled with pathos—all the earthly beauty and ugliness, the sadness and humor is there. The dreams, reality, and randomness, the crazy happenstance of this life."

—*Please Kill Me*

"Drawing on his unruly genius . . . his raucously frank, sardonic, sex-saturated, compulsively detailed, and hard-charging memoir is incandescent."

—*Booklist*

"A fantastic read . . . Lurie is an ace storyteller with perfect pitch."

—*Shelf Awareness*

"An energetic, raucous reprise of an adventurously offbeat life."

—*Publishers Weekly* (starred review)

THE HISTORY OF BONES

THE HISTORY OF BONES

A Memoir

John Lurie

RANDOM HOUSE | NEW YORK

2023 Random House Trade Paperback Edition

Copyright © 2021 by John Lurie

All rights reserved.

Published in the United States by Random House, an imprint and division of
Penguin Random House LLC, New York.

RANDOM HOUSE and the HOUSE colophon are registered trademarks of
Penguin Random House LLC.

Originally published in hardcover in the United States by Random House,
an imprint and division of Penguin Random House LLC, in 2021.

Library of Congress Cataloging-in-Publication Data
Names: Lurie, John, author.
Title: The history of bones: a memoir / John Lurie.
Description: New York: Random House, 2021.
Identifiers: LCCN 2021004403 (print) | LCCN 2021004404 (ebook) |
ISBN 9780399592980 (trade paperback) | ISBN 9780399592997 (ebook)
Subjects: LCSH: Lurie, John | Composers—United States—Biography. | Jazz
musicians—United States—Biography. | Saxophonists—United States—Biography. |
East Village (New York, N.Y.)—Social conditions—20th century. | LCGFT:
Autobiographies.
Classification: LCC ML410.L96365 A3 2021 (print) | LCC ML410.L96365 (ebook) |
DDC 780.82 [B]—dc23
LC record available at https://lccn.loc.gov/2021004403
LC ebook record available at https://lccn.loc.gov/2021004404

Printed in the United States of America on acid-free paper

randomhousebooks.com

987654321

Book design by Susan Turner
Photo inserts design by Stephanie Greenberg

Contents

THE HISTORY OF BONES

1

Boy Boy

Just a speck. At the top of its arc, a mystical thing suspended against blue. Then it would come hurtling down and thwack to the earth. Always out of my reach.

My father could throw a ball, incredibly high, straight up into the air. I loved being hypnotized as it hung up against the sky, this thing that was no longer a ball. It wasn't really even a game of catch, because I could never catch them at that age.

We used to sit on the couch listening to the stinking Red Sox on the radio. I loved the smell of him, there was warmth in it.

"You're a foxy little newspaper."

My dad laughed. He was waking me up to go fishing, and this was something I said that was left over from a dream.

When I was a kid we used to go fishing on Saturday mornings. He'd wake me really early and we'd go out, both so tired we'd be laughing like idiots at everything. Boat stuck in the reeds. Incredibly amusing! You had to be there.

On the drive home, we saw an old lady in a fur coat hunched over the wheel of a convertible sports car. Her white hair flapping wildly in the wind. She pulled alongside us, hovered there for a moment, and then whizzed off, like we were standing still. Tears rolled down my dad's face.

He wasn't much of a fisherman and didn't take it seriously. He just liked to be out in a boat with his son on a nice morning. He called me "Boy Boy."

"You want to go get something to eat, Boy Boy?"

The throws got lower and lower until it wasn't so exciting anymore.

I went to high school in Worcester, Massachusetts. A horrible place, Worcester has a dome over it so that God is not allowed in.

The first thing that emerges when I think of Worcester is a metal pole.

I am familiar with its molecules. I know its deepest essence.

The pole was a railing around someone's front yard on Pleasant Street, near Cotter's Spa. It was about two and a half feet off the ground. Steve Piccolo and I used to try to balance on it and then walk from one end to the other. We'd get halfway, wobble, and then fall off. We never made it all the way to the end. One night, when I was fifteen, we took mushrooms and crossed it several times with ease. That was how I got to know the metal pole on a molecular level. That was the same night we went into Friendly's, grinning insanely, and said, "We'd like to exchange these quarters for ice cream." We held the quarters in the palms of both hands, displaying them like they were gold doubloons.

They threw us out.

The first time I had sex was with a girl named Crystal. I was sixteen and Crystal was, I guess, twenty-five. We were in a hippie crash pad, sitting at this filthy kitchen table strewn with pot seeds and Twinkie wrappers. After the last person had passed out, we found ourselves alone. Crystal was a groupie and very proud of it, so I thought I had a good chance, but had no idea how to go about it. I sat there for a long time, not knowing what to do. Finally, I summoned the courage to take her hand and put it inside my fly. Crystal, not resisting, said with complete indifference, "I guess we can ball." We went into this crummy room with a mattress, with no sheets, on the floor. She took off her clothes. I got on top of her and came in eleven seconds.

Crystal was rumored to have slept with Jimi Hendrix the week before. She gave me gonorrhea. It was nice to have this connection to Jimi through bacterium *Neisseria gonorrhoeae*.

But at that time, my girlfriend was Jeannie, who lived in the neighboring town of Leicester. A waif of a girl with a beautiful face. My parents had rented a cottage one summer on Thompson Pond and that was how I met her. Though I don't remember meeting her or how she became my girlfriend.

After the summer was over, to go out and see her, I'd borrow the family car and drive about thirty minutes. This is how I learned to play the harmonica, driving with one hand and messing on the harmonica with the other.

I'd pick her up at her parents' and we'd drive around. Jeannie would jerk me off while I was driving, but only if I used a certain kind of cologne. I don't wear cologne anymore. I believe that cologne is a good way to gauge somebody's intelligence: The amount of cologne being inversely proportionate to the IQ. But this was high school and I had to have my hand jobs, so I'd splash on enough to kill a small animal before going to see her.

Jeannie called my cock "Everett." She would say that she didn't like Everett because he was always spitting at her.

By this time my dad was on oxygen. The guy who brought the tanks came and went twice a week. Friendly little guy.

The tanks were set up next to the black chair in the TV room. A thin, blue-green tube ran up to a little thing under his nose. When they said that he was going to be on oxygen, I expected he'd be stuck under a tent or have a big mask. I was thankful that this was a little more dignified.

He hated TV. Thought it was stupid. Evenings, before he got really sick, he would sit out by himself in the living room, reading, but the rest of the family was always in the TV room at night. It would have been strange if he was stuck out there by himself in the living room, so we moved the tanks into the TV room with us.

One night, it was just me and him in the TV room. Aretha Franklin was on the TV, performing live at a college.

It was the first time I had heard Aretha and something shocking happened to me—chills went up through my body. I had never had that happen before, heard a piece of music or witnessed something so brave or so beautiful that it made chills happen.

What is this? This sensation?

I was embarrassed to be moved like that. It was so out of my control.

I didn't want my dad to notice.

She finished the last song with an explosive crescendo and the audience of white college kids leapt to their feet in a simultaneous roar. The reaction was organic and completely correct.

My dad looked so sad and disappointed when he said, "I can see they are legitimately moved. But I don't feel it at all."

Isn't that wonderful? He doesn't go, "You kids, your music stinks," because he doesn't feel it. He sees there is something happening but he doesn't have the receptors for it, like evolution has been cruel and left him behind.

He was ugly handsome, like Abraham Lincoln.

I was supposed to watch my dad one night but instead went to a club downtown. When I was fifteen, I was mostly hanging out with the black kids, who lived on the other side of Main Street. Playing basketball, going to dances. The black kids were cool.

This wasn't a dance for kids. Most of the people there were twenty to twenty-five. I was always the only white person there, except for maybe the odd, horrifying blond woman. This was a fairly wild crowd. There were fights. A very muscular air. There were knives and guns.

The next day, Sunday, there was a big scene because I hadn't stayed home to watch my dad. My mom was always on the warpath on Sundays and she was holding a family council, going on and on about how I had to be aware of my responsibilities to the family. I thought she was being overly dramatic, per usual—my dad was upstairs asleep, she was playing bridge, what's the big deal, I just decided to go out. This was my dad, did someone really have to stay home and take care of him?

He sat there in his robe and pajamas, not saying anything, looking at the floor.

My dad was beautiful. He was a beautiful man.

When he was in college, he was the bright star of NYU's literary scene, bursting with potential. He wrote the entire literary magazine under multiple pseudonyms, the other young intellectuals deferring to his greater talents. But when he got out of college, instead of becoming the next James Joyce, as was expected of him, he went off into the South to organize unions for miners. It must have been incredibly rough. But, at sixteen, I didn't see the bravery in it, nor the altruism. I didn't know what altruism was.

He started to write his memoirs, but his sickness caught up with him. I thought he had failed. Not because he didn't finish the book, but because he'd never really done anything of his own. He'd never written any book, when he was supposed to be this great talent. I can't say that it was disappointment that I felt. It was all the scorn and disgust that a seventeen-year-old psyche could muster toward one's parents. And he would, now, never be able to do anything about it.

But about a year later, after he was gone, my scorn and confusion were lifted. I was at my cousin's wedding and all these old guys were coming up to me, showing me great respect. One of them, a short, tough New York Jew with something sweet under the hard cragginess, like Edward G. Robinson, looked me in the eye and said, "You Dave Lurie's kid?"

"Yes."

"He was my hero."

Thank you, tough craggy old man. You freed me.

My best friend at that time was Bruce Johnson. Bruce was incredibly thin, six feet tall, and about one hundred forty pounds, maybe even less. His skin color was more Native American than African American.

He had a lot of brothers and none of them looked remotely alike. He had a brother, Dickie, who hated me because I flirted with his date at a dance once, and another brother, Craig, who had the perfect physique of a Nuba tribesman. In junior high school, I was being disciplined for something and was told to stand in a specific spot and wait to speak to the principal, John Law. For real, the new disciplinarian they had brought in to tame our school was an angry, angry man named John Law.

John Law's way of controlling the school was to take whoever was brought to his office and hit them really hard in the ass with a paddle. He didn't even ask what you had done. He just told you to put your hands on his desk and then began flailing away at your ass with his paddle.

Craig Johnson was in his office, and I heard Craig yelling, "You aren't going to hit me!" And I looked into the office to see Craig and Principal John Law wrestling, each holding the other by the wrist, trying to get the paddle.

Craig Johnson was only fourteen then. But John Law couldn't get the better of him and he finally let him go. I didn't move from my specific spot for one moment. That was how scared I was of John Law.

Bruce was the fastest runner in the group we hung out with, and he could jump. He had won the state high jump championship. But he hated sports. I used to have to beg him to play basketball.

One spring night, we were outside a church dance. Someone had bought a bottle of whiskey. Wayne Boykin was making fun of me and the others were laughing. Because of Wayne's bizarre way of talking, I couldn't understand what the hell he was saying.

Later that night we were walking by the high school and someone cut up this path into the woods and started to run. Everyone fell in behind him and we were all running blindly through the woods. Someone would just start it and then it would all be happening. Running. There was none of this white kid shit of, "Hey, you guys, let's go and run in the woods."

Bruce was coasting way at the back, not interested. When we came out of the woods and onto the empty football field next to Doherty High School, the thing really broke into full speed. Bruce just gently turned it up a notch, came all the way from the back and beat everybody easily. Some of these guys were big deal track stars and Bruce just decimated them.

Karen Lubarsky sat in front of me for five years of junior high and high school. Every day of that five years I would borrow a pen from her that would always, somehow, disappear before the end of the school day.

I wanted to be on the football team. I wanted to play end but needed to gain about twenty pounds, because I was rail thin. For breakfast I would drink a Nutrament with five raw eggs. At 10:10 A.M. every morning, during third-period French class, I would get these stabbing pains in my stomach. Karen Lubarsky got to the point where she could time them and would turn around with an amused smile just before they occurred. I got even with her by biting off my fingernails and dropping them, lightly, on top of her black, frizzy hair. But you know what? In the end, fuck the cool kids, Karen Lubarsky was the best.

I was with John Epstein, otherwise known as Running Red Fox. We all had idiot pothead nicknames. We were hitchhiking somewhere and a state trooper stopped to tell us that we couldn't hitch there. This was 1968, hippies were hitchhiking everywhere, and the troopers were always telling you that you couldn't hitchhike here. They would take you to a back road in the middle of nowhere and say, "You can hitchhike here all you want."

John had a plastic bag of some pills—I don't remember what—hanging out of his breast pocket. The trooper said, "What's this?" and pulled them gently up out of John's shirt. Then he unrolled John's sleeping bag and there was a fat bag of marijuana.

He drove us to the station house and put us in adjoining cells. They took our belts away so we couldn't hang ourselves. We thought this was hysterically funny and attempted to hang ourselves with our shoelaces.

Toward the end I'd have to dress my dad. He slept in his own room now. Liz, my older sister, was in Boston at college. Evan, my younger brother, got my room, I got Liz's, and my father moved out of the master bedroom into Evan's little room. He never complained.

It must have been clear that he was dying, but my brain couldn't hold that. He certainly knew. I was down on the floor helping him on with his slippers, and he said out of nowhere, "I've led a full life." At the time, I had no idea why he had said that. Was like a non sequitur. But, in later years, when that moment would cross my mind, I thanked him quite deeply. It really helped.

The house had a weird feel to it. Liz was gone and Evan and I were running wild. Evan invented a pipe for smoking weed, made out of a gas mask, that he called "The Eliminator." He had hair all the way down his back and had to hold his head out the car window on the way home to get the marijuana smell out.

On the news a bunch of uncomfortable, geeky kids with glasses were burning their draft cards. They were being punched and beaten by normal, red-blooded American boys. I didn't really understand the whole thing, but I was impressed by the violence. The guys who were beating them were just like the guys on my high school football team. The kind of guys that I thought were idiots but desperately wanted to be in with. This was way before opposition to the Vietnam War was commonplace.

That night, I was in my dad's room and asked him, "What could I do to make you proud of me?"

"If you could show as much courage as those boys who burned their draft cards today, I'd be enormously proud of you."

I got a suspended sentence on the drug thing. The lawyer went off and discussed something with the judge and it was all settled. My dad looked so sick, it was difficult for him to walk. That was the last time that he left the house.

There was a nineteen-foot-long flag that flew at the end of the downtown part of Worcester, in Lincoln Square. It was supposedly one of seven flags in the country that flew at all times. We had decided to steal it. I talked about it all the time.

One night, motivated by this guy Wayne, we go out to steal the flag for real. Everybody else chickens out, so it's just me and Wayne. Wayne was a little too handsome and never smoked pot because he "didn't want to change his personality." We didn't really trust him.

But Wayne is serious about the flag; he really wants to do it. I'm surprised because I really assessed him as a phony and didn't think he had the balls. We park the car around the corner, out of sight. The flag is situated in a big grass roundabout, with traffic going around the outside. It's late at night. There are no cars. The flag is all lit up, and the light feels soft but strong, like an evening baseball game. We walk onto the roundabout and are completely visible from hundreds of yards in every direction.

Wayne takes a knife and cuts the rope. I'm not ready for this. I'm not ready at all.

The flag starts floating toward us in fast slow motion. You can't believe how big it is. We're engulfed. We're underneath the flag, like it's a tent and we can't find our way out. I'm terrified.

We—mostly Wayne—gather the flag up. Wayne starts to run toward the alley where the car is. My legs are frozen, I can't run. I want to call time-out. I really didn't think we were actually going to do this. I have to run stiff-legged to the car because my knees won't bend.

We bring the flag to my house and stretch it out in Evan's new room. It's too big and parts of it have to go up the walls to the ceiling on either side to properly display it.

When my dad wakes up, I go into his room, beaming. He knows something is up.

"What did you do?"

"It's very big."

"What did you do?"

"We painted city hall red."

"You couldn't have or I would have read about it."

"You'll read about this. We stole the flag at Lincoln Square."

I thought that he would see that this was like the kids burning their draft cards, only better because it was funny. But he didn't. He said, "That's just stupid," and went back into his room.

We had a blues band called Crud, and there was our larger entourage, also called Crud. This was mostly with the white kids in Worcester. We each had a Crud number. So if you were in the pizza place you'd write, "Crud 33," if that was your number, on a napkin and then put the napkin back in the middle of the napkin container. Hopefully it would be found later by another person in the group. With spray paint, we changed the sign that said "Entering Worcester" to "Entering Crud." We changed the name of the beauty shop in Tatnuck Square from "The Imperial House of Beauty" to "The Imperial House of Crud."

At least, that is how I remember it.

Crud played its first show, and I was playing the harmonica. It went okay. It was pretty messy, and some of the attempts at humor were pretty pathetic, but it was the first time I'd ever played in front of people and I was excited.

My dad was in the hospital. He was dying. The next day after the gig,

I went to see him. This was something that my mom had set up, the last meeting, the farewell, but I didn't know this. Had I known, I certainly would have behaved differently, but my head was full of excitement about the gig.

He asked me when my show was going to be. I said with great pride that we had played last night. He looked away from me and cringed. He was disgusted with himself for not knowing what day it was. He had accepted what was happening to his body, but his mind was going and this was not okay. He took a lot of pride in his mind.

A couple days later, I was still in bed when my mom came to the door of my bedroom and said, "It was all over at seven o'clock this morning." Just like that. I like the way she did it. My mother, who could be overly dramatic and find problems when there were none, in the face of real tragedy was levelheaded and stoic. I miss them both.

Three girls from my class came to the funeral. They weren't close friends. I was surprised to see them there. I hardly went back to school after that, so I never got a chance to tell them how grateful I was. And the worst part is that now I can't remember their names. I made this mistake through a large part of my life, gravitating to the cool people and ignoring the real ones.

After the funeral, there was a reception at the house. My father's job was selling Israeli bonds, and there was a lot of the Jewish community there. My parents were devout atheists and they had decided in advance that he would be cremated.

There was a rabbi who was chasing my mother, who was raised Protestant, around the house, saying, "Forty-five minutes, forty-five minutes to save him!" Then, "Thirty-five minutes!" My mother was in a state, she didn't know what to do. My mother, who wasn't Jewish, thought that maybe, just maybe, she was damning my dad to whatever the Jewish version of Hell was.

I didn't catch any of this. I knew something was going on because people were ushering me around the house in a weird way. I think people thought that it wouldn't be good if I started punching the rabbi. It's a shame because I really needed to punch somebody, and punching the irritating rabbi would have been perfect.

* * *

It was a beautiful fall day and the little guy came and took the oxygen equipment and extra tanks away. Didn't say anything.

No jokes today.

My mom was upset that he didn't offer his condolences. I imagine he didn't want to get into it. Brings oxygen for sick people, and then eventually they die and he can't really make a thing out of it. But I remember that my mom was upset. It was kind of cold, but I'm sure he just didn't know what to say. Kindness is a higher form of intelligence that this guy just didn't have.

I lost touch with Bruce Johnson. I was on Pleasant Street, near my house, and he came walking down the street. He was so thin and loose that he looked like his body was made only of disconnected bones. It was about noon and he was never in this neighborhood when he wasn't with me. He was disheveled and his eyes were red.

He mumbled something:

"I told her to put my balls in her mouth and sing 'The Star-Spangled Banner.'" Then he laughed his little Jimi Hendrix–like laugh.

"What's wrong with your eyes?"

He didn't answer. Just walked past, toward downtown, laughing.

About a year later, I was driving near Main Street in the area where the prostitutes hung out. I saw a ravishing girl standing on the corner. Her skin had a scarlet glow. I had to stop at a light and was staring at her beauty for about twenty seconds. Suddenly, I realized that this was Bruce. This was Bruce Johnson dressed as a woman.

My brain turned over.

I didn't understand. I didn't know anything about the concept of drag queens or transgender people at that time.

Later, I realized that he'd only played basketball to placate me and he wasn't interested in it at all, though he had massive skills. I guess the others all knew he was attracted to me, and that's why they were teasing me outside the church that night. That's what it meant.

Steve Piccolo was in Crud, our blues band. Steve, Evan, and I decided to hitchhike to New York to see Canned Heat play with John Lee Hooker.

They'd put out this double album with Alan Wilson, who had recently died, playing harmonica and all kinds of other stuff. We listened to it all the time.

My uncle Jerry lived on West Fifty-seventh Street, so we stayed at his place. It was right next door to Carnegie Hall, where the concert was held. After the show, we're just hanging out on the corner of Fifty-seventh and Sixth in the summer air when Bob Hite, the singer from Canned Heat, comes out. He's fat, with long hair in a ponytail and a beard. They called him "The Bear." I go up to him, I'm excited to meet him, and tell him that I play the harmonica and I'll hitchhike to wherever they are playing next to show him that I'm serious. He's surprisingly friendly and says okay, that they're playing tomorrow night at the Spectrum in Philadelphia.

Me, Steve, and Evan hitch to Philly, find the Spectrum, and sneak into the giant arena in the middle of the afternoon. We're hours early, and we hide in the Spectrum's basement and wait there. When the band shows up, we're in their dressing room waiting for them.

Bob Hite asks to hear me play, so I take out my harmonica and play a bit. He says okay, I can play, that the first two songs are in E. I have an A harmonica, which is what you need for the blues in E, and I'm all set.

This is incredible.

Me, Evan, and Steve stand back and try not to be a nuisance. Henry Vestine, the guitar player, is very strange. His mind seems to be fried; he's sitting in a corner playing the strangest guitar: *reooom, reeoooom,* like the Shaggs' version of a raga.

Next thing I know I'm standing out onstage in front of twenty thousand people. They're out there screaming. I play my two songs—I get a solo in each song—play my ass off, and split the stage. We watch the rest of the show from the wings and then hang out in the dressing room after it's over. The guys in the band tell me I did great. My head is swimming.

A roadie comes back and says that there are two women here to see John Lee Hooker. John Lee Hooker says, "Shit, I don't need but one." He was probably around fifty, but I was seventeen and he seemed like this old, old man. How can he still have sex?

* * *

Mark Pluff, Steve Piccolo, and I were going to start a band playing Hendrix- and Beatles-like material that we had written. I was playing guitar. Mark was on drums and Piccolo was on bass. I imagine this was 1971.

We practiced a couple of times in Mark's basement in the afternoons. Steve couldn't make it one day, so Mark suggested that we take acid and then write some music.

I haven't taken acid before, but Evan has. Evan told me much later that he was tripping during one of our family dinners. He just watched the roast beef being passed around: *whoosh, whoosh,* roast beef, *whoosh.*

Mark offers me this little orange barrel, Orange Sunshine, which looks like a tiny marshmallow. We take them. Today he's set up his drums in the garage and we play there.

I have this beautiful Les Paul guitar, which may have been made as early as 1950, my prize possession. As I start to play it, my hands feel very odd and my fingers are purple. I can't really manipulate my fingers to do anything that makes musical sense, and I suddenly am not sure what musical sense is. It doesn't make any difference anyway, because the neck of the guitar has turned into a liquidy rubber and it's bending away from me. Seems like a swan's neck that's trying to get away and could bite me in a moment.

I gently lay the guitar down on the concrete of Mark's driveway and walk away.

Wandering around, I hear a strange, unearthly mechanical sound rising up into the air behind a school, and then the next thing I know, I'm at my house, which is odd because Mark doesn't live close to me.

I walk in and my mother has her sacred bridge club going. They're all seated around a fold-out bridge table in the living room. I'm not around the house much anymore and I haven't seen any of these women in a couple of years. There's a big mirror over the fireplace and I'm staring into it and I'm grinning from ear to ear. Can't stop grinning.

The bridge club are all looking at me and I'm looking over their heads into the mirror.

"Oh, he's getting so handsome."

"Yes, he is handsome, isn't he?"

I don't even acknowledge them, I'm looking over their heads and past them. I'm staring into the mirror, grinning from ear to ear. The smile goes past my ears, I'm grinning from neck to neck. I'm really grinning.

My mom, who has always desperately tried to keep us away from the bridge club, actually offers me some of the sacred bridge club's sandwiches that they are not going to eat. This is very unusual. We never, ever, get any of the bridge club's food. Never. Maybe it's because I've been declared handsome, or maybe it's because my mom senses that something is up and I'd be better off shepherded into the kitchen with some food.

Well, how nice. I go into the kitchen and say hi to Max the dog. I really feel like I can talk to the dog. I sit down on the kitchen floor and start trying to eat the sandwiches. I'm talking to Max, and clearly, if he had the right vocal equipment, he would answer me.

"How are you, Max?"

Max comes over to me and I hold out the plate of sandwiches for him to have a bite.

"How is it being a dog, Max? Is it okay for you?"

Max demurely eats half of one of the sandwiches. He's looking at me kindly and we're intimate on a level that we haven't previously experienced. Max has another sandwich.

"They're good sandwiches, aren't they, Max?"

I don't think there is anything strange going on here. Maybe this is strange, I know that I've never sat on the kitchen floor and eaten with the dog before, but my mom's never offered me the bridge club's food before. This is a new experience, that's all. No, this is okay. In fact, it's great.

My mother comes into the kitchen and says, "You're acting very strangely." I can see she is not an ally, so I go upstairs to my room, but not before stopping at the mirror and grinning at myself for however long.

Upstairs I find Hendrix's *Electric Ladyland* and put it on the record player. I don't notice, but the stereo is turned all the way up to ten. It doesn't seem loud to me, but I'm sure the house must have been shaking. We never listened to anything higher than three or four, even when my mom was out. Ten must have been deafening.

My mother comes flying up the stairs, but before she can say anything, I run past her, down the stairs, and out of the house. I don't say goodbye to the bridge club, I'm laughing too hard.

I find myself back at Mark's. My guitar is lying in the driveway where I left it. I put it in its case. I knock on Mark's door, but his mother answers. Mark's not there.

"Can I use the bathroom?"

"Of course."

I go into the bathroom and start looking in the mirror again. This time it's not as much fun. In fact, some of my skin is peeling off my face. This is scary. I try to take a shit, but the muscles in my stomach are not mine to control. There's a weird electric jolting feeling, and I think I have to move my bowels but am incapable of figuring out how to do it.

I start looking in the mirror again. Now it's a little more fun. I hope my face doesn't start peeling away again. This is better. I start grinning again.

Suddenly it dawns on me that I've been in the bathroom for two or three hours, maybe longer. I can't go out, I can't handle seeing Mark's mother. And it seems like it must be around eight P.M., his father must be home by now. I'm going to stay in the bathroom until they go to sleep and then I'll sneak out of the house.

That doesn't make sense. No, I have to walk out no matter how scary. So I get my courage together and walk out. I sense nothing from Mark's mother's face that suggests there is anything wrong. Maybe I was only in there for ten minutes. Everything's fine. I say goodbye and leave.

Later that evening, I run into Mark downtown, miles from his house. This always seems to happen when you're tripping: You get high with someone and, inevitably, you get split up. Everyone goes wandering in different directions, but, miraculously, some force brings you back together.

We walk around for a while. Mark has very strange eyes, and he wears sunglasses all the time because light hurts them. I can see his strange eyes behind the dark lenses, and they're bugging me out. Mark's psyche had always seemed like granite to me—nothing fazed him—but now there's something evil lurking in his eyes.

We stop in the middle of the street and I look at him.

"Mark, you're freaking me out."

"You're freaking me out, too, John."

I'm freaking him out? I'm amazed. I feel so disoriented; I can't possibly have the power to freak anybody out, particularly not Mark.

"Oh, okay. Maybe we should split up."

Then there is a very nice moment between us, unsaid.

"Okay, I'll see you later."

We walk in opposite directions. I go over to Larry Preston's apartment and tell him that I'm tripping.

There's a party going on in the building next door, do I want to go?

"I don't think I can."

Larry leaves me alone at his place. Next door someone is having an epileptic fit. I hear screaming.

"Get a spoon! Get a spoon!"

The police come; the red light from the top of the car is circling the walls in Larry's apartment. I slink down onto the floor.

Larry comes back and starts to play this flutter thing on the guitar. Going down chromatically. Whatever he was playing, or whatever I thought he was playing, has influenced my own music forever. Colors were coming off of his fingers.

I was in the school cafeteria waiting to take my college boards. Jody Queen asked me, "John Lurie, are you really going to go to college?" This wasn't an insult, as I was the school rebel; she was actually surprised that I would do anything so mundane. It had never occurred to me that I didn't have to go to college. I wasn't forced to go. So when I went into the examination, I answered a few questions and then drew a goat or a chicken over the boxes where the answers should go. Snakes were chasing pharaohs and giant penises. When the scores came back I still got 500s on the verbal and math.

After the test I walked downtown. The whole downtown area was under construction and there was a thirty-foot hill of dirt piled in a little park behind city hall. I climbed to the top, unnoticed, and sat there. I watched people rush around as they went about their business. It all seemed so futile. Empty. Gray. I wasn't thinking about my dad, but I was feeling the loss of him. I stayed there until it got dark.

Then I got sick.

2

The First Time They Arrested Me,
I Actually Was Drunk

The doctors couldn't figure out what was wrong with me. I had lost all the weight that I had gained for football and gone from 180 to 135 pounds. They put me in the hospital. I was vomiting bile. That this luminous green color could exist in nature didn't seem right. Like a color this ridiculously plastic looking had to be man-made.

A very pretty nurse came into my room and asked if I wanted a massage. I was shy, said no, and then regretted it for days and hoped she would come back.

I had a little record player in my room, so people brought me blues records. Even now, if I hear that James Cotton record, a vague, queasy recollection of that illness floods over me.

They released me from the hospital, but I wasn't right. If I didn't go to college, it looked as though I'd have to go to Vietnam. But that was only a small part of what was really bothering me.

I started to walk around at night. There was nothing to do in Worcester after eleven P.M. Everything closed and I would walk. I'd just walk. I'd walk around the deserted streets. I would look at my feet and walk. If I went to school, I'd stay up all night and go in the morning.

I was so lonely that I used to stand on corners at two A.M., hoping somebody would just stop their car and talk to me.

I liked the quiet of the night. I thought that I might see answers that I couldn't find in the daytime. My mind constantly caromed with torment: *Why am I here? Who will have sex with me? What does it make sense to do? Does it make sense to do anything at all? Does this life make sense? Who will have sex with me?*

I was looking desperately for answers. I had read about people making breakthroughs on psychedelic drugs—Huxley and Castaneda. I thought I would try that.

I bought a hit of ecstasy. Ecstasy wasn't the same thing as it is now. It was much more like LSD. But it doesn't matter what ecstasy was then, because this turned out to be a horse tranquilizer.

I wasn't doing so good. I was staying at Dean Cohen's house. My mother and I had had another fight. I had my own little room at Dean's house and I loved his mom.

But I was really thinking about checking out. I was talking into a tape recorder when Dean came in and found me, hunched over in terror on the floor, as I studied the hideous death flower pattern that used to be his wallpaper.

There were two cops who hated me. Whenever either of them saw me, they would arrest me for drunkenness, whether I was drunk or not.

In jail, in the morning, they bring you a bologna sandwich on white bread and coffee with fourteen sugars. Fourteen sugars to propel you to do more crimes as soon as you are released, so you can come back for another visit.

Once, I was in a cell by myself, and from around the corner I could hear someone yelling down the concrete corridors, "This is Craig Johnson, does anyone here know me? This is Craig Johnson!" I yelled that I was there. I thought this was kind of fun. Craig apparently did not.

Three months later, the Worcester police beat Craig Johnson to death.

* * *

The first time they arrested me, I actually was drunk. I was maybe sixteen and hanging out with these older guys, Larry Preston, Bill Shirley, and Willie something-or-other. They were extremely wild and a lot of them ended up in jail. My mentor was Larry Preston, who was a great guitar player. You can't always be certain that something that impressed you as great when you were that young was actually great, but in this case I'm sure it is true.

Larry Preston's crowd was a strange group. Some were criminals, some were artists, and some were both. Many were clearly insane.

There was Pierre, who Larry loved, but I could never, for a moment, understand why. Pierre's claim to fame was that he had cut a hole in a large ham that was for a big family dinner. After he cut the hole, he jerked off into the ham and then put back the piece that he had cut out. His family ate the ham.

That this was something that Larry found amusing bothered me. But if you heard him play the guitar, that would vanish in a second.

Pierre was also constantly telling the story of when he was in the hospital and got an erection when the nurse came into the room. The nurse said, "I did nothing to provoke that," and poinked his hard-on with a spoon, which, to Pierre's amazement, made his erection immediately shrivel and die. We'd be sitting on the steps of the church near Larry's house and Pierre would flick his wrist and say out of nowhere, "I did nothing to provoke that." And make a little poinking sound.

We had crashed a party of these preppy high school kids. Clean boys and girls, well adjusted, on their way to fancy colleges. I had sex with a red-haired girl in the closet. She had a pony bottom, hard and round. Pony Bottom decided that this was a good opportunity to slum for a moment and cuddle up to one of the bad boys.

God knows what Bill Shirley had been doing, but when I came out of the closet, the police were there. Bill and Larry and Willie were in handcuffs. I got pointed out and we were all thrown into a paddy wagon.

Spent the night in jail. About a week later Bill Shirley and Larry Preston were arrested again. When the police opened the paddy wagon door, one of them—I can't remember if it was Bill or Larry—punched the first cop in the face. The cops beat the shit out of them and then, by association, hated me, and I was arrested every time they saw me. That and the fact that I was one of the few guys in Worcester at that time with the audacity to have long hair, which was seen as a great threat to the established order.

At around five in the afternoon, I was talking to a friend at the swing set in Duffy Field. A squad car stopped, and two cops came walking across the field, announced I was drunk, which I wasn't, and ushered me into the squad car to spend the night in jail.

It happened a couple more times. I don't know why I wasn't more outraged about it. I kind of found it funny.

Bill Shirley was amazing, an unbridled force of nature. Before I had even met Bill Shirley, I had heard many stories. He went to a different junior high school and shared his homeroom with my friend Bill Noel.

Bill Shirley, who was probably thirteen at the time, came in late; the teacher said that he needed a note.

"But I'm here now."

"You have to have a note from your mother explaining your tardiness."

"My mother's at work."

"That's not my problem."

So Bill just stands there, with his head down. Doesn't move and the teacher ignores him.

Finally, "Young man, I don't know what you think you're doing but you can't stay here without a note."

"My mother's at work."

The teacher goes back to ignoring him. Bill walks over and punches out the glass in the first window with his fist. Then moves to the second window and punches out the glass with his fist. One by one, slowly and methodically, he punched out every window along the wall. Blood and glass everywhere.

When I was seventeen, at Larry Preston's wedding I'd smoked this pot that was so strong, I wasn't capable of having a conversation. I'm sitting there. The party is an odd mix of the older guys I know and this other crowd of people in their thirties. Tough guys in leisure suits. A guy bets Bill Shirley that he can eat a shot glass. Bill bets him. The guy eats the glass. Does he really eat the glass? I certainly remember it like he did.

Bill scrunches up his face in bewilderment, like he's been tricked; the lines in his forehead turn into the Thai alphabet. If it was that easy, Bill would have done it himself. A frozen moment of stares passes, and then Bill's face scrunches up to another level of confusion and amazement. He then pulls back and punches the guy square in the face. All hell breaks loose. Everyone's fighting. I'm so stoned it's just a blur.

The last I heard of Bill Shirley, he had been arrested and was working on a chain gang in Florida. He had been in a McDonald's and cut ahead of a woman in line to use the McBathroom. The woman said, indignantly, "Young man, you have a lot of nerve."

"Yeah, and here it is," Bill said as he whipped out his cock and waved it at her as he hopped up and down. When the police arrived, Bill was behind the counter and attempted to hold them off by hurtling a constant barrage of buns and uncooked hamburgers, as the police ducked and held on to their hats.

Around that same time I was at the Kitty Cat Lounge. This was the only late night hangout in Worcester; they had music there, and it was filled with people drinking and dancing, pimps, prostitutes, and musicians. Felt like a throwback to the 1950s.

I had wandered in by myself, and to my surprise found Alex there. It was a mostly black club, and Alex was a white bass player from Boston who sometimes played with the drummer Michael Avery. Alex was twenty-five or so. He was smart and different from most of the dopier blues musicians from Boston. He seemed to have a wide range of consciousness. There were a few guys like that, Michael Avery and the amazing piano player David Maxwell, who could play anything but was hiding in the dim world of blues bars.

I was asking Alex all kinds of musical questions. The thing that struck me was when I asked him who was more important, Coltrane or Hendrix.

"Coltrane." There was a long pause and then he said, like he was discovering the answer for himself, "Coltrane, because he lived longer."

What did that mean, because he lived longer? I didn't really understand, but it had a certain impact. Alex went completely mad a year or two later.

When I left, it was two A.M. Across Main Street, walking slowly, was a three-hundred-pound woman I had seen earlier in the club. That I was drunk now, and that I had caught her catching a glimpse of me, gave me the courage to cross the street and start talking to her.

We went back to her place. This was not an easy deal, the layers of rolling fat created a barrier, and I could only manage an inch or so of penetration.

When I woke up hungover a couple hours later, the kitchen was full of yelling kids and one very large, angry man, who was not her husband or boyfriend, but very angry nonetheless. I slunk out of the house as quickly as I could, bumping into blurry objects on my way.

I decided to hitchhike across the country. My first night I arrived in Baltimore with hardly any money and nowhere to stay. I was in a deserted part of town, everything was a wreck and dismal. I saw a greasy creature that made me want to gag. My first rat.

I had a couple of White Castle hamburgers. A little white dog came out of the rat's alley, vomited, and then keeled over and died. A couple of white guys getting out of a car saw the dog keel over and laughed.

How does one laugh at that?

There was nobody anywhere and it was only about eleven P.M. This barren landscape was Baltimore? How could there be absolutely no one? I heard a roar and went around the corner to see what was happening. A block or so away, there were hundreds of people all walking fast, all going in the same direction. Everyone was black. Insane activity, the bursting energy of a parade no longer able to contain itself.

There'd been nobody on the street and suddenly there's a mob.

I walk toward the crowd. There's a huge woman in a very colorful dress coming toward me. I ask, "What's going on?"

She looks at me in amazement. "Don't you know? The roller derby just got out!"

About six months before I landed in Baltimore, Larry Preston, Evan, and I had hitched down south to go to a rock festival in South Carolina. When we heard on the radio that the festival might be canceled and that Canned Heat was playing in Roanoke, Larry thought it made more sense to go to Roanoke so I could sit in on harmonica. When we got there, it turned out that I couldn't play because Magic Dick from the J. Geils Band was already sitting in. I was jealous, particularly because Bob Hite seemed really taken with the idea that Magic Dick could play in third position, way up high, using a different key on the harmonica, which I didn't know how to do at the time. Actually, I was never that interested, because it sounded so shrill.

And who names himself Magic Dick?

I don't remember so much about that trip. I remember Larry laughing in amazement when he heard Henry Vestine playing in the dressing room. Larry, who is one of the best musicians I have ever met, was in the dressing room with musicians who were a huge deal at the time, and Henry Vestine was sitting in the corner, droning away on his guitar like, like . . . I don't even know what to call it.

Larry was laughing really hard. "Oh! Oh, his brain is fried!"

I remember the giant star on top of a hill in Roanoke that they lit up whenever there had been a fatal car accident.

I remember when we were hitchhiking back to Worcester, we were awoken by devouring mosquitoes at dawn, when we had tried to sleep a couple of hours along the highway.

And I remember Gloria.

Backstage at the Canned Heat concert there had been this sassy Southern girl named Gloria, who was flirting with the guys in the band. Flirting isn't quite the word.

We'd gotten her number.

Before I left Worcester on this trip, I called her and said I might be coming down that way. I don't think she even remembered who I was, but Gloria was a nymphomaniac, and I guess it was slim pickings in Roanoke, so she said, "Okay, why not?" I went to Roanoke, Virginia, to see her.

I was very excited about the idea of having sex with Gloria, but I was also scared to death because she seemed so sexually worldly. I was so shy at this stage, I could hardly go into a restaurant and order without being terrified, never mind the idea of dealing with a devouring vixen.

Gloria was about twenty-five and had a wonderful drawl that floated out of a sultry mouth. She had short, curly hair and a pert little bottom that she used to full effect. She waved it like a flag. She hailed cabs with it.

To my great disappointment, when I got to Gloria's, this German guy was already there. He was a couple of years older than me, taller than me, and had an incredible physique. A little sleazy and completely amoral, but I liked him somehow.

The second day, the German guy was out somewhere, and Gloria came into my room and sat down on the edge of the bed while I lay there. We talked for a minute, and then there was a little awkward silence. She picked a pen up from the floor and started going up and down on it really fast with her hand, like she was jerking it off. I didn't know what to do and so I did nothing.

Gloria, disgusted with my shyness, got up and left the room.

Instead of hitchhiking across the country, I let the German guy talk me into taking a Greyhound bus with him to San Diego. Said it was great, that he did it all the time. He was going to visit this guy who owned a restaurant, and we could stay there and eat for free.

Taking a bus across the country is one of the most unhealthy ventures that one can put the body through. Especially if you only eat ham sandwiches and drink bottles and bottles of apricot brandy. By the time we got there, I had boils all over my back and face, and my hair was coming out in handfuls.

At one point, in Texas, government agents got on the bus to inspect all of the Mexicans' IDs. They were really rude to the Mexicans, and the German, giving them a hard time, asked why they hadn't asked for his ID. A couple hours earlier he had threatened and pushed this big Texan who was trying to take one of the Mexicans' seats, so I thought he might really get into it with these agents, but he didn't. Because he had seemed so scuzzy, I was surprised to see him stand up for somebody and was kind of proud of him.

We got to San Diego, and the restaurant guy made us his special sandwich. I have no idea what was in this sandwich, can't remember, but I can still somehow invoke the taste of it.

It became clear that this was some kind of weird sexual deal between the two of them. I guess the groovy restaurant guy supported him in return for sexual favors. It felt creepy and I left the next day. I hitched up to San Francisco. I heard that there were friends of mine hanging out there in Berkeley. It was all happening on Telegraph Avenue in Berkeley.

Berkeley didn't do me much good. It was over. What was left was mostly hippie burnouts, at least on the street. Air filled with the smell of burning, rotted synapses.

We'd found out after my father died that we had a half sister, Ella. She had a family and lived in San Jose. I stayed with them for a while, but it was very awkward. I was grieving my father and she resented him deeply. He'd left before she was born, and she was certainly entitled to this feeling, but I couldn't cope with it. It was eerie because she looked just like my dad.

I got introduced to a houseful of people living in Berkeley. They were older, sort of ex-hippies. They were intelligent and organized. They tried to guide me along, but I was so dark that they mostly kept their distance.

I had a mad crush on this woman who was with the second-oldest brother in the household. He was respected and they, as a couple, held a position of honor.

People were constantly coming and going. They had a sort of open door policy and tried to be tolerant of all the wayward misfits that they allowed to crash there.

There was this blond guy who stayed for a few days and kept telling the same story about how he had whipped his dick out at a police officer. He told it over and over. The woman I liked, Jane, said to him, "Next time I see a policeman, I'm going to whip my cunt out at him." That shut him up. And deeply amplified my crush.

I decided to hitchhike down to L.A. The guy who picked me up was going all the way. When we got close to Big Sur, he pulled out a joint and we got very high. He started swerving his van really fast through the cliffs, with the sea smashing against the rocks hundreds of yards below.

We got to L.A. and stayed at a flophouse filled with miscreants. The guy who brought me there was cool, but these other people I could have done without. We smoked some more of his very strong pot.

I was having trouble smoking marijuana at this time. I had adored getting high before, especially when playing music, and thought that it was essential to my development and understanding, but now it was driving me mad. Every time I smoked, I felt ugly and small. I kept smoking it and trying not to go to this hideous place, but it happened over and over.

I decided to smoke a lot with this guy and see what I found. I brought a notebook back to my cot and started writing. This way in the morning I would have something I could learn from, from when I was high. When I got up in the morning, the notebook read: *hoooufhd thiee b*—then just a bunch of squiggly lines.

The guy with the van had left. I got my knapsack and went outside. I walked for a while and found a diner. I had ham and eggs and then had only about $20 left.

There is nothing to walk to in L.A. There is nothing to find and no people to meet. At least not that I came across. I walked around from morning until it started to get dark without seeing the slightest sign of refuge or kindness. I bought an Arby's roast beef with change and thought that one day I would have enough for two Arby's roast beefs, and then things would be better.

On Sunset Boulevard I found a free paper. There was a number listed for kids stuck without a place to sleep, so I called it. They gave me another number and I called that.

The guy who came to the phone sounded nice. I told him where I was and he came and picked me up about forty-five minutes later. He stopped at Jack in the Box; it was a drive-thru. I'd never been to a Jack in the Box before.

We go back to his place and there are photos everywhere of the young and old Jay North. Jay North is, or was, Dennis the Menace from the TV show. This guy was his manager, and he was trying to help the career of the now-thirty-year-old Jay North, with little or no success. It gave me my first glimpse into the desperate world of show business.

He offered me a massage. I let him rub my neck and then told him I had to go to sleep. I lay there on the couch for hours pretending to sleep. The next morning I left him a note saying he was very kind and hitched back up to San Francisco.

I stayed in San Francisco for another few months, a pretty uncomfortable time for me. I wasn't getting any closer to making a breakthrough and decided to go back to Massachusetts.

I got a ride from a couple with a van. I found them off a bulletin board.

These people were the original yuppies. They dressed in all the correct hippie garb, were super clean, and looked like they each did their hair with a hundred brushstrokes every day. They charged each person they took and made a profit on their trip back east. I couldn't stand them.

I was staring out the window as we drove through flat Oklahoma. Lost, rigid, and unhappy. I said to myself, "If there is a God, let me see a red light in the sky as a sign." Two seconds later we drove under a giant radio tower with a red flashing light, thousands of feet off the ground. Does that count?

Among the passengers was Charlotte, a very sweet, very plain hippie chick. We started making jokes at the expense of the Hair Brushers.

The van broke down in Tennessee. We were pushing it and I just stopped helping. Now, after laying down all these rules about their van and dictating when we would stop and when we would eat, the original yuppies were putting forth this attitude like, *Come on! We're all in this together!*

It just didn't seem like I should have to push their stupid van when they were charging me more than Amtrak. And we clearly were not all in this together.

The guy couldn't turn his neck. To look around, he had to swing his whole torso. This added to his general demeanor of uptightness. He and his wife were fifteen feet ahead of me, pushing the van. When he realized I was not helping, he did his little mannequin move, swung his whole body around to glance back at me in disapproval.

We got to a gas station and there was a guy in army fatigues going north, so Charlotte and I took our stuff out of the back of the van and split with him. The guy turned out to be a psychopath. He had just gotten back from Vietnam and would rave, while he drove, that he was having recurring dreams where he died: "Holding my guts in my hands! You're not supposed to die in your dreams! You almost die and then wake up! You're not supposed to die!"

We stopped at a motel, the three of us in one room with two beds. It was decided that I'd share the bed with Charlotte.

I took my first shower in four days. I came out of the shower naked. People in the house in Berkeley were always walking around naked, so this is how it's done.

This didn't sit very well with Vietnam Vet Psycho. When we were leaving the next morning, Charlotte took me aside just outside the motel room.

"He was going to kill you when you were sleeping."

"What?!"

"He has a big hunting knife and he wanted to cut your throat. He didn't like that you came out of the bathroom naked."

"That's crazy!"

"He thought it was disrespectful to me."

"How? Do you think that? I didn't mean to be disrespectful to you."

"No, of course not. It's perfectly natural and I kind of enjoyed it, but I had to stay awake for hours begging him not to hurt you."

"Oh, great."

"I think it will be okay."

So for the rest of the trip, I only pretended to sleep. I heard him saying to her in the front seat, "There's a group that I think you would like. They're a brother and sister team called the Carpenters. They're very unaffected."

As we drove north, it was beginning to snow. Psycho Vet told me to throw my shoes out the window. I was wearing sneakers that were falling apart.

"Why?"

"Just throw them out the window."

I didn't really want to get murdered without my shoes on, but the guy was demanding that I do it in a really threatening way. I threw my sneakers out the window as we sped along the highway. He reached down into a bag at his feet and pulled out a relatively new pair of army boots that did me quite nicely.

When I got back to Worcester, I called my mom from the neighbor's phone, pretending to still be in Berkeley. I asked her to hold on for a second and snuck in the front door. I said, "Hi, Mom," from behind her.

When she realized that I was standing behind her, her glasses came flying off her head as she rushed toward me.

3

Inside God's Brain

At four A.M. on Main Street, in Worcester, Massachusetts, the universe gave me my first saxophone. There was hardly any pretense or shrouding it in the mundane. It wasn't *this happened* and then *that happened* and I turned that way and there it was. Just a man with a wheelbarrow gave me my first saxophone.

My sister, Liz, had given Evan a harmonica for his fifteenth birthday. I had taken it and become obsessed. I played all the time and was getting good really fast. I had heard the better known harmonica players in Worcester and in Boston and I knew that I was faring pretty well.

The drummer Michael Avery was my sister's boyfriend. I looked up to Michael. He taught me a lot about music, just by playing me stuff when I would go to visit them in Boston. He was the first person to play me Coltrane. I didn't understand it and was fascinated by the idea that there was music that I didn't understand.

It was like hearing someone speak Chinese. How could there be this music that I didn't understand?

* * *

Michael came to Worcester to play at a dive called the Ale 'n' Bun. Evan and I had been at the Ale 'n' Bun a few months before when this giant guy was acting like a complete asshole. The bouncers tried to throw him out but couldn't. The police arrived and the giant picked up a barstool and heaved it at the wall of bottles and mirror behind the bar.

Only a couple of bottles broke.

Evan turned to me and said, "I was disappointed at how little damage that did," as the police dragged the guy out.

Michael was there playing with Babe Pino, a harmonica player from Boston. Babe Pino had a reputation as being the best harmonica player in the area, which, to me, was bullshit. It was solely based on the fact that he had lived on Maxwell Street in Chicago, which, at one time, a long time ago, had been the hotbed of blues in this country. He had a few fancy licks that he played but didn't have any heart or imagination in his playing. He wore shiny clothes, had ugly hair, and I couldn't stand him.

On guitar was a misshapen white guy who had played with Muddy Waters. Muddy had named him Guitar Goony.

I ask Michael if I can sit in, and he says he'll ask but doesn't seem thrilled about the idea. It's Babe Pino's gig, and Babe Pino is a harmonica player. Halfway through the show they call me up. Babe is not friendly. He hands me a mic—not his prized bullet mic, which is made for the harmonica, but some cheesy thing. He says he's going to sing and I can play harmonica. I'm nervous, but I know that I'm good.

They start, and I join in but I can't hear myself. I can't hear a note I'm playing and I feel uncomfortable. This is not going as I imagined, where they would play and I'd come in behind them and, "Wow! The kid is good!"

I can't hear myself. I have no idea what I am playing. I start playing so hard that I can basically only play one note at a time, one note per breath. It's a disaster. I'm horrible. I feel that hot prickly sensation on my back and neck, that thousand mosquito bite feeling that accompanies making a complete asshole out of yourself. But what has happened is that my mic is not in the monitors, there was no way I could have heard myself. I didn't know anything about monitors at that time. (Monitors are the speakers that face back toward the musicians onstage, allowing them to hear what they are playing.) I don't know why I can't hear myself and I'm thinking that Babe Pino must be some kind of a monster to be able to be heard. I don't have the power that it takes. I'm playing harder and harder, to the point where nothing I play makes any musical sense.

I can see their derisive glances. Who is this jerk kid who thought that he could compare to the great Babe Pino? Even Michael is snide afterward.

I'm walking. Late that night. I'm inconsolable, my depression has been verified because I stink. Vietnam is looming, my dad is dead, and now it turns out that I am not the great talent that I thought I was. In fact, I'm a fraud. Nothing. I really am nothing.

I'm walking and just staring at the pavement. I'm not even hoping for an encounter with a frustrated housewife, as I used to do.

At about four A.M. I find myself alongside a guy casually pushing a wheelbarrow down Main Street, near Clark University. This is odd because nobody is out at this hour and he has a wheelbarrow.

I ask him what he's doing and he tells me that he is going to plant an organic garden on the roof of his apartment building. He also says that he's just seen a statue turn into an angel and fly off. He says it in such a way that it sounds like something he suggests I do if I ever get around to it. He's very odd and very gentle, he's black and a little on the plump side. He is that kind of person who has no actual awareness that he is in a physical body.

I find him fascinating.

He explains to me that it's possible to make amplifiers out of cotton. That it has a higher vibration. This man may be crazy, and I knew then, as I know now, that it is not possible to make amplifiers out of cotton, yet he is so warm and so human and he isn't crazy, he's just something else, and he's just mistaken about making amplifiers out of cotton.

I walk him to his mother's house to help him with the wheelbarrow full of dirt. We have to be quiet, his mother is asleep. There is an enema bag hanging on the back of the bathroom door. I wonder what this object is.

I wait by the door while he goes deeper into the apartment and comes out with a tenor sax. He's going to lend it to me and I can bring it back when I'm done with it.

He also lends me his bicycle so I can get home. Just like that. He doesn't know me, I've hardly said a word, and he gives a complete stranger who he's met at four in the morning a horn and a bike. This is not usual.

I can't remember his name. I've been trying for years to remember his name. I think it was James Washington. I only met him twice, and a third time I saw him from a car as he was walking down a side street in Worcester, one foot on the curb, the other in the gutter, like a kid, shirt-tail hanging out. The other people in the car knew him and laughed when they saw him ambling down the street. He was clearly not of this world. The reason that I am not sure that his name was James Washington is that later there was a man named James Parker Washington, who also seemed to drop out of the sky for a visit, who helped me when I was lost. He set me up with a job and apartment in Brooklyn, which was how I first got to New York. So I am not sure if I somehow later imagined the man with the wheelbarrow to be named James Washington or if they were both named James Washington, which then would make it certain that they were not people at all.

There are moments when some force in life parts the clouds and says, "Hi, it's me, God. I was hiding, but now I'm back. Here's a little something to nudge you in the right direction."

So now I have this tenor. I'm not going to study other saxophone players. On harmonica I had listened furiously to Little Walter, who is an absolute genius. His big scarred head staring out from the album cover. On guitar I had studied Hendrix so deeply that it may have been impossible to ever find my own sound. On the horn I was going to start from scratch. I wasn't even going to buy a finger chart to learn which notes were which.

There is a place in Worcester called Newton Hill, which is a wooded area. It's near Newton Square and Doherty High School, and at the bottom of the hill are basketball courts where we used to play. Newton Hill is centrally located yet isolated, so at night I would take my borrowed horn and go up into the woods and blow my brains out.

Nothing made musical sense, as I didn't know what the notes were. This was complete unadulterated energy. I played until the night darkened trees spun around me in a warm, inviting way.

One night, I was up there at about three in the morning. I used to play in a clearing at the top of the hill. Blowing as hard as I could, for as long as I could, with my eyes closed in the woods. I'm on the hill and I'm playing and I notice that the ground is trembling. I stop playing, something weird is happening. I hear engines, and the sound is coming closer, which is really strange because I'm in the woods at the top of a hill and it's three in the morning. I grab my case and back off into the brush.

I see five or six motorcycle cops on their bikes come blazing into the clearing. They are all yelling, like, "Yahoo!" kind of shit. One of them has his gun out and fires it into the air. Do they think that bullets just disappear into the atmosphere when you fire a gun into the air? They are riding around in a circle like madmen.

I hide and wait for them to leave. They are only there for a minute. After driving madly in a circle three or four times, they go rumbling back down the hill.

Then I start again.

I was back staying at my mother's, though I was hardly there. She had a boarder now in one of the rooms, a graduate student. One night I was sitting there on a nice August evening and decided that I was going to go for a bike ride naked. I don't know what I thought this was going to accomplish. But I knew that now that I had thought of it, I had to accept the challenge and go ahead and do it.

We lived at the top of Chamberlain Parkway, which is a very steep hill. When Evan and I were kids, we used to walk home from school, and I would start at the beginning of the hill with my arm around his shoulder in a brotherly way. About a quarter of the way up, I would have all of my weight supported by Evan, who couldn't understand why he was having such a hard time getting up the hill. Evan would slowly realize and whine, "Don't lean on me," with the *ee* sound in *lean* drawn way out. This happened daily. Whenever Evan complains about anything today, which he rarely does, I go: "Don't *leeen* on me."

If you have never ridden a bike naked, it's fantastic. I think it's the breeze on your bare skin. As I came flying down that hill, toward the bottom, as it opened onto Pleasant Street, which is a main street in Worcester, it was thrilling. The wind, the speed, and the sheer abandon and recklessness of it opened me.

I'm naked, it's about four A.M. and there are some cars. One follows me. This is a little scary. I later find out that it's Mr. Crotty, who was the father of a friend of mine, Richard Crotty. Mr. Crotty was apparently quite amused and followed me, I assume just to see what the hell I was doing. I wonder what Mr. Crotty was doing out at four in the morning.

I get all the way down Pleasant Street past Newton Square and go onto Lee Street, where I sneak onto Bill Noel's wooden porch. Bill Noel's mother is an absolute terror, so I have to be very quiet and not wake her. I tap gently on Bill's window until he finally wakes up.

"What are you doing, John?"

"I'm naked. Do you want to go for a bike ride?"

"Okay."

We ride around until it started to get light out. I'm nervous now about getting caught, because there was a star athlete named John McPartland who had been having sex with this girl behind Doherty High School. The girl ran off when the police came and he was found there alone and naked. He was forced to go in for months of psychological observation. If the police find me, they might not recognize the sheer genius of my act.

I go into several backyards until I find one with a clothesline that has clothes on it. I finally find a tiny pair of orange shorts that must have belonged to a ten-year-old. I shimmy them on, say goodbye to Bill, and ride home.

When I get home, the boarder was making his breakfast.

"I saw your clothes on the floor in the living room and I just shook my head."

More than once I have witnessed the inexplicable. Once when I was walking home I heard the sound of thousands of bells in the sky. Kind of beautiful, like gentle sleigh bells. I couldn't identify the direction. It sounded like the bells were spread across the sky.

Another night, when I was about twelve, I was in the dining room listening to the Red Sox on the radio, while the rest of the family was in the living room watching TV. I saw hundreds of red flashing lights, coming through the bushes in the backyard, from up in the neighbor's driveway. They looked like car brake lights, but there were way too many and they were at varying heights and flashing very, very fast. I ran into the TV room but didn't say a word to anyone about whatever phenomenon I had just witnessed. Not sure why I am telling you now.

One morning, as the sun was coming up, I walked down from Newton Hill after playing the horn. I was standing in the middle of Doherty High School's football field. I love football fields and basketball courts, especially when they are empty.

I saw a woman dressed all in black leaning over and picking something, halfway up the hill. I didn't think anything of it and turned to watch the sunrise for not less than four seconds when I realized it was odd that this witchy-looking creature was out picking something on Newton Hill this early in the morning. I turned to see what she was doing and she had vanished. And there was no way for her to have just disappeared like that, it was open terrain in all directions.

I went to a shrink to try to get out of the draft. He was a squat beast of a man whose trademark must have been his steady gaze.

A toad who could stare.

My mother was from Wales. While she was there visiting her mother, we were not supposed to drive the car. But I searched through her room and found the keys.

We went for a drive out into the country. I sped up on a dirt road with pebbles pounding up underneath the car. Then the car froze. Died in the middle of nowhere.

We walked back to a farmhouse to ask for help. A couple of guys in overalls walked over to the car with us.

One got down under the car and had a look.

He said, "You got a big hole in your oil pan. You can put all the oil you want in there and it will just run out onto the ground." A line that Evan repeated for years after.

So I guess that by driving with no oil, I had broken the engine of the car. Something my mom could hold over my head on any occasion that suited her.

I went for a bike ride with Al the Rat. We were talking about having kids and Al said he would never bring kids into this fucked up world.

We were riding down Highland Street, it was late and there were no cars. It was summer but not too hot, in fact, it was perfect. Light air blowing against my face on the bike. I love breeze. Breeze can make you fall in love. Breeze can make you fall in love with life.

I'd let Al get ahead of me as we got onto Main Street—he was about a hundred yards ahead—when I had this moment. I remember the exact spot. I felt the benevolent connection of all things in life. I was filled with an optimism. Just in a moment it came over me and things changed for me after that. I can't explain this moment, certainly not in a way that would do it justice. Particles were all part of one bigger thing and were floating and touching. Things that were solid were not solid at all.

Particles floated. Just like that, life was everywhere. Prana, light from the tree, concrete was not solid nor inanimate. Caressed.

This was not God saying hello. I had been invited.

I was inside God's brain.

I spent the next few years trying to recapture whatever had unveiled itself and passed over me during that experience. It is abundantly clear that all beings and things are part of one life. During various periods of my life I have been very far and divorced from this philosophy. I have seen it as folly and wishful hallucination. But at that time, I wanted to repeat this experience more than anything. I just didn't know how to go about it.

Years later, Al the Rat came to one of The Lounge Lizards' shows. He has lots of kids.

I moved into a Kundalini yoga ashram. We got up at three A.M. every morning and took a cold shower, in an apartment that was always freezing because they were saving money on the heat. Then we did three hours of strenuous yoga exercises and chanting. These exercises were yoga postures done with a really violent approach. If the normal yogic pose was sitting on the floor with your legs in front of you and then bending to touch your toes, in Kundalini yoga, you would reach out as far past your toes as possible and then recoil, in a rhythm of about forty times per minute, over a ten-minute period. All the exercises were done with the "Breath of Fire." This is something like the breathing one learns in Lamaze class, but faster and heavier.

The basic idea behind Kundalini yoga was to have a Kundalini experience. According to them, at least at that time, it was not an experience possible for women. This is the rising of one's sexual energy from the base of the spine up to the third eye. The purpose of sleeping very little and rising at three A.M. was to avoid having a wet dream. An orgasm was a loss of the sexual fluid and energy needed to achieve this cosmic event of a Kundalini experience.

I didn't know anything about raising my sexual energy. All I wanted to do was repeat the feeling of oneness and well-being that I'd had on the bike. I was eighteen and just at a period when releasing some sexual energy might have done me a world of good. I already suffered from acne, but the intense concentration on the third eye before I was ready caused me to be constantly afflicted with giant boils on my forehead, particularly between my eyes. I have scars there today.

I was going to high school as a postgraduate student. I'd learned that if one's father dies and one is still in school, then it is possible to receive Social Security benefits. When I found this out, I went to Mr. Connor, the principal, and told him I wanted to register to do another year of high school to improve my grades. He was suspicious and had been happy about the idea of getting rid of me. When Ted Kennedy came to speak at our high school shortly after Chappaquiddick, I was locked in the principal's office by myself because they were terrified of what I might do or say.

I convinced Mr. Connor that I was sincere about going back to high school as a postgraduate student in the hopes of getting into a better college. This way, I'd go to homeroom and cut out the rest of the day and then collect my $200 a month.

The yogis all wore turbans. These were all white college students who dressed like Sikhs. They actually got me to wear a turban for a couple of days. This ended after I went to practice with our blues band and it was suggested with a snicker that we should change the name of the group to Turband.

While I lived with the Kundalini people, I actually started going to school, because it was so cold in the apartment and because I liked the music teacher, Miss Giannini. Sometimes I'd practice the alto at the ashram, but they hated it. One younger yogi in particular hated it and felt it was sacrilegious for me to play my horn in the meditation room. The others disagreed and they had a big fight about it.

I moved out after a couple months with acne welts all over my head.

4

I Come from Haunts of Coot and Hern, or, I Didn't Kill Yogi Bhajan

I still wanted to recapture the experience that I'd had on the bike. I wanted to have it all the time. It was the only thing that made sense to do because it was the only thing that made life make sense.

I wanted to find my soul and live in it. All the time. That is all that concerned me. I became a monk of my own order, an ascetic, making up the rules as I went along. I put myself through the fire.

I slept on the floor. Practiced yoga, didn't smoke, didn't drink, didn't eat meat, no sugar, no TV, no sex. I questioned everything. An ice cream sundae was a sin.

I tried to do incredible feats of endurance, to challenge myself and force a crystallization. I'd practice the saxophone until my lips bled. I would hold a chair at arm's length for as long as possible—really as long as possible—causing blinding pain. Twice I fasted and kept silent for ten days.

I read everything I could about religion, mysticism, the occult.

While other boys in their early twenties were out drinking, chasing girls, or developing careers, I lived like a hermit and drove myself close to insane. The realm of this world was not only an illusion, it was a waste of time. I wanted to pass through the veil.

During a fast I had a dream that revealed to me the meaning behind the mathematical and geometric symbolism of the cross. I knew exactly what it really meant. But when I woke up, it was gone. I had lost it.

I read somewhere about a woman who had fasted for a week and then eaten a potato and died, but it didn't matter. I read that garlic cleansed your blood. I took ten cloves of garlic and put them in a blender with a few tablespoons of water. I was listening to Coltrane with big studio headphones and sat down to drink the garlic juice. I was a kid and had no idea how intense drinking ten cloves of garlic would be. I gulped it down and my brain rewired. For a moment I was tasting Coltrane and hearing the garlic.

I'd leave the house, walk left, and turn left at each corner until I got back in front of my house. Then I would walk two blocks, turn left, two blocks, and do that until I was parallel to my house. Then three blocks, then left, in ever-widening concentric circles.

I was completely uncomfortable with every facet of society. I couldn't buy a pair of pants. I was incredibly shy. No girls. If a waitress looked at me, even if she clearly was no brighter than a shoebox, I would have to avert my eyes, as somehow she would know how unworthy I had become. If I wasn't able to go into a restaurant and order a milkshake without being terrified, then let me move on from here.

My mother was Welsh, and after my father died, she moved back to Wales. My dad had been stationed in North Wales at the end of World War II. The first time they met they were at a party playing charades. They were partners. My father drew a quote from a poem: "I come from haunts of coot and hern." He stood there looking at the piece of paper, gathering his thoughts. My mother, without hearing a clue, blurted out, "I come from haunts of coot and hern!" I don't know what poem that's from or what the fuck it means, but they were married shortly after, and I owe my existence to that line of poetry and some psychic event at a party in North Wales, 1945.

* * *

So my mom decided to go home. She went back under the guise of taking care of my grandmother, who didn't really want or appreciate her help. Grandma was tough as nails. It was odd to watch my mother go through that thing of the daughter trying desperately to get her mother's approval.

I thought it bizarre that my mom just up and left the United States with me and Evan being so young. Of course, we pretended that we were old enough to take care of ourselves, that it was no big deal, but at seventeen and eighteen, that's what you're supposed to do. It was just a pose. But my mother called our bluff and took it to heart that she was no longer needed here. She sold off all the stuff from the house, including my baseball card collection, which would now be worth $8 million, then sold the house itself and moved back to Wales. This freaked me out a bit. Now Ev and I didn't have a home. There would be nowhere to return to, nowhere safe to go when things got out of hand.

I moved to Brookline, just outside of Boston, and lived in an apartment building, down the hall from my sister, Liz, and Michael Avery. I had no furniture. None. Lots of roaches and a tiny bathroom across the hall.

I'd practice, read, listen to and study music, do yoga, and try not to masturbate. I started finding bits of myself in music. Tiny little breakthroughs.

Devouring music from Bali and Tibet, Stravinsky, Varèse, Mingus, Messiaen, Dolphy, Monk, Ornette, Bird, Hendrix, Coltrane. Looking for something where colors were buzzing, something otherworldly or with a link between this realm and one less mundane.

What I wanted most was my own voice on the alto. A sound that was me—not so much to be unique, but to find the person who seemed to be in danger of not appearing when standing in front of a mirror.

I didn't have a TV, but Claire Mallardi, the grande dame of dance at Radcliffe, where my sister taught, had asked me to take care of her cats and plants for a few days in her nice apartment on Beacon Street.

"You have to run the water for a long time to make sure it is clean and cold."

I was practicing but had the black and white TV on with no sound. It was Martin Luther King's birthday and they were playing a lot of his speeches. I turned the sound on and sat down on the bed, with my horn next to me, for a moment.

It just hit me like a ton of bricks. *Look at this man. Listen to him.*

And I said, out loud, as I sat there, "Well, there is a God. And he is coming through that man."

Even more than what he was saying, it was the sound of him that struck me. The honesty resonating through him. Honesty in sound. That became everything to me.

There is a line attributed to Mark Twain: "When I was a boy of fourteen, my father was so ignorant I could hardly stand to have the old man around. But when I got to be twenty-one, I was astonished at how much the old man had learned in seven years."

I had something very similar to this. When I was twelve, of course I didn't listen to anything my parents had to say, but they would always speak of this Martin Luther King with great admiration. The only other thing that I remember their talking about with this much respect was *The New Yorker* and their impeccable fact-checking department. After the Martin Luther King experience, I was idiotically hopeful to think the magazine was still what it once was, some forty years later, and it almost ruined my life.

On a freezing cold night in December, I decided to ride a bike back to Worcester, about forty-five miles away. It was midnight and it was fifteen degrees. The bike was a piece of shit. I pushed myself beyond what I could endure. It wasn't anything I'd planned. I was watching TV with my sister and Michael and just got up and left.

I was wearing a long gray coat with a little fur collar that I'd gotten at the thrift store in Coolidge Corner. I had to hike the coat up over my thighs so I could pedal.

The wind was biting into my bones. At first it was exhilarating, then my eyes started to water and the tears froze to the sides of my face.

The bike was so sluggish, and with the coat and long underwear, every stroke of the pedals felt like I was going up a steep hill. For about ten minutes I went as hard as I could, the harsh, cold air hitting my lungs so fiercely that I thought I was going to have to stop, but I was approaching an incline and coasted down for a while. A car drove by. A guy screamed out the window and it made me jump. *Assholes, very funny.* Then another car went by and someone threw a beer bottle at me. *These people are having fun.*

After forever, I could look back behind me and see the sun was coming up. I was three miles or so from Worcester. At that time I had a big Rasputin beard that was frozen solid with drool. I could have given it a tiny smack and it would have broken off and shattered on the road.

I got off the bike for a moment to look for the sunset and realized my legs had really had enough. I had to call Dean Cohen and ask him to pick me up.

The next day I could hardly walk. The muscles in my legs were a gnarly, striated mess. Dean drove me back to Boston.

Bill Noel came to visit me. He was in worse shape than I was. Something had happened to him when he had gone to Las Vegas to visit his brother. Now he was afraid to sleep and he thought that if he took a shit he would die. The way Bill told the story, his brother had the ability to make objects, like dice, move from several feet away without touching them. The Mafia was now holding his brother hostage because this talent was obviously beneficial to them in Las Vegas. I went back and forth from believing it to thinking it was totally absurd, but didn't let Bill know. Everything he said was deeper than his normal voice, his head tucked down into his bearded neck. Once, when I had gone to Bill's house in Worcester, he was standing on his head and smoking a cigarette.

"Hello John! This is the smoking man's yoga."

I finally got him to go to sleep on his second night in my place. In the morning, I felt there was some credence to his stories because about fifty flies were flying in a circle over his hunched up body.

I smoked some pot with Michael and walked to the corner, where there were a bunch of guys playing basketball. I got in the game and played the best I ever had in my life. Could not miss, wild weird shots, all went in. The guy who was guarding me was good and clearly respected by the other players. He had played college ball somewhere. He was disgusted by this shit I was throwing up, but it just all kept going in, kept going in. And it wasn't luck, it was something else. It was right. It was Zen in basketball.

Michael and I were high and watching the news on TV. There was a ceremony of some kind and the mayor of Cleveland was using an acetylene torch to cut a wire or something, marking the grand opening. The sparks from the torch bounced back and set the mayor's hair ablaze. You could hear this guy in the background screaming, "The mayor's hair is on fire! The mayor's hair is on fire!" The mayor stood there oblivious as his hair crackled, in flames. Michael and I were laughing so hard we couldn't breathe. To this day I will just say, "The mayor's hair is on fire!" and expect people to find it funny.

There was a friend of my sister's named Matia. She and I spent some time together, I guess as boyfriend and girlfriend, but I was so stuck in my turmoil that it seemed hopeless.

I went cross-country with Kaz and his girlfriend Nancy to the Kundalini summer solstice, in Arizona. I thought I should give Kundalini one more try.

Kaz was a harmonica player and was a few years older than me. I knew him through Michael Avery. I knew Nancy a little better than Kaz. She was a friend of my sister's.

We stopped at Kaz's relatives' somewhere on the way. We had dinner with Kaz's aunt and uncle, or whoever they were, and I sat there in silence while they carried on polite conversation. At one point, Kaz's uncle was eyeing my Malarski pants. One of the women from my mother's bridge club was Ann Malarski. She had a son who had been in the navy. He must have been a large fellow, because the waist and length of these pants were enormous. Forty-six-inch waist, forty-inch length. My waist must have been twenty-eight inches around at that time, so I was swimming in them. I rolled up the bottoms of the pants and used a piece of white rope to tie them around me, so that they wouldn't fall down. In big black handwritten letters, just above the ass, was written the identification "MALARSKI." And that is why they were called Malarski pants. I felt shy to have him staring at my pants. I was shy to have him even acknowledge my existence. I had the feeling that they thought I was a heathen or perhaps even dangerous in my strangeness.

After dinner, they were sitting around having a drink and the uncle turned to me and said, "So, John, what's your story? What do you do?"

I said—and this is probably the most uncomfortably awkward thing that has ever exited human lips—"I am in pursuit of a yoga that suits my metabolism."

A pained and confused grimace floated across everyone's face in unison and then they, mercifully, didn't try to include me in the conversation further.

We drove and drove. I was fascinated by the dead animals on the highway in the desert. Every time we saw something, I would go, "What was that?"

Kaz said, "You're really into DOR."

"What's DOR?"

"Dead On Road."

We had an empty two-gallon plastic water container in the back. I was nervous about getting there because I knew that I wasn't going to wear a turban. I knew everybody else would be wearing them, but I wasn't going to do it. I put the plastic container on my head and kept saying over and over how jealous those yogis were going to be when they saw my turban. I kept the thing on my head for hours because I knew it was annoying Kaz, and Nancy found it funny.

Finally, we reached the spot in the desert where they were holding the Kundalini yoga seminar. This thing was based around a form of tantric yoga. We all kept silent for seven days and slept in tents. Everyone was required to have a partner of the opposite sex. Kaz hooked me up with his beautiful ex-girlfriend Vicky Kennick, so that I could do the exercises with her. I think Vicky was there to do this thing with Kaz and he had brought me along as a replacement, since he had a new girlfriend now.

During the day we would line up in scores of long two-by-two rows, with men on the right and women on the left of each row. There were easily a thousand people there, so the rows stretched out forever. In the morning we would hold three different postures for an hour each, while staring into our partner's eyes.

After a very short amount of time, while holding these difficult yoga postures, I would be looking into the beautiful face of Vicky Kennick and orange flaming lights would be bursting from her nose.

Three sets of one-hour postures in the morning and then three sets again in the afternoon. And every one of these thousand or so yogis was keeping silence. The only person who talked during the whole thing was Yogi Bhajan, who sat up on a makeshift stage with a microphone, giving instructions and explaining that mung beans and rice were the meal for the Aquarian Age.

I realized years later that I had gained something from this seminar. Previous to this, I had been terrified of women, and because I was terrified, I hated them. This changed all that. But then, at seventeen or eighteen, being in the desert, being told what to do at every moment, and being under the incontestable authority of Yogi Bhajan made me get weird. I had heard that the year before, Yogi Bhajan, guided by light, was randomly marrying people who had never met before. I didn't want to be under this massive authority. Everyone there was wearing a turban but me and I was wearing Malarski pants. I was the obscene, lost renegade.

I lay in my tent one night, very unhappy and more confused than I have ever been. I was, of course, madly in love with Vicky Kennick, who was not interested in me as I was some four years younger. But that is not what made me crazy. What made me crazy was being part of this enforced community, with its enforced spiritualism. It wasn't that the thing was that phony, I just didn't fit in and I was going through giant changes. Maybe I just wasn't getting it. Maybe it was me, I was too dark in my soul.

One night, I lay there on the cold desert ground, in my tent, and decided that I would kill Yogi Bhajan. I would sneak over to his tent and hack off his head with a cleaver from the kitchen. If he was enlightened, then he would know and stop me, or if he was enlightened, he would know and allow it to happen, or if he was not enlightened, he would not know and he was a sham anyway and I would have done the world a favor.

But I didn't kill Yogi Bhajan, maybe I didn't have the nerve, but I think I was just too tired and it was cold outside of my tent.

When it was over, I went back in another van. Went to Chicago and dropped off Vicky Kennick and then back to Boston. I hardly remember the ride back except that it was odd to be in a metal contraption as it hurtled forward at seventy miles an hour on a neverending strip of concrete.

Evan moved to Boston and got his own apartment in the same building as me and Liz. Had his piano moved in. He was going to high school for the seventh year in a row. I don't really know what he was hoping to accomplish by finishing high school at fifty-one years old, but he went.

He was in class with Michio Kushi's kid. Michio Kushi is the person who introduced the macrobiotic diet to America. According to Evan, Michio Kushi's kids' teeth were falling out because they'd never had milk.

We would eat dinner together and then play, wildly, in his apartment. Cecil Taylor on speed. Evan had the dog, Max. My mother couldn't take him because to go to England, the dog would have had to spend six months in quarantine, Great Britain being very proud of the fact that they had stamped out rabies.

I was walking Max when he got in a fight with another dog. I tried to break it up by grabbing Max's collar and got bitten by my own dog. You could see the bone under the blood.

Cotton blocks me from the world. I can't hear a thing, and what I can hear I can't understand. My mother talks for me.

We've landed in London and the pressure on landing has blocked my ears. That and the accent make it impossible for me to understand anything.

My mother, who must have been quite lonely, has convinced me that if I am to follow the path of a mystic ascetic, then I should truly seek solitude. It's winter and she knows of someone's summer home in Wales that I can stay in for free. This little home is up in the hills in Abersoch and there won't be anyone around for miles. She was daring me and I took her up on it.

The house is barren and concrete and not equipped for winter. I take all the electric heaters and put them in one room. With the heat, a giant black fly comes to life and bombards my solitude. I think that this is a bad omen. This fly could most certainly be the Devil.

During that period, I always slept on the floor. I had peanuts, porridge, and brown rice. The air was cold and damp, always cold and damp and gray. There were sheep in my front yard and no one around for about three miles. My mom and grandma lived in my grandma's little house in the village. My grandma had had this place for a hundred years.

Grandma was tall and strong, with an iron face that had been lived in. She'd sit by the fire and was quite pleased with her life. She had just given up smoking. My mom asked her if it was hard for her to stop, and she said that the doctor had asked her so nicely that she just stopped.

I don't know exactly what I hoped to accomplish by putting myself into complete seclusion. I was uncomfortable with myself and I was looking for some kind of breakthrough. I'd practice the alto and was reading all kinds of different books on religion, mysticism, the occult, and magic. I got completely lost in P. D. Ouspensky's book on George Gurdjieff, *In Search of the Miraculous*.

Matia came over for a few days; that was nice but had nothing to do with what I was trying to accomplish. We didn't get along very well.

She thought that what I was doing was nuts. Which, of course, was a fair assessment, I have to admit, except for this: I gained something from putting myself through this. Something deep inside me. A certain kind of strength in the essence that is me. Something I am continually shocked to find that most people do not have.

Also, people always talk about talent. But really, of this I am quite certain: There is no such thing as talent, there is only cleaning the mirror.

A few days after Matia had left, on my birthday, I went down into the village and had a miserable dinner with my mom and grandma. I broke my regime and had wine and cake. On the way back up the hill I felt awful, saw a shooting star, and then I cursed God.

I turned on the electric heaters and went to sleep on the floor. Cold, lonely, and unhappy. I was violently awakened by lights flashing into the room. I thought that I heard my mother calling outside and that the lights must have been from her car, but my mother wasn't there. Something was happening. I was terrified and ran out of the house. I had heard that the Native Americans had hugged trees in times of psychic peril. It was pitch black and I was stumbling on the gravel road. I found a tree and hugged it, but when I looked up I saw that it was dead, with a ripped piece of clothing dangling from one of the barren branches. This was really upsetting. I felt I was in danger, like I had taken myself too far into some unexplored psychic realm and had perhaps done irreparable damage. I found my way down the hill, toward my grandmother's house, but it was only four in the morning, so I went to walk along the beach. I thought about my dad. It was almost the first time since he'd died that I really thought about him.

Up in the cliffs along the shore, I saw something. Three creatures. I started to climb up the rocks toward them. I was sure this would be a sign for me. These creatures looked wild and mythic, like something out of Homer. I got close enough to see that they were wild rams. Tough, agile, fearless. I was jealous.

I go to London, stay in a bed and breakfast. I can't stay in that house anymore, I'm too afraid. In London, I go to a jazz jam session, one of those horribly annoying unmusical events where there are eighty-three saxophone players waiting to get up and noodle forever. It seems much more like an amateur competition than a musical event. Beer and cigarettes. A tough-looking little guy with an army jacket and long frizzy hair goes up to the stage. He looks like Sonny Bono marinated in beer. His teeth are bad. He looks mean and plays and plays, but not music. This should be a contest, it's all testosterone.

It seems a terrible thing—music being what I believe it is—these saxophone players who spend all their time trying to play as close to Charlie Parker as possible. What a horrendous way to spend your musical life, or your life at all, trying to do the same thing someone else has already done but far better than you ever will.

I drink a beer and have a hard-boiled egg. Things not allowed in my regime. In this very unpleasant atmosphere, I slowly, uncomfortably, descend back to this planet. I'm going to stop torturing myself and stay here for a while.

5

I Am the Supreme Totality!

There were signs all over his apartment that stated: "I AM THE SUPREME TOTALITY!"

I went back to Boston for a while and then went to New York to visit Matia, who I guess I'd have to say was my girlfriend. We went to the museums and to hear music. People seemed tough, with jagged faces, yet less mean in the petty way they seemed in Boston. It was exciting and weird and immediately felt like home.

I went to see the tenor player Sam Rivers in a loft somewhere. I was by myself. Matia and I had had a fight. Sam Rivers didn't show up and someone awful took his place. I actually remember who it was, but I met this musician years later and he was such a sweetheart, I won't mention his name here. In any case, I was there to see Sam Rivers, and when they announced that he would not be playing and who would be playing, the guy sitting next to me grunted in disapproval. I agreed and said, "Yuck."

We started talking about not wanting to see this replacement music and left. This guy was maybe forty-five, black, with a gnarly, muscle-clad body. Had a little beard and wore a knit hat. His strong fingers looked like they could pry open an oyster. He invited me out to his place in Brooklyn.

He lived in the basement of these two buildings on Caton Avenue, near Flatbush. You had to walk down a skinny alley between the two buildings and then pass through a courtyard before you got to a green door that was the only access to the foreboding basement and clearly not intended for tenants. Then you went into the hot concrete underbelly of the building and past the boiler before you got to the padlocked wire door that led to his apartment, which was really a storage closet vaguely transformed into living quarters.

He was the superintendent. He'd sweep and mop the corridors on all six floors of the two buildings and take the trash and put it in the compactor. A few other little jobs that went along with his duties paid him $14 every two weeks and he got this dwelling in the torrid basement for free.

I can recall exactly what the place smelled like, but I cannot put my finger on what that smell was. Maybe sweet incense trying to mask some fetid something.

There was an upright piano, a couch, and a bed in a second tiny room. All over the apartment were hand-painted signs that proclaimed, "I AM THE SUPREME TOTALITY!"

His name was James Parker Washington, and he had just gotten out of jail for murder. He had such a beautiful, unassuming gentleness that I was never nervous around him for a moment.

He offered me some tea and said that I could stay there with him as long as I wanted. So I slept on the couch and the next day, I went to Matia's and got my duffel bag and my horn and moved in.

He would make some kind of health food gruel and tea, and then we would play. Him on the piano and me on alto. Then late at night I would go through the empty hallways with him mopping the floors and talking about music and religion.

He explained the hand-painted signs to me: One night he had smoked a joint and was sitting back in a chair with his eyes closed. He was drifting, but not asleep, when he heard a loud voice giving him a message inside his head that said, "I AM THE SUPREME TOTALITY!" and he realized that it was true. This was not an egotistical thing—quite the opposite, it announced that he was part of God.

Ever since then he had changed.

A sweet girl with big breasts was always stopping by and bringing him food. She had a kid and was on her own.

She wanted Jim. Smiling at him. Beaming. She seemed completely smitten. He was very nice but apparently not interested in getting intimate with her. She was clearly disappointed. He seemed nervous. There was a part of him that was deeply, deeply wounded. You could see it when he looked off and down to the floor.

"Why don't you sleep with her?"

"Oh, no." But that was as far as he wanted to explain.

One night he started rubbing my shoulders. Strong hands, felt great. Like getting rid of those knots would add five years of health to my life.

"Here, lie down."

So I stretched out on the couch. I was disappearing under the massage when I felt him poke with deliberation at my anus through my pants. I sprung up from the couch and halfway across the room.

"What the fuck are you doing?!"

"I just wanted to . . . fuck, you know?" He was looking at the floor. He looked sad and ashamed.

"I'm not into that, Jim."

"Oh, okay."

His vibe was clearly straight, and there was that sweet girl who wanted him. I think that all those years in jail just made him want to have sex like how he was used to.

He showed me how to use the compactor. Then James Parker Washington announced that he was leaving the day after tomorrow and if I wanted his job, he would square it with the building manager.

So as simple as that, I had moved to New York.

It was kind of wonderful, in a way, to sweep and mop the floors in the middle of the night with no one anywhere. Long, empty night hallways. I liked having some specific menial task, and most of the time, I liked being alone. I had trouble making myself get up to sweep, but once I did, I always enjoyed it. I think that this kind of work is good for people, especially people like me, who are stuck living deeply in their heads.

The compactor scared me, a big, bellowing monster of a thing that inhaled the trash and spat it out in little squares, but I did all right with it.

So I would do these chores and then practice. One day, I was playing my horn and this man's voice came booming through the courtyard.

"Shut up!!"

I didn't know if he meant me, waited five minutes, and then started playing again, quieter. A few minutes later I heard someone walking in the basement. No one ever came down there. Hard shoes on the concrete floor. A tough-looking guy in a T-shirt was ducking under the low concrete roof and approaching the wire door.

"I need to sleep. You have to stop. I hate that kind of music."

How am I going to save the world with my music if that's the effect that it has on people?

It was during this time that I fasted for ten days and had the vision and understanding about the cross. I kept trying to fast to understand things further but would find myself walking across Prospect Park in the middle of the night to buy a gallon of Breyers ice cream, which I would eat in one sitting and then be overwhelmed with guilt.

I'm making oatmeal for my breakfast, I look up, and outside the wire door is a thin guy just standing there. Very clean, short blond hair. White, white shirt and glasses.

How do these people get so clean? I try to get clean, I wash, I wash my clothes, but I could never look that clean. It's like he's been boiled or something.

"Are you confused about the meaning of life? May I come in, to talk with you?"

I let him in because I was deeply confused about the meaning of life.

"Have you found Jesus?"

He goes on with his little fervent spiel. And at the end, somehow, he gets me to get down on my knees and pray to Jesus. He is very pushy and I am lost and I am searching, but this isn't right. This isn't what I want. But he is so insistent, I do it just to get him to leave.

After his conquest, he leaves quickly. I feel like he has stolen something from me. I feel violated and am filled with shame. Somehow I feel as though I have been soiled by this little creep in the clean white shirt, who honestly had no more interest in God than I had in pork belly futures.

After a few weeks I went up to Germantown, New York, where Steve Piccolo was living with his wife, Wendy. They both were going to Bard College, and during the summer they had rented a little cottage. I was only going to stay for a day, but Wendy kept convincing me that it was silly for me to go back to Brooklyn. She was very manipulative and I didn't like her, but I stayed because it seemed too hard to go back to being completely alone in a basement.

I stay almost a week, and when I get back, trash is piled everywhere and there is a note on the wire door saying that I have to come to the manager's office.

He fires me. I couldn't possibly blame him. He just looked at me like, how could I do that, just disappear after taking the responsibility? I can still see his face, and somehow, I have to thank him. He didn't yell or act pissed. He just, for a moment, looked right into me, and without saying a word, the message came through: *You know that's not right, kid. This is life and that is just not right.*

I moved up to Germantown, where Wendy insisted that Steve and I get jobs. She found me a job at a fruit cocktail packing company. The smell was horrifying. I will never eat fruit cocktail again, ever, and I think it is the reason that to this day, I cannot even eat fruit from the deli or anywhere else where it has been precut.

I was strange and skinny. I had absolutely no skills in dealing with people because I'd never really dealt with people. Everyone on the job site stayed as far as possible from the new guy. I thought that I could fit in, but no way. People worked in pairs and the foreman came to me.

"Lurie, why doesn't anyone want to work with you?"

"I don't know," I said, and tried to hide the fact that it was something that was really beginning to hurt me.

Then new guys came after me and they fit right in. It was me, they smelled something on me. I wasn't like them.

The foreman gave me a job where I worked by myself. I had to carry boxes of canned fruit cocktails in and out of a large freezer room. The stench was awful and my sweat would freeze to me as I went back in from the outside summer heat.

I will never eat fruit cocktail again.

I quit the job, had a fight with Wendy, and went back to New York. Wendy was trying to get us to all have sex together and I wanted absolutely no part of it. I had no money, so I couldn't take a cab, and all my shit was in a big army duffel bag, which got so heavy that I just started to drag it behind me, bouncing on the Manhattan pavement. I had no idea where to go, and the bottom of the duffel bag was tearing. Distributing socks and underwear all over Thirty-fourth Street.

I called my uncle Jerry, who told me to come over to his place on Fifty-seventh Street. He had a very romantic penthouse duplex on Fifty-seventh between Sixth and Seventh avenues. I slept on the couch. Jerry was moving to a much bigger place on Central Park West after living in his idyllic bachelor pad for a quarter of a century. The rent was $130 a month. I wanted to continue to live there after he left, but he said that that would be illegal. Jerry was a lawyer. And he was a good man. I believe the term is *a mensch.*

He gave me a job sorting his hundreds of books by category and then packing them up. I don't think that he really needed this, and often I had no clue what category some of the books should go into, but did the best I could.

There were steaks in the icebox, and by now I had started eating meat again. My skin was growing to be less the color of paper. I would fry up a steak and then down it with a big glass of whiskey from Uncle Jerry's bar. He didn't drink himself but had a full bar for visitors.

Then he said that his new place was under construction but that he supposed if I didn't mind the noise and the mess, I could sleep there. So I moved my horn and duffel bag over to this construction site that would eventually be a luxury apartment on Central Park West, with an amazing view of the park.

I slept in a sleeping bag in the front room, which had a big picture window that floated over the park. A cord with an ornate tassel hung to the ground from a contraption that closed the curtains. One night I dreamed that I had severed the cord with my teeth. I woke up and went out to Central Park, and when I got back to the apartment, workmen were moving sheetrock from one room to the other. Over in the corner I saw the severed curtain cord. I was sure that there must have been some significance to this, but I didn't know what the hell it was.

My uncle got me a job at the Plaza Hotel. I was the new night housekeeping dispatcher. If Milton Berle needed more pillows, I would call Elsie or Beverly and have them bring some pillows to Mr. Berle.

I loved the maids. They were mostly Jamaican and Haitian, and they were wonderful. We would constantly tease one another back and forth. I felt like one of them.

There was a big, older, angry Irish guy named John who did the maintenance work. His response to pretty much everything was, "They can go pound sand up their ass."

I worked from four in the afternoon until midnight, which was fine with me. From four P.M. to six P.M. there was a lot of work, making lists of checkouts and rooms to be cleaned. Then at six P.M. it would slow down, and unless a guest needed something, there was nothing much to do. I would bring my horn and practice or steal Plaza stationery and draw in my little cubicle, surrounded by fresh, clean towels.

My pursuit of mystical transcendence was still there but not a constant preoccupation. I would flirt with the maids. But oddly enough, the person I ended up sleeping with was my boss, Miss Andrade. She was fifty-two. This is 1974, so I must have been twenty-two. She was Swedish and quite pretty for any age. Other guys at work were always hitting on her and couldn't figure out why she was with that weirdo when people caught wind of our little fling.

I never stopped calling her Miss Andrade. Even after I'd slept with her two or three times, I still called her Miss Andrade. Her real name was Guri, but I just couldn't feel that. Evan met her and found it extremely disconcerting that I didn't call her by her first name. Mostly, we just had sex in the housekeeping department when nobody was around, but a couple of times I went out to her place in Jackson Heights. She put maple syrup on my cock and licked it off. She really had no zest whatsoever in sucking my cock. This was something that she had clearly read about in a magazine: "Interesting Ways to Perk Up Your Sex Life!"

But she was fun. I spent one very weird New Year's Eve with her. Somehow the idea of New Year's Eve with her pointed out the complete gulf, and it made me sad for her. My God, Miss Andrade, if she is still around, must be close to a hundred. If you are still around, Miss Andrade, a warm, heartfelt hello to you.

* * *

My first real place in New York was a railroad apartment on Fourteenth Street between First and Second avenues. There was no shower and only a tiny little bathtub that I never used.

I joined the Jewish Y next door so I could take showers there and started to play a lot of basketball.

The apartment was on the top floor of a six floor walk-up. The building was owned by the Puerto Rican family who had the bodega on the ground floor.

There was another mattress for Evan, who wasn't really living anywhere at the time. A woman downstairs ranted on and on for hours at a stretch. She was screaming at her husband, and she would scream and scream until her voice had cracked and broken and then keep on screaming. It was unbelievable, I've never heard anything like it. I used to take a baseball bat and smash on the pipes to get her to stop. It never worked.

The screaming was so intense it was clear the woman was raving mad. I didn't want to have any direct contact. I never saw either the husband or the wife on the stairs, and I don't think that they ever left their apartment.

Pretty much every day I would get up, go play ball at noon, eat, and then go up to the Plaza by subway. When he was around, Evan and I always got along really well. The only thing we ever fought about was socks.

Then one time the shrieking was just too much, and I went downstairs and knocked on the door. That was a mistake. The husband answered the door, but what I remember was her. She stood lurking behind him, in mostly darkness, with this malicious half smile, the face and power of a true demon. The smile said, *You want to mess with us, honey, go right ahead.* Her fingernails were a full three inches long and curled toward her palms. The madness was terrifying. I never knocked or banged on the pipes again. She had me beaten with a glance.

I had bought a flute and a clarinet and was working on them a little bit. When I came home one day, someone had come through the window off the fire escape and stolen them. I had my alto with me and didn't really feel that bad. I'm not that fond of the flute, and the clarinet fingering was different from the alto and a little confusing. But I knew that Life or God or whatever controlled how things went, would never let my alto get stolen. That just couldn't possibly happen, and even though I had just been robbed and the window still didn't lock, I didn't think that much about it because I was sure that anything that I really needed in life would not be taken from me.

It was summer. I'd saved a little money and I was just about to quit the Plaza to work on music full time. I went to the Museum of Modern Art, and when I got home my alto was gone. I couldn't believe it. I just couldn't believe it.

I was heartbroken, but not only was I heartbroken, I was shocked that something like this could happen. It wasn't like I was fearless, but I just believed that somehow one is protected. I used to practice, every night, in the subway station on the corner of Fourteenth and First. I'd go in about midnight, walk all the way down to the end of the platform, and play until two or three in the morning. I was never even nervous about it. The Canarsie line didn't come that often and there were few people using that stop at that hour. But really, New York on the Lower East Side was one hundred times more dangerous then than it is now, and if I heard about someone doing that now, I would think they were insane.

There was one moment when I was on Second Avenue near Thirteenth Street that is just sort of frozen in my memory. I had the same thing when my mom died, just this one spot, during one stride on the pavement and a glance at the sign of the store that sold nurses' uniforms, where it really hit me. Just one moment in time. Just how horrible it was and how deep it went into me that my horn was gone.

I go in to tell the landlords, the Hispanic couple who ran the bodega downstairs. I tell them that I was robbed. They just stare at me like, *So? What do you want us to do about it?*

I go up to Forty-eighth Street to see if I can get a decent alto with the money that I had saved from the Plaza. My alto was a beautiful Selmer Mark VI; old horns are much better and more expensive than new horns. They were made better and have more warmth and resonance. I am there at the counter and I can see the price tags, and this is nowhere near what I can afford. There is a guy there talking about these six soprano saxophones that somebody is selling in this little shop downtown for three hundred apiece. So I go down and buy one. It's a silver Conn, a straight soprano.

Now I've got a little money left but not much and decide to move back to Boston. I can't remember why. I had hated Boston.

Rudy has a car, and he says if I get a U-Haul he'll drive me up to Boston. I had met Rudy in Boston when I was a few years younger. He was round and black and had a grin halfway between the Cheshire cat's and Buddha's. He had gone out with my sister, but just for a minute. Rudy introduced me to the music of Lester Young, Billie Holiday, and others. Beautiful, magical worlds that became part of my being. He was maybe five years older than me. Rudy was very into Ramana Maharshi, Meher Baba, and other mystics, as well as the Bible. He used to have a job running the projector at a theater in Boston's Combat Zone, which was then a porno district.

I would go down and visit him and watch *The Devil in Miss Jones* and *Deep Throat* five times in a row, back to back, from the little booth. Leave the theater with him at dawn, have some greasy eggs in a diner, and then go watch a gaggle of Bruce Lee movies in the neighboring theater. Like to wash the porn from our brains.

A few months after that, Rudy wrote religious slogans all over the walls of his apartment and disappeared.

I moved back into the building with Liz and Michael and got a job driving a cab. I didn't really know my way around. I'd get a call from the dispatcher on the radio saying car number 314, go to such and such a place, and I would look it up on a map.

The second night, around three A.M., I picked up a go-go dancer outside of a strip club. She wouldn't tell me where she wanted to go. We just drove with the meter off. She was sexy in that dirty sort of way in her purple scanty outfit. Her eyes looked odd and somewhat empty. I realized years later that they were pinned because she was on heroin. Finally she said that she wanted to go to my place. I said okay. I brought the cab back to the garage. The guys at the garage wondered where on earth she'd come from but didn't say anything. I walked her back to my apartment, which was right down the block on Harvard Avenue.

We had sex once and then I wanted to fuck her in the ass; I'd never done it and thought that she might be into it, being older and obviously more experienced. She reacted with horror, like she'd never heard of such a thing. There was something very strange about her, maybe because her eyes were pinned. I was afraid to go to sleep. I was convinced that she was from outer space and might kill me.

I dropped a passenger in Roxbury. There was a basketball court, all lit up with a serious game going on, and the bleachers were fairly packed with people watching. I parked the cab and watched for a while.

All the players were black. Everyone in the stands was black. I didn't think much of it.

I had played in the black game in Worcester and it was fine. It was better than fine, it was pretty much the most fun I had ever had. And I could hold my own.

I was completely unaware of the racial tensions in Boston.

There were some really good players, but I assessed it and thought that I was as good as the players on the low end out there.

So when the game ends, I go out onto the court, start shooting around with the players who're going to play next, and get into the game. One guy with a beard nods at me as we shoot around, and I think maybe it's okay.

But I'm not welcome. The vibe is heavy. And what makes it worse is when the game starts, the ball deflects off someone's hand right to me, and I put up a fairly easy ten-foot jump shot and, *swish*, it goes in.

I hit the first basket of the game and seem to have crossed all kinds of lines here.

Someone on my team shoots and I go underneath to get the rebound, and BLAM! this guy elbows me hard in the eye. I think probably on purpose. I can hear people in the crowd gasp as the *thwack* to my eye echoes through the outside court. My eye is fucked up. One of the older, kinder players comes over to see if I'm okay.

I can't open my eye. This kinder guy helps me off the court.

I take the cab back. I'm doing a lot of yoga and the book says that a headstand cures everything. So I decide to do that; this will bring blood to the afflicted area. When I come down there's a lot of pressure on my eye and I reach up to touch it. I look at my hand and there's blood. A lot of blood. In the bathroom mirror, I see that my eye is swollen up to the size of a racquetball and blood is gushing out of my closed eyelid.

Michael Avery takes me to the hospital, where they get the swelling down and then give me drops for my eye. The drops will mess with my depth perception, so I'm not supposed to drive. The next day I'm sitting outside of the building on Harvard Avenue and this kid is coming down the street on a bike. A car is coming the other way. They can't see each other! I scream, "Look out!" The kid and car pass each other a full ten feet apart, both of them staring at me in bewilderment.

I liked driving a cab but it was very time consuming. To make any money I had to drive fourteen hours a day, I was always getting lost, and didn't have time to practice the horn.

I get a brilliant idea: There must be a program for people who are insane but not so insane that they have to be institutionalized. I do some research and find out that there is. I can get $250 a month if I qualify.

I find a young social worker who shows a deep concern for my case. I refuse to ever look her in the eyes. I stare at the floor. I talk from the back of my throat. She asks lots of questions.

"Do you hear people calling your name?"

"Right now?"

"No, maybe when you're out on the street, do you hear people call your name who aren't there?"

In actual fact, I did. "Yes."

She asks more questions and I don't really answer, I just kind of murmur at her. Then I take a deep breath and rock my head back and forth.

"It's good."

"What's good, John?"

"I can't, I can't really."

"I don't understand."

"Am I okay?"

"Yes, John, you might be schizophrenic."

I try to discern how she wants me to answer different questions, throwing in an occasional moan or bark. I have to see her twice more, but it works. She's going to recommend me for Supplemental Security Income.

It takes about two months, but after I go to this government office, I will start getting checks. I go down to the agency that handles this deal. They make you wait forever. I'm a little worried that my symptoms will change because I don't remember exactly what I did the first time.

I'm tired of waiting in this place. It's a big, hot room with all the charms of governmental bureaucracy. A guy comes in with a filthy shirt, torn jeans, and a very hostile look on his face. He comes in and walks to the middle of the room and gets down on one knee, pointing his finger above his head toward the heavens.

"I WANT THE MONEY! I WANT THE MONEY!"

He gets immediate attention, bureaucrats scurrying everywhere, telling him he has to go to this line and then that line.

"I WANT THE MONEY!"

Okay, no lines.

This guy's a genius. My act is nowhere near as good as his. He's getting immediate attention.

"I WANT THE MONEY! I WANT THE MONEY!"

I was very impressed. A little jealous, to tell you the truth.

So I started getting the checks. I felt a little guilty about it. Maybe this wasn't so moral. I should work. Why should I get this money?

I went to see this evil psychic I'd seen before. He was a suspicious character but very accurate. He said that I was an artist and that they were the enemy, and I should definitely take the money. So I did.

But you know what? If this society had really taken a look at me at that time, they would have decided certainly that I was not one of them.

I met a girl named Andrea. We were both insecure and depressed and it was a dismal thing of a relationship. She was studying dance and not doing so well with it. She would have sparks of wonderful life to her and then just get so lost she would bump into walls.

I started playing music for the dance classes at Radcliffe College, where my sister taught. I had a tambourine under my foot and would play the sax to "step-brush-land, step-brush-land."

Andrea and I moved into a place together in Allston, right on the Mass Pike. It was not really a neighborhood, just a few old three-story tenements sitting off desolately by themselves. A solid wind would have crumbled the building to the ground.

The landlord was an alcoholic, with a big head and white hair that was so healthy and perfect, it seemed to belong to a politician. He lived on the first floor and never left. The building was in complete disrepair, and for some spooky reason, we were always finding dead crows scattered about the barren yard.

There was a woman, with not many teeth, constantly around the house. She was really out there. Usually she was drunk, but she was so insane that it was hard to know if she was drunk or not. I came into the house from the cold one day and she was standing on the landing.

"They put their fingers in my cunt! They put their fingers in my cunt!"

She was spitting as she wailed and wiggling her fingers around up in the air.

On one of my many trips to New York, I had somehow started smoking. I was twenty-four now. Matia was in Robert Wilson's *The $ Value of Man*, which I saw, and it hit me really deeply as something important and different and completely modern.

Andrea and I were always depressed. I was a weirdo, at least for Boston, and she was a not-very-talented dancer. We had no confidence alone, and together we were worse. The low point came when I was with her in Coolidge Corner. She was wearing some fabric thing that she had wrapped around her as a skirt. The trolley came and as she ran across the street to catch it, the fabric thing opened up, revealing her undancerly, plump bottom with no underwear.

These two ten-year-old kids were standing next to me on the corner and one said, "Look at that lady."

At least thirty people saw her ass as she hopped onto the train. I yelled but she couldn't hear me. Then I just walked away. It was too sad, somehow.

Evan was in London now. He was living in a squat and made it sound very glamorous, so I decided to go. A couple days before I was planning to leave, Andrea came home late at night, escorted by her brother. She was crying hysterically. The look on her younger brother's face made me think that this had been going on for hours. She was already on the verge of a breakdown but had had sex with a lesbian friend of hers, and it had put her over the edge.

I thought I would only be gone for a month or so. I left my record collection, my good tape recorder, and most of my stuff at that apartment, on Lincoln Street, with her. Of course, when I came back to get them, it was a year later, she was gone, and no one had any idea where she was.

6

Dancing Hitler

I've got mashed potatoes smeared all over my face. The British couple are staring at me in horror.

I left Boston and went to New York on my way to England. Spent three or four days on a mad binge, saying hello and goodbye to everyone. I didn't sleep.

Rick Morrison gave me a Quaalude, a real one. I'd never had one before; he said to take it twenty minutes before I got on the plane. I was anxious to take it and swallowed it down at the water cooler in the terminal, an hour before the flight.

Twenty minutes later I was incredibly horny. I called Rick on the phone and said, "What is this pill? I have to sleep with somebody. Right now! Who am I going to sleep with in the airport?"

Rick, with a leer in his voice, said, "Anybody."

I got on the plane. I had the window seat and was trapped in by a lovely British couple in their midfifties who'd just had their first vacation in years. They offered me a cigarette after the plane took off and we were talking. They'd had a wonderful time. "It's our first visit to the States. We've seen the Statue of Liberty and the Empire State Building."

I must have been pulling it off that I wasn't completely droolingly trashed, because they were going on and on. They were really very sweet.

The stewardess brought a drink and then the meal. It must have been the drink that did it. When I wake up, my head is on the pull out tray thing and my meal is gone. I sit up and don't realize that I've got mashed potatoes all over the right side of my face. My head must have just gone *plonk* on the tray.

The squat Evan is staying at is horrible. No heat. Everything dirty. A bunch of lunatics, with bad teeth, trying to run a household; they would have meetings to discuss the orders of business and it was just nuts. Once, a government official came by to challenge their right to stay in the abandoned building. He knocked on the door and got no answer. He went around to the window and saw a bunch of scraggly people, sitting around. He knocked on the window and yelled, but nobody looked up. He went back to the door and buzzed. He went to another window: more people with tattered clothes sitting around in chairs who didn't look up when he pounded on the glass. He came back the next day and was greeted, congenially, at the door.

"Why didn't you let me in last night?"

"Were you here last night?"

"Yes! I was pounding on the window and nobody looked up. Is that some kind of joke to you people?"

"We didn't hear you."

The amazing thing was that they really hadn't heard him. They were all high on this or that and just sat there in their lunkhead stupor not hearing him for real.

I was pissed at Evan. This wasn't glamorous, like at all. This was kind of disgusting. Ev himself seemed to be doing quite well, though. He had cut his waist-length hair and wasn't wearing jeans anymore. He had a short army haircut and had changed his fashion to look sort of like an out-of-work college professor, tweed sport coats with elbow patches and hard brown shoes. There was something more solid and positive in his walk.

Somewhere around this time, he had confided in me that he was gay. I know that he actually told me when we were walking around in New York, but it was certainly around this time. I know that he told me in New York because I know the exact spot where he told me. Lafayette Street between Bleecker and Bond. It's that same thing of a frame in my memory that goes *click* and something from that moment holds it.

He was clearly nervous to tell me. But it was bizarre how little impact it had, though I was very surprised. It hadn't occurred to me.

I think I just said, "Really? Okay."

And it was okay, perfectly okay, and Evan could see I meant it and we just went about our evening.

When he told my mom, she said, "Oh, I always thought it would be John." I don't know what provoked that. Actually, I do know. She wanted to piss me off, which she did for a minute, but then I just had to laugh. "I'm not gay. Evan can be gay and that is fine, but I am not gay and you know it. You just said that to make me angry, which I'm not."

There was a girl in London named Wendy, who I guess had spent some time with Evan and was still into him. Wendy was the sexiest thing I had ever seen. I asked Evan if he minded if I got together with Wendy and he said, "I'd rather you wouldn't."

I tried to wouldn't, but it was not possible. I was smitten. And, Evan: I really am sorry about it to this day. But only a little.

Wendy lived in a one-room council flat. These are provided by the government. She didn't have a phone—no one had a phone. If you wanted to play with Roger Turner, the drummer in Portobello, and Mike Block, the piano player from Sandringham Road, it could take a week of traveling on the tube to set it up. Wendy's place was right behind the London Coliseum in Covent Garden.

At night, I would be outside talking to sweet little eighty-four-year-old Ben, and Rudolf Nureyev would come walking out of the stage entrance of the Coliseum. Just me, Ben, and Rudolf Nureyev in the brisk London air. Ben loved World War II, he loved to talk about how awful and hard it was, but if it weren't for the war, I don't think that Ben would have had much to say.

The whole floor shared a communal bathroom, which was very cold but clean. You would stand there freezing putting five pence into the water heater to get enough water for a third of a bath.

I started playing on the street—busking, they call it. I played in

Piccadilly Circus, on weekends, or near the Tottenham Court tube station at around five P.M. as people were rushing home from work. People would throw money in my case, sometimes quite a lot. I tried it in New York, down near Wall Street, a couple years later when I was broke. I didn't get a penny. What was so bizarre was how the stockbrokers would avert their gaze, embarrassed that you were there. I finally started to just scream into the air, standing behind my alto case, to make them as uncomfortable as possible.

London was different, and it was accepted—there were lots of buskers there. Many of the guys had their territory marked out and it was understood that you couldn't take their spot. There were two or three different one-man bands, guys who wore a bass drum on their back, hunched over, and played the guitar, with a harmonica in a holder and maybe cymbals clanging between their knees. There was a spindly old guy Wendy called Hitler, who dressed up in a tuxedo and top hat and danced about in a way that seemed he would soon either catch his ride on a spaceship or burst into flames. There was the Budgie Man, who had a bunch of trained white pigeons that would do not very interesting tricks.

One night, I was playing in Piccadilly Circus and this somewhat official looking guy, in a uniform, came by to warn me, very politely, that all the buskers were getting arrested. He almost was apologizing for it. The police never bothered you, so I ignored him, but twenty minutes later I was arrested.

The police are so civil in London, exceedingly polite. They processed me through and put me in a cell for the night filled with other street musicians. Dancing Hitler wasn't there, and they didn't arrest the Budgie Man because they probably didn't want to deal with his birds. Other than that there were five or six of us in this kind of holding area with bunks. One of the one-man bands that I saw all the time was there, cursing and cursing. These guys were so mean. I thought that there would be a certain camaraderie because we were all street musicians captured together, but these people were just ugly. I had encountered weirdness from British musicians toward musicians from the United States, a jealousy thing, so I stayed back and didn't say anything. Thought they might not appreciate the Yank on their turf, but they were not speaking to each other either. There wasn't a sound from anyone, all night, except for the one-man-band guy I recognized, just going, "Fuck! Fuck! Shit! Fuck!"

London, at least then, was the most violent place I have ever seen. Not guns, just sheer out-and-out brutal shit. There were always fist fights in Piccadilly Circus like I never saw in New York. Groups of guys fighting each other, fans of different soccer teams. Two wrong looks and it would just start. I was walking home late one night and walked past an alley where I could hear this girl's shrill, ugly voice, screaming, "Hit him again." There were three guys standing around a car, and as I looked to see, this guy's head was hanging out the open car door, facing upward. He looked like he was only partly conscious; there was a guy kneeling on his chest, just punching him in the face every time the horrible girl demanded it.

I was playing in Piccadilly Circus on a weekend night. Very crowded. I was playing with my eyes closed, when—*blam!*—out of nowhere some football yobbo punched me full in the face. I didn't even know what had happened for a moment. I just looked up from the ground to see a bunch of drunken assholes walking away, laughing. They weren't even looking back.

Destroy something every ten yards and move on.

I figured out a great trick for weekends. When the idiot drunken football fans would start coming in, I'd get them to sing their team song. They're standing there drunk and singing and I just put my saxophone case, open, in front of them, so that other fans of that team would come by and jokingly throw money into the case. I made a fortune like that. Then when the fans of another team came by, a fight would start, and I'd pack up my case filled with money and scurry with my saxophone in one hand and my case in the other to the next corner.

My mom had bought a house in Anglesey. You could see the cold water of the Menai Strait rushing by from her front window. Always seemed cold, and the air was so clean and brisk that it hurt. Now she had Max the dog. She had put him in a kennel for six months' quarantine. WE THE BRITISH ARE PROUD OF HAVING NO RABIES!!!!!

The house was a nice little house, but there was a horrible green and yellow rug that was left over from the last owner. My mom couldn't have had a lot of money, but she had some from the insurance and some from selling the house. I was shocked that she, who had always had such good taste, would leave that ghastly carpet in her living room.

She was drinking a lot.

The neighbor had a dog that her son had named Franco's Dead. The son was off at college and you would hear the mom, with her sweet little voice, out on the porch calling the dog in: "Franco's Dead! Franco's Dead!" Trying to get the dog to come home.

I always felt sluggish around then, and I found that if I stayed awake for a couple of days it would break the cycle, and by the second day I would feel more alive. I had been up all night drawing and my mom came down in the morning. It was Sunday and she was reading the London *Sunday Times*. There was a contest: The idea was to add the funniest or cleverest caption to a photo from the paper. My mother was working hard on her entry. I found a picture of a farmer in a field with rows of cabbages, and there were little bubbles coming out of the cabbages like they were singing "Rule Britannia!" My caption was "Lettuce Sing."

I kept telling my mom, "You can stop now, I've already won." I was so punchy from not sleeping, I was laughing my head off.

"Oh, you are daft." When you were being silly and she didn't want to laugh she would say you were daft.

After she went to sleep, I would practice in the little cold kitchen. It must have been loud for her upstairs, but she encouraged me to keep playing.

She was a good sport about stuff like that. When I was eleven or twelve, I thought I was going to be a pitcher in the major leagues one day. I would be out in the backyard, throwing a hard rubber ball against the side of the house, over and over again, as hard as I could. It must have been incredibly loud inside the house, but she never complained about it once.

I went back and forth between Wendy's and my mom's for a while. Evan was hanging out with a brilliant priest named Liam. Liam would drink whiskey in his council flat and get really mean. But he had a wonderful evil twinkle in his eye and could be really funny, when I could understand what he was saying through his accent.

Wendy was as violently nasty as she was sexy. They kind of went hand in hand. We would have fights where we would each be standing at one of the two windows of her apartment, throwing each other's stuff out into the street. The blue scarf that my mother had knit me, Wendy took scissors and cut it into tiny little squares.

We had a fight—we were always fighting—then went to sleep, and I woke up to being punched hard in the nose. We would fight like mad and then have sex. She would look at me with this impish grin and say, "You can do anything you want to me." Which was irresistible.

I wrote and played music for Wendy's dance and some other dancers, and then just got tired of damp, cold, poor London, where nobody had a phone, and decided to go back home to New York. Wendy was at the train platform with me before I went to my place and got my stuff to go to the airport. This was basically goodbye, but we were fighting and fighting.

She could say something like, "You stupid sod!" with so much venom in her voice it made me want to kill her.

So the train pulls up and we're fighting. I get on the train and she is on the platform telling me that I am selfish or stupid or some such thing. Then, as the train started to inch away, I realized I wasn't going to see her again. Or if I saw her again, she would be with her husband and two kids. I just yelled, "Oh, Wendy," like, *What have we done?*

7

Crushed Bandit

I moved into a place with friends on Second Avenue. A big apartment on the third floor between St. Marks and East Seventh Street. All my friends were actually moving out soon. They had qualified for government housing at Cooper Square and were moving into fifty-five dollar a month apartments on Third and Fourth Street that were given to people who could prove a low enough income.

I used my status as an insane person on SSI to apply myself, but it took months, even a year, to get approved. Pretty soon I was living in the Second Avenue apartment by myself. In 1977, rents weren't like they are now. It cost $270 a month for this enormous, halfway decent apartment.

When I was still in Boston, Rick, Francie, and Gerri, the people who were at Second Avenue when I moved in, had all lived in a loft on Bond Street. When I would come to New York, I would crash at their place. They lived on the second floor. The fourth floor was vacant, and I used to go up there to practice so that I wouldn't bother anybody.

The person referred to as Rick preferred, in later life, to be called

Richard. Richard Morrison. I have to say this somewhere, so I will say it here: I have met countless amazing people in my life, but I learned more from Richard Morrison than, perhaps, anyone else. He was a true artist. And he was an artist with so much integrity that, of course, no one has ever heard of him.

But somehow try to grasp this: Things Richard Morrison passed on to me are things that I passed on to Jean-Michel Basquiat a few years later. While you can have some understanding of the strangeness of a painting selling for $110 million, you may not understand this. But I was there and I know. You read this stuff and see these movies where people try to glom on to Jean-Michel and his value and what it can do for their lives, but I know this: Richard Morrison was the real deal, and indirectly, Jean-Michel, who was also the real deal, got a ton from Rick, through me.

I had begun to find myself musically, and what I was doing was different. This guy named Vance heard me playing and was fascinated. Vance was black, overly groovy, and "in control." His clothes were always freshly pressed. Even his jeans had a crease in them. His Afro was perfectly round. He had a horribly affected voice and was so intent on appearing sane, the way he would enunciate words or slow down to construct a sentence, that it seemed obvious to me that he was completely out of his fucking gourd.

Vance had bought a saxophone and been playing for three years. But you knew immediately that this was not now, nor would ever be, a horn player. What Vance was, in his actual life, was a drug dealer.

I ran into him on the street, soon after I got back. Vance first wanted to know about my sister. He had met her somewhere and wanted to hook up with her. Right. Like I was going to hook up this phony, insane person with my sister. He talked to me, at length, about not being able to get an erection if he wore a condom, information that I really didn't want to think about.

But Vance had an interesting offer. He wanted to front me pot—lots of it. Like twenty fucking pounds of pot. Whatever I didn't sell, I could return. What he really wanted was a safe place to store it, but he wouldn't come right out and say that. That became clearer two nights later when I got a call from Vance at four A.M., saying his brothers had to come over immediately.

I was disappointed because I thought that he was going to take his pot back, but his brothers came running up the stairs ten minutes later and had garbage bags full of marijuana. Another twenty pounds, maybe even more. They must have been expecting a raid.

Vance's brothers did not say a word to me. Came into my place, dropped the weed in bags on the living room floor. Didn't even make eye contact. On the way out, they stopped, reached in their pockets in unison, held their guns out for a moment for me to see. The display was so well timed, I thought they could have been synchronized swimmers with dreadlocks. Then they left without speaking, still not making eye contact.

I decided that I wanted to do a performance in my giant apartment. All I had to do was knock down the double walls that held the big wooden doors in the living room and I could fit twenty-five people seated and have enough room for the play that I wanted to make called *Crushed Bandit*.

Rick, who used to live in the apartment, said that he didn't think that these were structural walls and that it would be easy to knock them down.

These were big, thick walls in the middle of the place. Smoking tons of Vance's pot, I spent hours and hours, and then days and days, smashing at the walls with a sledgehammer. At first, it was a blast to smash away at the walls like that.

Then it got awful. Dust was everywhere. I came home with groceries and as I walked up Second Avenue, I could see billows of dust floating out of my windows hours after I had stopped.

It was 1977, incredibly hot that summer. I would be naked in the apartment, stoned and smashing away with all the windows open.

I find out that the mean Albanian guy who runs the newspaper stand down the block wants to kill me. The people in the store downstairs say I better be very careful. I have bought cigarettes from this guy and I know just from looking at him that his wacko eyes are wired for violence. I also saw him go nuts on somebody twice his size.

"Why does he want to hurt me? I didn't do anything to him."

"His fourteen-year-old daughter is watching you naked in the apartment. She is home from school and he keeps catching her watching you."

I'm so stoned all the time that it has never occurred to me that every single person in the buildings on the other side of Second Avenue can see right into my place. New York always seemed such a blur of activities and people that it never dawned on me that, in a sense, each block is still a neighborhood, and that some people know every little thing that is happening.

I have been lugging all the debris down and throwing it into a dumpster right in front of my place on Second Avenue. Apparently, this is no good. I just thought, *There is a dumpster full of trash, I'll throw my shit in there.* But I am throwing barrels and barrels and barrels of wall and dust and plaster into this thing and filling it up all with my own debris. Whoever has rented this dumpster for their own job is really pissed off and also is looking for me.

All the pot is making me paranoid. I feel like I am being watched at all times. Then Vance calls. He needs the twenty pounds of pot that he dropped off plus whatever I haven't sold back immediately.

It's unbearably hot, 104 degrees, as I lug a suitcase filled with forty pounds of marijuana over to Vance's house. I am a little nervous. If everybody knows everything, I am going to get arrested. Plus, forty pounds in a suitcase starts to get heavy after a few blocks.

The suitcase is getting heavier and it's 104 and it feels like big particles of New York are bombarding me and sticking to my face. What is all this guck? Then the only thing that I can think about is, *How many people get cremated in New York City every day? Is this them floating around and sticking to my face?*

Then, I'm about halfway done with the wall and the downstairs neighbor tells me that he has a crack in his wall. Do I know what I'm doing?

Well, obviously no.

I hire someone to come and look at the wall and tell me if it is structural. He tells me no, it isn't, but a couple of days later there is a report that there is a crack that is going down from my place on the third floor all the way to the first floor apartment.

I am very stoned. I am destroying an entire building.

I began to freak out. Francie said, "Five years from now this won't mean anything to you, you'll look back and laugh."

I could not imagine this to be true, but it absolutely turned out to be.

Tom moved into the apartment. Nice, smart little gay man from Provincetown. Rick and Francie's friend. I cleaned up the wall a bit and then just tried to ignore it.

Tom had tons of Quaaludes. I loved them. All my anxiety and self-hatred dropped away, and although they were supposed to be a downer, they gave me energy. They were perfect. I only allowed myself to take them once a week or on special occasions in between.

Watching our little black and white TV, we discovered this show that was on at four A.M., *The Jeanne Parr Show.* Jeanne Parr was six foot two, with a bouffant of blond hair. She hosted a type of show that was a sort of precursor to *Jerry Springer.* She discussed controversial subjects like, "Should gays be allowed to teach in grade school?" Jeanne Parr was a reactionary and quite strange. Her guests were usually bizarre. For example, for the gay teacher one, she had a gay teacher and a bald guy who had nothing to say except to scream at the top of his lungs, spitting, "I won't allow it! I won't allow it!" Then Jeanne would go out into the audience and interview them about what they thought. Tom and I would smoke pot and laugh hysterically. We even reenacted our favorite scenes from the show, with Jimmy Jenkins, by tape-recording it and then learning the lines. Then we would make our own tape recording of the scenes with Tom and Jimmy playing Jeanne Parr and the women guests, and me, in different voices, playing the men.

I wonder where those tapes are.

The show was on live at noon and then the same episode repeated at four A.M.

Tom said, in his delighted, quippy voice, "We should go down there. We should go down and be in the audience, they'll think we're wonderful and ask us all the questions."

So a troop of us in sunglasses and white shirts would go down and be in the audience as often as we could get up by eleven A.M. When the camera panned across the audience we would all be there waving blenders and pineapples or whatever else we had collected on Fifty-seventh Street, yelling things like, "Aardvark! Aardvark!" Later that night we would smoke more pot and proudly watch ourselves on TV.

Eventually, they let us know that we were not welcome. It took them a while before they mustered the nerve to ban us from the show, but then they did. Tom did get asked a question once. It was a great success.

My apartment on Third Street came through.

8

Men in Orbit

I moved into an apartment on East Third Street in 1977. Government-run railroad apartments for $55 a month. I suppose for some people it would have been a drawback having the men's shelter directly across the street, but it didn't bother me. I felt a certain kinship with these people who had chosen to or couldn't help but live outside of a hopeless society.

The building was full of characters. Besides Eric Mitchell, who lived above me, and the porn star couple on the top floor, everyone else was, like myself, government-certified insane. At that time I was still living on Supplemental Security Income.

Demi Demme, the guy on the first floor, wore an eye patch and had long, matted hair with a little beard. He was skinny and nervous. Usually he was pleasant, but on more than one occasion he would curse and hiss at me in the hallway like I was responsible for the downfall of his people.

One night he came up to my place on the third floor and pounded on the door.

"John, John, come here. You've got to come to my place." He was very excited. I thought it was an emergency.

"What's wrong, Demi?"

"Nothing's wrong. You just have to come downstairs."

I said I didn't really want to. But he started pulling on my arm, yelling, "Come on! Come on!"

He opened the door to his apartment. It was set up like my place with a tub in the kitchen. Standing in the tub was a plump, naked blond girl, ankle-deep in water. She was about twenty-two or twenty-three years old. She wasn't moving, she was just standing there, in profile, with her glasses on.

Demi looked at her and clapped his hands. She didn't say anything but glanced at me for a moment. Then Demi jumped in the air, giggled, and clapped his hands again.

This did not seem like a sexual encounter. I don't know what it was. It was more like a viewing. I wasn't sure what I was supposed to do, so I shrugged and thanked him, and told him I had to go back upstairs.

Across the hall was Hannah. She'd been a normal, middle class housewife, married to an accountant or something in Connecticut or somewhere. Then she had taken LSD, or lots of LSD, and her life had gone on a little detour. Now she lived alone in the East Village, saw words on her forehead, and made poems out of them.

Years later, I was in a used book store and actually saw her book. There was a picture of Hannah's pleasant, loppy face beaming out from the cover. Written on her forehead in crayon was, "I See Words on My Forehead." I wonder how many copies were sold.

She started having a problem with her hearing and got it in her head that my playing the saxophone was making it worse. I have a tape somewhere of my playing this beautiful, soft, fragmented melody while Hannah pounded on my door shrieking, "John, stop hurting people with your music! Stop hurting people with your music!" She started wearing a headband around her ears. She even threatened to report me.

Back then, because my SSI benefits were not enough, I was doing a lot of petty crime, dealing pot, traveler's check scams, a bunch of stuff. When I moved into Third Street I got this cheap insurance because the block was so unsafe.

I got the idea to steal my own horns and collect the insurance. I locked my door and went out into the hallway with a hammer and a crowbar. I couldn't believe how difficult it was to break into my own apartment. I was out there flailing away with the hammer and crowbar, making a racket, when I sensed something and I stopped. It was the porn stars on their way upstairs. I stood there like a fool with the crowbar cocked over my head.

"What are you doing, John?"

"Uh, I locked myself out."

"Do you want to come to our place and go down the fire escape?"

"Um, no thank you, I'm almost finished."

I could sense Hannah watching me through her peephole and scurrying away every time I looked at her door. Somehow she figured it out, maybe when the insurance adjusters came. These poor guys. I had prepared an elaborate story for them, but they took one look at my block, were terrified, and no explanation was necessary. They wanted to get out of there as fast as possible. They looked like they were about to break out into a dash. They approved the claim.

Through the ceiling, at all hours, I could hear the minotaur clomping of Eric Mitchell. His rotting wooden floors had no carpet. He was working on Super 8 films that he shot in his apartment, one after the other, like Fassbinder. He would pace back and forth furiously as he worked out ideas in his head.

His apartment was barren and painted all one color: gray. He slept on an army cot. He had found a rusted industrial clothes rack on the street, which acted as a closet. I loved the idea and found one for myself. He threw the butts from the cigarettes he bummed from me into his kitchen sink, making an unsightly mess, but his apartment, in general, was spotless. Like an army barracks in an impoverished country.

He would come down to my apartment and I would play the guitar while he would sing stories that he made up on the spot, sometimes with an empty bucket on his head.

He was French, with a thick, bizarre accent that felt more like he was from Romania. For about eight seconds Eric had been a punk movie star in an Amos Poe film. He was connected up to things that seemed exciting—the punk, anti-art world. He knew all these smart, interesting oddballs, who appeared to be living uniquely on a ferocious edge: Richard Hell, Arto Lindsay, James Chance, Alan Vega, James Nares, Tina L'Hotsky, Pat Place, Patti Astor, Steve Kramer, and tons more who were just fascinating. No bullshit. I had never seen anything like it. This was a tough artist community that I had to be part of, and I followed Eric around like a sidekick.

We found a crate of giant rotting avocados on the West Side Highway. I took half the avocados and worked my way through the traffic to the other side of the street. Then we had a war. Hurling avocados at each other over the speeding cars. Eric was French and I had a good arm, so I pulverized him. Splatting rancid green avocado bombs all over his pants.

On the corner of Fourth Street and Second Avenue, a storefront opened up that sold ice cream. There was a banner outside that said, "Free Ice Cream Cones." We both ordered cones and started eating them. The guy behind the counter said, "Two dollars."

"But the sign outside says they're free."

"That was yesterday."

"Well, then you have to take the sign down."

The guy shrugs and says, "No ladder today."

Eric, who was incredibly tight with money, plopped down $2. I was shocked that he was paying for me. He laughed that infectious laugh and slammed the ice cream cone into the middle of his forehead. He just let it stick there as he walked out of the store, making a sound like he was drowning as he inhaled his laugh.

Twenty-third near Eighth Avenue, where there is now a multiplex movie theater, used to be the home of Squat Theatre, a Hungarian theater troupe who had been exiled from their home country for their wild performances filled with political outrage and humor.

Everybody was talking about this exciting new group. They all lived upstairs, sprawlingly, in this fairly large building on Twenty-third Street. They did their theater pieces on the ground floor, which had a huge picture window out onto the street. Passersby outside became the backdrop to the play.

I thought they were brave and interesting and went upstairs into their kitchen to hang out with them. Everything was very matter of fact with them. Peter Halasz, who, in a way, seemed to be their leader, sat at an enormous grungy dining table cutting into a raw onion with a sharp knife and eating it, like it was an apple. He beat me in a game of chess.

I went back a couple of days later to ask if I could perhaps use their theater one night. They talked about it for a second, surveyed me, and then said yes. They had not let anyone use their theater previously. It was nice to be surveyed and approved like that.

I could have the theater for one night in August. I started to work immediately.

As a form of exercise, I used to do Rocky Colavito stretching with a baseball bat. Then swing the bat back and forth in rhythm, over and over again, as fast as I could. I decided to extend a little farther for the second section of the performance, entitled *Fear Strikes Out*, in honor of the baseball player Jimmy Piersall. He was a bipolar baseball player who had a nervous breakdown and did all kinds of unusual things on the field before being institutionalized for a spell.

I went to Rick's place on Third Street with my tape recorder and made a recording of several layers of static on his broken TV and broken radio. I swung the volume up and down and created the music for *Fear Strikes Out*, a roaring symphony of whooshing.

For the performance, instead of a baseball bat I used a wooden curtain rod that I shaped to look like a baseball bat because it was easier to swing faster and longer as the static sped up, and then finally just became a white roar, while I danced and flailed wildly about.

The first part was called "Baby" and was just me softly playing the soprano saxophone.

The third part was "Anthem," which was me playing the alto over the sound of smashing glass.

I went over to the abandoned dock buildings, on the West Side, at five in the morning with my tape recorder. I took every large sheet of glass out of every window and brought them to a large, empty concrete room, up on the second floor.

I turned on the tape recorder and started to smash the sheets of glass in the middle of the room. I wanted this part to be about fifteen minutes and had a stopwatch on top of the tape recorder. It is difficult to calculate the time that has gone by as you are smashing giant sheets of glass in a concrete room.

As I was getting to the end of the sheets of glass, I could just see the stopwatch and that it showed only ten minutes had gone by. So after the last seven-foot window was smashed, I ran into the pile of broken glass, picked up two of the largest pieces left, and dragged them in a circle along the cement floor, in the middle of the field of broken glass. It created a hellacious sound.

My arms were bleeding everywhere as I headed home, proudly, amid the morning traffic.

Between the second and third acts, I ran offstage, where Julie Hanlon waited with clippers and a line of coke. Julie shaved my head as fast as she could, leaving odd rows of misshapen hair. I'm not sure why I did this, other than to prove my commitment.

The smashing glass was used as bass and drums behind this major melody that I played on the alto. I loved that melody. It later became a Lounge Lizards song called "Party in Your Mouth," which we never recorded.

Someone swung the spotlight from me to the audience to mimic the earlier swinging of the bat. Evan and Rick and a few other people in the packed house were instructed to start screaming about eight minutes into the smashing-glass section, which they did. Then the whole audience began to scream.

The piece had a number of different titles but was finally called *Leukemia*, probably not the best choice. But it was for my father, who had had leukemia when I was very young, which then magically disappeared.

The posters said, "Leukemia by one boy," with the address and date.

The piece, though youthful and silly in a way, was a success for me. All the parts worked, it was certainly powerful, and the feedback was fantastic. It was the first thing that I had done in front of an audience that had worked. And it was the first thing I had done in New York.

I celebrated with my friends and then went back to Third Street, where Eric Mitchell was finishing the one-night shoot of his movie *Kidnapped*. I went upstairs, all excited and wired, and Eric was exceedingly unfriendly.

"That's great, John," he said sarcastically, but it hardly fazed me. I had done something great.

In the summer of '78, a group of us—James Nares, Becky Johnston, Michael McClard, myself, and Eric—all made Super 8 movies. Everybody acted and worked on each other's films. They cost five hundred to a thousand dollars, and most of the money was raised by crime. Eric was the driving force behind all of this. Then he got money from Michael Zilkha for an Advent projector and opened a storefront on St. Marks Place called the New Cinema. He wanted me to make a film for it.

I had already made one film in Super 8 called *Hell Is You*, which was me interviewing James Chance from the Contortions, with a ridiculous grin on my face the entire time. Trying to emulate some combination of Joe Franklin and Tom Snyder.

I asked James incredibly inane questions as he played a sort of a famous woman punk singer. But the highlight of the film was a three-minute version of *The African Queen*, where I was Humphrey Bogart and James was the leeches who attacked me every time I got out of the boat, which was a cracked full length mirror on the floor. If you are thinking, *Oh, I would like to see this*, let me suggest that you probably wouldn't.

There used to be this great place on Stanton or Rivington called Young Filmmakers, and if you could put down a deposit equal to the value of the equipment, they would loan you cameras and mics and lights, then give you back your deposit if you returned the equipment undamaged.

What I had wanted to do was a movie with Jack Smith, where James Chance and Christopher Knowles are his sons and they go on a road trip. These were, by far, the most compelling people I had encountered since coming to New York.

Christopher Knowles was the autistic kid in several Robert Wilson pieces around that time. He also wrote a lot of dialogue for things like *Einstein on the Beach*. "If I could get some wind for the sailboat." "Windbreakers. Windbreakers. That's where it's at! Windbreakers!"

I went to a workshop where he was featured and he stayed out of the room. At the end he came running out with this enormous roll of graph paper. He unrolled it on the floor and it went out over forty feet. It had a red line down the middle that he had drawn with a crayon.

This was majestic in and of itself. But then he announced, quite loudly, "The red line is the airplane line." Then went back to his room.

This kid was something else. A true artist who lived in it.

I wanted him badly for the film, but he was a teenager and had people who handled him. Perhaps that is unfair and they actually cared for him but it felt more to me like they coveted him as an artistic force with a great deal of value.

Smith, if you do not know who he is, is hard to describe. You could look him up. His movie *Flaming Creatures* was a big influence on Warhol and John Waters.

But that was not why I was so interested in him. Much like Christopher Knowles, it was the wondrous, magical world that Jack Smith seemed to inhabit at all times.

I first became aware of him when he was with Henry Flynt and his Brend project. I saw photos of them where they were standing outside the Museum of Modern Art wearing sandwich board signs that said, "BOYCOTT ART." I fucking loved it.

Richard Morrison took me to see a play Jack Smith was doing in a loft on Broadway near Thirteenth Street. I wonder now if this was Rafik's place.

That play was what really hit me about Jack Smith.

There were just a handful of people there, in fold-out chairs. There was some odd music that I believe was from a Maria Montez movie that was almost like Egyptian Muzak. Very slow melody that was almost campy. It played on a record player, which Smith would go over to and carefully pick up the needle and start it in another spot.

The play never started. It was Smith amid a bunch of props—plastic flowers, plastic flamingos, some colorful vases, a table with the record player. He was wearing a robe and a turban, which he took off and put back on from time to time.

Smith would carefully, with much consideration, move the props from one place to another. Then go back and stand over the record player and try to pick up the needle without scratching the record. It often took quite a bit of time.

It was mesmerizing. I know it doesn't sound like it, and even as I think back to it I wonder how it was so fascinating, but it was. I can say that when I think back to it, it is etched in my memory stronger than almost any other performance I have ever seen.

Getting Jack Smith, Christopher Knowles, and James Chance in one place was impossible. I doubt anyone could have pulled it off. No matter how much money or power or will one had.

I got Jack Smith's address and was told that he was open to visitors. I went over to his place on the East Side. There were a couple of people there. He wasn't interacting with them. He was painting a tiny corner of his apartment.

His place was decorated as a mad, plastic, tropical paradise. He had painted the walls in tiny blotches of turquoise and green and yellow. There were plastic flowers everywhere. I want to say there was a stuffed boar's head hanging off the ceiling, but I am not sure if that is true. It just felt like that.

He was pretty cantankerous, rude to people, but if you brought him some marijuana he would be much nicer.

I went by a few times. He would be carefully plastering in some little corner, adding just the tiniest amount of plaster until he felt it was perfect. He explained that he had to work constantly because it made him feel cleaner. Less guilty. He seemed to like me and would confide in me. Then a moment later he would be snarling at my stupidity. And as I was twenty-four and said a lot of stupid things, he was probably fairly accurate.

I ask if I could film him. He asks if I have a script. I say that I have one, with him driving in a car with James Chance and Christopher Knowles as his sons, but that project has fallen through.

He agrees to do a film with me. But every time someone stops in, he says in snide tones, "This guy wants to make a film with me. He doesn't have a script."

So it is set up that I will come by his place around five the next day. I get there and he is doing his normal . . . I want to call it puttering, but that would be an injustice to it. It is puttering, but there is something magical to it.

He takes forever to pull together the things he wants and we go up on the roof.

He takes a blanket and puts it down to crouch on but wraps half of it around his body. He moves a couple of his props.

He rearranges the blanket over his shoulders.

He rearranges the blanket again.

I start to film.

He screams at me, "Don't film now!" So I wait for a bit as he moves things around. But I am thinking, *Shit, the most compelling thing I know about this guy is the performance where he tries to set things up and never gets started. I should film this. It is fascinating.*

He screams at me again, "Don't film now! You are wasting film!"

Then it dawns on me . . . he is fucking with me. He is going to wait until it gets completely dark and then say, *Okay, you can film now.*

And fair enough, as I think back on it. I have been in this situation many times in my life: Some young "artist" approaches me about doing something where they have nothing—zero—to offer into the mix. The rationale is, *I am an artistic person like yourself. I have never actually done anything but I have artistic feelings, so I would like to use you.*

But they don't bring anything to the table. Nothing. And then expect you to donate your time and talent to their unformed project, and they are vindicated in this because they have artistic feelings. It is parasitic.

I start to film again. He screams, "You are wasting film!"

I say, "It will be dark in a minute. Let me film."

He doesn't respond as he rolls the blanket one way and then the other.

I start filming again.

He screams again.

I finally just started shooting into the air at this point. It was dark.

I was yelling, "Waste of film! Waste of film!"

He jumped up from the blanket and came charging at me.

I dodged him, laughing, and kept shooting in the air, yelling, "Waste of film! Waste of film!"

My basketball skills were finally coming to some use. I swear he would have killed me if he had caught me.

I finally went running down the stairs, laughing, with him charging after me. "Waste of film! Waste of film!"

* * *

So Eric wanted me to make a film and I explained that I had no money to make a film.

"It's easy. I'll show you. Come on."

He gave me his driver's license and told me to start practicing forging his signature. At that time, the New York State driver's license didn't have a photo. It was just a card with a signature. After a couple of days, he came down and inspected piles of scraps of paper, on my desk, with his name scrawled on them.

"Okay, this is good enough."

Eric went out and bought a thousand dollars' worth of traveler's checks. He thought I didn't look straight enough, so he made me wear his penny loafers that were three sizes too small.

I waddled into bank after bank cashing Eric's checks, in one hundred dollar amounts, by writing his name at the bottom, while he waited impatiently outside. I couldn't sign his signature quickly, so I would sign them at the glass desk that holds deposit slips and then walk up to the teller and pretend to sign them there.

The first few went fine. I was a little nervous, but not too bad. The fifth bank, I signed the check and it didn't look remotely like Eric's signature. I was told that I would have to see the bank manager. He asked me to sign it again, but because now I had to do it quickly, it looked even worse. He asked me to sign again and it was looking less and less correct. I announced that I was very nervous because I was going to Europe in a couple of hours and I had never flown before. The manager smiled at me and said, "I understand, that's fine," and gave me $500 in cash.

After I finished, Eric reported the checks stolen and collected a thousand dollars.

With my $500, I was supposed to make an astronaut movie, *Men in Orbit*. But I ran into a little problem. I had just gotten through a course of antibiotics and it was the first night I could drink in ten days. Not drinking for ten days was very austere for me at that time and as soon as I could, I got drunk.

Stumbling home, I ran into Ann Campbell and her white friend.

"Hi, John. Want to take two girls home?"

Ann Campbell was a prostitute who had once tried to shoot me through my bathroom door with a tiny pistol she carried, because she was jonesing for coke and I wouldn't pay to have sex with her. But that was all forgotten now.

So I had $500 and thought I would spend some of it on these two women. When we got to my place, I went into the back room, took some money out for them, and hid the rest in the vest pocket of my coat. Ann asked what I wanted. What I wanted was for one of them to blow me while the other licked my balls, but they were older and I was too shy to ask. Ended up me and the white girl on the living room floor with her on top.

On the way out, Ann looked at me in a way that made me sense something. I went back to check and the money was gone. I threw on my clothes and ran out to Second Avenue, but they were nowhere to be found. Then I remembered that she had given me her address once, over a year ago, and ran upstairs to find it.

She lived on the corner of Avenue B and Fourth Street. Back then, Avenue B was like a war zone. Could be really dangerous, especially at night. I got to her apartment and knocked on the door. A sleepy giant answered. He didn't know where she was. He held his head in a way that indicated both that he wanted to go back to sleep and that I was clearly out of my mind to be knocking on doors on Avenue B at two in the morning.

I start walking around the neighborhood and see two plainclothes policemen sitting in a car.

I ask if they are cops.

They seem shocked by the question and start stammering.

First they say no, they aren't cops.

But I go, "Come on, you guys."

They ask, "How did you know we were cops?"

And I am thinking, *Are you kidding? The hair. The shirts. The car. The feigned nonchalance sitting out here at two in the morning.*

But I don't say any of that. I just tell them what happened.

They drive me around for a bit and when we don't find her, they drive me home.

So on the day I stole $500, it was now stolen from me. Makes sense.

But a month or so later, I get a call saying my court case against Ann Campbell is tomorrow morning at nine. *I have to get somewhere by nine A.M.?*

I didn't know I had a court case.

In this enormous room, I see Ann go by with two policemen holding her by the arms. Some courtroom person tells me to wait on this bench.

Ten minutes later, he comes out and tells me it is all settled. She has to pay me back my $500 or she will get an eight-month sentence.

I say, "Wait a minute. How is that right? I didn't speak to a judge or a lawyer or anything and you are just taking my word on this?"

"Sir, are you saying that what you told the officers is untrue?"

"No."

"Well, then I see no problem."

The unfairness and horror of the whole system hit me, but the last thing I needed to do was stand there and argue with this little court person who just wanted to get me out of there and go on to the next pile of shit he was going to deal with.

So I let it go. I let the whole thing go. I had stolen the money anyway. This all made sense.

In the end, my uncle Jerry bailed me out and lent me the money to make the film.

Originally, what I wanted to do was an astronaut training program movie, a set of exercises that I had made up, with autistic barking, done by a bunch of us young men, with short haircuts.

Eric, Arto Lindsay, James Nares, Seth Tillett, and I would jam. These guys were all very talented but knew nothing about music. We would take turns on guitar, bass, drums, the saxophone, and shouting into the microphone. The result was unbelievable and it was better than any music I had ever done with normal musicians. I wanted to capture the dynamic of that rigid fervor in the film. Like Robert Wilson in ferocious military training.

We would do these sort of tai chi movements that I had invented and then spout out a series of syllables in unison. Take a step or make a movement and spout another group of syllables. Then freeze.

But Eric thought the idea of the astronaut training film was about as bad as any he had ever heard in his life. So it turned out to be a simulated documentary of an Apollo spaceflight, filmed in my apartment. Mission control was built over the tub in my kitchen, with all kinds of electrical stuff I had foraged from the street. People sat in white coats over control panels that looked legitimate, except that you could see a bit of my bathtub in the corner of the shot.

The capsule was built in my living room. A piece of cardboard, painted gray, standing upright, was the outside of the capsule. I found a car seat that I spray-painted silver and used a bunch of junk and semi-working electrical stuff for our control panel. The cardboard was about three feet off the ground, with James Nares, who was a genius, bending down into the set and moving his arm around like a snake. With the camera constantly moving above and around our heads, we were actually able to simulate a feeling of weightlessness.

I did have an outline for the film, but it was abandoned immediately. In place of writing a script or bothering to actually act, we would just take LSD instead and see what happened.

We shot the opening of the movie while visiting Steve Kramer in the hospital. Kramer had a party trick. He would walk on the ledge of rooftops, drunk, and never fall off. Vito Acconci was out of town and someone threw a party at his loft. Everyone was up on the roof and Kramer was doing his party trick, while his wife, Patti Astor, screamed at him to get down. Her voice sounded like she had swallowed an angry cat. "Steven! Get down! Steven!"

This had the feeling of something that happened all the time. Kramer did his party trick and Patti yelled at him.

When we left the party, Kramer was still walking on the ledge. No one gave it a second thought.

We got back to Eric's and the phone rang. It was Patti Astor on the phone. I could tell by the screaming. Eric hung up and said we had to go to Bellevue Hospital.

We arrived in the lobby of Bellevue to see Kramer being whisked through on a gurney. You could see the bone from his leg jutting through the skin and his lower teeth coming through his upper lip. It is funny how your mind works at twenty-five: You see Kramer being wheeled through looking like some kind of bloody frog monster and you don't think, *This is horrible.* You look at it and think, *Wow, how unusual.*

* * *

We went back to see him a few days later. James came with a Super 8 camera and Eric and I were dressed as astronauts in jumpsuits. Kramer was trying to pull the IVs out of his arm and Patti was screaming, again. Patti really loved him and Kramer was impossible.

On the way out, James sat facing backward in a shopping cart that we had brought to use as a dolly. Rick Morrison pulled him as fast as he could, while James filmed Eric and me marching, invincibly, down the long hospital corridor. We stuck out our chests, nobly, and waved at the nurses and attendants as they screamed at us to get out. That was the opening sequence to *Men in Orbit*.

That night we shot a little bit of stuff in my kitchen for mission control. Next day, I had to get our costumes together, buy the LSD, borrow two motorcycle helmets, and finish the set so we could shoot the movie that night.

I was running around like mad. Jeffrey Cantor lent me his very expensive motorcycle helmets. I bought two Mylar suits for $9 each at a store on Bowery. Then I popped some LSD.

Everybody was there in my apartment: Michael McClard, the voice of mission control; Becky Johnston; and James, who stood above us gyrating the camera as we tilted way back in the silver car seat.

All the rushing around and the LSD was making me feel a little odd. We shot one three-minute reel of film, but Eric was goofing around too much. He kept blaring disco music from the broken boom box behind his head.

This was not what I had in mind but I cannot control him. I want to say something to Eric to try to get the thing back on track but feel the words *Cut it out* getting buried in my throat, like the sound cannot enter the room.

I feel very strange. I am too high.

I stand up and get out of the capsule. I try to tie my shoes but can't figure out how to do it. Becky has to come and do it for me. I am catatonic, and Eric is laughing his head off and blaring music.

I cannot talk. Eric is getting mad, because we've done all this work, this is the big night, and I am an LSD vegetable. He jumps up from the capsule and kicks a boot-size hole into my apartment wall.

"I am really mad at you! I am really mad at you!"

I stand up again and look at everyone's faces. This film, what is it? Is it good for the world? Maybe it's evil, and who are these people in my apartment? Can I trust them?

But the question I keep asking myself is, is this film good for the world?

Somehow, I wind up on the roof of the building in my space suit. I don't know how much time has gone by before Michael McClard appears out of the darkness in his white lab coat. He gives me a handful of Valium and I am ready to go in no time.

Eric and I get back in the capsule. I ask him if he has a light.

"Not since John Glenn died."

We find this hilarious. An enormous leap from: "Do you have a match?" "Not since Superman died." But we liked the joke very much.

Michael thought it might be more comfortable for us if he set up the mixing board in the capsule and gave us two sets of headphones. This way we could hear and control the sound ourselves. There was feedback everywhere. If they had given the mixing board to monkeys it would have sounded about the same.

As mission control, Michael talked us through the trip.

"All right, gentlemen, you are now in orbit. Why don't you relax and enjoy the flight?"

We leaned back in our seats for about two seconds and then simultaneously realized that a movie of two astronauts relaxing was not very entertaining and started to laugh.

There were a bunch of McDonald's hamburgers and Filet-O-Fish sandwiches taped to the wall of the capsule since early that afternoon.

Michael said, "Perhaps you should have something to eat." We started to giggle; the idea of food was ridiculous. The idea that anyone had ever eaten food was ridiculous.

Eric groped behind his head and pulled a hamburger off the wall.

"Mission control, mission control, the food that you have prepared for us seems to have come out of the container cold."

Eric's laugh had become a high-pitched gurgling that sounded like he might be drowning.

"They are really, really good, mission control. Bob is having a Filet-O-Fish and I am having a hamburger. They are really, really good."

Mission control responds, "They look really good and we think we'll send out for a bunch of them ourselves."

I couldn't eat my Filet-O-Fish. It just sat there in my mouth; I had no idea how to swallow. Eric was talking into a ketchup package, thinking it was the microphone. We could not stop laughing. Anything either of us said, even just one word of a phrase, was met with sheets of laughter from the other. This was then amplified ten times and distorted through the mixing board run by monkeys.

We called Evan, who also lived on Third Street. It was late and he was asleep but I told him to come right over. I asked him to stand outside the capsule and play little beeps on the harmonica, which he did gladly.

There was so much electrical noise from the lights and equipment and broken stereos that were part of the capsule that when we finally stopped to take a break and shut everything down, there was a *whoosh*, a big contained cloud of *whoosh*, that you could see as it floated out the window and bounced around the East Village night.

We stopped shooting when we ran out of film. It was light out and we went for breakfast.

We were all sitting in Veselka on Second Avenue. Eric and I were still tripping and laughing. James started to cry. I wasn't sure why, but it somehow made sense.

I went over and hugged him.

After that we went for a walk over to the West Side. There were cherry blossoms. I love the second half of tripping when the crunch goes away and you start seeing things you have forgotten, and there are cherry blossoms.

We were so sure of ourselves, we never doubted anything. We were powerful, smart, energetic, confident, egocentric, and astoundingly naïve. Nothing outside of our fourteen block radius mattered. From Houston to Fourteenth Street, from the Bowery to Avenue A, that was the only universe.

9

The John Lurie School of Bohemian Living

I had disappeared into hermit mode to edit *Men in Orbit* when I met Leisa Stroud. Nobody remotely like her had ever been interested in me before. She was only twenty but years more worldly and sophisticated than I was ever going to be.

Editing Super 8 film is horrible. At least for someone like me who is not neat. The film is tiny, about a third of an inch wide, and you have to pick your frame, splice it, and then glue the little pieces together. Glue gets everywhere: on your shirt, on the middle of the frame, in your eyelashes, on your sandwich.

You have to view the footage through this little viewer thing that you crank by hand, which makes a loud, unpleasant, metallic wobbling sound as you turn it. Then you cut the bits out that you want and keep it all organized. It is a nightmare. It was taking forever to weed through all the footage and make a story out of it.

One night, Michael McClard and James Nares and some others were going for a drink and yelled up to my window for me to come down and go out with them.

Leisa was there. This was the first time I'd met her. I had my soprano with me and somebody convinced me to take it out and play for a minute on the street. Hearing me play for just that moment had her completely taken. Leisa had just gotten back from London and started asking everyone who this interesting new boy was.

A couple days later, I ran into her again. I have the feeling she was lurking around near my place to meet me.

I had gone out only to get cigarettes after a couple of wild, drunken days with Madge.

When we got to my place, I looked in the mirror and saw that I still had on the makeup Madge had drawn on my face. I hadn't been able to wash it off because Madge and I had had sex against the sink, which was now sitting on the floor, where it had crashed to pieces.

Leisa looked at the sink and laughed really hard and somehow, as women often seem to, knew the entire story without my telling her a word.

I was still playing the horn, but at this stage, in the East Village, nobody was doing what they actually knew how to do. All the painters had bands. All the musicians were making little movies. I had worked hard for years on music but had to hide the fact that I actually knew how to play or that I practiced every day.

My band, The Lounge Lizards, first played on June 4, 1979. We had two other possible names: The Sequined Eels and The Rotating Power Tools. Now I kind of wish that it had been The Rotating Power Tools.

When you have a gig on Wednesday and you are on the way to the Xerox shop to make your first poster, it seems like it will just be that one concert. It will last twenty-four hours. It seemed most of the bands then lasted twenty-four hours.

I didn't imagine that years and years later we would be dragging this inappropriate name around that no longer matched the music as it got more serious and more elegant.

Jon Ende gave me the name. I was on the way to make the Sequined Eels poster when Leisa came flying down the street, behind me, to tell me that The Lounge Lizards was better, that she had just talked to Jon Ende and that The Lounge Lizards was a better name.

Leisa was the fastest runner. When we had no money, we used to dine and dash. I hated to run after eating, so when I was finished, I would walk out and head up Second Avenue about eight blocks from the restaurant. Leisa would come dashing up behind me. We'd run back to Third Street, giggling, and hide in the apartment. It was a good thing that she ran so fast or the band would have been The Sequined Eels. We rewrote the band's name by hand at the Xerox place and ran off the posters.

Leisa had the best ass. The best ass ever.

She was whiter than me and she dyed her hair platinum blond, which increased the effect. I didn't really believe that she was black until I met her dad. He was black. He was also short, bitter, and angry. He was an artist and an aikido master. I didn't like him and he didn't like me. He asked Leisa if I had spent a lot of time around autistic people, which I took as an insult and compliment all in one.

Leisa and I would go to the Mudd Club every night. The Mudd Club was infinitely cooler than Studio 54. It was wilder and there was a better mix of rich and poor, and black and white. We'd go to a gallery opening or some other function, eat all the free cheese and hors d'oeuvres, and then go out to the Mudd Club, and Leisa would finagle us drink tickets and cocaine.

I had discovered 1940s clothing in the thrift stores and would go out looking all fancy in my three dollar baggy suits and slicked back hair.

The most absolutely willful person, Leisa had the ability to make a room full of people get up and go to a different party on a moment's notice. I have to give her a lot of credit for pushing me to persevere when I was feeling down about running the band. She was largely responsible for getting the band off the ground. She could network.

Leisa was incredibly sexy and energetic, and she was smart. David Byrne, Brian Eno, Larry Rivers, and a host of others all had crushes on her. That Talking Heads song, "This ain't no Mudd Club, this ain't no CBGB, this ain't no fooling around," whatever the name of it is, and some other songs they did were also apparently about her. At least, Leisa claimed that this was what David Byrne had told her, and by the way he acted around her, I think it was most likely true.

The Lounge Lizards had a song for her too. It was called "Leisa's Too Short to Run for President." And another: "I Want a Basketball, I Can

Bounce," which was written in yearning homage to her incredible ass when we had split up for a day or so.

Leisa brought me into the world of glamour and cocaine. Then later into heroin. She insisted that I shave every day and hold cab doors open for her.

After *Men in Orbit,* I wanted to make a real movie. I was working on ideas for a film that was going to be called "Fatty Walks," stories of the odder occurrences that I had had in New York. I watched Eric Mitchell and others run around desperately with scripts, trying to raise money, and I didn't think this was going to be any fun at all.

This was before The Lounge Lizards started. Instead, I was going to write and record the music for the movie, then bring the music in to the money people and play it while I explained the story. This would be more real and exciting, and I'd get the money easily.

Yes, I realize this was naïve.

While I was in the process of writing this music, Jim Fouratt asked me who was a good band to open for Peter Gordon's Love of Life Orchestra on a Monday night at Hurrah, a club on Sixty-second Street.

I said, "Oh, my band."

"You have a band?"

"Of course."

I didn't have a band, but Evan had just moved to New York. Arto Lindsay and I had been having these great jams with Seth Tillett and James Nares, and sometimes Eric Mitchell. We had played in front of an audience once for Glenn O'Brien's *TV Party.* We did Thelonious Monk's "Well You Needn't." James played drums and Arto and Seth thrashed wildly about on guitars. I played the alto and actually played the head of the song over the confusion they were conjuring. All the girls rushed to the front of the stage and were screaming. This is very nice, when girls do that.

We only knew the one song, so when it was done and the girls kept screaming, we played it again. I was in the cab with Leisa and some other people on the way home, all full of exuberance. We passed a hardware store with a big sign that said "Rotating Power Tools." I called James when I got home and said, "We should call the band The Rotating Power Tools!" James liked the idea, but then we never played again.

So The Lounge Lizards, on June 4, 1979, were: Arto on twelve-string electric guitar, a Danelectro that I think he got at Sears; Evan on Farfisa organ; and me on alto and soprano. Arto brought in Anton Fier to play drums, and I called Steve Piccolo, who had been in my band Crud in high school, to play bass.

Steve Piccolo was a bona fide genius. His IQ was 170 or whatever number makes one a genius. At twenty-four, he was already a vice president at Merrill Lynch on Wall Street. Steve was incredibly musical and just an inch behind Paul McCartney in his ability to write melodic bass lines. He showed up for the first show in his Wall Street suit and carrying his bass in a plaid plastic suit bag. Piccolo was so stiff and so straight we used to joke about putting heroin in his coffee. Six months later he was strung out and dealing, with syringes in a cup on his desk like one that would normally hold pens.

We had one rehearsal. Everybody brought something big to this situation. I had written the melodies already, but what everybody added—Arto, with his cataclysmic guitar, Evan's odd choices on the organ, Anton's solid drumming, and Steve's melodic and harmonic sense—really made it something unique and special. I had learned something from James Chance and the Contortions that had freed me up a bit. The undercurrent roar of wild dissonance by part of the band helped it escape the drudgery of what jazz had become. My heart and roots were mostly in jazz and classical music, but after Coltrane, I felt there had been nothing, no big voice to push it along. Now jazz was played to people eating their dinner. The word *jazz* had become synonymous with *boring.* It seemed anachronistic to think about trying to do something really musical in this world.

The rehearsal was a little vague and shaky. What was this? I didn't really know what it was or what it was supposed to be, and it didn't fit together. The night of the gig, we pitched in and bought a gram of coke, which we snorted at my uncle Jerry's place around the corner from the club, while he was out of town. The music, magically, force-fully, came together onstage. It really came together, and I am sure that it was helped by the reckless force of the communal cocaine. Though cocaine ruined dozens of subsequent gigs, it certainly solidified the first one.

We are in the dressing room after and the door flies open. People are freaking out. Smashing things. Nobody had ever heard anything like it. There hadn't been anything like it. Leisa has done what she is great at and gotten everyone down to see it.

"What do you call this music?"

And I say, without giving it any thought, "It's fake jazz."

At that moment, I thought to myself that that was pretty good off the top of my head, just throw that out there. But it stuck, for twenty years. It stuck—for forty years, it stuck. It is still stuck. When the music had nothing to do with any notion of fake jazz, 2,473 lazy journalists would look up The Lounge Lizards and see it and go, "Oh, that is colorful, I'll call it that." That stupid tag of fake jazz stuck like some horrible gum in my hair.

Peter Gordon did the first and last generous thing that has ever happened to me in the music business. His band was the headliner and we were supposed to get like a hundred bucks. But, because we were so good, and because he realized that so much of the crowd was there to see us, he gave me an extra $75 out of his own money. Might sound like nothing, but it was a big deal and incredibly generous.

We were in all the papers. It was very exciting. I remember walking with Arto a couple of nights later. We were glowing in our success.

"If we could just get two hundred bucks for the band, each gig, and play once a week, we'd be all set."

We started playing around. Tier 3, Hurrah, Squat Theatre. We used to play for thirty-five minutes. That was our set. That was all we knew. I made the whole band dress in thrift store suits. All the white shirts and ties were crumpled. It was kind of elegant but it was also off; for example, if there was gray gaffer's tape holding your black shoes together, that was better than if there wasn't.

Lisa Rosen was standing in the audience one night next to a man who looked at us, five very white, emaciated guys, and said, "My God, they look so unhealthy."

Lisa said, "I know! Isn't it wonderful?"

There was Lounge Lizard Madness. Lines would go around the block with people scrambling to get tickets. Andy Warhol would be in the front row.

It is amazing how fast one becomes arrogant.

The cocaine had worked so well the first time, we kept using it. I was also so shy that I couldn't imagine getting up onstage without the help of drugs and alcohol. But coke, which had worked so magically on the first gig, never seemed to work as well after that. In fact, it ruined a lot of shows. I'd be up onstage gnashing my teeth. I'd feel that nice thing of the coke dripping down into the back of my throat, but then my mouth would go numb and I couldn't control my lips, and the mouthpiece would come flying out. We'd play everything too fast. "Too fast" isn't even a way to describe it. It was frenetic and often as confused as it was powerful. It should have been called "Car Crash Jazz." Melodies hopping out of great smashing turmoil.

Cocaine is a bad, horrible drug.

Sometimes we were great, but not consistently. We didn't really know what we were doing yet. One of the most important things about playing music live is hearing yourself onstage and knowing how to cope with monitors and dealing with what you cannot hear. It is a constant problem, especially with loud bands, at least the poor ones, and we were very loud and very poor.

Despite the inconsistent performances, we were getting a lot of attention from the press. Record company people would come into the dressing room and we'd tell them to get lost.

"Hi, John! I'm from Columbia Records and—"

"Get the fuck out of here!"

Guy would stand there in his fashionable hair and outfit for a second, looking confused.

The whole band would just scream, "Get the fuck out of here!"

I wish we had never stopped telling them that.

Leisa and I were broke. The band would play sometimes, but then after a week, we wouldn't have any money left. They kept turning off the electricity or the phone. I had a bag full of sunglasses that I had bought to give out to the audience at the *Leukemia* piece at Squat Theatre but never organized it. So I had about a hundred pairs of cheap sunglasses. Leisa painted them and got $3 apiece from the local punk stores. She scampered home with $300 in her hand.

We never ate enough food and drank too much. Liquor was usually free, but food was harder to come by.

* * *

I met Jean-Michel Basquiat at the Mudd Club. He was just a kid—couldn't have been more than seventeen—with a funny haircut. He used to grin with absolute delight while he danced. I called him Willie Mays. It wasn't so much that he looked like Willie Mays, which he did a little, but how much he enjoyed his silly dancing.

In 1949 or 1950, before I was born, my family was living in Minneapolis. They had a minor league baseball team before the Twins. A young Willie Mays came through there on his way to the pros, and my dad used to go see him play. He said they were all heartbroken when Willie Mays got called up to the majors because he was so wonderful to watch. And part of what was so wonderful was the ease with which he played and the joy that emanated from him. Jean-Michel's dancing wasn't graceful or elegant—in fact it was awful—but he certainly enjoyed it, immensely, in an abandoned way. Because of this I dubbed him Willie Mays, and he called me Willie back.

Jean-Michel and Danny Rosen used to sleep on the floor in my front room. It was called the John Lurie School of Bohemian Living. We would stay awake for days and then crash. They didn't seem to mind sleeping on the carpet. I had splurged and spent $100 on carpeting for my front room. I don't remember either of them ever bathing. After being out all night, I would make Jean-Michel come out and shoot baskets with me at six A.M., in the morning light. He never liked shooting baskets, but I made him come anyway.

When Jim Jarmusch was making his first film, *Permanent Vacation,* I let him use my apartment to store the film equipment in the front room. Jean-Michel was asleep on the floor after being awake for days.

He was often in their way and they couldn't wake him up.

Jim and two crew guys finally picked him up and moved him to the side of the room to get at the equipment.

Kind of pissed me off, how they grimaced with disgust when they had to touch him and moved him like he was a stinking homeless person.

But, damn, Jean-Michel slept right through it. I cannot tell you how jealous I am of someone who can sleep like that.

Jean-Michel and I would smoke marijuana and paint and draw all night. I had a box of oil pastels and we would paint on anything. Cardboard. Shopping bags. Anything.

Jean-Michel made a portrait of me out of a catcher's mitt that I really liked. He had taken a catcher's mitt and painted on it, held it up, and said, "This is John Lurie." He also made me a big button that said, "Hello My Name is Lee Harvey Oswald." Which he also claimed was a portrait of me. I have no idea where these things are.

I still have one thing that we painted on a card together, but I took it to a gallery one day to see what it was worth. They took it to some expert who then declared it was not by Basquiat.

Who are these experts?

He was really messy and would leave his stuff everywhere. I kept telling him to do something with his drawings, but he never did.

But damn, the kid just had that thing. He was compelled to make the stuff. It wasn't even work. It was a thing. Like the autistic kid who has to spin the cardboard box in circles over and over. It was that thing.

There has been so much bullshit about him, in films and books and stories told. Attempts by so many to aggrandize themselves or make a living off his legacy, by people who were not there or barely there. I don't want to address it. Cheap is cheap. I don't want to visit cheap.

Arto came up with the idea that we should use our newfound underground buzz to apply to do something at the Kitchen for their fall season. The Kitchen at that time was almost on the scale of a small Brooklyn Academy of Music, as far as being a prestigious art place. Arto wanted to do it because it paid two hundred bucks per show.

I asked, "What are we going to do?"

"I don't know."

"Let's do a dance performance."

We laughed so hard at the idea that we had to go through with it.

We proposed a modern dance piece entitled *I Love a Tornado*. To my amazement we were accepted, I suppose because we were in all the papers as the hip new thing. We really just wanted the $400 that we would get to perform there two nights, and to stick our tongues out, as far as they would go, at the hopelessly serious and untalented world of bureaucratic art.

In the program it said, "John Lurie and Arto Lindsay premiere their new modern dance work, *I Love a Tornado*.

"Two lanky fellows jump up and down for their money. Come for comfort and fun."

We came out in cowboy outfits and just stood there, against a sunset projected on the wall, trying to look tough and squinting. We used the great spaghetti western music by Ennio Morricone.

We stood there for a long time. When the music changed to a cloppity-cloppity piece for percussion and banjo, we pretended we were on horses and pranced about for a bit. Then we changed into white shirts and black pants and did five minutes of contact improv that we did not rehearse. It probably looked more like a two person mosh pit. Arto and I would hold a posture that we assumed was dancerly and then smash into each other.

After that we had a tape of a severe wind. We were supposed to have a wind machine, but it was broken and only sputtered out a small stream of anemic air. When the wind started, we built a tornado shelter from junk we had found on the street fifteen minutes before the show and then went inside.

We hid inside there for a few minutes, shaking the shelter now and then, to the sound of the wind. That was the end. The whole thing took twenty-five minutes. When we came out of our shelter and bowed, a confused and somewhat depressed audience just sat there. There was no applause, no sound of complaint, nothing. When they realized it was over, they picked up their coats and left.

Evan came over to us after the show. He smiled and said, "You guys have a lot of nerve."

It actually left me with a bad taste in my mouth, to do something that was intentionally not good. After each show, I went and bought an enormous steak and washed it down with expensive whiskey.

The upstairs level of the Mudd Club wasn't officially or legally part of the club. It was more like a sprawling, illicit VIP room. There were two bathrooms without locks on the doors. Neither was designated for men or women, as they were only used by people fucking or taking drugs. One night, Leisa actually had to use the bathroom for real. I go in there with her to hold the door. Wendy Whitelaw is also in there putting on makeup.

There's a pounding on the door. This always happened, as people were very impatient to take their own drugs. I tell them to wait and a voice comes from the other side saying, "No men in the women's room."

This is ridiculous because there is no such thing as a women's room upstairs. I'd been in these bathrooms a hundred times, and if I didn't know which was the women's room, then nobody did.

I tell him to fuck off and continue to block the door. We're in there for at least another five minutes. Now both girls are taking their dainty time putting on makeup, as the door pounding continues, this in the true fashion of Rebels Without a Party Dress.

Finally, when I open the door, I see four or five guys standing there. They are all the same shape, five foot ten, two hundred ten pounds, and all have the same mustaches and the same suits.

They see an emaciated wise guy leaving the ladies' powder room with two beautiful women. I guess this seemed unjust to them. As I came down off the stair, one of the Mustachioed Security Men grabbed my arm. I laughed and said to the girls, "They all look alike."

I'm thinking, *Nothing can happen to me at the Mudd Club.*

But this is a new security team that Steve Mass, apparently, has been strong armed into hiring; this is their first night and they don't know how cool I am supposed to be. One holds me as another one punches me in the face.

I feel my front tooth resting in the middle of my tongue.

Soon everyone in the club has heard that John Lurie has been punched in the face and is rushing up to me, giving me coke to numb the pain. I have never seen such an outpouring of cocaine.

"Here, rub it on your tooth, it will numb the pain."

One night, years later, I was in a booth somewhere with Steve Rubell. I was trying not to do drugs and I guess Steve found me to be a drag. He took a bag of coke out of his pocket and flung it over toward me. The bag opened midair and I was covered in three grams of cocaine. So much for quitting. If you are suddenly covered in expensive cocaine, it would seem you must take it.

Anyway, the tooth was severed in half and the nerve was just dangling there. Later, at Bellevue Hospital, they took out the nerve with tweezers.

It took me months before I could play again. I tried several dentists who couldn't make a new front tooth that fit like the old one, that didn't screw up my embouchure.

Many people were suggesting I see this dentist known as "the musicians' dentist." He took a quick look at my tooth and said he couldn't do anything about it, but was there anything else that I needed? Kept saying, "Is there anything you need from me?" I didn't realize until I was two blocks away from his office, "Oh, the musicians' dentist! I get it! Drugs! Maybe even pure cocaine!" I turned and rushed back to his office, but when I asked him if he could give me something for the pain, he said, "I can't now. If you had asked before . . . but I can't now."

I had to have seven different front teeth put in and taken back out before I had one that worked. Where I could play the saxophone without air leaking out.

Haoui Montaug managed us for a little while. He cried when I told him it wasn't working out a few months later. I felt bad because I liked Haoui. Haoui years later contracted AIDS and had decided that he was going to take certain pills to save himself the pain and indignity of a long, drawn-out death. He had it all planned out and was saying goodbye to people. He had it set for Friday. The IRS called him the Thursday before he was going to do it and told him that he was in serious trouble because he hadn't paid any taxes for four years. Haoui asked them if they would mind calling back on Monday and hung up the phone. He went through with it. That was rough.

Haoui had set up our first gig outside New York, in Toronto. We were playing in a small room at something called the Spadina Hotel for three nights. The promoter's name was Robin Wall. We'd played two nights and hadn't gotten paid yet. We were supposed to get paid after each gig. Robin invites me to lunch the next day, explains that there have been some miscalculations, and says, "Well, why don't you and the guys come over to my house for a barbecue tomorrow? It'll be fun, we'll cook up some snakes."

Snakes? Did he mean steaks? But he says it again and again, *snakes* instead of *steaks*, and soon the slow horror sinks in. He's nuts. Somebody told me he was later institutionalized. We never got paid.

Our first gig in Europe is just one night in Bologna, Italy. When we arrive, the band nearly loses it with the Italians, who are in a frenzy at the luggage carousel.

They are pushing and shoving to get at their luggage.

We are New Yorkers and not used to this touching. "We are not used to this touching. You have to stop this bizarre touching."

They weren't touching us in New York at JFK before we got on the plane. They weren't touching us on the plane. Why the fuck is it supposed to be okay that they are touching and pushing us now?

Honestly, it even seems like some of their mustaches are suddenly two inches longer.

Then it gets much weirder.

We get picked up in a van that's driven by a normal-looking guy, but with him is a man—I think I have to call him a man—with a neck beard; waist-length hair; a high, irritating voice; and breasts.

He gives me the creeps, not at all because he's flaunting a mixture of genders, which I found somewhat courageous, but because he is just really creepy. And creepy is creepy. Neck beards are creepy.

Anton Fier takes out a joint that he smuggled in. Anton always has very, very strong pot. That weed that makes someone turn to you and say things like, "If your knees bent the other way, what would chairs look like?"

The driver smokes some and is not used to anything like it. He's way too high.

We have to stop for gas.

There are six or seven guys hanging outside at the gas station on the pavement. It seems they all work at the gas station. Though there is no sane reason for this many people to be working at this gas station in the middle of nowhere.

They hear us speaking English to one another and don't like it. The attendants start to grumble among themselves.

The driver feels he's too high to drive and switches places with Neck Beard.

When our drivers get out of the car and switch places, the attendants really don't like what they see.

This doesn't feel so great.

They all start moving, slowly, threateningly, closer to the van. It feels like it might turn violent. They're all holding wrenches and some other metal tools.

We are all very stoned. Too stoned. *What's happening here? Are we in real danger?*

We are very, very stoned.

Neck Beard tries to drive away but can't seem to face the idea of driving back onto the highway because he's so high, so he just drives in circles, round and round the gas pumps.

The gas station attendants are getting closer and closer. I have been in this country for twenty minutes and this is happening. I am sure you could live in Italy for several hundred years without anything like this happening.

And then I think, *Fuck you, you dumb motherfuckers. This shit is on now. You are going to step to us because we are speaking English on your little speck of turf in the universe and are threatened or offended or God knows what by us and our little friend with a neck beard and breasts? Fuck you. Fuck you, bring it on. We are going to fuck you up now.*

And I look around at the guys in the band, who are not the toughest guys in the first place, but now they are so high I suspect they might understand the language squirrels speak better than what is happening in the situation here or what they should do next. This is not going to end well.

The Italians have crowbars and wrenches that they are beginning to show us as they approach. Neck Beard is driving in circles around the gas pump with this kind of gurgling sound, halfway between terror and singing, coming out of his throat.

Then suddenly he speeds up and drives over the curb with a loud thump, and we are in the middle of the highway with whizzing cars desperately trying to avoid us.

A driver is screaming something in Italian, which I am sure is close to, "Are you fucking idiots?? What is wrong with you?"

To which we could say in explanation, "We were about to be killed with hammers and crowbars and are too stoned to defend ourselves and are being driven by a neck beard who gurgles." But it seems an unwieldy sentence to translate.

We get to the hotel and take a nap, then have an astoundingly great dinner.

We're in Italy! It's stunning. I love Bologna.

I am going to move here when I get old.

Piccolo and I decide to go for a walk.

"Let's write down the name of the hotel, walk as far as we can, and then take a cab back."

We write down the name on the neon flashing sign outside the hotel: "Albergo."

We walk for hours. We're exhausted from jet lag and walking and hail a cab. It's good we wrote down the name, because we are completely lost. We hand the driver the piece of paper with *Albergo* written on it. The driver is confused. He doesn't understand.

"Dove?"

"Hotel Albergo."

"Quale albergo?"

"Yes, yes, Hotel Albergo!"

But he doesn't understand and we have to spend hours picking our way through streets, trying this way and that.

Albergo turns out to be Italian for "hotel."

10

An Erection and an Alarm Clock

The second time I took heroin—not the first, the first time I just felt kind of fuzzy and tired—when I shot it, with Jon Ende and Leisa, it was perfect. It's funny now, to say this after what heroin put me through. I certainly don't want to be encouraging people to try it. Heroin leads to hell.

But this time was perfect.

The first time I took heroin I was with Leisa at Debbie Harry and Chris Stein's place. This was a pretty big deal, to be invited there. Like we had arrived in a way. They were for real celebrities and had invited me to their home. And they were quite kind and supportive.

Debbie asked if I wanted a line. I thought she meant coke. She brought out these two little lines on a mirror. I thought, *What? That is the smallest line of coke I have ever seen. Are they really this stingy?*

I snorted it, and it tasted so much purer than the shit I had taken. Fifteen minutes later I asked for another line. I hope Debbie doesn't mind my telling this. She is someone I have a lot of respect for and very much would not want to offend in any way. But it really wasn't like Chris and

Debbie were drug people. This was elegantly done, like it was a glass of exceptional wine.

I walked out onto the street thinking that it felt like I was made of rubber. Leisa started raving in an excited hush, "That was heroin! Really! I think we just took heroin!" She was saying it like we had won the lottery.

I thought that there was no way I'd get into it. I didn't like the feeling and it certainly wasn't going to help me work or have insights. And this is what I was interested in: I wanted drugs to give me insight, a transcendental experience, or to help me concentrate. I didn't think that heroin could come close to helping me, at all, with what I was interested in.

A few weeks later, Leisa and I were in Jon Ende's dingy apartment on Second Avenue, with his stinky cats and his pet frogs. Jon Ende's apartment is the place we used for my apartment in *Stranger Than Paradise*. Whenever I see a photo or clip from *Stranger Than Paradise*, I don't think about the movie, I think about Jon Ende.

He was quite brilliant. One of those people you might know who is brilliant but doesn't really do anything. Doesn't really want to do anything. And certainly would not put up with the kind of bullshit one must go through to get a project done. I have known many people who exploded into enormous celebrity, who are household names now, or others whose minds are considered to be very important. Jon Ende, like several others I knew, was not that. He was brilliant. Simple as that. And someone whose opinions on things I would listen to deeply.

The first time, I snorted heroin. This time Jon and Leisa convinced me to shoot up. This took quite a while, because I really didn't like the idea. They were so excited to do it and almost made it like I was being silly not to. I had the flu and was lying on Jon's couch. I didn't want to move.

They kept saying, "This will clear up your flu in a moment! You have to do it!"

I was just lying there on the couch and would have said yes to pretty much anything to feel different than I did at that moment.

Leisa tied up my arm and injected me while I looked the other way.

Warmth. Warmth and sinking, just a nice sinking. Soft. Things were far away yet very clear. I'd passed through some exotic veil that only the initiated were allowed to penetrate. Pain dropped away from my body that I had never realized was there.

My nerve endings were coated with pleasure as I lay on Jon's sofa.

I wanted to do this more often. I was absolutely fine. My cold and fever gently dropped away and were forgotten. At some point, I threw up, not unpleasant, whatsoever. God, I felt safe and warm, and it seemed like all my neuroses and self-loathing had floated off. But I think that safeness is what, in a way, is so appealing. You feel like nothing can hurt you, and if it does, it no longer matters.

I felt like, *This is the evil thing they have warned you not to do? They have been lying to you. All along, they were lying.*

At this exact moment my spiritual quest was gone. For years after, it was gone.

This shit was for real.

Then there were another several years trying to get away from it. That shit was even more real.

I started doing it once a week. This was the plan. Only do it once a week and you won't get strung out.

Pretty quickly after that I would do things like set up the tape recorder with my horn out, reed wet and ready to go, shoot a speedball, coke and dope, and then rush to record whatever the drugs brought out. The disconcerting thing is that, in the beginning at least, what was coming out was different and amazing. Not *You thought it was good because you were high*. I would listen to it days later and it would be good—actually, *good* doesn't do it justice, it was fucking great, the odd rhythms, the otherworldly overtones.

Four of us were shooting speedballs at my place on Third Street. Leisa had mixed everybody's shots and put in too much coke. I went first. It was really cold out. One of those biting New York February days. All the windows were closed and taped.

I needed air! Immediately. Too much coke in the shot. I jumped up on the windowsill, ripped the tape off, pulled the upper frame down—none of my windows opened at the bottom—and stuck my head out for air.

I held my head out in the freezing New York daylight for several minutes.

When I got down from the window, Leisa and our two friends were all standing on different window ledges with their heads sticking out.

My friends were wild. Bruce Balboni overdosed at his own birthday party. He was in the bathtub being shot up with saline, people trying to revive him.

Rene Ricard went around singing, "It's my party and I'll die if I want to."

There was this thing on the news about how all these junkies were ending up in the hospital, going blind with weird bumps on their heads. People I knew started to get it. Leisa was saying that she thought she had it but I didn't pay any attention. Thought that she was being silly.

The next morning she really can't see and she's got all these bumps under her platinum hair. This was so terrifying, I cannot tell you.

She really cannot see.

We're lying on my bed, a stinky foam mattress on the floor, and I can see by her gaze that she's half-blind. I run my hand past her face and there is no reaction.

Everyone got better in a few days. What had caused the condition was a lemon on a chest of drawers in a room at the Chelsea Hotel.

Bobo Shaw, the drummer who played with Miles Davis, among others, was living at the Chelsea Hotel. Bobo was selling this brown dope that was very thick, and in order to shoot the dope most people cut it with lemon juice from a half of a lemon that Bobo had saved for this purpose. The lemon had gone moldy and it was causing these odd symptoms. Amazing to me, the idea that there was all this concerned stuff on the news about a plague attacking junkies—"Scientists are mystified!"—when it was just this moldy half lemon on Bobo's counter because he was too lazy to buy another one.

Now I also knew that Leisa had secretly gotten high without me, which was not the deal. We were only supposed to get high once a week, together. Of course, along with massive amounts of sexual cheating, we were cheating by getting high without each other. If I got high the night before, I would have a line down the left side of my face from my cheekbone to my jaw. A line that lasted for twenty-five years and is still somewhat there today. It was like a road map, and early on, it was only there if I got high. You can see an example of these lines in the face of Chet Baker or Keith Richards.

Leisa would see it in the morning and yell, betrayed, "You have the drug line!"

Bobo had really lost it to drugs. There was a rumor that he had lost an arm when he was in jail, an even bigger tragedy for Bobo because he was a drummer. In the end, this turned out to not be true.

One time, when he had been sent off to Rikers, I sent him drumsticks and a practice pad. Seemed like a nice thing to do, so he could keep up with his playing. But when he got out he scoffed at me. Like it was a stupid thing to do. How could I be that corny?

The lemon story wasn't particularly revealing to me because I knew how unhygienic Bobo was.

A few months before, we had been taking drugs all night and as the sun was coming up, he asked if he could crash at my place on the floor. Bobo fell asleep, and I went out and braved Third Street to get some cigarettes. When I got back there was this strong smoldering smell. I thought the place was on fire.

"Bobo, wake up! There's a fire! Wake up! We have to get out!"

He rolled over and said, "No, that's okay, John, I just took off my shoes."

Bobo and Lindzee Smith were partners in crime. They were always together doing this scam or that. The odd thing was that they were both so talented, but whatever talents they had were put on the back burner for the pursuit and idolatry of heroin and cocaine.

There were lots of great stories about Lindzee, who was an actor and theater director of some repute. He had broken into an abandoned storefront on the Lower East Side to do a play. I think a Joe Orton play. Lindzee did everything himself: the set, the advertising, the music, directing, and acting. He had gone to his place on Seventh and Avenue D to pick up a boombox that he had borrowed for music in the performance. This was a notoriously bad block during this period. He gets held up. He hands over the $6 he has but refuses to give up the boombox because he needs it for the play. He gets stabbed in the side.

Lindzee comes back to the storefront with the boombox, does the performance bleeding all over the stage, and only after the play is over, does he go off to the hospital to have his wounds taken care of.

You think you're for real? Fuck you. Lindzee was for real for real.

Another, less noble story that I heard: Lindzee used to get dope for himself by copping for other people. If you came in from New Jersey and didn't know where to go, or you were a record company exec or something and didn't travel in this world, Lindzee would buy a bag for you and keep one for himself as commission. Lindzee had a certain contempt for these people, either because they weren't hip enough to cop for themselves or because they were from New Jersey—a crime in itself in those days.

This guy gets Lindzee to cop for him. The guy has nowhere to shoot up and asks Lindzee if he can use his apartment. They go up to Lindzee's second floor apartment and get high. The guy wants to get more. Lindzee warns him that it's strong, but the guy insists. Lindzee runs out and gets him another two bags.

The guy then ODs.

Lindzee tries to revive him but with no success. He can't call an ambulance because there will be police and Lindzee will go to jail. He can't just leave him in his apartment and he doesn't know what to do.

So Lindzee picks the guy up and drops him out of his second floor bathroom window. Because he uses the bathroom window, the guy will fall in back of the building and won't be found for a while. If they don't notice the bruises and broken bones from the two flight fall, maybe the police will just think that the guy was getting high in back of the building and OD'd there.

But the guy is still alive.

Some hours later he manages to crawl around to the front of the building, where he is discovered by the Puerto Rican dealers who run the block. They are furious with Lindzee because this kind of thing is going to bring unwanted attention to the neighborhood. Lindzee can't go back to his own apartment for weeks because he hears that the Puerto Rican dealers are going to kill him, and every time I see him during a several week period, he is wearing the same clothes. And then later, clothes he borrowed that look like they might fit a child.

I have been on a three day binge and finally go to sleep. I must have slept some fourteen hours when, from my sleep, I sense someone in the apartment. I spring out of bed, naked, with a big sleep hard-on. I have the alarm cocked over my head, as a weapon. *I will kill whoever it is with my clock.*

I see a fat man with a beard and Popsicle stains on his T-shirt. He's just standing there in my kitchen holding a revolver. I lurch forward ready to attack.

"I'm a cop! I'm a cop!" he screams at me.

I am not awake and it takes a moment to understand.

Then I say, "Oh," and put my hands up over my head. My hard-on kind of wobbling back and forth in the wind.

"God, I thought I was going to have to shoot you. You live here?"

"Yes."

"Why don't you put some clothes on? You've been robbed."

Someone had broken into my apartment while I was sleeping. Stolen my horns and been caught. The police saw this guy that they recognized as having been picked up before for breaking and entering. He was walking up Bowery with a saxophone case, and they stopped him because they didn't think he was a musician and wondered what he was doing with a saxophone. On the outside of the case was my name and address. The cops were very nice not to mention the syringes or the empty drug packages on the living room table.

They brought me outside to identify my stuff. The guy they caught was in the backseat of the squad car. He stared at me and smiled. His stare went right through me, like, *I could have killed you, you sleeping fool.*

11

Paris. Vomiting and Then More Vomiting.

B ack then there were only two channels on late at night. I would lie on my ragged foam pad that pretended to be a bed and watch a little black and white TV on the floor.

You could only watch *Mary Tyler Moore* reruns, which were fairly pleasant, or Joe Franklin.

Joe Franklin was this odd little guy who must have somehow been connected to Broadway in the real theater days but had no business being on TV.

When an author was on, and I swear he did this every time, he would hold up the author's book, so he, Joe Franklin, could look at the cover, but the camera could not see the cover, only the back of Joe Franklin's little hand.

He seemed sweet but very dopey, very pudgy, and very nervous.

Once I had seen all the *Mary Tyler Moore Show*s, I started watching Joe Franklin. Which I have to admit was fairly fascinating in a bizarre kind of way.

One night, he had on Sri Chinmoy to celebrate his fiftieth birthday. Sri Chinmoy was a guru I knew a little about but not much. I know he emphasized doing extended, austere physical exercise to put one into an exalted state, but didn't know much else.

I found this an odd pairing, Sri Chinmoy and Joe Franklin. It just didn't make any sense. Who set this up?

Then something really amazing happened. They brought out a cake with like fifty lit candles on it. Joe Franklin explained, "Well, Sri, it is our custom in America that when it is your birthday, you make a wish and then blow out the candles."

Sri Chinmoy just sat there without speaking. His eyes rolled up into his head.

Joe Franklin was going, "Come on, Sri, blow out the candles! Blow out the candles!"

Then, without even visibly inhaling, Sri Chinmoy just went *pffttt*. There was no effort in the exhale. The sea of candles went out like they had been hit by a tornado. *Whoosh!* Gone out. Only smoke rising off the cake.

It was just nuts. It was so nuts I started calling people and asking if they had seen it. It was four in the morning. No one appreciated the call or understood the importance.

I remember one of the people was Evan. I seem to have always been waking up Evan, in the middle of the night, for most of his life. He said, "John . . . ," in that way he has for all these years, and I laughed and hung up.

One night, I was lying on my little pad watching *Mary Tyler Moore* at four in the morning.

Outside, the bum who yelled, "Armageddon, Armageddon!" over and over was yelling, "Armageddon, Armageddon!" over and over.

The monk with the drum came through. There used to be this monk who walked around Manhattan, shaved head and robe, and popped on this little drum the size of a Ping-Pong paddle. I am sure he never spoke. You could hear him coming, and the pitch of the drum would change as he got closer.

So outside, the sound on the street was *Pip Pip Pip Pip, Armageddon, Armageddon, Pip Pip Pip Pop, Armageddon, Armageddon, Pop Pop POP POP, Armageddon, Armageddon.* Charles Ives had nothing on Third Street at four in the morning.

I can't tell you how much I appreciated that monk. Just a little tiny breath and funnel to some kind of light.

A few years later, I was on East Tenth Street on my way over to play ball at Tompkins Square Park but was in the middle of hideous negotiations on a movie score deal with Hollywood. It was eating up my mind. *These people are monsters, they are taking the soul out of culture. I don't care about the money, well, I do a little, but they cannot fuck with the music. They don't know what they are doing, they cannot fuck with the music because some producer who is the nephew of some movie mogul hears the score at nine in the morning and pronounces that he doesn't like violins because he hasn't had his special drip coffee with almond milk yet. So all the violins will be removed and the piece will be left with bongos and banjo* (which has actually happened to me). *No, they cannot do this.*

My head was locked into this awful thing and wouldn't stop.

I was walking by a mosque when the imam stepped out on the street, with the call to prayer.

He had a beautiful voice. And his call to prayer was right there with anything—the imploring beauty of it was right there with Nusrat or Coltrane or whoever you want to pick. Kurt Cobain? It was beautiful.

I stopped in my tracks in front of him and said, "Oh. Thank you. From the bottom of my heart. Thank you."

He looked at me funny, as probably he should have done, and I went over to play basketball.

Anyway, it was four A.M. on Third Street, when the phone rang. It was some guy calling from Paris named Fabrice. He ran a club called Les Bains Douches and he wanted to bring The Lounge Lizards over to play.

We talked about it for a minute and he realized he couldn't afford to pay for the hotels and flights for five people. Seemed a little odd to me that he had not thought that out a little further before he called me at four A.M., but okay.

I called him back the next night and suggested that I could come and do a saxophone solo.

I had done a couple of solo concerts that had gone very well.

He said okay, and I was going to Paris. This was pretty exciting, or at least it was then; someone would pay for me to come to Paris to play. Later it became, "Fuck, I have to go to Paris?"

But back then, how exciting could it get?

A French journalist, Patrick Zerbib, who wrote for *Actuel*, was in New York, had seen the band, and wanted to do an article.

Zerbib was a decent guy. I could tell this as I stood on my radiator to toss him down the keys when he was out on Third Street amid the mayhem of bums. He was out there smiling. He enjoyed it. Third Street was really out of control by then. It smelled of piss and uncollected garbage, and urine and more uncollected garbage, and more piss. On the southeast corner were three very nice brownstones, one of which was Phil Glass's home, and I think he still lives there. But that was closer to Second Avenue and not in the pit of the avalanche of stink in the middle of the block where I lived.

Zerbib goes out on a limb writing this giant article on me called "King of Third Street." *Actuel* had a lot of clout then, and if they said I was cool, it was verified that I was the hip new thing.

I suppose this is good. Is this good? I am still not sure. But this is what it was.

I'd been to Paris before. I was living in London and had gone to see my friend Rick Morrison perform in *Einstein on the Beach* by Robert Wilson, first in Avignon and then later, a second time, in Paris.

I took the train to the ferry and then another train and ended up in Paris. Wilson's early work really floored me, and I thought that the original production of *Einstein on the Beach* was great. What had really stuck with me was going to watch the rehearsals in New York.

I was staying in a cheap hotel on Barbès. I got food poisoning and was vomiting my brains out.

I was too sick to travel back to London, but I only had twenty English pounds left. If I paid for the hotel for another two days, which seemed about how long it would take for me to be able to travel, I wouldn't have enough left for the ferry. I stumbled out of the room to change money for the ferry ticket and stood in line at the currency exchange, shivering. I handed over my twenty pounds and the woman gave me back something like five hundred francs. She had given me double what I was owed. I normally would have pointed out her mistake, but this was a blessing beyond blessings. I went back to my room and slept with a smile on my face until the next morning.

This kind of thing happened one other time, when I was completely broke and in trouble because I was so broke. I was living on Third Street, in my apartment with no electricity because I have not paid Con Edison. A large pool is collecting under the refrigerator. I can receive calls but not make them. This so the phone company can have the pleasure of calling you to harass you, but so you can't call anyone to say what assholes the phone company is.

I woke up with no food, no cigarettes. This is no good. I go downstairs and open my mailbox to find a letter from Pete Liardi. Pete Liardi is from the Elm Park days in Worcester, and I have not talked to him in some eight or nine years. I open the letter and there is a hundred dollar bill in there, with a note saying, "The C-note is for cigs." Which is the first thing it went toward. Pete had read something about the band somewhere and sent me this. I don't even know how he got my address. Isn't that strange? This is the most broke I ever was and then out of nowhere is a hundred dollar bill in my mailbox.

I go to the airport to fly to Paris for my solo concert, but when I get to the airport, my ticket is for Brussels. I find out later that New York–to–Brussels is infinitely cheaper than New York–to–Paris, and this little skunk has flown me to Brussels without even telling me.

I'm at the Brussels airport expecting somebody to pick me up, but there is no one.

I've got no French money, the banks are closed, and I don't speak much of the language. I manage to get to the train station in Brussels and change enough money to buy a ticket to Paris and have a few francs left over for a hot dog and a beer. This was really a great hot dog.

Eventually, I get to Paris and stay at the writer Jackie Berroyer's house. He's told Zerbib that I can stay at his house because he thinks it will be interesting. His English is horrible, but I can see that he's very bright and he is a very sweet little guy.

Berroyer and I spent hours trying to talk to each other in broken French and English. He introduced me to *chevaline,* raw horse meat. At first I thought it was a hideous idea and then I thought, *Is there a reason it is okay to eat a cow and not a horse?* And it was just fucking delicious.

Heroin was very cheap and much better in Paris. Everybody I knew was taking it. So for three days I pretty much only took heroin, cocaine, ate horse meat, and drank champagne.

Life seemed really unusual and wonderful and exotic. I knew I was tempting some kind of edge, but what could go wrong?

A few months before, I had done a saxophone solo at Carnegie Recital Hall. It was the perfect room for this. The acoustics held the tone of the saxophone like a warm glow.

This was not the case at Les Bains Douches. I remember every bad concert that I ever did. They are etched in my brain, never to go away. This one was one of them. This was a disaster.

I step out onto the stage and there is just this cheap microphone. There are no monitors and no reverb. I start to play. Each note sounds thin and icky and comes out and dies immediately. There's no resonance, there's no tone. If you are playing by yourself and there's no resonance, you have to play harder and harder and faster and faster to fill the room with sound. I was exhausted fifteen minutes in and I could see that this crowd of ultra-hip French people had already pronounced me a bore after the first three.

I know it isn't going to get any better, so I just say thank you and good night and go into the dressing room, which is filled with people taking drugs.

A guy I knew a little bit from New York is on the floor, frantically looking under the couch for his works. He's screaming. Someone comes backstage and says that everyone is going to be furious unless I play more. People have paid a lot of money for their tickets. I say, "No, they hate it. Why do they want more of something they hate? And it sounds like hell, they should hate it."

Zerbib comes back and says he had gone out on a limb recommending me so highly in the article and please would I play a little more. So I go back out and play some more, really only for Zerbib, and then quit.

This wasn't a music venue, this was a place to see and be seen. I learned then, very painfully, to be careful about where I played in the future and to make sure that the equipment was going to be acceptable, although it is pretty much impossible to control.

There were three more concerts booked: one in Poitiers, one in Lyon, and one in Geneva. I had a fight with Fabrice from Les Bains Douches about money for airfare and left Paris for Poitiers. I was starting to not feel so good. I had no appetite.

I had taken heroin only ten times before, over a pretty long period of time. I had never taken it three days in a row, as I had in Paris. After taking it ten times or so, I had just begun to feel like, *This stuff is great. It can really be used to create things. They have been lying to me about heroin.*

But now I didn't feel so good and started to assume it was dope sickness. I didn't really have any idea what dope sickness was like and didn't have anyone to ask, out on the road as I was.

I took the train to Poitiers and did a show there. On the way there on the train, I was thinking, *Shit, I am in Europe, they paid me to come here, they paid me to play music. This is something special in one's life. It really is.*

I was opening for Carla Bley. Since this was an actual music hall and because it was Carla Bley, the equipment was good and the sound system was good.

D Sharp, a sweet little drummer who had played once with The Lounge Lizards, stopped by my dressing room. I told him about Paris, how badly it had gone, and that I was vomiting all the time and didn't know what to make of it.

We all know these moments, where things are going so wrong and you just need one human being to hear you. Well, D Sharp did that for me. He heard me. He sat there and heard me.

He died shortly after that and it broke my heart. I was never able to repay him for the human being he was to me at that moment. I did send his widow all the money I had at that time, but fuck money, money isn't a real currency when it comes down to it.

I don't feel so good. I take the train to Lyon and am booked to play at a college. *What's wrong with me? Am I dope sick? Is this what dope sickness is like?* I drink a bottle of Pernod and go out to do the concert. Students have booked this show. It is disorganized and there are only about a hundred people in a giant auditorium.

Three guys sitting about halfway back are heckling me. I play a phrase and a big sound comes from under the guy's coat, which is covering his face. Tonight it is going well and I'm pissed to be heckled. I need to redeem myself in my soul for Paris. I am not going to put up with this.

They make another farting sound and I stop playing. I lay the horn gently down on the stage, then hop down into the seating area, walk out into the audience, and stand in the row in front of the three guys who are making all the fart sounds. They are about twenty, not big but not small either.

"If I hear one more noise from you, I am going to come out here and fuck you up. *Est-ce que vous avez comprendu,* you petite assholes?"

They look terrified. I mean it and they can see it. The audience applauds wildly.

After the show I still cannot eat, and every time I try, I throw up. I'm by myself in Europe, and as much as I am enjoying the excitement of this, something is wrong. The college kid who has promoted the event comes back and says he forgot to make posters, so nobody knew there was a concert. Would I mind taking half of the money?

"Yes, I fucking mind. You have to pay me the whole thing."

He calls me an American businessman, says I'm not an artist, but he finally pays me. I've got one more concert to do, in Geneva.

I arrive in Geneva and they are expecting the artist/patron relationship. I am invited to dinners at the houses of incredibly wealthy people. Very snobby, they have to be the first to meet the new hip thing from New York. And they are stiff. Sometimes when I meet these kinds of people, who are so frozen behind the idea that their money makes them better than other people, they are so stiff that I wonder how they manage to procreate.

So, I can't eat, and I appall everyone at these dinner parties by asking if they know where to get heroin. I am convinced that I am dope sick.

But even if I weren't sick, I never did well in these kinds of situations. Every painter I know—and if you look at a list of top-selling living artists, the people I'm thinking of will be four or five of them—I won't name them, but that is their real talent. They can go to dinner with these people and be patted on the head and smile. It doesn't matter if they are good painters or not. It just matters that they are wearing the right clothes with the right hair and will bend over at the right moment.

I am vomiting all the time now and I don't know how I can possibly play. But I have to play this concert because they are paying my flight home, and if I don't play, God knows what will happen to me. Sometimes I wonder if most of the homeless people one sees are musicians whose tours went bad and they got stuck somewhere.

There are a lot of people in the dressing room. I am not paying attention to them. I wish they would leave. I am playing at the New Morning in Geneva, a nice big jazz club that is sold out.

I play for about a minute and then have to rush offstage to vomit. I come back out and start to play. I have modified what I am playing so that there are enormous gaps in the music. I introduce a phrase, then play it again with notes left out, then again with more notes left out, until I am just standing there in silence for ten and fifteen second intervals. This actually has some theatrical and musical merits. I think I might be the first in "it is about the notes I am not playing." But what is really happening is that I am looking down at my shoes and trying not to vomit right out there on the stage. So that they will pay for my ticket and I can get home.

You ever had a tough day at work? Imagine trying to not vomit onstage while playing saxophone or you will end up a homeless person in Switzerland.

I get through it. It is a bizarre success. Some famous poet even writes a poem about how odd and saintly I am in the dressing room after the show. How I just stare at the ceiling as annoying people try to talk to me.

I call Leisa from the hotel.

"Get some heroin! I get back tomorrow, I'm dope sick. Get some coke and some heroin and meet me at the airport."

So there is Leisa, on the other side of customs. She is bouncing around in her buoyant way. When I finally get through customs I start to run to get to her and they stop me. If I am running I must have something to hide.

They want to go through my suitcase. I tell them that I am just excited to see my girlfriend and, "See . . . ?"—for some weird reason I pull out all the press I acquired in France and show them my photos in all these magazines. I guess the idea is, "See, I'm famous, I can't be smuggling anything."

Well, this, believe it or not, works, and they let me through.

As buoyant as Leisa was a minute ago, she is now slumping over in the cab. She suddenly does not seem so excited to see me.

"You're high!"

"Yes, when you told me to get coke and heroin, I bought it last night, so that I could get to the airport in time. Then once I had it in the apartment I couldn't just let it sit there."

I'm a little disappointed that she didn't wait for me, but this is a fair explanation.

We get back to Third Street and get high. I feel great. The band has a gig on Thanksgiving, which is tomorrow, and they are rehearsing without me. The idea being that I'll be too exhausted from jet lag to make it, but now I feel fine. So, I go over to Anton's house to rehearse with them.

About an hour into the rehearsal there is a call from Leisa.

"The apartment is on fire."

"Are you all right?"

"Yes, the firemen are here now. They want to smash everything with hatchets."

"Well, stop them!"

"There might be fire still in the walls."

"No, stop them, I'll be right home. You sure you're okay?"

"Yes."

I tell the guys I have to leave and rush home. I see the fire truck pulling away from outside my building as I come up the street. I see the firemen slumped back against their truck with the satisfied, satiated look they get out of a good, big meal or unnecessarily smashing a lot of stuff with their hatchets.

Leisa answers the door, and her hair, which is normally blonder than blond and tied tight back against her head, is now jet black from the smoke and expanding in Don King rays in every direction. I crack up. She looks hysterically funny to me.

Leisa bursts into tears. I go into the apartment and see that she has actually had a close call. The mattress is burned. The walls are burned. There are ax holes in the walls.

Having been up all night, Leisa nodded off with a cigarette in her hand.

"You okay, hon?"

"Yes," she whimpers. Then we have sex on the burnt mattress.

The next day is Thanksgiving and Leisa is going upstate to her grandma's. Her grandma is elegantly old-style black. She used to call me Fandooley, because I reminded her of a pimp named Fandooley she knew in Harlem in the 1930s.

I still haven't eaten, and Leisa walks with me up Second Avenue to Schatt's Appetizing Treats so I can get food for myself. She feels bad that I am going to be alone, but I am perfectly happy. I've got money from the tour—otherwise we would never be able to afford to go to Schatt's—and this roast beef and stuff looks delicious.

Leisa goes off and I settle in to watch football on my little black and white TV with all the fancy delicatessen stuff spread out before me like a picnic.

I'm hungry. I eat a ton of different stuff—pickled herring, roast beef, smoked salmon—and wash it all down with ginger beer. I'm having a wonderful time. Then I get up and puke my guts out.

I go to sound check and then do the gig with the band. Some people come back to my place after and we smoke opium until the morning. I go to sleep around seven A.M.

I wake up and can't tell what time it is. Clock says eight. Shit. I must have slept thirteen hours.

But it's not dark out, it's morning. What's going on? Have I only slept an hour?

It's Saturday morning. I've just slept twenty-five hours.

Raging Bull opens today and I am going to go and see it. I'm the last person in line and it's sold out. Roger Grimsby, the local anchor person on the news, is in line ahead of me, but they only have one ticket. He's pissed because he is Roger Grimsby, and can't they let him in with his date? No. So I end up getting the ticket.

The only seat is in the front row. I get some popcorn and a Coke and watch this great, great movie. The movie ends and I can't get up. I am honestly just too tired to stand up. So I watch *Raging Bull* a second, and then a third time.

Monday morning, Leisa takes me to the clinic on Second Avenue to see what is wrong with me. We run into Marc Cunningham, who says,

"You look pretty yellow. Maybe you have hepatitis. Pull down your eyelid."

Marc looks under my eye and sees it's the color of a legal pad.

"Yep, you got it." Then he smiles and walks off.

We go to the clinic and the next day the blood work confirms Marc's diagnosis. I have hepatitis.

12

Udder and Horns

I have hepatitis. My apartment is burned out. I am supposed to stay in bed for at least a month. Maybe two. The bed—the little foam pad, really—is burnt. The pillows are burnt. A lot of stuff is still soggy. There are ax gashes in the wall. None of this really bothered me at that time. I actually kind of liked the ax gashes.

But as I write this, I cannot believe how unbearably grim it must have been. Yet I never once thought about it being grim.

While I was sick, Lisa Rosen did one of the nicest things anyone has ever done for me. Robert Rauschenberg, the painter, had a fund for artists who were ill and unable to make a living. Lisa applied for me and got me $400, which got me through the next couple months after the solo tour money was gone.

Leisa had a job at an architecture firm with a friend building miniatures of the places they were working on. I bet she was really good at that. She'd stock me up with food and leave me at home in front of the little black and white TV perched on the floor in front of my foam pad.

But she kept coming home later and later, and I knew she was fucking some guy at work. Since the hepatitis, my cock just lay there, like some squishy newborn puppy. But her excuses for being three hours late from work were just becoming too ridiculous.

One day, I threw a plate at her. I couldn't possibly have gotten up, so I hurled a plate that went sailing through the air like a Frisbee and hit the wall. The plate remained perfectly intact, but a huge section of the wall crumbled to dust. That can't be normal.

I mean, it was all fair. A few months before this, one night I had slept with Maripol. The next night I was at the bar at the Mudd Club with Leisa, and Maripol came running up. She said in a loud voice so that at least thirty people must have heard her, "I sucked your cock! Why?"

You need the full effect of the French accent to really get the impact of this wonderfully strange moment.

After a couple of months I was well enough to play with the band on New Year's Eve 1980 at Squat Theatre. We decided to play "Auld Lang Syne" to open the set at midnight. We worked it out in sound check and it sounded great. It's a beautiful melody, actually.

We get up onstage and are sorting stuff out, getting ready to play. We are going to count it down, "Five! Four! Three! Two! One!," and play "Auld Lang Syne" right at midnight.

I walk up to the mic and say, "Okay, who has a watch? What time is it?"

"Twelve oh three! It's twelve oh three!"

"We missed it?!"

Anton (Tony) wanted to make a record, whined about it, said we'd get better gigs. But I didn't want to do it. I didn't want to let those people into my life. Piccolo finally convinced me that it was just a way of documenting what we were doing.

Tony wanted us to go with EG Records, a British label, because he knew their New York rep, Ed Strait, and said we could trust him.

Strait was not straight at all. Maybe he was an honorable guy in an impossible situation because his bosses, Mark and Sam, were dodgy creeps, so he had to lie to us or lose his job.

We had to find a producer. I didn't know why we needed a producer but we had to have one. We got Teo Macero, who had produced a lot of the more famous Miles Davis and Thelonious Monk recordings. And he certainly knew how to record a saxophone so that it sounded like a saxophone.

We didn't know what we were doing. Teo was hardly ever there because Miles was recording in another studio in the same Columbia building, and Teo was also working that project as well. But it went okay. We had only two days to record everything, but we got it.

Teo kept calling Arto "Crunch" and never learned his real name.

Now we had to master the record. I didn't know what that meant. If we went to the mastering it would cost more, and we were told that the record label was not going to pay that and that it didn't matter anyway, it wasn't an important part of making a record.

When the mastering engineer heard Arto's twelve-string crunching, he thought the sound must be a mistake and turned Arto's clanging and thrashing into something much more polite and conventionally acceptable. Teo had had Arto up pretty loud in the mix, where he belonged.

Arto somehow got it in his head that my ego had thwarted him and went to all the press saying that I had mixed him off the record. Which I had honestly not done.

EG did such fucked up stuff. Evan and I both had ideas for the album cover that they rejected. It was the first time I'd seen things like this, which I later encountered in grand abundance in Hollywood. These guys were saying no to everything we did only because they could. For no other reason than it gave them a sense of power. Then they took the cover that Evan designed, which they had rejected, saying it was no good, and used it as the artwork for another, much more famous band on their label.

A few years after the album came out, my tour promoter at the time investigated how many copies of the first album had been sold. He reported to me that it was over six hundred thousand. The EG statements reported less than a twentieth of that.

Steve Piccolo changed for the worse rapidly. I was dabbling in heroin, but Steve took up residence.

He was living with this very sweet guy, Jerry, and his wife and their six-year-old little girl, and he was selling dope out of his room. I remember going to visit him and being disgusted by a glass of water that had about eight filthy syringes soaking in it.

Before we went on our first European tour, I told Piccolo that he was going to have to kick before we went. I know he was trying but he kept falling off.

Anton never liked him in the first place. Thought his time was bad. Piccolo's time wasn't bad and he was melodically brilliant. No way was I going to fire him, and not just because he was my friend and going through a hard time. He hadn't done anything to deserve getting fired, his playing was great, and we were going to be humans and stand behind him while he went through this heinous dope thing.

Anton is basically a sweetheart, but he could also really be a prick, especially back then. In a lot of ways, that's what allowed us to become a band. He kicked our asses in the early rehearsals, made us work and pay attention and not fuck around so much. Anton wanted to get rid of Piccolo and hire this friend of his to play bass. Felt his rhythm was stronger, but this guy had nothing close to Piccolo's melodic brilliance, so it wasn't what I wanted.

What really upset me was how strongly Arto took Anton's side. Like he was the great arbiter when it came to rhythm. Arto tries to promote a reputation about himself, that his rhythm cannot be questioned because he is from Brazil. But this is nuts. Just because he cannot tune the guitar does not mean his rhythm is of value. What was of value was his concept and his sound.

Arto, throughout rehearsals as the music was getting more complicated, would sit there unconsciously strumming along and reading a comic book. Honest, we would be working on a complicated piece of music and Arto would be there, engrossed in a comic book in his lap. Strumming.

What Arto and Anton did to Piccolo was grotesquely cruel, and I don't mind throwing a little shit Arto's way.

I've known a lot of musicians who can be really macho about time. Certain guys think their time is great and some other guy's time sucks. For the person in question there's no way to defend oneself or prove your time is good.

Time is everything in music. Where you place the beat and how your feel is, that's what puts the soul in it, the sex in it. How you feel the beat is everything. But there is no such thing as someone with perfect time, or if there is, what value is that? A metronome has perfect time.

And your time in music has everything to do with your confidence and ease in playing. If you start worrying about your time, then forget it.

Piccolo is really wobbly at rehearsal. He's trying to kick and not doing it.

We're rehearsing and I notice that Anton is purposely speeding up and slowing down. Steve is desperately trying to stay with Anton, thinking that it's him who's screwing up the tempo. This is one of the meanest things I've ever seen. Piccolo's confidence is completely shaken, he's trembling.

Anton throws down his sticks in disgust, says he can't play with this guy anymore, and storms out of the room. He's set the whole thing up to convince me that Piccolo sucks and should be replaced.

Steve is in tears: "I just want them to like me."

This could be seen as just Anton being unreasonable, which he often is, but Arto backing him so hard is what makes it ugly.

Piccolo misses a rehearsal. He claims that he was getting acupuncture for heroin withdrawal and fell asleep on the table. Nobody woke him. When he did wake up rehearsal was already over. His lies kind of go back and forth between things one could just let go and things that make you go, "Oh man, come on."

I stick with him. We fly to London to tour supporting the first album. We've checked into our rooms. This is all very exciting. There are lots of interviews. Lots of girls.

I get a call from Piccolo, who says I've got to come to his room, right away. There's a problem.

Great, what now? I go to his room and he shows me his arm. It's blown up and looks like it's been pumped full of Jell-O. It is, literally, four times its normal size. His arm is so big, he's carrying it around the room with his other hand.

What's happened is that he shot up with the water in the airplane's bathroom—the water that the big sign says "DO NOT DRINK"—and he's had some horrible reaction. So the water is not safe to drink but he has injected it directly into his bloodstream. Holy Human Fuck.

I find him a doctor and his arm is back to normal the next morning.

I can tell on the phone, immediately, if somebody is high. The person is on the other end, denying it, but their voice is raspier and has a different rhythm and pattern. It's a funny thing, because even if they are trying to hide that they are high, it's one of those things that you feel is being enjoyed, which makes it infinitely more annoying.

Long after I stopped using, I would still have all the usual reactions to heroin. After sound check, which is always somehow rushed and irritating, I'd think, *What do I have to do now? I have to cop and then go home and change.* When I hadn't been high in six months.

I'd kick before going on tour, maybe go out with just a chippy and get straight on the road. By the end of tour I'd be completely fine. My suitcase would come off the conveyor belt back in New York and there would be a shooting pain in my knees. Then my stomach. My eyes burned. I was dope sick! After three weeks of being straight! It doesn't make any sense. I am Pavlov's dog.

The European tour is fishy. It's been set up by the record company EG records, run by Mark and Sam. We were told in New York that we'd be getting twenty-five pounds a day, each. That wasn't much but it was fine. We were opening for their darling, Robert Fripp, and we were blowing him off the stage night after night. We were getting all the press and all the energy from the crowds. Mark and Sam didn't like these upstarts from the colonies not understanding their place.

They decide that we've misunderstood what we were told in New York and that, in fact, it's $25 a day, about two and a half times less money at that time, and oh, by the way, we have to pay for the transportation of the equipment, so we actually lost money to go on tour. This was the first time I'd encountered shit like this.

We had Sam's address and I tried to talk the rest of the band into breaking into his house, but only Piccolo thought that it was a good idea. Piccolo started sending them postcards from all over Europe:

Dear Mark and Sam:

Tour is going splendidly. Audiences in Italy love the band and I'm sure they are buying tons of records.

Yours truly,
Steve Piccolo of The Lounge Lizards

It reminds me of that story that may well be an urban myth. The story where a band steals a lawn jockey from somebody's front lawn in Michigan and takes it on tour.

The band takes photos of the lawn jockey in front of the Eiffel Tower, in front of the Berlin Wall, at the Acropolis, and sends the photos, like postcards, back to the address where they stole him. The postcards say, "Having a wonderful time. Wish you were here."

When they get back to the States they put the lawn jockey back in the yard where they found it.

I don't want to hear that that story is not true. It may be absolutely untrue, and you may know for sure it is not. I don't want to know. And fuck you for being the kind of person who would need to point that out.

We're playing at Danceteria and Piccolo wants me to pick him up in a cab on the way. I don't want to. I have all these rituals I do before a gig and this is not one of them. He's also out of my way and I don't want to get him, but this is a way that at least I can make sure that he makes the gig, and so I go and get him.

He gets in the cab and doesn't make me wait for him before coming downstairs. He seems fine.

"I have to make a stop."

"Oh, no."

I want to get to the club and find a reed, warm up before the show.

I give in and he directs the cab where to go. He knows that if he says Fifth Street and Avenue C, I'm going to say no. So, he leans forward, and in this sneaky little voice he says to the driver, "Take a left here, okay, now straight, okay, left here."

We do go to Fifth and C. He says he'll be right back. I'm nervous and hyped about the show, and the driver is nervous because we are in what looks like a war zone. The streetlights don't work, the buildings look like they've been bombed. Anybody who is actually out on this street has to be a murderer.

He's gone a long time. The driver is really nervous and wants to leave. I can't leave Piccolo here and I don't want to go down that alley where he's just disappeared. We wait. The driver starts to drive away and I scream at him to stay put.

Finally, Piccolo arrives. I'm so angry that I don't say anything.

We're playing, it's going okay, and then the rhythm goes sideways. Really sideways and I'm not sure what's happening. Usually when we play and the music takes that amorphous drop, it means that there's a broken string or drum or something's wrong. I can't turn around when I'm playing, I'm always in front of the rhythm section. There's a part in the music where I'm playing in phrases that make it possible to turn around, and I see Piccolo. He's leaning way over and standing on one leg. His torso is parallel to the floor. He's balancing in a way that challenges the laws of gravity and physics. His mouth is wide open and he looks like he's asleep. He's gone into a complete junkie nod. If you live in a big city, you've probably seen this: A guy on the street so bent over that he's about to kiss the pavement. He's not unconscious but he's certainly not conscious either. It's not possible to balance like that. But they never fall. Never. Just like you never see a bird fall out of the sky when they die, you won't ever see a junkie on a nod fall down.

Piccolo is in complete nod. One leg, mouth open, but he's still playing. I could fucking kill him.

Steve Piccolo has since moved to Italy and is straight, married, and now, at least according to him, the highest-paid translator in Italy. He also really is a genius. His *Domestic Exile* records, which he did in the early eighties, were truly some of the best pop things I've ever heard.

When we went on another tour, we were in a small white van. Five boys from New York City looking out on the French countryside. When you are with the same people twenty-four hours a day in close quarters, the smallest thing begins to irritate you beyond belief. "I hate his ears! I hate his ears!" I heard a story from Tony Levin where the guitar player couldn't stand the way the drummer chewed, and so one day in the middle of a roadside meal, with no warning, took his fork and stabbed the guitar player in the knee.

We got into a big debate about whether or not cows had horns. It became very heated and almost led to fist fights. Two of us emphatically believed that cows had horns and the other three didn't. We did agree that only cows had udders.

We'd drive past a herd of cows and the two of us who believed that cows had horns would point madly and scream, "Udder and horns! Udder and horns!"

"No! No horns!"

"Yes! Yes! Look! Udder and horns! Udder and horns!"

We had a manager for a little while. Nice enough guy, Paul Trautman, who looked like a mild-mannered Jimmy Connors. He had kind of a weird speech thing, not exactly a stutter but something like that. How he got it in his head to try to manage us, God only knows.

Trautman contacted me and I said sure, we'll give it a try.

Pretty quickly, Piccolo wanted to start a magazine called the *Trautman Intelligencer*.

Later Trautman set up our first Japanese tour, which was great, but his first tour was in the States. He had gotten some kind of cheap ticket for us to travel all over the United States, but only if every other flight came out of Atlanta. So when we did the West Coast, we went from L.A. to San Francisco, and then the following day was in Portland, but we had to go via Atlanta. Then to Seattle and then to Vancouver, via Atlanta. Every other day we were flying all the way across the country and back. Danny Rosen, who was playing guitar then, took a locker at the Atlanta airport and kept his bag there. He'd dress for the gig in the bathroom of the Atlanta airport. He told me that he didn't need a hotel room if he could just keep the locker.

Trautman had come to our rehearsal to present the tour to us. He was nervous in general, and the guys in the band, a bunch of wise guys who would torture him, didn't make it any easier. The venue in Seattle wasn't going to cover the hotel expense and we couldn't afford to pay for hotels, but Trautman didn't present it like that. He somehow did this brilliant Tom Sawyer maneuver where we were all actually looking forward to the adventure and not angry at all. Instead of having a hotel, we were going to all sleep in sleeping bags on somebody's roof. "Oh, boy!" It did actually sound like fun at that moment and we never gave it another thought. I remember us all trying to sleep on this freezing roof, cursing him. When the sun came up at six A.M., we cursed him some more.

During this meeting at the rehearsal, there was some confusion about the dates and whether we had a day off or not. He didn't have an itinerary and was giving us the dates verbally, from memory. He was getting flustered, and Piccolo kept asking what day we were playing in Vancouver.

"The sixth."

"You just said we were playing in Portland on the sixth."

"That's right."

"So what day are we playing Vancouver?"

"On Tuesday."

"What day is Tuesday?"

"The fifth."

"We're playing Vancouver before Portland?"

"No, Portland, then Vancouver."

"Well, then we can't be playing in Vancouver on the fifth and then Portland on the sixth."

"Oh, I see."

"What do you mean, 'I see'?"

Trautman was sputtering, "Oh, that's right, that's right, the Tuesday is a Wednesday."

"Oh, I see. It's confusing because that week the Tuesday is a Wednesday."

"Yes. No!"

13

Mutiny on the Bowery

Martin Meissonnier lost most of his money because Fela Kuti and his eighteen wives and enormous band roasted an entire goat in their hotel room.

They did that and a lot of other things.

Martin was a French promoter we worked with for a while. He also booked Fela's tours at that time.

Fela traveled with his whole village, seventy people, who were running perpetually amok. Fela had a witch doctor who would tell him not to play if there were evil spirits onstage. Unless the tour manager paid the witch doctor a substantial bribe, evil spirits were declared and the show would be canceled. Cancellation by a witch doctor not legally being an act of God, this also cost Meissonnier a great deal of money.

The band—with Piccolo; Danny Rosen, who replaced Arto; Anton Fier; and Evan—did another tour of Europe, which was set up by Martin. I liked him a lot. What was great for us was that on the tour bus, we had all these videotapes of Fela playing live. Unbelievable music.

That infectious neverending beat that just pulled you in. They did concerts that went on for hours.

The videos showed his eighteen wives gyrating on the floor as they sang backup. They would be on their hands and knees, wailing, and would do this little bump-up thing with their asses going into the air that is the most arousing thing I have ever seen.

What The Lounge Lizards were doing musically had never been done before. In our way, for sheer ferocious energy and concept alone, we were great. We were tumultuous, irreverent, and exciting. But Fela's music, with that incredible rolling rhythm, was so noble and organic, it made me think that what we were doing was maybe phony and I started to rethink it.

We played Paris and it was wonderful. We started our opener, "Incident on South Street," and after the first two notes came climbing out of Evan's Farfisa organ, the crowd roared in recognition and approval. Beautiful young women all up in the front, giving knowing, smiling nods.

There was a show canceled in France, in Clermont-Ferrand. We had a day off in this little village. The tour manager and driver, who had been jerks the entire time, left us with the van and went to their hometowns.

So when they were three hours late getting back, we stole the van and drove through the Alps to our next gig, in Lyon. It seemed insanely dangerous to have Piccolo driving at high speed through the winding mountain roads. On each curve, the centrifugal force would press my face against the window. As the van leaned out over the precipice, I would look down at the jagged landscape a mile or two below.

Later on that tour, we had been booked to play at this beautiful casino in Deauville. It was the kind of elegant room we'd envisioned playing one day.

But something seemed very odd.

We looked out from backstage and saw a rectangle of tables, with crisp, white tablecloths, around the stage. A lot of older people in formal attire, politely eating.

"What the fuck?"

"How are we going to play for these people?"

"I don't know."

We attempted to modify what we normally do and play music that would not ruin these people's evening. We did a slow blues. Then we cut out the dissonant parts on a couple other things to be tamer, so as not to scare them. We tried, we really did try.

But about ten minutes into the music, almost in unison, everyone quietly folded their napkins in front of them, stood up, and left the room.

After they left, we played our normal set for ourselves in this beautifully ornate, empty room.

Turns out that this was a reunion dinner for a group of older veterinarians and their wives. It was sponsored by Meissonnier's older brother, who was in charge of the event. I don't know what their relationship was—I imagine it was not much of a relationship—but Martin's brother, knowing he was in the music business, must have asked him for a band for this veterinarian event. Martin, having a sense of humor and I suspect not liking his brother so much, had booked us, the wildest, weirdest thing he could get his hands on.

The last gig of that tour, we were scheduled to play the Philharmonie in Berlin. This was a modern, fancy concert hall that we were playing as part of the Berlin Jazz Festival. Outside, as we were rushing in to do the concert, I met Stephen Torton, who became an integral part of my life later.

I was completely groggy. We had to soundcheck at nine in the morning and we were playing at eleven that night. So I had been sleeping.

Torton was waiting outside the hall trying to get in. I guess we had met before in the East Village, and he said, "Hey, John, can you get me in?" So I did.

The Berlin papers had said we were supposed to be funny, so any time there was a change or segue in the music, the audience would laugh. The "I get it" laugh of the pretentious modern art aficionado.

But they were laughing in a lot of places that weren't funny. So I started stopping songs in the middle and then having the band point and laugh at them.

Crowds in Europe's bigger cities seem to grasp the music in a more real way, but this was not that kind of crowd. These were people who buy their culture for the season and go to every event because that is their social life. They don't understand a thing, they don't care to, but their clothes are very expensive.

So we laughed at them and pointed.

Perhaps I have not managed my career so well.

We have done shows at cultural centers in Europe, especially smaller towns in France, Italy, and Spain, where we were part of a cultural series at the fancy theater in town. It is an event, but the freaky thing is that the first two or three rows are filled with the bigwigs of the town, the mayor and his wife, and the idiotic chief of culture, and whoever else is the most bourgeois in that town. They couldn't care less about the music, but these people in the front rows have the honor of getting these seats, so they are there with these sour faces, looking down at their bellies, fingering their ties, and fondling their jewelry.

The one thing that I really remember about that night in Berlin was that it was live on TV, but in Berlin that station at that time went off the air at midnight. We are playing past midnight to a crowd of some five thousand people and the television crew is packing up all around us. Evan is playing this quiet, beautiful solo and this guy is dragging a cable across the stage.

"What are you doing?"

"TV finished. Go home."

"Great, but we're still playing!"

He shrugs.

Hard to hold the violence down sometimes. I protect Evan and music with the ferocity of a mother bear.

After the tour, Danny and I got an apartment in Paris, near the Bastille, for a couple of months with Vincent Gallo. We knew Vince from New York. Danny and I were getting high pretty often. We'd go to the fancy clubs and meet sexy girls and get high. We'd come home late at night to find Vince sitting in front of a mirror wearing a three-foot-long fake beard in a rabbi outfit or some other equally bizarre thing.

Danny's head would turn sideways and he would say, "Vince, what the fuck are you doing?" Vince would continue to stare into the mirror and say, slowly, "I am working on my acting."

Poor boy. As oddly confident as Vince seems now, he was equally insecure and uncomfortable then. Like a lot of sensitive, intelligent young people, it seemed as though his energies and thoughts were not his to control and moved sideways at painful cross-purposes to his being.

Vince was also a liar. A compulsive liar, one of those people who start to believe their own stories halfway through. He would come home and say that he had beaten up a train conductor or had lunch with a senator from the United States or God knows what. And you could see that halfway through the story, he now believed what everyone else knew was absolutely not true.

A few years later Vince and I were on the same softball team. We played over on Hudson Street.

Vince was on deck with the bat over his shoulder when somebody asked, loudly, "Vince, when you lived in Paris with John Lurie and Danny Rosen, were you a junkie too?"

"No, I was a liar."

The idea that Vince's lying was as problematic a vice as Danny and I getting fucked up on heroin was absolutely on the mark, and it created a soft spot in my heart for Vince that I am still trying to hold on to, though he sure makes it rough.

We actually made some money on the Meissonnier tour. Danny, Piccolo, and I all bought Borsalino hats. The one I wore in *Stranger Than Paradise*.

When I got back to New York I had a fancy umbrella, my new suit, and my hat, and strode into Uncle Jerry's law office, on Fifty-sixth Street, thusly attired and paid him back a chunk of the money he had loaned me. He was really pleased.

EG Records killed the first band. All the little devious, insidious things they did just took the life out of it. The thing with the album cover Ev designed. Stiffing us on the money for the first tour so we all went home broke. The worst thing was the equipment thing in London. We had done the whole tour opening for Fripp, using his sound system, which was really good and sounded great onstage, and I assume in the house. When we got to London we were doing a final gig for our own fans as the headliner. It was a pretty big deal.

EG was so upset about our getting so much attention and excitement on the tour and overshadowing Fripp that they had the sound guys turn in all the good equipment and rented the shittiest mics, monitors, amps, and drums, so that it just sounded awful. We had played a ton of times with shitty equipment and overcame it, but we had gotten used to having this really nice sound onstage, so when it sounded that bad, we just couldn't quite pull it off. I felt like we had lost the World Series.

They had booked a tour of the United States that had to be canceled when my hepatitis relapsed, and they were angry because they had already paid for the ads in those cities. They called and threatened me that this would be the end of the band if I didn't go. Then they went to the other guys in the band and said that, according to their doctor I had seen in England, I wasn't that sick and could do the tour if I weren't being such a prima donna. Then two months later they came to me and said that I was the band and that I should consider dumping the other guys. Just sick stuff with no real reason.

I thought it was over. I started getting pretty into heroin and cocaine, and a bunch of time just disappeared.

Jean-Michel Basquiat, Willie Mays, got really famous and really rich, very quickly. He didn't handle it so well. Just six months before, I was his mentor and had been for a few years. He was following me around, asking my advice, and sleeping on my floor.

Suddenly he was this giant art star, hanging out with celebrities and really flaunting the money.

I suppose I didn't handle it so well either, was kind of jealous, but mostly I felt like he was buying into this thing that we had sneered at. Or maybe he just sneered at it because I did.

I felt the currency of what we had, the things we could create, that no one else could, was infinitely more valuable than money and this kind of glitzy nonsense that he was now parading around in.

He had left a bunch of artwork at my place. It was constantly in the way. I told him he had to come and pick it up.

Danny and I go over to see him at his new loft on Crosby Street that was supplied to him by his gallery. There is a girl hanging around, smiling out from his bed. I'd never actually seen Willie with a girl like that before. Where she was actually there with him and not told to leave before we arrived.

Danny is telling this girl how great her show was the other night at the Mudd Club. I didn't know what the hell he was talking about. I guessed she was a singer. This amazes me, because Danny was always snide to everyone who tried to accomplish anything. Partly because Danny, who was as handsome as a young man could be, if he ever dared apply himself, could have done pretty much anything better than anyone.

I didn't think much about her. She later turned out to be Madonna.

Funny thing with Madonna, how she can look awful with that nose crooking down and then you see her and, wow, she is an exquisite beauty. This isn't video lighting. It happens in real life. She just changes.

Six months later, I am with Tony Garnier, who gives me a chaw of chewing tobacco to try. We're standing on the corner of First Avenue and Seventh Street.

"Don't swallow the juice."

"Of course, I won't swallow the juice."

I've got this enormous wad of tobacco in my mouth, and I'm spitting into the gutter when this young woman comes up behind me and says, "Hi," all flirty.

She is stunning, but I don't know who the hell she is and she can see this from my face. But she is really nice looking. I don't want to spit the tobacco juice out in the street, so I swallow it.

"I'm Madonna, I used to go out with Jean-Michel."

Swallowing the tobacco is making the shit just burn me up and I can't really carry on a conversation. I want to gasp for air but won't do it in front of this beautiful girl. She mistakes my not talking for disinterest and walks away.

Tony is off to the side, can see exactly what is happening, and is laughing at me. Tony always seems to be laughing at me, and it is always exactly fair that he is laughing at me, so I can't ever get angry.

* * *

I decided not to be crazy anymore and canceled the SSI money. The checks kept coming for six months. So I kept cashing them. Then I got a call from some government bureaucrat saying that I was going to have to pay that money back.

I went ballistic on the guy.

"I'm just getting better! Why are you bothering me? You should be happy for me, not asking for money!"

He gave up and said that I didn't have to pay them back, but that my checks would stop now.

Out of the blue I got an offer to do another tour with Martin Meissonnier. But I didn't have a band. I had to find a new one. Piccolo was in Italy and Anton Fier was just too cranky to continue playing with. And Danny Rosen, as talented as he was, just didn't want to do it or take it seriously. He thought it was no fun.

For a short period the band was Dougie Bowne on drums, Peter Zummo on trombone, Tony Garnier on acoustic bass, and, of course, Evan on piano.

That was a pretty stinky period for the band. As I tried to get back to the original reasons that I had started playing, the music seemed to get stiff and self-conscious. I couldn't find how to do it. I was making the music more difficult but not more beautiful or soulful. Part of the problem was that most of the stuff was written on heroin. For a year or two, I thought I had to get high to write, and there was nothing in it. No heart.

I was asking around about drummers and everyone was recommending Dougie Bowne. I met him, by chance, at Binibon late one night. Binibon was on the corner of Fifth Street and Second Avenue. It was the only place, back then, that was open all night in the East Village. Maybe there was Kiev, but Kiev sucked. There was a coffee shop on the corner of Tenth and Second, but I didn't go back there after I was in there by myself one night at three A.M. and saw someone get shot in the ankle. I didn't actually see it. I heard the gunshot and then saw this guy hopping around on one leg. The guy who shot him was gone, immediately, before I even looked up.

If you run a coffee shop where the food is truly awful, it can be bad for business if people get shot at the counter.

Binibon was more central. When we got back from tours, we'd get high and stand on that corner outside Binibon and run into forty people we knew in about half an hour, and soon knew pretty much everything that was going on. It was really like being in a village, but a village that had gone mad.

So nights when nothing was going on, I'd go and hang out at Binibon. They'd let you sit there for hours just drinking a tea or coffee. They'd let you hang out, but you absolutely could not use the bathroom. Employees only.

Binibon was the restaurant where Jack Abbott had horribly stabbed a kid waiter to death. Abbott was the author of *In the Belly of the Beast* and had been released from prison through the efforts of Norman Mailer and others because he was supposedly a great talent. He was living across the street from me in the men's shelter.

Jack Abbott went into Binibon late one night with two women. When he asked to use the bathroom, the waiter told him that this was not possible. Jack Abbott thought that he was being disrespected in front of the two women and stabbed the kid just under the ribs, the same exact way that he'd described in his book. It got a lot of attention.

It's too bad Jack didn't know that they don't let anyone use the restroom. We used to beg them to use the toilet there.

"It's the law, a restaurant has to have a restroom for the clientele."

"No! Employees only."

Evan said, "How many more must die before they let you use the bathroom at Binibon?"

This wasn't a scheduled meeting with Dougie. He came up to me and said, "You're John Lurie, I'm Dougie Bowne."

Dougie is hardly five feet tall, and when he shook my hand, I noticed that he had these tiny, tiny little hands. Tiny like a doll's hands. *You've got to be kidding. How can this guy possibly play loud and hard enough to play with The Lounge Lizards?*

But we got together and played for a bit and he had incredible power. I was thinking about using Denis Charles on drums, who was a great jazz drummer and a true sweetheart, but Denis couldn't play in odd time signatures and Dougie was a master at it. Dougie was great, actually better for the gig than Denis, so Dougie got the job. Dougie is also a sweetheart.

Tony Garnier, who was with me for only a year or so, has now been Bob Dylan's bass player and musical director for years. Tony is, I think, one of the great bass players. In a way, it's a shame that he's spent all these years playing with Bob Dylan, because even though Bob Dylan is obviously Bob Dylan, it doesn't really give Tony a chance to play like he can play. He is up there with any great bass player you can name. Richard Davis comes to mind.

When I was writing film scores, I would write a fairly simple, unembellished bass line to go with whatever else was going on and then Tony would take it and turn it into something very special. Not by changing the notes, but just the way he turned the phrase into something really musical and right.

I have been kind to some people in this book who, years later, when I was in trouble, were heinous to me. They also spread horrendous gossip about me on top of it to cover the tracks of how they had behaved. But this was how I felt about them at that time. So that is what I will write here. I will be gentle.

But Tony is not that. A tough guy with heart. I fucking love Tony Garnier.

We were playing in Paris at New Morning, a jazz club that holds about seven hundred people. When we'd play there, we'd get a funny mix of intellectuals, jazz fans, models, and the hip French. It was a bit of a dive, but the sound was good. The dressing room was this tiny ten-by-five-foot room right off the side of the stage.

Rickie Lee Jones is there after the show to see Tony. He introduces her to me by saying, "John, you know Rickie Lee Jones, Tommy Lee's sister." Then he laughs by himself.

We hang out for a while.

The local chapter of the Hells Angels shows up after the show to see Tony. Some of them are French and some of them are expatriate Americans who, because of warrants, can't go back to the United States.

We go to their clubhouse and stay there until late into the next

Theda and David Lurie boarding train in Minneapolis, heading for New Orleans

John Szarkowski

My dad and Liz

I am a cowboy

My mom

My dad and Evan, Rockport

The world didn't stand a chance

My dad and me as camels

Uncle Jerry, our backyard in New Orleans, photo by me, age five

The Jeanne Parr Show, Tom asks a question

Jeanne Parr Interrupted

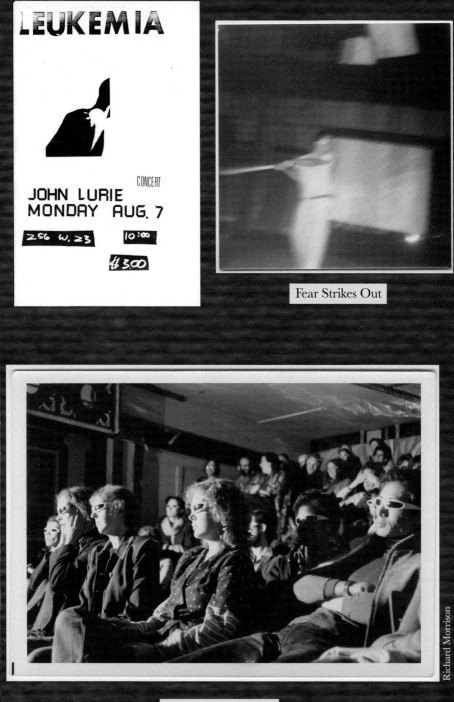

Fear Strikes Out

Audience Leukemia

Richard Morrison

Leukemia program notes

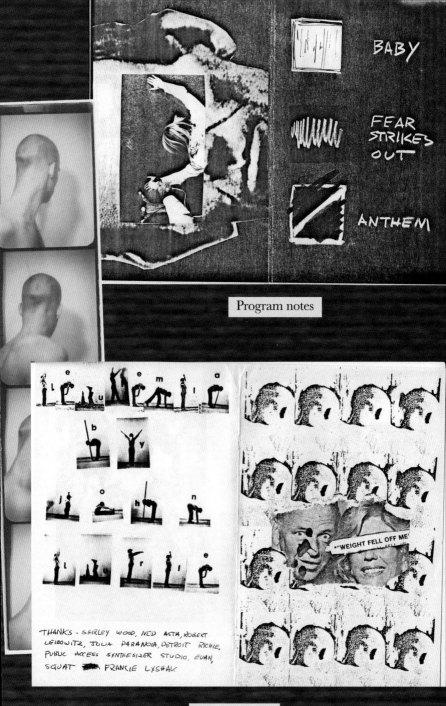

BABY

FEAR STRIKES OUT

ANTHEM

leukemia

"WEIGHT FELL OFF ME"

THANKS - SHIRLEY WOOD, NED ASTA, ROBERT LEIBOWITZ, JULIA PARANOIA, DETROIT RICHIE, PUBLIC ACCESS SYNTHESIZER STUDIO, EUAN, SQUAT FRANCIE LYSHAK

Wendy

Danny Rosen and Vince Gallo

Danny Rosen and me as
trustworthy Italian merchants

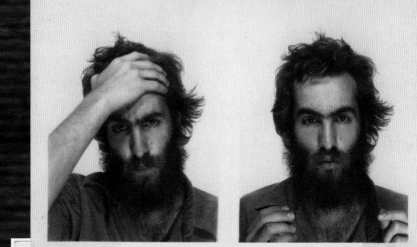

The most stoned I ever was, Avignon, 1976

Tibetans on Venus, wardrobe

Richard Morrison

MEN IN ORBIT

A JOHN LURIE PRODUCTION

FEATURING: ERIC MITCHELL JOHN LURIE MICHAEL McCLARD JAMES CROSBY

MARY LOU FOGARTY BECKY JOHNSTON ARTO LINDSAY RICHARD MORRISON

CAMERA:
JAMES NARES

WED. THUR. FRI.

FEB. 21, 22, 23   9 PM $2.00

NEW CINEMA 12 ST. MARKS

I built a capsule in my living room

Leisa is too short to run for president
and not good at checkers

With Richard Morrison

Hack license after basketball

With Steve Piccolo

The Kind and Lovely
Evan Lurie on Farfisa

James Nares

Stephen Torton

María

John and Evan Lurie. Brothers.

LOUNGE LIZARDS
SQUAT
FOR $5

256w23 _ fri.7 _ sat.8

Jack Zaloga

James Nares

The Fabulous Fucking Lounge Lizards

morning. Tony is a little nervous about my coming because he's afraid I'll say something or make a joke that won't be appreciated. That kind of awkward feeling when you introduce two groups of friends from completely different planets. And this, after all, is me, who will say anything at any time, to anyone, and they're the Hells Angels. We're all taking a ton of coke, so he's probably right to be a little nervous.

I'm having a great time. I love these guys and I am very high. It's getting light out and suddenly I jump up and announce:

"I want to join! I want to join!"

There is silence.

"What? Am I too skinny to join?"

"No, a skinny guy with a gun is fine."

Tony tries not to look up from the table.

But at this moment at seven A.M. in Paris, high out of my mind on cocaine in the Hells Angels clubhouse, I am very serious. I want to join the Hells Angels.

Well, the Hells Angels decide that I'm okay and they want to come to the show the next night. I try to discourage them, telling them that they wouldn't like the music, but they feel I'm talking down to them and say they will definitely be there. We can count on it.

We're onstage playing. The place is completely packed—people are standing all the way to the back of the club. The entrance to the club is at the other end of the long, thin room from the stage, so that the band faces out toward the entrance.

There's a big commotion. I can't really see what's going on because the stage lights make it difficult, but I can see that people are being jostled all over the place, like a herd of bulls is coming through the crowd.

It's the Hells Angels and they've decided that, as a show of respect, they're going to guard our dressing room door.

Altamont!

About eight of them just stand there with their arms folded, blocking the door to the tiny dressing room. This way the models, intellectuals, and poets can't break in and steal the rotting cheese.

That same band played at the Montreux Jazz Festival. I didn't think we were any good that night, but the head of the festival, Claude Nobs, was taken with us and invited us to lunch. I didn't want to go but Rene, the tour manager, said it was a big honor and we had to go.

"You cats." Claude Nobs kept saying "you cats."

Somewhere around that time, Bruno Denger set up a couple of our tours. Bruno was from Basel and he also used to say "You cats" when referring to us. It made my fucking skin crawl, "you cats" said with a Swiss accent. It made my skin crawl even further when, halfway through the second tour, he announced that a couple of shows were canceled, and because of that we were only getting about two-thirds of what I had been originally promised. Now, how it works is this: I get offered a tour for X amount of dollars per week by the promoter. I then call the musicians and offer them X amount per week based on that figure. If the figure changes in the middle of the tour, I can't pay the musicians less than I've promised, so I end up working for a month on the road and actually losing money to pay the band. This shit happened over and over, so that in the early stages of the band, I was losing money, sometimes a lot, on every other tour. "You cats."

Claude Nobs is bringing out cheese and fancy bottles of wine. We'd drink anything, especially if it was free. Telling story after story.

Tony goes into his "Really?" mode. Tony has the ability to zone out during a conversation that bores him and say, "Really?" at the appropriate pause in the conversation. He sounds slightly amazed and interested, when his brain is actually five miles away somewhere.

It's getting late and Rene is getting nervous about our catching the train. We've got to go all the way to Vienna, it's an overnight trip. Claude assures him that everything is fine, he'll send us with his drivers. We get to the station and do a mad dash with the bags. The band always has tons of luggage because of equipment.

Evan, who is bombed from all the wine at lunch, is standing on the train, and we're throwing all the bags up to him. We get the last bag on the train and it starts to pull off. Rene is running along the side of the train, banging on it and yelling, "Wait! Wait! Hey, wait!"

Evan grins out the window at us as the train pulls away. Tony is laughing.

I ask, "What happens now?"

Rene screams, "The money! All the money is in my bag!" He's wearing these skimpy little shorts that only a Frenchman would wear.

Rene is frantically trying to figure out a train route that will get us to Vienna. A couple hours later there is a train to Geneva, we can get that. There isn't another train to Vienna until the next morning, but we can get cheap rooms in Geneva, spend the night there, and then take the long trip to Vienna first thing in the morning.

Meanwhile, I'm a little worried about Ev, who is drunk out of his mind with thirty bags. I don't think Evan even knows that he has to switch trains in Geneva.

We get to Geneva. No sign of Evan and no hotel rooms. There's a sports convention in town and there are no rooms to be had.

Now what? We have no money, we're hungry, and Rene's legs are getting cold. This is also only the second day of the first tour these guys have done with me, and they're all looking a little nervous. I also find out that this isn't really Meissonnier's tour. He's sold it to another promoter I've never heard of in Switzerland.

It's now about midnight. We're cold, tired, and hungry. We're just standing on the street with our instruments. At about two A.M. I think that it would be better to be in jail than just standing here on the street. So we take out our instruments and start to play. Tony's got his acoustic bass, Zummo is on trombone, and I'm on soprano. Dougie is smashing a metal railing with his drumsticks. We play a New Orleans kind of blues.

We don't get arrested, but out of every alley, from all directions, drunk bums are appearing. They are all dancing, flailing their arms and legs around. Almost like they were waiting for this moment.

Now we are surrounded by our new friends. We can't understand anything they're saying. Rene can speak their language but won't talk to them because they are bums.

Morning comes and Rene wants to take a train. I insist that we fly. "We haven't slept, we haven't eaten. Even if we fly we're going to be a wreck. If we take a train it's hopeless."

He has to approve it with the new promoter but can't reach him. I force Rene to get the plane tickets with his credit card and we fly.

Evan somehow figured out that he had to switch trains and managed to move all thirty bags by himself. When he gets to Vienna, there are people from the festival to pick us up. Evan unloads all the bags from the train and waits there, not knowing what else to do.

The people from the festival are waiting for a band. Once everyone has left the station, there is just them and Evan standing on the platform. Evan goes and asks them if they are there to meet The Lounge Lizards and they say, "Oh, oh."

We get maybe an hour's sleep before we have to soundcheck. We're on a bill with Joe Pass, who plays solo and is amazing, then Benny Golson, who is also amazing.

Freddie Hubbard is playing with Tony Williams and seems like he wants to kill him, with Tony Williams playing over everything.

I'm really tired and getting loopy. We get up onstage in front of some five thousand serious Viennese jazz fans and they're not loving us. Which is fair because what came before us, with both Joe Pass and Benny Golson, truly was amazing.

I tell a joke to the audience. In places like Vienna and the bigger cities in Germany, I can talk to the audience—they understand enough English—but I'm pretty fucking loopy and my jokes are obscure. I tell a joke and five thousand people sit there in silence. I can hear Tony giggling behind me. I tell another joke, five thousand Viennese jazz fans sit there in silence. I can be very obstinate and weird. I tell more jokes, I'm not going to stop. Tony is doubled over, he's laughing so hard. He's not laughing at the jokes, he's laughing from exhaustion and he's laughing at me.

After the show they have delicious hot dogs, the best hot dogs, served from chuckwagons by very pretty Austrian girls who smile. A TV station asks if Evan and I can interview each other. So we do it as close to Bob and Ray as we can:

"How do you find the audience here in Vienna?"

"Well, when I'm at the piano, they are just to my right. They are usually just standing there in front of the stage. They aren't hiding."

The people from the TV station don't know what we're talking about, but we manage to crack each other up quite a bit.

Rene comes running over and says we have to leave immediately. We have to check out because we're taking the overnight train to Holland. We all start to complain but there is no other choice. This apparently has always been the plan.

Rene says, "Don't worry, we have sleeper cars." This sounds very exciting to me and Ev.

Pretty much nobody has slept except for Evan, but put a bunch of young guys in a train car right after a gig, and there is sure to be a certain amount of fooling around.

Dougie goes right to sleep. Dougie is little and can scrunch up on a chair and fall asleep. Over the years I have grown extremely jealous of Dougie's ability to sleep anywhere, at any time, and usually wake him up out of spite.

Tony and I develop a game called Kick In The Face. We sit across from each other with our feet up, each poised to kick the other one in the face. On the count of three we are both supposed to kick each other in the face as hard as we can. We count to two and then laugh hysterically.

We finally all manage to fall asleep. The trip is over twenty hours, so we can sleep all afternoon. I'm not asleep an hour when the door to the compartment comes smashing open and it's an enraged German conductor screaming that we have to get up immediately. At least, we assume that this is what he's saying, we're not really sure. The only thing that is completely clear is that we can't sleep anymore or he's going to continue to scream at us. A little frightening as our first moment of consciousness ever in Germany, and every Nazi movie starts flowing through my head.

We get to Holland and then have to take vans to the North Sea Jazz Festival. This is an enormous festival with hundreds of acts. There are a lot of great people playing and we're excited to be there. We're also excited to prove ourselves in this environment, because we are seen with a great deal of skepticism by a lot of the jazz world, most of which has probably never even heard us play.

The North Sea Jazz Festival, unfortunately, has all the charm of a car show. There is music going on everywhere and the vibe is somehow very sterile.

We're playing on the roof of this building. We don't get a sound check. We go out to play and the sound of each note just disappears like it's sucked off into a void. We haven't slept in three days, we're very tired, and we play horribly.

We've played at the North Sea Jazz Festival twice, and they are two of the absolute worst shows that the Lizards have ever done. I remember every bad gig we ever did, and these were two of them.

That tour taught me to study the itinerary months in advance to try to avoid whatever obscene tortures the tour promoter might have in mind. It got more and more gruesome as it went on. There was no time to sleep. We would finish a show and get back to the hotel, when there was a hotel, really late, and then have to get up in an hour or two, pack, and then travel for fourteen hours to the next gig.

We were exhausted beyond exhausted. Tony and I would go in and out of bouts of hysteria. We were somewhere in Germany, driving through the countryside, and U.S. fighter jets were flashing across the sky, doing test flights.

Tony would put his head out the window like a little kid and yell, "Jets! Jets!" and then collapse on the floor of the van laughing.

"Jets, they're so beautiful."

Right before the show a couple of radio journalists came into the dressing room to interview us, live, on the radio. Anwar Sadat had just been assassinated. They wanted to know what we thought about it. Tony and I couldn't stop laughing long enough to tell them. Must have been something else to hear that over the radio.

The tour was really hideous, everything about it: the travel, the hotels, most of the venues, the equipment, the food. It was unendurable. Because Meissonnier had sold the tour, we didn't even know who to blame. Rene kept saying that we would meet the promoters when we finally played in their town, that they would make it up to us, that we would probably get some kind of a bonus.

We finally get to their town—I can't remember where it was—and we have dinner with these assholes. There is this big, six-foot-tall, sexy young woman who is positioned to sit next to me at the dinner table. She speaks no English and is not interested in putting up with my attempts at French. Her eyes are pinned. Halfway through dinner, she puts her hand on my thigh and runs it up into my crotch. This girl is not interested in me one bit and I don't know what to make of it. Then it occurs to me that she has been hired for me.

She's the bonus.

Her pupils are just two tiny dots. I am sure I can get some dope out of her. We go back to my room. She pretends she doesn't know what I am talking about.

She takes off her clothes. She is incredibly sexy as she stands there. A sex beast.

But at the same time, she's totally uninterested in me. And really what I want is a fucking line of heroin.

So, of course, I have sex with her. I'm not sure why. I didn't really have any desire to. She was like a nonperson.

An hour later, I have to check out because we have a ten-hour train ride to Brussels before we fly back to the United States. The train is packed and we have to stand next to the stinking bathroom the whole ten hours.

Get on the plane and I don't feel so good. This is a super cheap flight and the food is bad. I am really nauseous. Maybe I'll feel better if I vomit. I get the airsick bag out and go to open it. There is someone else's vomit already in it from another flight, which is now all over my hand.

When we arrive in New York, Zummo's wife and Garnier's girlfriend are at the airport. I see their mouths move from a smile to a gaping exclamation of shock when it registers on them just what horrible shape I have returned their men in.

14

Look Out! The Anteater!

I met Jim Jarmusch on the aforementioned corner of Fifth Street and Second Avenue. I had known him only vaguely before. He had been the bartender in Eric Mitchell's movie *Red Italy*, one of the films we made for the New Cinema. I was in the scene, first as part of the band, and then later on dancing in a spaz attack. I didn't think much about this white-haired guy; in fact, we sort of sneered at him. "He's a film student, ick." That really was unacceptable to us.

"If you want to make movies, then make movies. You are going to school for it? Are your parents paying your rent?"

But I ran into him late at night, outside Binibon, and he started talking to me, seemed nice enough and very sincere and thoughtful. He had some hash, and we went and sat on a stoop on Fifth Street and smoked it. He talked about Nick Ray.

We became friends and started hanging out a bit. Then he paid me $200 to store his film equipment at my place when he was shooting *Permanent Vacation* and I gave him some music for it. He used my apartment to shoot the scene where Chris Parker is dancing. I am also in the movie for a moment wearing some very white shoes, playing the saxophone.

Soon after I met Jim and his girlfriend, Sara Driver, I ran into Sara on the street. She was with this tall girl with blond hair who was so movie star beautiful, it made me a little shy. She seemed shy, too. She kind of hid behind Sara and smiled out at me.

That was María Duval. We got together shortly after that.

María was light-skinned Cuban, tall with phenomenally generous lips. She had a real apartment on Seventeenth Street near Park Avenue. Maybe it wasn't that nice, but compared to the squalor I was living in, it was completely civilized and dazzling. I was getting high a lot. María was very straight, a little on the *Mary Tyler Moore Show* side of things. Polite, proper, and very serious about her acting career. I would come to her place late, fucked up, and show her a bit of how the wild people do it.

She had been the lead in a couple of plays, and though they had been successes, I felt bad because I just couldn't get behind it at all. I thought they were corny and predictable.

The band was rehearsing at Squat Theatre and I went upstairs to make phone calls. I called Jim, because he had been working on a futuristic script called "Garden of Divorce," which was going to star María and me.

It was a futuristic sci-fi romance. He had been working on it forever and it didn't seem to be going anywhere. The idea seemed fairly forced and not particularly inspired. He was trying to finish the script but was stuck. For months he was stuck.

Wim Wenders had given him a half hour of black and white film that Wim had left over after *The State of Things*. But Jim didn't want to do "Garden of Divorce" in black and white. He didn't know what to do, and he was agonizing over it for quite some time. He was paralyzed.

"So, what do you want to do?"

"I'm not sure." It really sounded like this was causing him pain.

"Let's just use the film from Wim and make a little movie."

"Oh . . . I don't know."

"Come on, man, what's wrong with you?"

"Oh . . . I don't know."

"If you made a little movie, who would you want to use?"

"Ah, you and Eszter."

I had known Eszter Balint since she was twelve, when she was the very bright daughter of Pisti Balint, one of the heads of Squat Theatre. Now she was a seventeen-year-old, wisecracking terror.

"How about this: I'm a low-level gambler. Eszter is my cousin and she comes to New York from Hungary. I get a call from my aunt saying Eszter is coming and I have to take care of her. I don't want her there, and I especially don't want anyone to know that she is my cousin or that I am Hungarian, though I am quite taken with her after a bit."

"Um. Okay, I guess."

"So let's just shoot that and see what happens."

"Okay. I think you need a buddy."

"Okay, we'll figure it out later, I gotta get back to rehearsal."

That really was pretty much the conversation verbatim. Not like it was some earth-shattering idea that I had come up with, but that was the seminal moment of *Stranger Than Paradise*. Right there in thirty seconds. Perhaps proving this is the credit right before the copyright: "Part One from an idea by John Lurie and Jim Jarmusch," in such tiny little letters only a dog can hear it.

But really here the credit goes to Eric Mitchell. This was what I had gotten from Eric: Just shoot it. Just do it now. You have the film? Just make something. Roll up your sleeves and attack. Kamikaze style.

Funny how credit works, but I can tell you for certain that without Eric Mitchell's influence on me, I would not have influenced Jim and pushed him the way Eric had pushed me.

So, all you film school students, understand that *Stranger Than Paradise* would have never existed without Eric Mitchell, because Jim, to this day, would be sitting in his apartment, smoking joints and rewriting "Garden of Divorce" and saying, "Um, um, I'm not sure." Would seem truly bizarre a couple years later when he was declared an auteur.

I recommended Christopher Wool to play the part of my pal, but we met with him and Jim thought he was wrong. Jim was probably right— I think Chris would have been a little tight. Richard Edson has seven sides to his nose, so he got the part.

We shot in Jon Ende's Second Avenue apartment, right around the corner from me. I think that it just took three days. Acting seemed a breeze to me; I didn't think much about it. There was one scene with Eszter where I get mad at her, and when I saw it, I didn't like the way my face contorted, but otherwise it seemed fine. I wore the Borsalino hat that I had bought with Danny and Piccolo. It had shrunk a little and fit the dopey character.

I was playing saxophone solo, the same three nights we were shooting, for a play on Forty-second Street. I wasn't going to get paid anything from *Stranger Than Paradise*, though Jim had promised me three points of the gross, should it do anything.

I'd grab my horn after we finished shooting and rush out to get seventy-five bucks for two shows a night for this improvised theater thing. I played along behind a curtain, mixing with the actors.

I thought that the title was *Monologues*, but Torton would laugh at me and say that the name of the play was something else. I'd get a little high before the shows and then a lot high after. I was straight when we shot *Stranger* during the day.

Torton was around all the time. He has the best mind, full of great ideas. He also had the capacity to make things happen, not for himself, but for other people. He was helping out on *Stranger* and it seemed like if Jim had said, "I need a fire engine," Torton would bring one back with ladders and a Dalmatian fifteen minutes later.

On the other hand, it can easily be said that Torton has the worst mind. He is a complicated fellow.

The first half hour of *Stranger Than Paradise* was shot in no time, and I didn't think much more about it, while Jim went off to find the money to complete it.

I was working on various things and Torton was helping me. We made a pretty good team. But he is as nuts as he is brilliant.

The band is playing the Purple Barge, which is exactly what it sounds like: a barge painted purple that had a sound system. The deal is that instead of the normal thing where the club pays you a flat fee of—I think we were getting five hundred per show at that time—the Purple Barge is going to pay us a percentage of the door from dollar one. As I'm up on stage, I begin to realize that we are going to make a fortune. I think we were getting two-thirds of the door—I don't remember the figures—but it seemed clear to me that we were going to make two or three thousand dollars, if they didn't screw us on the head count. And they didn't.

Stephen Torton was recording the show with an expensive tape recorder and mics that he had commandeered from somewhere.

Stephen and I were getting high on and off then. On this night he was very, very high. I looked out at the crowd to try to surmise how much we would be making and saw Stephen standing in the middle of the crowd. Each hand was holding a mic a hair more toward us, but basically straight out above his head and to the sides. His eyes were closed and his mouth was wide open, you could fly canaries in and out and he would not have noticed. He's standing, nodding out in the middle of the crowd recording the show. This lopsided V-stance makes it look like he has been crucified by some very incompetent crucifiers who have put the hands too high and the body has slumped down.

Willie Mays invited María and me over to his house. He painted my portrait, made me look like Simon Bar Sinister. While he was painting, Willie and I took tons of coke. María didn't take drugs.

María was completely taken with how much money Jean-Michel had. Was in awe of it. That bothered me, seemed cheap, and he was playing into it.

The heroin I had taken earlier started to wear off and the coke was making me feel really creepy. Jean-Michel didn't take heroin then. Scoffed at me about it. He took lots of coke and smoked weed so strong it would have killed Bob Marley. He could read me really well and knew the cocaine was starting to make me uncomfortable. And he kept pouring out more and more.

He gave the painting to María. This was definitely a poke at me. He knew that I was hurting for money, that María was taken with his new-found wealth, and that this thing he had just whipped off was going to be worth, at that time, at least ten thousand. Of course, now it has to be worth maybe a million.

He most certainly had a cruel streak. But more than anything, we were just so competitive all the time. I have never been competitive like that with anyone else, before or since. We loved each other like brothers, but whenever I showed any weakness, it disgusted him. Maybe it stemmed from disappointment, his hero losing his spine.

* * *

Things began getting grim. People started dying. Many were very sick or had died from what at the time was called the Gay Cancer. People were OD'ing. People died in car accidents. People fell out of windows.

For real, Martin Futant had died when he fell out a window while trying to steal a typewriter. All the girls competed in their grief by counting the number of times they had slept with him.

What had been a year or two of the most relentless fun ever on planet Earth was no longer that. The urgency and impunity were gone. Things suddenly felt dangerous.

The drugs weren't doing me any good. At all. Most people were just getting high all the time and living the junkie life, but I kept kicking, over and over. I wouldn't let myself go more than two or three days in a row. So I was spending half my life kicking.

When Thelonious Monk died, I was kicking heroin for the fiftieth time on my little mattress on Third Street, watching my black and white TV on the floor. I was really upset that the news was all about Lee Strasberg, who had died on the same day, and not about Monk. Our culture weighing the importance of things in a very wrong way.

Any news station that even mentioned Monk at all only did so like he was some insane cartoon character of jazz.

That night around seven, Teo Macero called me to ask if I would go to Monk's funeral with him the next day. He really wanted me to go. But the only way I could have gone was to get high or I would have been too sick to go. But to take heroin to get straight enough to make it to Monk's funeral was desperately pathetic and disrespectful. I couldn't do it. And I told Teo I couldn't go.

If I have made drugs seem glamorous at any time in this book, which they can be from time to time . . . if you can't make it to Thelonious Monk's funeral because of your heroin problem, you are a pathetic loser.

Now I wasn't the coolest guy in town anymore. That was last year. As I tried to make the music better, to get closer to the concept I had always had, it seemed to get worse. This was immediately seen as uncool. Faster than my star was plummeting, Jean-Michel's was rising. He skyrocketed past me in a second and sailed by. Suddenly his hero, me, was someone to look down on in disgust. Danny Rosen, another member of the John Lurie School of Bohemian Living, who at one time had also gazed up at me with abandon, now sneered at me along with Jean-Michel.

And I was poor. Really poor. And now to be a poor artist was not cool. Just like that, money was the thing, and Jean-Michel had tons of it. You would go over to his place and there would be stacks of hundred dollar bills lying everywhere. Flaunt it, why don't you?

Jean-Michel and Torton were poking at me and I got pissed. Said, "The fact that you are actually a great painter has nothing to do with your success. These people don't even see your stuff. It's because you're black and handsome and your name is Jean-Michel and you were a poor graffiti artist at exactly the right moment. It's a fluke that you actually are good, but you being good has nothing to do with this success you're having.

"You have great promise. You are a true artist, you can't help but be an artist, but if you keep getting lost in this fashion parade you aren't going to get there."

He snapped back, "Anyone who works as hard as I do would make as much money as me. I work really hard."

I'm sure I said something equally stupid in return. But we had big fights; he started surrounding himself with an entourage who told him his every thought was genius, and I was not having it. The stacks of hundred dollar bills were constantly being nibbled on by his idolaters.

Like I said, we were really competitive. I loved him. And he loved me. But we were always fighting, and really he had more power than I did. And he had that go for the jugular thing, where if he saw that I was insecure he would eat me alive. When he was in trouble, he would fly to me in a second, begging for help. And I would always let him off the hook and look after him.

A couple weeks later, the night before his first big show, he calls me at three in the morning. He's crying, he has to come over. So he comes to Third Street and he has been snorting so much coke that his nose is bleeding. He's terrified because his father is coming to his opening tomorrow. I don't know exactly what their relationship is, but it's some twisted shit. And you know that that weird voodoo power Jean-Michel has is most likely, through fatherhood, even more potent in his dad.

Willie Mays is crying and crying. He is terrified. I'm not sure if he's afraid his father won't like his paintings or will somehow take from him, or if his father being there might expose him somehow to an art world that up to that point has found him to be just the perfect evil little darling.

Then, at the party after the show, he's all fine and smiling.

Jean-Michel gives Torton a couple hundred bucks to act as a bouncer. He wants Steve Kaplan kept out of the party because he'd insulted his work.

A couple of days later I flew down to Cozumel. I was about to turn thirty and I wanted to kick dope, once and for all, before I did. With the sun and the water, I was actually fine the first couple of days and thought that I might get through okay. The other side of the island was deserted, and I would ride over there on a motorcycle and watch the giant iguanas. I was going through a roundabout when I skidded on sand and went down. My leg was all scraped up. Every missing endorphin raged a complaint. I was not so much hurt from the crash as immediately overcome by dope sickness. Spent a day in my room, shaking, staring at the ceiling.

Dope sickness is amazing because you can't even really just lie there. The parts of your body that are touching the bed hurt from the contact. Your hair hurts.

I finally was able to get up and go a half block away to get some food, from a not particularly hygienic looking café. I got food poisoning. Puked my guts up for another day and a half, and when I came out the other side I was okay.

I moved to the deserted side of the island. A cheap row of tiny concrete rooms. Otherwise there was absolutely nothing on that side of the island, except for hundreds of huge iguanas.

I'm there on the beach, have the whole beach to myself—just me and the iguanas and the crashing waves. When this woman comes walking toward me. She is someone I know from New York. Actually she is not someone I know, she is someone I barely know who has leered at me from time to time. I don't know how she knew that I was going to be in Cozumel. I keep asking her how she knew but she just smiles coyly and will not answer.

Much more incredible is how she found me on the deserted side of the island.

People think celebrities are aloof and insulated, but often it isn't because they are assholes but because they have no choice. There is something really terrifying about these superfans who do not see you as a person, only something that lives inside their mind but moves around in the flesh from time to time.

No matter how hard you try to treat them as human beings, they do not return it. They just burrow into you like a parasite.

Every time I'd met her, she announced that her name was no longer the last name that I'd known her by, which I didn't remember in the first place, but now it was something else. So I have no idea what to name her here. Sally? Anna? Valerie? Sue? Table? Porcupine? Porcupine, I guess.

Porcupine suggests a deal, that I accompany her to the ruins. She is nervous to travel in Mexico alone. After that I can keep her car when she goes back.

I don't have a credit card and I can't rent a car, so I take her up on this so I can drive down to Belize.

I spend a day or so with Porcupine Table and then put her on a bus back to Cancún. Then I drive around in the jungle and get lost. After a few hours, I hit a clearing and there are people everywhere. Right in the jungle. Film crews, vendors, busloads of tourists. I have stumbled onto the Mayan ruin of Chichen Itza and it is the day that the sun casts a giant shadow of a serpent across this long football field of very green grass.

But something is wrong here in my memory. I think that the serpent comes out on the first day of spring, and this trip ends in about a week, on my thirtieth birthday. How can this be the first day of spring if my thirtieth birthday is December 14? Oh well.

I am somewhere near Tulum and get a bungalow for the night. I read that there is a ruin near the hotel and go there in the morning. It is really a towering thing, and I climb and climb the stone steps, out of breath, to the top. When I get to the top platform, with jungle spread out all around beneath me, there are two other people at the top. It kind of wrecks it not to be alone up there and I stand on the other side, away from them.

"Hey, John!"

That is weird. No one can possibly be yelling out to me, here in the absolute middle of nowhere jungle.

I turn to see that it's Jeffrey Cantor, the very sweet guy from Young Filmmakers who loaned me his motorcycle helmet for *Men in Orbit*. And he's with Rhonda Ronin, who is a good friend of Richard Morrison's. These people could not possibly know each other. Rhonda is wild and a sexy, two-fisted drinker, and Jeffrey is quiet and sweet. They are just from different worlds. It's odd enough that they're together, never mind that I should run into them on top of this tower in the jungle.

We have an awkward conversation and then they head back down. I continue on my way to Belize. There are warnings all over the rental car papers that say that one cannot take the car into Belize, that you will not be allowed to come through customs, but when I get to the border they look me over and wave me through. On the other side of customs there are groups of guys flagging down my car. I think that they are official and roll down the window.

"Mister, you want to sell this car?"

"It's not mine, it's a rental."

"Yes, I know. You say is stolen from you."

He tells me to meet him after dark at this park along the water. I go, but it is deserted and feels not so safe, so I drive away.

I spend the night at a hotel that has a three-inch-long water bug on the bedcovers. I lift up the sheets to discover his cousin.

In the morning, I look at the map. Belize City doesn't look so far, at least not by miles. What is not clear is that, at least at this time, these are not really roads. They are trails. Miles and miles of muddy trails, with big patches of water, fallen trees, and rocks. Vegetation grows out onto the road, determined to reclaim it. I am driving a little stick shift car not meant for anything like this kind of travel.

I am driving for hours through the jungle. Lots of birds, armadillos, anteaters all over the place. I get to a clearing, I think it was Orange Walk, and a soccer game is taking place in a field with what seems to be the whole village watching.

They see me in the car clumping along and someone yells, "White Man! White Man!" Everyone starts pointing and yelling, "White Man!" and they all start to run toward the car. I speed up and bounce out of there. They may have just been intrigued; maybe I am the first white man they have ever seen. It did feel kind of like that, but I didn't want to wait to find out.

I drive through the night and arrive in Belize City the next afternoon. Stay in a filthy bed and breakfast with a bunch of American expatriates who all seem to be hiding from the law.

A guy, with long dreads, on the street whispers to me, "What you need, man?" I ask for opium, thinking surely he can't get any.

"You wait here."

"I don't want to wait here."

"Where you staying?"

I tell him.

"I come tonight, at eight, meet me outside."

At eight P.M. he is sticking his head out from around the corner, waving at me to come. I go out and he says to come with him. He leads me somewhere, goes inside, comes back, and is all flustered.

This is all starting to take forever. He takes me to a downtown area and tells me to wait here at the corner. Forty-five minutes later he returns and stretches his cupped hand out toward me.

I take what he has concealed. It is a vial that says "Omnopon."

"What's this?"

"Omnopon."

"What's Omnopon? I don't want that. I wanted opium."

"Yes, I already pay."

"How much?"

"Ten dollars."

It sounds like a question. I give him five and let him keep the vial.

Have one lovely day snorkeling with a group of wacko Americans at the island of Caye Caulker, where we are devoured by mosquitoes at night in a little hut.

Mostly, though, Belize just seems to be teeming with criminals, and I have my horn and can never leave it anywhere and feel safe, so I decide to drive back.

It takes thirty-six hours to drive back to Cancún, where I have to drop the car off. I don't really know how to drive a stick, and the transmission is getting fucked up from the roads that are not really roads. There is wildlife everywhere, mostly anteaters. Anteaters. Anteaters. And I am deliriously tired. Anteaters. Thirty-six hours later, I leave the car, with its transmission dangling on the pavement, in the parking lot of the rental car office.

It is my thirtieth birthday. I sit on the beach watching the sun go down. I am very, very sad but not sure exactly why.

I got back to New York and Torton was working for Jean-Michel. Doing the same kind of thing he had done for free for me, but now he was getting five hundred a week. I felt a bit betrayed. Stephen had given me a sense of buoyancy that was wonderful. I really couldn't blame him for working for Jean-Michel, but they were starting to gang up on me and were making me even more insecure than I had become.

"You're not so great. In fact, you're a bit of a joke, aren't you?" Which for a moment really was turning me into a bit of a joke.

I was pissed. Got high a bunch with Gabrielle. She had a bunch of art supplies and I would draw while she would do other stuff at the end of her loft. I would get so into drawing that when I would look up at the clock, five hours would have gone by.

Gabrielle came to my end of the loft after watching the news.

"It is so cold in Alaska that when people exhale, their breath crystallizes and falls to the ground."

I was drawing and not really listening. "Yeah?"

"It must be really loud there."

Gabrielle was one of the funniest people I have ever met.

I bought a rubber ball for twenty-five cents and was walking around New York bouncing it off buildings. Really depressed.

Jean-Michel and I were sleeping with a lot of the same girls. Wayward model types. I was walking by his place and buzzed the buzzer. This girl I had almost been with a month before came to the second floor window and yelled out, "He is very busy. You can't come up." She didn't even say hello.

When she closed the window, I threw the ball up and hit it, really hard. The glass was still wobbling when Jean-Michel came barreling out of his front door with his chest out.

He wanted to fight. I wanted to fight. We stood about fifteen feet apart from each other without saying a word. Then he turned and went back inside. Stephen watched from the window.

Willie Mays and I almost got in fist fights a bunch of different times, but one or the other was always too high or too depressed.

So we decided to have a boxing match. We were both really excited about the idea. We'd go into training, and I was most excited about making the fight card. We could make an actual fight card with us both staring out, wearing Everlast shorts. A couple of years later he took the idea and used it with Andy Warhol for a combined painting show they did. I was not pleased at all about that.

The band went on the Bruno "You Cats!" Denger tour. Got stiffed and went home. Of course, Tony and I never slept. The last show was in Switzerland, where Bruno lived. He gave us the keys to the van and asked if we minded just driving ourselves to the airport and dropping off the van there.

This is crazy to me. The promoter never lets the musicians drive. It just doesn't seem safe, but Zummo is driving and he, for sure, isn't going to crash. I am fucked up, been up for days. But I am responsible for the van, even if Zummo is driving. I am trying to pay attention as he drives.

We're on the highway, and this must be some kind of a flashback to the month before, but I see a giant anteater hop the railing and come running across the Swiss highway.

I scream, "Look out! The anteater!"

I don't think anyone in the band even made a comment.˙

* The World's Longest Footnote
They Are Trying to Disappear Me. Good Luck with That.

When I was nine, I was on a Little League team, Shebro Builders.

They gave us each a uniform, which even at nine I knew was a wool piece of shit. It had "Shebro Builders" written across the chest and my number on the back. It itched like mad.

I would never play. I was nine, and the kids who played were eleven and twelve.

I would come home to our place on Elm Street in Worcester, in my itchy uniform, and inevitably run into Mr. Pasowitz, the superintendent of the building, who lived on the first floor.

Mr. Pasowitz was a large, strapping man. Almost handsome in a Burt Lancaster kind of way, but his face was a bit more swollen. I think he drank a lot. Kind of Burt Lancaster if he had been hit in the face with a board several times.

He would see me in my uniform and ask, in his booming voice, "How did you do today?"

I would say, "I hit a home run!" Though I had not even stepped to the plate.

It felt horrible to lie like that. It made me feel creepy inside, but every week when I came home and he saw me, I would say, "I hit a home run!"

After a while he seemed bored with this response, so I said, "I hit two home runs!"

But he knew I was lying. I knew he knew I was lying. He knew I knew he knew I was lying. It just felt awful.

I was nine years old. Jim Jarmusch is now sixty-seven. His uniform must really itch.

Sometimes the bullshit rises so high that people don't seem to see it. Like fish don't see water.

I didn't want to take a left turn here. I wanted to keep the flow of the book. I want this book to be real and honest but not be ugly or negative where it doesn't have to be. As much as possible to have it filled with love. I really didn't want to allow someone else's pathetic bullshit to influence what goes into the book, so I have made it a footnote. A long footnote.

A string of things happened, right as I was writing this chapter, that were just really too much, and I felt that I had to address them. Felt phony not to.

I knew the Barbican Centre was about to have an enormous show of Jean-Michel Basquiat's work.

A few months before, I had been asked to speak with two young women concerning the show and the program they were working on. I usually say no to this stuff but felt like they should speak to someone who actually knew Jean-Michel, who had firsthand insights into the person. His history is getting out of hand, from the Schnabel movie onward. And in a way I felt like I owed him that much, to try to set the record straight where I could.

Jean-Michel was for real.

All the time. He was for real. And it is really awful to see these people who are very much the opposite of real legitimatizing themselves by pretending to have been close to him or understand him.

I went to look up the Jean-Michel show and saw that it was happening. I sent an email off to the Barbican lady and said, "You were going to run my quotes by me, before you published your program."

It honestly hadn't occurred to me that they hadn't used anything I had said. I had given them over two hours of my time, and I think I really shed some light on him in a way that no one else could have possibly done. What it was like to be with him from a very young age and watch him transform.

But they had not used anything from me. That was strange, but okay, no big deal.

But then, in conjunction with the Jean-Michel show, I see that they are screening a Jarmusch movie, *Permanent Vacation*, like this is connected and pertinent somehow.

They are also having several evenings of concerts under the banner *The Music of Jim Jarmusch!*

To advertise *The Music of Jim Jarmusch!* there is a photo of me, from the movie *Stranger Than Paradise*, a movie made from an idea by me.

I don't know how many movies Jarmusch has made, but I believe I must have scored at least half of them.

So they are using my photo, from a movie that was my idea, for a night of my music, and my name is not mentioned anywhere?

I feel like I have to hurry up and get this book published before Jim Jarmusch gets hold of it and puts it out as his own memoir.

What seems insanely rude is that the Barbican, who I was in touch with, never informed me that they were playing my music in several nights of concerts.

To be candid, I am not bothered that the Barbican did not use any of my quotes in their program, but I am angered because places like the Barbican should be having enormous shows of my paintings. Of course, the art world will not get too close to an actual artist until they are dead and safely not moving. Just like what is happening with Jean-Michel or David Wojnarowicz now. It is all part of the Conspiracy to Maintain Mediocrity.

I looked into the music thing further. The musical director, Coulter?, who was putting it together, said in an interview something along the lines of "John Lurie's music was not particularly interesting to us. We liked that he played with Marc Ribot and Naná Vasconcelos but otherwise we weren't interested."

So my name is finally mentioned, to insult me.

What in the holiest of human fucks is going on with this?

Okay, even though Jean-Michel used to follow me around like he was my kid brother, and I certainly had a great deal to do with who he became, I don't want to glom onto him like so many people are doing. It is sick, but true is true; this shit is becoming like Stalin rewriting history and it appears they are trying to disappear me.

Still. I was going to let all this go. Honest, I was really going to let it go. It seemed like a negative thing to pursue it.

Let me work on what is positive. I will finish chapter 14 and then go work on this painting I have going. Concentrate on what is positive.

The thing that made me just throw down the towel and say, "Oh fuck, this cannot stand," is how *Permanent Vacation* is advertised:

> Famously, when Jarmusch was filming in a flat on East Third Street, the painter Jean-Michel Basquiat took to using the set as a crash pad. "Every time we did a reverse angle, I'd have to drag Jean-Michel in his sleeping bag under the camera so he'd be out of the shot," reported the director. "He'd grunt and go back to sleep."

And what Jarmusch is saying in interviews is even worse and more untrue. He is saying things like he supported the young artist by allowing him to sleep on the set.

Jean-Michel, on and off, for about two years, used to sleep at my apartment.

Jim was making his student film *Permanent Vacation*. And basically, as a favor, I let him store the equipment at my apartment. It was not his set.

Jean-Michel was not even there the day Jarmusch shot the one scene they did at my apartment, where Chris Parker is dancing.

Jim and his NYU film crew needed to go through equipment and maybe change reels or something like that one day, and Jean-Michel was there sleeping on the floor. Jim had never met him prior to that and Jean-Michel never woke up.

Jean-Michel was plopped in the middle of the way. At one point, eventually they decided it would be easy to drag him in the sleeping bag to the side of the room.

What really offends me now, as it offended me then, was Jim's NYU colleagues' being so put out and somewhat disgusted that they had to deal with and touch this "homeless person." Jim has a pretty good heart with things like this, he wasn't disgusted, but still, he didn't know Jean-Michel then, and now he gloats about it? Like he was supportive of the young Basquiat. HOLY HUMAN FUCK make it stop.

As much disdain as I have for Jarmusch, I feel sorry for the guy. Can you imagine what it must be like to invent stories about yourself to vindicate who you are? I remember how I felt with my Shebro Builders uniform.

It felt pretty awful.

15

Gaijin Sex Monster

After a few months, my on and off girlfriend María moved to L.A. She rented a little house on Hammond with a dry backyard and a lemon tree. The house used to belong to TV's Grandma Walton. You could imagine her in the kitchen with an apron on, or maybe I am seeing Granny Clampett. María wanted me to come out, so I booked a solo concert and went out for a week or so.

Jean-Michel met me at the airport with a limo and insisted that we stop at Fatburger. He was in love with Fatburger. Jean-Michel was staying at the house of his art dealer, Larry Gagosian. We snorted some coke and smoked some of Willie Mays's strong pot. Then I practiced while Willie painted on the floor. I was doing this chromatic thing that slowed down and got to a whisper in the higher register and then came back down. What I was doing on the horn was really nice. I had been practicing a bunch for the solo concert and had a really good hold on the horn. It was doing that pot thing where a phrase of music can tickle a spot in your brain. Willie looked up from his painting and gave me a big grin and nodded. That grin was amazing. Had such an approving warmth in it.

He had that thing some babies have, that thing where they look at you and it seems they are seeing right through you. If you are doing something phony or there is something phony in your soul, the baby will see it. If you are doing something real and right, they will see that, too, and beam with delight.

He was amazingly powerful and could make me feel insecure in a way that no one else ever could. And now that there was all this money flying around and I was so broke, he was kind of ugly in how he was always putting that in my face.

But then I was playing and I was really hitting this thing, this beautiful strange thing, and there was that grin. I could be playing that music for a million other people and no one would grasp it like he did.

I fell asleep on the couch. I suppose it was the fat from Fatburger being pushed out by the cocaine, but when I woke up, there was a pool of grease sitting on the right side of my stomach, perfectly mapping out my liver.

With the fame and the money, Jean-Michel at times seemed to be turning into Idi Amin.

His girlfriend, Suzanne Mallouk, was there in L.A., and on a tirade. She was clearly really hurt and angry, crying and yelling about something he had done. It was disturbing me quite a bit but didn't seem to faze him at all. Wouldn't look at her. Or if he did it was only with a momentary, ice cold stare.

He threw $500 at her and told her to fly back to New York. What is odd is that a few years before, he had come to me in the middle of the night, with a lot of yearning and angst, wanting advice about how to deal with this girl he loved, Suzanne, who wouldn't go out with him because he was poor and homeless. We actually recorded our conversation about how he could go about making a living. I still have the tape somewhere but don't want to listen to it.

María didn't know how to drive. You can't live in L.A. and not know how to drive. She had a car but couldn't drive it. I would drive her somewhere and then watch hours of TV on her bed and practice a little.

I went back to New York, but Third Street was becoming insane.

I started getting fucked up as soon as I got back. Hang out with Rockets Redglare and freebase.

* * *

Still, I was not getting high all the time. I would go three days on a binge without sleeping and then shut myself in to kick. Over and over. Kicking has many levels. At this point it wasn't so bad—like I had a bad flu and my hair hurt and I'd get really insecure, but after a day or two I'd be okay and start over. Not exactly start over; in between, I would have a day or two where I just felt too fucking good. Exorbitant energy and unbearably friendly.

I had been cast in Martin Scorsese's *The Last Temptation of Christ*. The book, by Nikos Kazantzakis, is brilliant. Somebody had told me that Scorsese and De Niro were talking about me on the set of *The King of Comedy* and that I should call Cis Corman, Scorsese's casting agent, about getting a part in the film. *Raging Bull* and *Taxi Driver* are two of my favorite movies. *Raging Bull* is perfect, frame by frame, perfect. At this time I thought that acting was, in most cases, completely superficial, but to be in a Scorsese film was something else.

So I got the number and called Cis Corman. She scheduled me to come in the next morning at ten A.M. It would have been impossible for me to go to bed and then get up in time to make a ten o'clock meeting in the morning, so I just stayed up all night and went in.

I like Cis Corman and she seems to genuinely like me. She tells me that *The King of Comedy* is already cast but that I should get the book *The Last Temptation of Christ* because that's what Marty is going to do next.

The book is hard to find. It's out of print. Suzy Lawrence has a copy I can borrow. The band played the night before. I don't remember why, but I haven't been home, and I haven't paid the band yet. I'm still in my suit from the night before.

So I go around the East Village with about $1,500 in my pocket and pay the guys in the band. Then I go to get the book. I start reading it at Suzy's place and it just hits me really hard. And what really hits me is that my life doesn't have to be like this. I don't have to live on Third Street with all these hideous, murdering people from the men's shelter. I don't have to take drugs every night. It is possible to get out of this squalor. Even if I do live on Third Street, I can direct my consciousness. I can find a purer light in the midst of all this.

So I come down Second Avenue and turn onto my block. Now, Third Street, because of the men's shelter, at this time has to be one of the ten worst blocks in the world. When I first moved there in 1978, it was kind of great and fascinating. Partly because I'd always felt a kinship with people who led their lives outside of the normal modes of society and I was certain some—though certainly not all—of these people were actually in touch with a higher reality that made being part of normal society both incongruous and ridiculous.

There was that one guy who would say, "Armageddon, Armageddon," wait maybe five minutes, and then say it again, over and over, all day. All day. Every day. I'd hear him from my window, and the weird thing was that I never actually saw this guy. I just heard him all day long. Like those frogs in the jungle you can hear but never see. There were a lot of great characters. The block was not dangerous.

Then at some point, I think in '81, Rikers Island had become overcrowded and they released a lot of prisoners who definitely should have still been incarcerated. The block changed overnight. These people were cold-blooded predators, and the sweet, defenseless bums who had previously occupied my block were chased away, or literally killed off. There would be people screaming outside the window, being beaten or robbed. Call the police and they wouldn't show up. So I'd throw things out the window. I had a big bag of blue lightbulbs that I'd found on the street. I don't know what I was going to do with them, make a sculpture or some such idiot thing, but I'd keep these lightbulbs near my third floor window so I could throw them at these marauders when they were attacking someone. The smashing of the bulbs on the street would usually deter whatever was going on for about three seconds.

Third Street has turned into a prison yard, and it's ruining my life. I live in the middle of the block, and going to the corner to get a pack of cigarettes is hell. It's terrifying. I literally have to be prepared to defend my life every time I walk down that block. Second Avenue is okay; I think the police have a sort of deal with them that, if they stay on Third Street, they can do what they want, but if they come out onto the avenue, they're in trouble.

I've developed ways of looking completely insane so I can walk down the block without being accosted. I'll have wild, bugging eyes or twitch spasmodically and violently as I walk. This usually works, but if I'm dressed nicely, then it doesn't.

So I come around the corner. I'm in this green suit from the night before. There are maybe forty people on the corner. Loud. Usually, if I walk down the block, I'll scope everyone out as I walk. If someone speaks to me, I'll show respect and try to keep moving. But now I've just had an epiphany and I don't want it soiled. I don't want this debauched circus to enter into my consciousness. I'm going to see the higher light.

I'm smoking a cigarette. A woman from against the wall asks me for a light. I don't stop, I don't acknowledge her. Now, as I write this I can see that, in fact, I am a complete asshole, this guy in a suit who's too good to stop and give someone a light. But the harassment was so constant and so brutal, an unceasing attempt at intimidation. But not today. I'm not going to put up with this today. And *blam*!!

I'm out, unconscious. I find myself on my hands and knees. My shoulders are wet. I put my hand back behind my neck to see what the wetness is and it's blood.

The bottle of cranberry juice I just bought, the expensive kind, is broken in the gutter. I see the book in front of me and pick it up. My head is cracked open. Blood is spurting out of the top of it like a little fountain. I've been hit over the head with a full quart bottle of Colt 45.

I stand up and reel. There are people around me. The initial primordial thought that happens when you are really hurt and really in trouble is that people will come to your rescue. Someone is handing me my keys, but at the same time he's got his hand in my pocket. I push him away and suddenly I'm surrounded by, at least, seven or eight guys, and they are holding me against the wall and going through my pockets. They're filthy. Humans help other humans. But this is Third Street and I'm being preyed on. Thank God this didn't happen half an hour ago before I paid the band.

A giant man with a club comes running out of the men's shelter and chases them off. I'm woozy. I start screaming at them. "What the fuck? I was just walking down the street!"

They stare at me blankly. Nothing. I couldn't possibly know the rules.

I get to my house and the police show up. Someone has called them. They insist I go to the emergency room. The police ask if they can call anyone for me.

"Rockets Redglare."

"That's a person? Rockets Redglare?"

"Yeah."

The policeman makes a face, like he doesn't really want to call any-one named Rockets, and says, "I don't want to call anyone named Rock-ets Redglare. Anyone else?"

"No, I'm fine."

When I get home, my jacket and the book are drenched in blood. The jacket becomes so stiff that it is like cardboard and I have to throw it away. I take the book and separate the pages, and when Scorsese finally makes the film some eight years later, that's the copy that I read, the one completely stained with my blood.

The band was booked to go to Japan. First we were going to stop and play one show in L.A. There wasn't much money for the L.A. gig and they weren't paying for the hotel. I put half of the band up in a pretty bad hotel on Sunset, and Dougie and Evan stayed at María's with me.

Tony couldn't make it, so we replaced him with Fred Hopkins, who was a well-known upright bass player from the serious avant-garde jazz world.

After I'd gotten hit on the head, I'd moved up to my uncle Jerry's place and slept on the fold-out bed in his spare room. I couldn't go back to Third Street.

In Uncle Jerry's medicine cabinet was a big bottle filled with codeine. Every time I was a little dope sick, I would take a few. Now the bottle looked suspiciously low. I couldn't take any more and get away with it. Before the trip I just said fuck it and threw the whole bottle into my carry-on bag. I figured maybe Jerry would be less likely to notice that the bottle was gone than how few were left. The codeine got me through the first few days pretty well.

Jerry had always been so sweet to me. He had loaned me the money to buy my beautiful Balanced Action Selmer alto from 1949. He always helped me every time I was in trouble, and he used to handle my legal stuff for free. I felt really guilty coming back to his place high, and steal-ing his codeine was even worse. I felt low.

We played an awful club in L.A. on the corner of Pico and Bundy. I think it was called the Music Machine. The first couple of times we played in L.A., it was at the Whisky a Go Go, and that had been pretty good. But after that, almost every L.A. gig, except that one we did in '98 at the El Rey, was a nightmare. This place felt like it was a Texas bar in Vietnam. Nuts, violent, and stupid. Not a place for music.

You just walked in there for sound check and the smell alone told you that it was going to be a disaster. That horrible stale beer smell that had never been ventilated. The sound guy was a psychopath. We couldn't hear ourselves onstage and waved wildly trying to get his attention during the show. He obviously had more important things on his mind. After the show, he flexed on Dougie for trying to get his attention. Dougie was waving desperately at him because he couldn't hear the bass, and the sound guy felt that he had been disrespected, like Dougie was showing the audience that he didn't know what he was doing.

I really do remember every bad gig we ever did, and nine out of ten times it was caused by not being able to hear ourselves onstage. This was a bad gig.

The next morning a guy knocks on the door of María's house. It's the driving instructor. María doesn't want me to drive her car anymore without a license and she has booked an appointment for me. I vaguely remember her saying something about it on the phone before I came out. I am drinking a beer at eleven in the morning when the guy walks up to the screen door. I invite him in and offer him a beer. Dougie can't stop laughing, thinks my offering him a beer at eleven A.M. is the funniest thing he has ever seen, but I pass the test.

Fred Hopkins was snorting coke the whole fourteen-hour flight to Japan. How is that even possible? I cannot do coke without dope. It just makes me too wired. I gnash my teeth and waves of weirdness go surging through my body. So to take it in a confined space like an airplane? That is just insane. Fred offered me his package when I was on the way back to the bathroom, but I refused. I think this is the first time in my life I ever refused a drug, but it seemed clear to me that if I took it, fifteen minutes later, I would be trying to pry open the airplane door to get outside. The plane landed and we all had a hot dog and a beer at the airport. This is now a mandatory custom for all members of The Lounge Lizards, a hot dog and beer upon arrival in Tokyo. The strong beer just knocks you into a coma after the flight. The hot dogs are inexplicably delicious.

Jerry's codeine got me through the beginning of the Japan tour, and when it was gone I was fine. We were all drinking a lot. Japan just seems to be set up like that. But I was shocked when I came down to the hotel breakfast area in the morning and saw Fred sitting there, pretty as you please, reading the paper with a big glass of Jack Daniel's at ten in the morning. My having a beer at eleven in the morning at María's was a rare event, but the somewhat disconcerting thing was that this appeared to be Fred's usual breakfast.

Tokyo was a blast. There was a crazy band that opened for us called The Trombones. They were just so nice and they had tons of girls with them who immediately jumped ship. I was actually pissed at Dougie for sleeping with this girl who was clearly the girlfriend of one of The Trombones.

I met this lovely creature named Mamiko. The Japanese promoter wanted me to stay away from her because he was grooming her for stardom. He didn't want her defiled by the Gaijin Sex Monster. Maybe he had a crush on her himself. But for a minute there I really thought that I was in love.

We were lying in bed in the morning and Dougie walked into the room.

"So, John, is this your first trip into the Orient?"

The band played pretty well. Fred Hopkins didn't take it seriously and never learned the music. There was a section during one song where we had an up-tempo duet and Fred just left the stage, leaving me to play all alone with nothing to play to. I confronted him later and he said that he had to take a piss. I was furious. I had given him a lot of leeway because he was older and well respected. But to leave the stage like that, right before we had a duet, was so disrespectful that I was furious and knew I would never hire Fred again.

The band went home and I went back to L.A. to stay with María.

After about a month in L.A., the coke and heroin really left my system. I took out the horn and started to write some stuff: the melody for "Big Heart" and then the melody for "The Blow Job," the name of which Island Records made me change, so on the CD it's called "It Could Have Been Very Very Beautiful."

The thing is, the drugs were gone and beautiful things were starting to emerge.

16

Hung There Against the Sky and Floated

I was sitting on María's couch looking out the back window at Grandma Walton's lemon tree when the phone rang. It was Evan. *That's odd, we can't afford long-distance calls.* There was a pause and then he said, "John, Theda's dead."

We used to call our parents Theda and David, even when we were little. I don't know why. It was something my parents decided.

I could tell by the awkward pause that he had thought for a long time about how he was going to say this to me and then it just came out like he was saying, "Today is Friday," but with a little wrenchiness in his throat that made the words go up.

I didn't feel anything. I was in a haze and just thought, *So this is what it is.*

I have to tell Aaron Lipstadt immediately.

This made no sense. It could have been, "It's time to set the towels on fire right now." It's some kind of weird wall the mind puts up to keep from dealing with the onslaught of grief.

Aaron Lipstadt was making a movie that he thought maybe I could score. They hadn't even started shooting yet, but I thought I should tell him that I had to leave. His office was right up on Sunset near María's place on Hammond, and I just had to walk up the hill.

Right outside María's house, which is no longer standing, there is a block of pavement. About ten feet up the hill, toward Sunset, I looked down and had one of those moments. Hazier than the other moments, but still one of those bubbles. I looked down at the sidewalk and it burned a frame in my memory, like when Ev told me he was gay, or on Second Avenue when my saxophone was stolen, or when my mom came into my room and said, "It was all over at seven o'clock this morning," or the metal pole on Pleasant Street in Worcester.

An exact frame of existence.

A block of pavement.

My mom is gone.

I was completely numb and not really there. I walked into Aaron's office and told him that I had to go and he said, "Of course." He looked at me like he didn't know what else to say.

María tried to comfort me, but I wasn't having it. If someone wants to comfort me, they have to really bring it. It takes a big soul. You have to bring it big and real. Even if you are as sincere as possible, if you do not have the stuff to back it, I can't have any and I can get pretty mean if you try.

I had a ticket back to New York, a cheap ticket. I called the airline and asked if I could take a flight a few days earlier than my scheduled departure. They said yes. When I got to the airport they told me that I had the wrong kind of ticket and it couldn't be changed. I would have to wait to use it on Friday, my scheduled date of return.

I told them that my mom had died.

It is very strange to tell someone that you need something because your mom just died and have them think you are lying to them. You start to think maybe you are lying.

I got back to New York and went straight to Fabian's and got fucked up. Anna Taylor was with me. She wasn't into going to Fabian's, she was just being supportive, and this is where I wanted to go. I had been straight, and in honor of my mom, I thought that I shouldn't get fucked up, but I did. I just went and took heroin and smoked coke all night. It was not to ease the pain of my mom. I didn't really feel anything.

Me, Ev, and Liz all went to Wales. I wasn't so close with Liz then. The whole thing just felt cold. We had to deal with the house and my mom's stuff and the funeral and Ivy, my grandma, who was in a nursing home and fairly loopy.

As the three of us stood around her bed, Ivy kept saying, "Well, I don't know who you are, but you're all very nice."

Liz would say, "Ivy, we're Theda's children."

And Grandma would say, "Oh yes, Theda. Well, you are very nice." And then shake her head and smile. "But, I have no idea who you are."

My sister had brought her her slippers. "Here, Ivy, I brought you your slippers."

Ivy took her slipper in her hand, opened her mouth as wide as it would go, and then chomped down on it like it was an éclair that might try to get away from her. She looked confused and disappointed with the slipper and then bit into it again. It was so sad and tragic and funny.

Liz couldn't stop laughing. She tried but she just couldn't help it. It was all so awful. It was slowly dawning on all three of us that we were going to have to leave Grandma in this place until she just wasn't here anymore.

We, especially me and Liz, would crack up in a way that we couldn't stop laughing. I think it upset Evan, but he didn't say anything. My mom had a sort of a boyfriend who lived in London. They had been friends when they were younger and I think this guy, Ken, introduced my mother and father, thirty-five years earlier.

Ken was married. I didn't have any compassion for this married guy who was sleeping with my mom, but Liz or Evan said that we had to call him.

I wasn't going to do it. Evan said he would. Evan calls Ken, and Liz and I are in the next room listening, sort of crouching down, like we're hiding.

We hear Evan telling this poor guy that Theda is dead and we cannot stop laughing. We are laughing so hard that I am on my knees gasping for air, drooling, and Liz wets her pants. Poor Evan is in the other room, talking in this serious voice, and we can't stand it. I think Ken must have heard us laughing in hysterics in the background. He couldn't not have heard. I wonder what the hell he thought. Ev was really pissed that we did this. Fair enough.

The neighbor had convinced us that my uncle Mosten was not to be trusted, that my mom had told her that if anything happened to her, not to let Uncle Mosten in the house. We hardly trusted anyone already. We were being eyed by everyone in the little Welsh village and we were also going around to shops and antique stores trying to get anything that wasn't dear to us valued to sell. We were getting ripped off right and left but we didn't care.

I had loved my uncle Mosten, actually my grandmother's brother, when I was little. He was enormous, six foot seven, with a handlebar mustache. When we heard his car drive up and heard him come up the side of the house to knock on the door, we hid. All three of us—I have no idea why—hid behind furniture from Uncle Mosten. Even Evan laughed. Then we heard his footsteps walking away and that horrible ill feeling came back.

My mom had grown very bitter with her lot in life. She had met my father, this charming American man, during the war and had come to the wonderful land of possibilities and futures, the United States of America. But my dad couldn't get work, as he had been a communist, so there was trouble with that.

Then he got sick, so the whole thing just wasn't what had been promised. And she was talented. I had never thought much about it, but when we looked through her stuff and I saw her paintings, it was shocking to see how good she was.

I resented her bitterness. She was always sick with this or that, and as much zest and curiosity as she had for lots of things, she just seemed to never really get past the bitterness.

Every night when we lived in Worcester, my mom and dad would have a martini or Manhattan before dinner. Just one, which they seemed to enjoy. But there wasn't any problem. After my dad died she started drinking more. We even got her to try marijuana a couple of times. She didn't feel a thing, but I got high as a kite. I tried to explain why *Jaws* was a great movie. She didn't think anything that popular could be any good.

I went into this long thing about fear of the unknown. The monster under the water that you could just barely see. Then I digressed into making my left hand the girl in the beginning of the movie. My hand, with fingers for legs, ran across the arm of the couch and yelled, "Swimming!" only to be devoured by my other hand, the ferocious shark.

"Oh, you are daft!" she said, with her Welsh accent, which had completely returned.

I knew something was strange. Our last tour she was supposed to come and meet us in Paris and she just didn't show. I called her and got no answer. If you plan to have your mom meet you in Paris and she doesn't show, that is unusual. I didn't think that much about it, being embroiled in the tour. Evan's theory, later, was that she must have been drinking too much and was afraid that she would embarrass herself. I asked Ev why she just couldn't drink less when she was in Paris, but he explained that with alcoholics, sometimes a couple of sips makes them instantly drunk.

From what we could piece together, I guess she was alone in the house, upstairs. And Miffanwy, who was kind of a simple woman who wandered around in the village, came into the house and went upstairs. My mom was in bed.

"Miffanwy, something's wrong, it's time to go to the hospital."

Miffanwy just said, "Okay," and left. Not quite understanding.

I don't know how long she lay there by herself before she died.

At the funeral, almost the whole village was there. The priest was in the middle of his bit when he leaned over and put his hand on the coffin. He looked puzzled. Liz thought he was leaning over to say goodbye, but I didn't think that was it. He looked kind of panicked and was squinting down at the coffin, craning his neck. He was in mid-deal and he started to walk out toward us. This seemed very fucking weird. Why was he walking out here?

He leaned over to my sister and said, "What was your mother's name?"

"Theda." My brother answered for her.

"Freda?"

And then Evan practically spit at him as he hissed slowly, "Theeeeda."

Great. I love a well-prepared funeral.

They sang hymns. Those Welsh can really sing, boy, they just raised their voices to the sky and filled the church, in this strong way. I don't know how many people knew my mom or even if they liked her. Maybe it is just custom in the village. My mom was contentious and could be a real rascal. I know that she had had a problem with someone in her bridge club. She called me once to tell me, with great pride, that she had spray-painted "Gwyneth Cheats!" on the stone wall outside the house of her nemesis.

When I was sixteen and we were in Worcester, she washed my pants twice with my driver's license still in the pocket. The second time I went down to the Registry of Motor Vehicles, the little chubby man behind the desk said, "This is your third license."

"Yes."

"That is a problem."

"What do you mean?"

"Driving is a privilege. I am not obligated to give you another license. It is up to my judgment."

I said something like, "What the fuck?" and the next thing I knew I was being escorted out by two large men who told me not to come back.

I went home and my mom asked if I'd gotten the license. We had already argued about her washing my pants.

"No, they threw me out."

"What do you mean they threw you out?"

"I swore and this tubby bureaucrat had me thrown out."

"So you don't have a license? They can't do that, I'm going down there myself."

So my mom went down to the Registry of Motor Vehicles in an indignant huff. They threw her out too.

On the Welsh death certificate the cause of death was listed as alcoholism. Didn't sound very official or even medically correct. Not liver failure or whatever else. Just "Cause of death—alcoholism." That upset me for some reason, like it was a judgment.

Well, she drank so much that she died. Must have deserved it.

I had taken my horn with me but I hadn't played it in a couple of weeks. When I finally took it out to play, I expected it to be the most beautiful, lamenting melody. Something I wouldn't think about that would come directly from my depths and appear as music. I put the horn together and blew into it.

What came out just sounded ill.

* * *

She was cremated. We had a tree planted on the other side of the Menai Strait, off in the woods in a sanctuary. We took the ashes out to that spot to scatter them. Ev and Liz scattered some gently, and then I took the urn and jolted the ashes up to the sky. The white powder shot up, a lot of it, more than I thought, and then hung there in the air against the sky and floated.

17

Fifty Million Junkies Can't All Be Wrong

The time I spent attempting to find my soul and its place in the universe, that period covered a span of almost seven years; the drug period was roughly the same, less even, yet the amount of space the spiritual part takes up in this book is almost nothing in comparison to the drug days. A journey inward has less tellable tales. In music or painting I can maybe do it, but not in writing.

Unless you are Rumi or Lao-tzu, descriptions of journeys of the spirit perhaps should be left alone.

And one week of drugs leads to twice as many stories as a lifetime in a monastery.

Heroin is a predator. A barracuda.

Heroin goes out of its way to find you.

Once I had spent three days kicking in my place on Third Street and finally had my legs back enough to venture out and pick up some food. I get to the bottom of the stairs, outside, and there is this guy there I barely know—I just know him from nightclubs—and he says, "Hey, John, you want a bag of dope?"

I mean, this doesn't happen. Ever. No one offers you a free bag of heroin.

People who say "Just stop taking drugs" do not have a clue. It's an asshole thing to say. It is like saying "From now on you will not piss." At some point you absolutely cannot bear it any longer.

You have to trick the heroin away. And your own mind lies to you about it.

I didn't want to take dope anymore, but it just seemed to be everywhere.

Piccolo had recommended an acupuncturist named Danny Dunphy to help me kick. Danny was working at the Atkins Diet place and he would sneak me in a side door. This place was a hell of a lot nicer than the community-run acupuncture place that I had been to in the Bronx. A hundred skeevy-looking junkies, sitting around this giant room with a high rotting ceiling, all with acupuncture needles sticking out of their ears. No one spoke as they sat in the broken chairs.

Danny knew some stuff, but he was also experimenting on me. Once he injected me with this big syringe of red-orange liquid that I suppose was vitamins, but it just rocked me. I felt on the verge of having a seizure.

He gave me this stuff called Perfect 7 that cleared my bowels out. Opiates make one very constipated. My shit was just these tiny, hard rabbit pellets. After a couple of days taking this horrible tasting stuff, I had a trip to the bathroom that produced a two and a half foot long, perfect stool, all impressively in one piece, in the shape of my colon. I wanted to call people and have them come over for a viewing. A remarkable thing it was.

One thing he gave me that really helped me was one hundred grams of vitamin C intravenously over three or four hours. This works. It blocks out the dope sickness. Your eyes stop burning, your nose stops running, the pain isn't as bad. It amazes me that this isn't common knowledge.

I used to freebase cocaine with the bass player Sirone, born Norris Jones. Sirone was part of an extremely muscular, modern jazz trio called the Revolutionary Ensemble.

Jerome Cooper on drums, Leroy Jenkins on violin, and Sirone on acoustic bass. Evan and I used to listen to their records in the midseventies and hoped that they really might forge new territory for jazz.

Back in 1977, I went to see them at Lincoln Center. They were the first of three bands and they were wild compared to the more normal, geriatric or frighteningly academic groups that usually got booked at jazz festivals in the United States at that time.

I don't think it went well for them. They tried to do the show acoustically because they were playing at Lincoln Center, where the acoustics would theoretically work for their instruments, but the sound was small and didn't have the power that was required to achieve the ferocity that I'd heard them play with before.

I don't remember who the second and third bands were, but I got bored and walked out. As I was leaving, I ran smack into Sirone. For me, at that time, this was kind of like I was seven years old and bumped into Mickey Mantle, accidentally, all by himself outside Yankee Stadium, carrying a baseball bat and glove.

I told him how much I admired his group. He gave me a big thank you that sounded completely disingenuous and like he had thrown out this thank you, with nothing behind it, a thousand times before.

We ended up taking a cab downtown as he grumbled complaints to himself that I didn't really catch, but he felt the gig had gone terribly and was blaming someone for it.

I was dealing the pot fronted to me by Vance back then. I used to go over to Sirone's and we would play. It was more along the lines of teacher-student than two musicians jamming.

Sirone was always scamming something. Always running to the pawnshop or trying to get in the middle of a drug deal or scam a grant—anything. He was always hard at work chasing something that didn't really make any sense and never amounted to anything. One thing that always shocked me when I first got to New York was how these musicians, who were known and respected, with actual recordings in the stores, were usually broke and trying desperately to make ends meet and still do their work, as I had seen them as stars.

When Sirone found out that I had this pot, he somehow conned me into fronting him half a pound. This wasn't great pot and at the time was probably worth about $300.

He never paid me back. Once, when we had been smoking a lot of pot and playing, I tried to press him about when he was going to pay me back. Said it wasn't very revolutionary to rip off another musician.

It was hot in his loft and he didn't have a shirt on. He went into this diatribe about Michael Rockefeller, who had traveled into the darkest regions of Africa and disappeared. It was feared that he had been eaten by cannibals. Sirone stood there, eyes rolled into the back of his head. There was a wolf trying to escape from under his skin—his muscles rippling, sweat dripping off his body—and he goes off into this story about the Rockefeller kid but from the point of view of the African warriors who had discovered and eaten him. How he deserved it. I took this to be a threat, because it was a threat. I was a kid, and this money that I lost I let go as being a sort of tuition.

Once when I was over at Sirone's, the contentious Stanley Crouch stopped by. Stanley Crouch made it clear that he didn't like Sirone playing with a white kid. Would not respond to me directly. Wouldn't look at me. I sat on the couch while he and Sirone animatedly enjoyed each other's company. Stanley told a story about Louis Armstrong knocking out Jack Teagarden, a white trombone player, which was clearly meant to put me in my place.

But I grew to really like Stanley. I would always run into him in the East Village and we would argue. He had such a sharp mind, fast and funny, and he was really confident with his mind and his arguments. Though when it came to race, he was really a bitch.

He used to run the Tin Palace, a small jazz club on the corner of Bond and Bowery. I ran into him on the street at a time where The Lounge Lizards were really getting a ton of attention in the press and said he should book us. We would have easily sold out the Tin Palace for nights on end and there was often no one in there.

I would really rather have been playing jazz clubs than CBGB's. But Stanley said, "I saw you play, I can get twenty-five black alto players to play the tricks you play."

Okay, Stanley.

But still, I liked running into him. I was in Binibon when Stanley came in and I had posters for *Leukemia*. This was shortly after I first met him at Sirone's and before The Lounge Lizards.

Stanley saw the poster and said, "*Leukemia!* Perfect! The white cells overrunning the red."

I mean, it was an asshole thing to say, but still pretty fucking good.

I was just giving this book a once-over before handing it in to Random House and read that Stanley died today. I guess the last years of his life were really rough. Was really sorry to hear that. I don't think we ever had one civil conversation, but I was fond of Stanley.

Sirone and I fell out of touch. I think that he actually felt bad about the pot thing, but no way could he afford to pay me back. His money always had more pressing places to be.

About five years later, when my band had gotten off the ground and I was getting some attention, I ran into him again. The playing field was more level now and we started hanging out as equals.

Sirone introduced me to his drug of choice: freebasing cocaine. I'd usually take dope before I went to his place, get half the money from him—an improvement on our earlier relationship—and then go up to Gabrielle's and get a gram or whatever we could afford, then I'd bring it back downtown and Sirone would meticulously cook it up like an alchemist.

We'd smoke and then we'd !!!!!!!!!PLAY!!!!!!!!! for about ten minutes. Then we'd smoke some more and then !!!!!!!!!!!!!!!PLAY!!!!!!!!!!!!!!!!!!! We'd do this until the coke ran out.

Smoking coke has a particular kind of insanity that is all its own. There is something about smoking coke that does this thing to you: When it runs out, you crawl around on the floor and any little white piece of fluff or bit of plaster or paint chip is thought to be a little rock of cocaine and is snatched up and smoked.

We used to treat this shit like it was gold, so the idea that we might drop a chunk of it on the floor and forget about it was absurd. The funny thing is that after you've smoked a few times, you know that you are going to be scouring the floor for what we called "unidentified hits" after you've run out.

I wrote on a piece of paper: "I, John Lurie and I, Norris Jones A.K.A. Sirone do solemnly swear that when the cocaine is finished we will not crawl on the floor to collect and smoke unidentified objects." We both signed it. Of course when the coke was gone we were crawling around and smoking weird white things, but at least we were laughing about it, and Sirone had the greatest big full laugh.

I went to see an acupuncturist in Chinatown named Dr. Gong. He's supposed to have helped Keith Richards quit. On the wood-paneled walls are little framed pictures of Dr. Gong and celebrities. Though they are mostly of Dr. Gong and Dinah Shore. Dr. Gong and Dinah Shore buying a hot dog at Coney Island. Dr. Gong and Dinah Shore in a rowboat in Central Park, both smiling at the camera. Dr. Gong and Dinah Shore on a Ferris wheel.

He comes in smoking a Marlboro. As he picks up the needles, the long ash from the cigarette stuck in his mouth falls into the tray of sterile needles. He blows the ash out of the silver tray and smiles at me. Dr. Gong's technique is to insert the needles and then attach an electric charge to each one. You lie there for an hour with your muscles doing berserk twitching. The twitching is so violent, I wonder how he stops his patients from flying out the window and landing on the pavement in a pile.

Afterward, when I got out onto the street, it was dark, around eight at night. I felt surprisingly good. Looked around the street at Chinatown and felt a little alive for a change.

I heard the laugh behind me. That big wolf laugh. I knew immediately who it was, before I even turned around.

Sirone was with his little Japanese girlfriend. They just looked like the perfect, innocent couple coming from dinner at a Chinese restaurant.

Sirone leans in and whispers to me, "Let's get into some devilment."

He makes some excuse to his girlfriend and we drop her in a cab. Go to cop some coke and dope and get fucked up.

Whatever Dr. Gong had done to my nervous system made me enjoy the drugs more than I had in months.

I wouldn't have expected to see Sirone in Chinatown at night in a million years. But that is what always happened. I'd vow to stop and the drugs would find me.

When I first moved to the East Village, there was a girl I saw around who I had an enormous crush on. She had long, sinewy arms and legs and walked around the neighborhood with incredible pride and strength. She looked like a panther.

About two years later I met her in a club. Her name was Rebecca. I brought her back to my uncle Jerry's, where I was staying. My uncle was out of town, otherwise I never would have brought Rebecca there. She was like a wild animal, the way she moved, the way she sussed out a new environment. Her eyes darting.

Rebecca never ate. The only thing that I ever saw her eat was hot sauce or mustard.

She was hungry and asked if she could open this enormous jar of mustard that was in my uncle's cupboard. I said it was okay, I guessed, but we couldn't eat any of my uncle's food. She said that was okay, she just wanted some mustard.

When my uncle came back to town, he came into my room pissed about something. I was always nervous that he would discover that his giant bottle of codeine was missing.

"Look, I don't mind you staying here and you're welcome to anything you want. All I ask is that if you finish something of mine, replace it. Or just tell me that you've finished it and I'll buy more."

That's a weird reaction to me taking his codeine pills.

"I don't think I did finish anything." Man, I lied to my uncle. I never lied. Even when I was a junkie I never lied to anyone.

He held up the enormous restaurant-sized jar of mustard, which had been scraped completely dry. I was thinking, *Damn, Rebecca, how could anyone eat that whole giant jar of mustard in one night?*

My uncle would come home and eat Chinese food, watching the TV in my room. He screamed at the screen during football games. I thought it embarrassing. Of course, I now do the exact same thing myself.

I had to go to Texas to be in Wim Wenders's movie *Paris, Texas*. Wim was a fan of the band and friends with Jim and had asked me to do a part in the movie. Wenders had made *The American Friend*, one of my and Evan's favorite movies. It has the line "Throw a gangster off a train going eighty miles an hour, then you throw a second one: How much time passes between the two events, if the train doesn't change speed?" So I had to do it.

But now I couldn't find out what was going on. I kept calling the production office, and they would tell me to keep this period free, then when that time came I wouldn't hear from them. I would call and call again, not reaching anybody and getting the runaround when I did. Finally it was set to happen. But it was one of those things where they said, "Would you mind purchasing your ticket yourself and then we will reimburse you when you get down here?"

I didn't want to go down there being this strung out. Gabrielle, Rebecca, and I decided to go to Jamaica for a few days before, so I could dry out.

It was a good combination somehow. Gabrielle, who lived all in her brain and had this odd, nonathletic little body that she seemed completely unaware of, and Rebecca, the panther.

We go out to rent motorcycles. Gabrielle has money and credit cards but the guy doesn't want to rent to us because we must look like complete freaks. We have to lie to the rental guy and say that we all know how to ride a motorcycle. Neither Rebecca nor Gabrielle has ever been on a motorcycle before and I have only ridden the one I crashed in Mexico.

Rebecca and I fake it and get on the bikes and are starting to ride out of the parking lot when we hear the sound of a big clank behind us.

We turn around and Gabrielle, before she has even gotten it started, has fallen over with the bike. She's scraped her leg. We go back, reluctantly, to see if she's okay and the guy makes us give all the bikes back.

We sleep in three separate beds. I can't sleep because I'm a little dope sick. At about four in the morning Rebecca gets up. I'm hungry. So is Rebecca. She wants to go get something to eat.

"We're in Jamaica, you can't get food at four in the morning. Nothing's open."

"I'm going to go out, I'm sure there's something."

"Bring me something."

When I wake up hours later, Rebecca is still gone. Gabrielle is having coffee. She has that New York accent thing.

"You want sum cawfee?"

"No thanks, can't drink coffee when I'm dope sick."

Why isn't Gabrielle dope sick? How can she be sitting there drinking her coffee all pretty and composed like that?

About seven-thirty A.M., Rebecca comes back in. She's got a miserable looking mango and a coconut and some other unidentified piece of fruit. They look inedible.

"You want some?" She holds up this stuff like it's treasure.

Then she says something bit her arms. She shows me. There are angry red welts all over her arms. What she's done is gone out into the brush, climbed up trees, and picked this stuff herself.

Gabrielle is in her underwear; she has nice legs and a nice butt. Rebecca says, "You have a nice butt, Gabrielle." Rebecca is wearing her rubber pants and is doing contortion stretching, I am practicing the alto in my underwear. When the room service guy brings Gabrielle another coffee, he looks puzzled by the goings-on in room 104.

Gabrielle says she's going swimming. Rebecca and I wait in the room and Gabrielle is back in a second. She's whimpering.

"What's wrong, Gabrielle?"

"I went in the wawter."

The salt water has burned the scrape on her leg. Rebecca and I look at each other and try desperately not to laugh. When Gabrielle goes into the bathroom, I say, in a whisper, "I went in the wawter," and we burst into hysterics.

We say it for the rest of the trip, sobbing with laughter, "I went in the wawter."

Ray, who drives the glass-bottomed boat, stops by the room.

"You want to see the beautiful fishes?"

I say no, but Gabrielle goes. She's gone a long time. When she gets back, though she won't admit it at first, she's fucked the guy from Ray's Shell Boat on some island. Now she's complaining because he fucked her in the woods somewhere and her ass hurts from pieces of bark and pebbles.

Ray stops by to take us by boat to a restaurant. I love going out on the ocean at night in a boat.

We arrive at this fairly high stone wall with a metal ladder coming down.

The waves are high and the boat is rocking. Gabrielle can't get off the boat onto the ladder. She stands at the front of the boat trying to grab on but can't.

Rebecca goes and lies down on the front of the boat with her torso extended out, in a straight line, past the end, hovering over the waves. She grabs hold of the ladder and Gabrielle steps on her back like a gangway to get to the ladder.

Paris, Texas is odd. Gabrielle, without asking me, decides to buy Rebecca a ticket to come with me to Houston. I don't really want this. Rebecca is just a little too wild. It might be hard to concentrate. Rebecca can spend forty minutes making sure that the window is cracked to exactly the right height for draft and temperature.

We are in one of those towering hotels in downtown Houston. I go down to do wardrobe and when I get back, the lights are all off in the room.

Then Rebecca, from the darkness, turns on the lamp and then turns it off. Then she does it again.

"John, you have to see this. Come here." She has her face pressed against the big window and is peering seventeen floors below.

She turns the light on and off and then a car in the parking lot turns its lights on and off. She does it again and the car does it again. This is beginning to feel a little frightening.

Rebecca thinks that this is fantastic.

"See!"

"See what? Who is that?"

"It's Wim Wenders!"

"What are you talking about?"

"In the car, making the signals. It's Wim Wenders! I bet they are filming us right now."

For a moment, I look for hidden cameras, getting sucked into the madness, and then think, *No, why would they bother?* Later, Rebecca will find out that it was the parking lot attendant, who was watching her all along.

Next morning at the hotel breakfast, Wim makes his appearance at my table. He seems fascinated by Rebecca, who is indeed fascinating.

"She looks just like you."

Rebecca does look a lot like me. "Yes, that's the attraction," I say.

So I don't really know what's going on with the movie or what my part is. All I know is that I am Nastassja Kinski's boyfriend and that I have a big fight over her with Harry Dean Stanton. I haven't seen a script.

The next morning, early, the production moves en masse to a motel on the highway in the middle of nowhere and goes off to shoot.

Rebecca and I are just stuck there, on the highway, with no car.

I am thinking, *This is nuts. I don't know what my part is or what I'm getting paid, I paid for my airfare, and now I have just been abandoned on the highway for twelve hours.*

There is no food and the TV doesn't work. I am pissed. This is how movies treat people? This is worse than a music tour. I don't like being stranded in the middle of nowhere.

Rebecca grabs her dirty clothes and proceeds to walk out onto the highway in search of a laundromat.

She comes back four hours later and says she found a laundromat fifteen miles away.

The next day we move to Port Arthur, Texas.

My character is a high class pimp who runs the whorehouse that Nastassja Kinski is working in.

My outfit is a powder blue tuxedo. It's ridiculous.

"I can't wear this." It looks like an outfit from a prom worn by the most unpopular kid in school.

The production is completely out of money, they know this outfit is awful, but this is what they have.

I go out in Port Arthur and find a superfly pimp store, where I buy this purple suit. On the way back, I meet this strange guy who appears out of nowhere. I swear he looked exactly like Lee Harvey Oswald. I think he was Lee Harvey Oswald.

Wim says the suit is fantastic. No one reimburses me for the suit I bought but Wim sends Claire Denis, the assistant director, to buy two of the same for him. Claire uses her own money, and then Wim, according to Claire, never pays her back. Ah, the life.

Nastassja is breathtakingly beautiful. A woman whose beauty would make almost any straight man begin to stammer.

Harry Dean Stanton is a wonderfully cranky fuck with a mellifluous voice.

The three of us share a tiny little cubicle as a dressing room and are fooling around in there for a long time.

Harry and I are hanging in there. We are not stammering.

The wardrobe person comes and says Harry and I will have to leave because Nastassja has to change now. As it's our dressing room, too, and we have nowhere else to go, and as Nastassja has just appeared nude in thirty different magazines, Harry and I say in unison, "Why??" I bet it sounded like a couple of kids who've had their toy taken away.

My first scene, Wim and Kit Carson are discussing what I am going to say; the original script was written by Sam Shepard but they have abandoned that and are writing daily what will happen. I stick my head around a corner to see Harry Dean and tell him, "All the girls are downstairs."

I do it once. Something is wrong with the light. "All the girls are downstairs." Do it again, same problem. "All the girls are downstairs." Do it a third time and the boom is in the shot. Suddenly, I think that it's me. These aren't the problems, they are just saying these are the problems so as to not come right out and say, "This guy sucks, get someone else."

The next day my call is at ten A.M. I get picked up by the teamster driver. Karen Black, whose son is playing the little boy in the film, wants a ride to the set. We get into the car and she announces that she now wants to stop at the health food store. The health food store is miles out of the way. We drive there. I am late now. She disappears into the health food store for almost an hour. Comes back and we drive to the set. It's eleven forty-five A.M.; they are pissed at me for being late. Ah, the life.

The crew has not been paid in weeks and they are upset. There is a rumor that Wim is taking the money for their salaries and buying film stock with it. My big fight scene with Harry and my scenes with Nastassja are not shot because they have run out of money. The whole reason I took the job was this big scene with her, and then the fight with Harry, and now they are not shooting them. I'm told I can go home, but would I mind buying my own ticket and they will reimburse me? Ah, the life.

18

I Was Instructed to Slouch Down
to Eat My Sandwich

I had forgotten all about *Stranger Than Paradise*. I was growing a beard. Jim had persevered. It took him a year and a half, but he was finally able to find the money to finish it. I don't know how he did it. He had screened the first half hour and I heard it didn't play so well. Someone who was there, I think Gary Indiana, said that it was like watching cancer dry.

I had been cast in Scorsese's *The Last Temptation of Christ*, as Saint James, which was scheduled to shoot in a month. I was growing a beard for the part. Jim said that I had to shave, which I wasn't going to do, and we argued about it.

My character could have grown a beard. Then *Last Temptation* was postponed and I shaved.

I had sublet my apartment on Third Street. I didn't want to go back there after getting hit on the head. I wasn't living anywhere. I had gone to María's, in L.A., after *Paris, Texas* and then when I came back to New

York, I stayed sometimes at my uncle's or with one of a number of different women, but I really didn't have a home.

I had gotten back into heroin once again and had to kick before going to do Jim's movie. I had nowhere to do it. I couldn't kick heroin at my uncle's.

I rented a room at the Century Paramount. That hotel is now the fancy Paramount Hotel on Forty-sixth Street, but then it was a crappy place for forty-five bucks a night with ugly carpets. Carpets that smelled. Carpets that had absorbed twenty-five years of vulgar activity.

I stayed mostly in my room and then would go down to the bar and drink three or four sombreros. There was never a soul in the bar. The bartender eyed me with suspicion. I'm sure I was a wreck.

I couldn't eat. Tried a bag of pistachios, but no good. Sombreros were my diet.

We shot the last third of *Stranger* first, in Florida. I was still a little sick. I see those scenes where we are driving in the car, I look at my face, and I can feel exactly that illness I was in.

There was no script. Jim claims there was one, but I certainly felt like I was writing the dialogue as we went along, with Eszter helping. I certainly never saw a script if there was one. Apparently Jim put together a script after the movie was finished, but how does that count?

Jim would say that he wanted such and such to happen and I would map out the dialogue for the three of us, and then get Jim's okay.

Jim seemed lost. Eszter started mimicking him: Every time he left the room, she went, "Um, um, I don't know."

There was a scene at the airport where I was supposed to be drunk. I got drunk. And then terrorized the airport. Acting drunk is a mistake. I didn't seem drunk in the scene, I was just bad.

Rammellzee came down to shoot a scene. He was a painter who had an amazing thing with language. I think later he lost that thing he had, but at the time he was remarkable. He'd walk around wearing goggles as sunglasses or God knows what, inventing fashion moment by moment. His painting wasn't as good as Jean-Michel's, but he had something and he was an edgier, wilder soul than Willie. He used to call Jean-Michel "Scribble Scrabble." I thought his great thing was language, and his voice, like Sly Stone coming out of a cartoon wolf.

I drove Rammel to the airport and he was dressed so weird that they didn't want to let him on the plane. Rammel had a very big thing about traveling first-class. Always first-class, which was not at all in the budget. He was standing in line getting weirder and weirder and angrier and angrier because he just didn't understand, if he was going first-class, why it was taking so fucking long. Now they didn't want to let him on the plane at all because he was so strange and so angry. I took the guy collecting tickets aside and explained that he was a "special" person, and they let him on.

Eszter was angry and thought that I was fucked up to resort to that. Which I suppose it was, but they, for sure, weren't going to let him on the plane if I hadn't done that.

We finished in Florida and went to Cleveland.

It was cold in Cleveland. Brutally cold. Painful. There is a scene where we are looking at Lake Erie and we're wearing skimpy little coats. I could hardly think, it was so cold.

There were a lot of scenes in the car, and Drew Kunin, the six-foot-two-inch wonderful soundman, lay curled up all askew on the floor, all entangled in my legs. We spent days like that. Cold and uncomfortable, Drew curled around my feet.

Drew would mimic me from the floor of the car, saying, "Awful, horrible, terrible." I tend to not be the most positive person on a film set.

There was no money. I remember Sara Driver, who was producing the movie, bringing me a sandwich. Even back then my blood sugar was a problem, so I really needed to eat.

I was instructed to slouch down behind a car, in the freezing cold, to eat it. That way, no one else would see and want a sandwich for themselves.

The crew was miserable. There was no food. We were all sleeping on people's sofas. It was hideously cold. But I was straight. By the time we got to Cleveland, I was gaining strength and a hundred times more affable than I had been in Florida. No one understood why I had changed so radically. At the point where they were all miserable and ready to go home, I had become completely gung-ho about the project.

The thing did seem to get a momentum of its own. Seemed to gain a flow.

We finished it and again, I forgot all about *Stranger Than Paradise*. It was just two weeks working on a project.

If The Lounge Lizards Play in the Forest and No One Is There to Hear It . . .

Tony came into the rehearsal laughing. As tough as he was, Tony Garnier was just the cutest. Maybe the toughness made him cuter.

"That Michael Jackson, boy. 'The chair is not my gun.'" There was that little *boing* in his voice as he laughed.

"What are you talking about?"

We had decided to cover "Billie Jean" as a joke, and Tony had taken the record home and listened to it.

"Those are the words, 'The chair is not my son.'" We didn't believe him until we all sat down and listened to it together. It is true, the words are "The chair is not my son," or maybe even "gun."

We played at Danceteria in New York. The gig was awful. The crowd was creepy. We had played there many times before, but it hadn't been creepy like this.

After the show, we were in the dressing room and I was pretty depressed. My friend Liz sat on a table up against the wall, not saying anything, but watching me the whole time.

I was being drained. People we didn't know were filing into the dressing room. Rockets Redglare came rushing in, right after I had been paid for the gig. I'm walking around paying the guys with cash in my hand, and there's Rockets. He had an uncanny knack for knowing the exact moment there would be cash, and appeared, whining, "John, I need twenty dollars." Relentless: "I need twenty dollars, John." Following me around while I'm paying the band. Back then, in 1983, Rockets weighed three hundred fifty pounds. The high-pitched whine coming from this huge vessel was not making any sense. He would not stop, you knew he would not stop, he was somehow entitled. You really could not end up not giving him $20.

Later, right before he died, I heard Rockets weighed seven hundred pounds. For a while he had no teeth, having lost them in a fight, but later he had a big giant set of white, gnashing things in his mouth after the dentist had fixed him up. Rockets was a stand-up comedian and a very convincing actor. He's in a million movies. I was watching *Talk Radio* with Eric Bogosian on my VCR and heard Rockets's voice as one of the people who call in to Bogosian's radio show. I paused the VCR to call Rockets.

"Hey, I just heard your voice on *Talk Radio*."

"Yeah! I kill him at the end!" He said it very proudly as he ruined the movie for me.

Rockets was on 120 milligrams of methadone a day, and drank a bottle of Stoli and freebased a lot every night. If I hung around Rockets for one evening, it would take three days to recover.

When we would get high at his place, he would start talking about the Fire Escape Monster, late at night. Not that he was seeing the Fire Escape Monster at that moment, but you could tell there had been some real battles in the past.

I didn't mind Rockets mooching after the gigs so much. That was just part of the life. I loved Rockets. Though he was devoid of morals, certainly when it came to drugs and money, and though his stand-up comedy routine was horrendous, Rockets had something to offer. Rockets was the real thing. In my world, Rockets was a legitimate citizen.

What bothered me was all those people, pushing their way into the dressing room, who were just psychically selfish. They gave nothing, had no compassion, and just took. And what they took could not be quantified, but it was way more than money or drugs.

That night the crowd seemed to be only a sea of unconscious, leering cretins. We couldn't rise above it and I was lost. Trying to make the music beautiful was dangerous. When it failed, it just sat there vulnerable and flat. The only thing good, oddly enough, was "Billie Jean," because it was a joke, and we nailed it. Only a joke could have stayed afloat above that atmosphere.

Liz sat perched in the corner watching me as one asshole after another came into the crappy dressing room and took a little chunk of my soul. They'd ask for drugs or drink tickets. The inevitable guy who comes in right after the show and tells you that he used to play the drums, then stands there like this is the opening to an enlightened conversation. Now, as a fellow musician, you have a certain connection and you must respect him because he used to play the drums.

"Let's rap for a while, you go first."

Let me tell you something, unless you are Elvin Fucking Jones, do not ever go backstage and tell the band that you used to play the fucking drums.

People push in, in little groups, to snort their own drugs away from the rest of the club, in your dressing room, while acting like you're not there. The dressing room is supposed to be the performer's safe haven away from the crowd. A place to prepare oneself before the show and relax in peace after.

There was no sanctity. These people barging in were way out of line. There was nowhere to hide.

Someone came in and said, "How did you think you were tonight?"

"It was okay, but—"

"I didn't like it. I thought it was cheap and derivative."

I was too tired to punch him. They were coming in, in droves. A Bosch painting in my skin. Draining me.

Liz just sat up in her spot watching me. I went over to her and asked, "What are you going to do now?"

"I don't know. You want to get high?"

"Yes please yes, do you have any?"

"Yep."

Liz was sexy. Just writing this now and thinking about her gets a little tingle moving through me. She had red hair and eyes that were green and eight different other colors. She talked out of the side of her mouth.

I had moved back to my place on Third Street, and we went there. I was pretty ruined by the show. The band didn't make any sense to me anymore. A month before, we had played at Tramps, and they had screwed up the advertising. There were only nine people at the gig.

"Why were you sitting on that table the whole time?"

"I was protecting you."

That was perfect. I had needed protecting, I was being devoured. I had known her for a couple of years and we had never been close to being together, so I really didn't know if anything was going to happen or not. But after she said that, I reached over and kissed the back of her neck.

I really did not expect the sensation I got. You can touch or kiss some people in the exact same way, the same spot, and there is nothing, no spark. But that kiss on the back of her neck, sitting on my blue plastic couch, which Klaus Nomi had helped me carry home just a couple of days before, really exploded. I didn't expect that.

"Wow."

The next night I was lying in bed with a girl named Joy and the phone rang. It was Liz. She could immediately tell by my voice.

"Is there a girl there?"

"Yeah," I laughed.

"Tell her to get out, I'm coming over."

So I had to tell this girl to leave because I wanted to see Liz, and this girl was fairly annoying. Plus, Liz probably had dope.

This sounds harsh and heartless, which I suppose it is, but it was a time of sex and drugs. More than anything it was a time of "take no prisoners."

Liz was a stripper. This was 1983, and there was pretty much only Billy's Topless and the Baby Doll Lounge among New York's downtown strip clubs. Liz worked at both of those places. She would come to my place and we would get high every night. This was the first time that I had thrown caution to the wind and gotten high whenever I felt like it.

Before that I would get high for two or three days and then ride out being sick for a couple of days. On and off. On and off. I was either high or sick but never had gone the full way. In a way my friends were more courageous than me. I always had some level of self-preservation.

Now I was getting high every day and having marathon sex with Liz.

Hello, I Am a Dilettante and a Hack

Stephen Torton knew this guy who was being chased by Interpol who had tons of unbelievable heroin. Pure white dope from Thailand. Stephen set it up and got Gabrielle to buy a bunch of it. We ended up holding a good share for ourselves.

This heroin, and I am sorry to say this, but this pure, light heroin from Thailand was magic. If I could find it today, I would take it. Magic. Made you float, but what was really unique was that it made one brilliant.

Gabrielle was nodding so hard her face hovered inches off the floor for hours.

"Look, Gabrielle is reading her carpet."

It came time to do the music for *Stranger Than Paradise*. Eszter, who was a pretty decent violin player, and I used to listen to the Bartók string quartets and follow along with the score. Like a little weekly class we did.

Since my character in the movie was Hungarian—actually almost everyone was Hungarian—I wanted to write a string quartet as a kind of nod to Bartók. Jim thought it was a good idea.

At this point I had never really written music on paper before. I had only done it as notes for stuff I was working on for the band.

I snorted this dope from Thailand. My mind went completely clear. Without an instrument, I started to get ideas and write the score: two violins, viola, and cello on a napkin. People can write music without instruments; now I can do it myself. You can hear it in your head and you write it. But at that time, this was inconceivable to me. And a string quartet? Come on. I didn't know how to write for a string quartet.

This dope made me a genius. I drew lines on the napkins in pen and then started to fluidly write what was popping into my head. I could hear three moving lines at once and facilitate them with ease. It took more time to make the music staffs with a ruler and pen than it took to write the music.

Jim didn't want to give me a tape of the movie to score to. Suddenly, he was very secretive. If I needed to see the scenes, I should come up to the editing room, but even that seemed like something he really didn't want to let me do.

He wanted me to just record a bunch of string quartet music and he would plop it into the movie where he saw fit.

"That doesn't make any sense, I don't want to write the music without knowing the rhythm of the scene. Why can't I just get a tape?"

I couldn't get a straight answer.

Nothing makes me angrier than not getting a straight answer.

I said to Torton, "Shit, it was my idea, I starred in it, I wrote half the dialogue, where does he fucking get off hoarding it? How am I supposed to write the music without seeing it? And why can't I see it? Suddenly it's his secret film?"

Stephen played middleman and got Jim to let him tape the scenes I asked for. He brought a video camera to the editing room and shot off the Steenbeck, and I wrote the rest of the music like that.

I had written most of it on napkins at Gabrielle's the night before. Now I only had a day to write the rest. Jim needed the music immediately to mix it and get the film to Cannes by the deadline. This, you can imagine, is not normal, to give a composer two days to write and record the music for a feature-length film, but somehow I did it. Every step of that movie hung over a precipice that would have doomed it. It was an extraordinary thing that that movie ever got finished.

Liz got home from work and wanted attention. I had to write the music. She stood against the refrigerator, clad in her red G-string from work. Her eyes closed, lips moist and parted, hands cradling her yearning neck, back arched, breasts pointing skyward, and she was moaning a little.

But I wrote on.

I didn't have a studio or even a four-track tape recorder. I just used two shitty little handheld recorders, layering the tracks on one and then the other. Did all the work on the floor of my apartment on Third Street, bums wailing outside.

I watched the movie with Stephen's camera hooked up to my little black and white TV, while recording the cello line to one tape recorder on a tiny keyboard, then the viola line on the second keyboard while listening to the cello line, then playing that back and playing the second violin on the first tape recorder because you could still faintly hear the cello line from when I played the viola line. I layered all four parts going back and forth between the two tape recorders.

Jim snuck us into a recording studio where a friend of his was engineering. Jim slipped the guy some money and I had a string quartet, put together by Jill Jaffe, arrive at midnight.

They came in, set up, the engineer looking over his shoulder the whole time to see if the owner had come in and caught him.

What had I written? I was nervous.

A miracle.

I was amazed. It sounded incredible. I was really worried that it was going to sound plodding, but it was beautiful. The players helped it a lot, they really brought it to life, but I felt like I had invented the string quartet.

I got the call to come out to L.A. to meet with the film company about doing the score for Aaron Lipstadt's movie *City Limits*. I didn't really have the job, though I thought it was mine if I wanted it, but I had to go out there, watch the movie, and then pitch them after. I didn't really want to do it. I didn't want to fly to L.A. to sell myself to them as a composer. Somewhere along the way I'd picked up a manager, Frank, who talked me into going.

My flight is early in the morning. I try to go to bed at a normal hour but can't sleep. Liz is out. When she came back, she was supposed to bring me dope for the trip and leave it on top of the piano. I get up and Liz had come and gone. There's one little line of dope on the broken mirror on top of the piano. I had expected a package. How is this going to get me through the trip? I snort the line off the piano and head for the airport.

I get out there. I get the job. They hire this guy, Bob, because I have never done a full movie score. I don't really know what his function is but I can't stand him. They've heard the stuff I did for *Stranger*, which they were impressed with, and they know the band, but this is a full, big Hollywood film, and they think that I'll need help.

I don't have any dope and I don't know where to get it. During the meeting where I pitch the producers, my eyes are burning out. I tell them I have a cold and go to the hotel to rest. I call Liz and tell her to FedEx me dope immediately.

The package comes after a day and I rush down to the front desk to get it. I have no idea if it is safe to FedEx dope across the country and I am afraid I am going to get caught. The night guy working the front desk gives me a once-over.

"Hey, buddy, you need anything?"

I am a little paranoid, but in the end, I buy a gram of coke from him and rush upstairs with the coke and my FedEx package. I have the weirdest feeling that this is the guy at the SSI office who got down on one knee and pronounced, "I want the money!"

I snort a line of dope and then a line of the night guy's speedy coke.

Coke hits you first. While I am waiting for the dope to come on, I get so paranoid that I am squatting next to the toilet ready to flush everything when the narcotics agents bust down my door.

Liz wants to come out to L.A. It is not really over with María, but at the same time it's been over for a while. I snort the last line from the FedEx package and go out to the airport to meet Liz. I am nodding out as I drive, go right up on the median a couple of times.

I expected Liz to come out with heroin, but she doesn't have any. She is going to kick. She has a bag of heart medication called Catapres that is used, I think, to lower your blood pressure.

The film company has rented this apartment for me in this building for swingers in Burbank. They're all out by the pool. I feel like a giant bug and can have nothing to do with these swinger people.

I take Catapres with Liz for a couple of days and then stop. It makes me too tired and I hear that it can stop your heart. I find a place to give me a vitamin C drip and then after that I'm cool. In a way, I kind of already have kicked. But I just walk out of that vitamin C thing feeling cool.

Liz's habit is much worse than mine. Still, I'm a little sick and can't sleep. I'm flopping around so much in the bed at night that Liz takes the cushions from the couch and puts them in the middle of the floor to sleep on.

She takes a ton of Catapres. This surely can't be safe, but Liz just lies on those cushions for days, hardly moving. She is not bathing and it is like having a big, sick, stinky dog with red hair in the middle of the apartment. I come in to sleep. Now that I am feeling better I want to have sex, but if I try to touch Liz, I am attacked by the snapping alligator that has taken over her body. Otherwise I am gone all day at the studio they have set up for me on Sunset Boulevard right above their offices.

I cannot stand Bob. Poor Bob. He's from New York, so we are supposed to get along, but he says things like, "What's the prob?" instead of "problem." If you want to be my friend, one thing you can do is, while you're talking, use your fingers to make air quotes around interesting words in your sentence. That will go a long way toward making me warm to you.

I just can't stand him. I get ornery and drive him to quit.

Liz is coming around. Actually just like that, she is up and about and not so scarily cranky. We drive into L.A. and on the way back, the rent-a-wreck they got me, because it was supposed to be cool, blows up. I just leave it on the highway, smoke billowing out from under the hood. Liz and I walk back to our swingers' apartment.

I get them to get me a normal new car and move me to an apartment in Westwood. Not great, but it's not Burbank.

I do the score. It's so much work, and what doesn't help a bit is that the film is just awful. The people who did it are the nicest people, but the film sucks. It is right after *The Road Warrior* was such a hit, and so they've done a futuristic biker movie with gangs of kids. The movie has Robby Benson as some kind of evil higher-echelon character; Rae Dawn

Chong, who at one point, on the back of a motorcycle, actually yells out, "Knees to the breeze, cowboy!"; John Stockwell; Tony Plana; Kim Cattrall; and a whole slew of people who end up being somewhere years later. The movie is *The Road Warrior* with some of the less delightful elements of *Welcome Back, Kotter*.

I need an orchestrator and a copyist. I read a book about writing for film music. It says that a film composer who does not orchestrate his own score is a dilettante and a hack.

"Hello, I am a dilettante and a hack."

A guy auditions for the job and I am told that he wrote the music for *Hawaii Five-O*. Well, perfect, let's use him. I think it's funny and want to hire him but the production thinks it's a bad idea.

They bring in this guy, Jim Price, to orchestrate and conduct. Jim Price is kind of a Hollywood session guy by this time. He also is a bit of a cowboy. We are from different worlds and clash a bit, but in the end I grow to like him.

Jim Price used to play trumpet with the Rolling Stones for years, and Joe Cocker. I can tell he used to be wild but is trying to make the transition. We have to work like mad to get the thing done in time. I thought that the score came out great. They loved it at first, and then when the film tested badly, they took the score off. That was fine with me. I had learned to write for an orchestra and gotten paid for it. Earn while you learn. The movie was bad, but they had treated me nicely.

Rudy shows up! Rudy Graham! After writing religious slogans all over his walls and disappearing all these years, Rudy Graham shows up.

I think I found out from my sister, Liz, that he was living in L.A. and working at a publishing house. I get his work number and call him up. He has disappeared for ten years and it is like no time has gone by at all. A lot of people who are friends, if you lose touch for a while and then see them years later, it is different. Who are they? But with Rudy that is not the case. Not at all. It's like I dropped him off at his place on Friday and now it's Monday.

He looks great. That big Buddha laugh. He's wearing really straight clothes for his job, a bad white shirt and tie.

I get the movie to fly Evan out to play the piano parts. Jim Price doesn't want to do it, but I need someone in the studio who I can stand and Ev needs the money. I insist that there are parts only Evan can play.

Evan is in the room recording, and the engineer and Jim Price are making nasty comments to each other about his playing. Not so I can hear, but they're leaning in to each other whispering and then laughing. I'm livid, but it isn't blatant enough for me to call them on it. It's just stupid anyway. "He's not part of our L.A. session musician club. He can't be any good."

They can have their little club. I want to go home.

Frank, my manager, and his partner negotiated the deal. I got $15,000. This to me then is unfathomable wealth. Fifteen thousand fucking dollars. This is going to last a lifetime.

Frank gets me to wire his commission out immediately. He knows about Liz's and my proclivities and wants to make sure to get his money. I think he's acting like an asshole. How could Liz and I go through $15,000 before we get back to New York? I'm on the street talking to Frank on a pay phone on Sunset Boulevard. I'm pretty pleased with the money. In that same conversation he tells me that I have to sign the contract for *Stranger Than Paradise*.

I already know the deal. Jim and I talked about it. I'm certain that Jim isn't going to try to do anything dishonest or creepy. He seems like a really decent guy.

I am getting a thousand for acting and a thousand for the score. If the movie makes money, Jim has offered me three points of gross. Also, we'll take turns taking it around to festivals. I don't think much about the many-page contract when it arrives.

I told Frank the manager and his lawyer partner Wayne what the deal was supposed to be with Jim, and they've promised that the contract is fine. I can just sign it. I think they don't expect much from *Stranger Than Paradise*.

I'm in the middle of writing this score, working eighteen hours a day, and it just doesn't occur to me that Jim wouldn't make sure I got what he promised. A naïve mistake that I would never make again.

Liz and I are straight. We're a little wobbly and insecure but basically okay. She is pretty fucking bored stuck out in Westwood without a car, but things to me seem kind of like they could work out. Things are okay, except we're in L.A. and I am working day and night with L.A.

music people. Jim Price, the engineers, the musicians, the editor—they are all from L.A. and I just can't get next to it. Liz has made some friends who say that they will come and pick her up to do stuff, and then stand her up over and over again.

I take a day off, and Liz and I go for a drive out by the ocean. We head up into the hills in Malibu and get to a dead end with a roundabout. I glide the car in a circle. The windows are open, cool air flows through the car from the ocean stretching out below. This is how I know that a breeze can make you fall in love. I look at Liz and my heart opens.

Scoring a film is so much work, and Jim Price, in a way, is running the show. I have written this nice stuff for orchestra and it sounds pretty great. There are some sections for bass, drum, and guitar.

I want to find some guys who can play for these parts, so that Jim Price can't hire these rhythmically correct session guys, and I try to think who will know musicians in L.A. Matt Dike, who later founded the record label Delicious Vinyl, was a DJ who had a hip-hop club that moved from place to place. He was the first person to put on a Lounge Lizards record in a crowded public place when I was there. He put on "Harlem Nocturne"; I felt a little nervous. All the L.A. hip-hop kids looked bored. Then a young Max Perlich smashed into the DJ booth on his skateboard, scratching the record to a stop.

"Matt, I need a funky bass player for a film score. Who can I get out here?"

"You gotta get this guy, they call him The Flea! He's got a band called the Red Hot Chili Peppers. They're crazy! You gotta use The Flea!"

There are some things in 5/4 and 7/8, so I can't just hire some funk bass player without knowing if he can play in odd times. I schedule a meeting with this guy, The Flea.

The Flea is not The Flea but just Flea. He is short with an impish face and an L.A. punk feel. He can play the bass like a motherfucker. I play him stuff on the piano and he just shrugs, like, *No big deal,* and then nails it on the bass. He wants to bring the other guys from his band and I say sure. I'm excited to get some players in there with some gomph because Jim Price is hiring all these L.A. session guys who make everything I write sound like it is supposed to be music for *Starsky and Hutch*.

Flea sees some of the wardrobe from the futuristic motorcycle movie hanging in the office and says, "Hey, can I have this?"

He picks up a leather jacket with metal cups attached all over it. I tell him, "Yes, you can have it. You look stunning." I'm actually impressed that this kid just takes this ridiculous thing and wears it right out onto Sunset Boulevard.

For the band stuff, we have a smaller studio booked than the one we used for the orchestra. We're supposed to start at two in the afternoon. At two-thirty Jim Price is rapping his fingers on the mixing board. You can see smoke. "This is not how one does a session. One should get there a half hour early, set up, and be ready at the start time." I actually have to agree with him.

"The musician's dog comes in late, fucks the other two dogs, and leaves."

Flea, Cliff Martinez, and Hillel Slovak show up at three P.M. Flea is slouching. Like he knows he's done something wrong, but his posture also has that *I don't care* thing. Jim Price tells him that we don't need them.

They say, "Okay!," all chipper, and leave.

I am out at Jim Price's place a bunch, and then in the studio, and Liz is completely stir-crazy. Maybe my feeling for her isn't reciprocated. Liz wants to go back to New York, so I get her a ticket to go back a couple of weeks before I do.

I'm in this apartment in Westwood and the place just goes to hell. I guess I'm depressed. Don't wash the dishes for a week. The trash is piling up. I can't get myself to take it out and I have no energy.

From the couch I can see roaches traveling over the tops of the garbage bags.

21

Fifty Million Junkies Are Probably Wrong

I get back to New York and Liz is getting high every day. I go back to my struggle. Try to do it only once or twice a week. But now that I have been really strung out, I get sick every time after I get high once or twice. I am determined not to fall back into taking it every day, so I am kicking all the time.

When we were trying to quit, sometimes, on Fridays, I would go with Liz and wait on Third Avenue in the East Twenties, while she would go and buy Herbert Huncke's methadone. I didn't really know who he was at the time, but I did know he was a respected beat poet. Liz might have been in and out of there in ten minutes, but it seemed like hours. I would stand on the corner, shivering and looking into the coffee shop window. The people looking out at me knew that I was a shameful and terrible person.

Anyone who glanced at me knew in an instant that I was a loathsome creature to be avoided at any cost.

The methadone worked in a way. I didn't like it, but it worked. It made me incredibly hyper. I would become Mr. Gregarious. I noticed that people would back away from me while I was talking.

Liz had a truly inspired suggestion, that we take LSD to kick. That would help us transcend the addiction. She claimed that she had done it before. It seemed like a brilliant idea.

We were back living on Third Street and I had mice. For a little while we used normal traps using peanut butter as bait. You'd be sleeping and hear this sklakity racket. A mouse in the trap but not dead. Sputtering and twisting like mad. I'd jump out of bed and throw the trap out the window.

This was too gruesome and cruel. If the trap killed them straight out, I was okay with it. But this maiming was unacceptable. We tried balancing a ruler on the edge of the bathtub, with a bit of peanut butter on the end. The mouse was supposed to travel out on the ruler and then when it got past the middle, the mouse's weight would make it, and the ruler, fall into the tub. The mouse would be trapped and I presume then I would catch it in a towel or something and let it go outside. Every morning we'd find the ruler in the bathtub with no peanut butter on it.

So fuck it, we'll live with the mice because I can't maim them in these traps. But the thing is that the mice get braver. They start doing outlandish things. Running across the bed while you're still awake. Walk out into the middle of the floor and just plunk down like your dog would and then rest there for a spell. Just stare at you like it was their place and you were only a bit of a nuisance.

So Liz has bought some LSD. I'm already dope sick. Liz should be sick, too, but I never know with her because she's always getting high on the sly. I've got the bulk of what's left of the fifteen thousand from the film score in hundred dollar bills hidden in my coat, and I am in denial as to the reason it is inexplicably short every time I count it.

As I start to feel the acid coming on, it seems like there are mice everywhere. I'm not hallucinating mice. They *are* everywhere, and they are watching me. I get a chair and put it in the middle of the kitchen and sit there naked with a broom. I'm going to sit there, patiently, the kind of patience that only comes with religious insight or when you're high as a fucking kite. As soon as a mouse gets close enough I'm going to smash it with the broom. I don't mind killing them because now they have disrespected me.

The mice are very smart. The mice are really smart. They are toying with me. They stay just out of reach and stare into my soul. They calculate my striking distance at five feet and are hanging out five and a half feet in all directions. They stare at me and then ignore me. I am not a threat. I sit there for—an hour? I don't know how long. I'm tripping my fucking brains out, how can I know?

As I am sitting there naked with the broom cocked over my head, I suddenly realize that I don't feel so good. In fact, I feel horrible. PANIC. This is absolutely not good. We have to get heroin immediately. I'm racked with pain. My nerves are shredding. LSD and dope sickness is the worst of all possible combinations.

It's late but Liz calls this creepy, yuppie dope dealer who lives in a high rise. He wears designer tinted eyeglasses. I've never been to this guy's place and I'm not supposed to go up. He's already pissed that Liz called him so late, but there is no fucking way that I'm waiting out on the street, tripping and dope sick.

I just remember the really bright fluorescent lights in the elevator and that the elevator had this loud, piercing ring as it registered going past each floor. Each horrifying beep shattering my neurological core.

He begrudgingly sold us a package of heroin and we snorted it in the elevator, on the ride down.

The world seemed relatively safe again.

22

Werner Herzog in Lederhosen

I t's so weird how it went. I wasn't prepared for it.

Stranger Than Paradise wins the Caméra d'Or at Cannes. *Paris, Texas* wins the Palme d'Or.

I am suddenly the hot new independent film star.

This is very strange. Do I want this? One is supposed to want this.

Jim is declared a genius. And the genius that is Jim explains to the world that I am not an actor but an odd person he has discovered and coaxed into a wonderful performance.

I do not want to be an actor. I am a musician and composer. But I would rather be an actor than an odd character Jim Jarmusch has coaxed into a wonderful performance. Does he keep me in a box and let me out once in a while? If I am not acting, then that nitwit in *Stranger Than Paradise* is me.

Stop the presses! Stop Jim!

I had done the music for *Variety* and another movie that was at Cannes that year. And another movie had used a bunch of Lounge

Lizards songs. I've got five movies at Cannes and I cannot afford to buy the plane ticket. I can barely afford to do my laundry.

Jim was supposed to take me to Cannes and then took Sara Driver instead. At least if I were there, maybe I could stop this insane arc that is twisting my fate through the press in such a horribly wrong way.

It's kind of hard on Liz, who wants to act and takes it seriously. I don't give a shit about acting and suddenly I'm on the cover of all these magazines.

All I care about is the music. And the band is now finally starting to be something great.

The Lounge Lizards had a couple of gigs in New York when there wasn't really a band. For Bette Gordon on the *Variety* music score I had used Tony Garnier, Dougie Bowne, Evan, and a bunch of added horns. Most of the guys I used were street musicians. This great blues alto player who called himself Mr. Thing, from the South somewhere. Really irritating guy, but he could play the shit out of the alto in a way I never could. Tight, hard blues sound with facility. The lead alto on "Million Dollar Walk" is him.

There was a tall, oafish Nordic guy named Anders who could also play like mad on tenor or baritone.

There was one cue in the movie that was just an up-tempo thing in G. Someone had to play the solo. Mr. Thing kept saying, "Let Anders do it! Let Anders do it!" I looked at this six-foot-four guy standing there with the heavy accent and quiet little voice and thought, *Nah.*

But motherfucking Anders kills it. Kills it. Tony starts a fast walk and Dougie is with him and then Anders comes in and I get goosebumps. Ended up calling the cue "Anders Leaps In."

The budget for *Variety* is next to nothing. Bette Gordon is sweet and I manage to give her a nice score for about $1,000, paying all the guys $75 for the day.

The Lizards have a couple of nonserious gigs in New York and I just throw this thing together with like ten horns, Dougie, Tony, and Evan. And there is Roy Nathanson on soprano, alto, and tenor.

I had known Roy ever since I moved to Second Avenue, five years earlier. Roy was friends with Jon Ende, and he had keys to La MaMa theater, on Fourth Street. We would go there late at night to practice and play together.

Roy was supposed to be gay. For years he lived with his boyfriend, Ray. In fact, Roy was a closet heterosexual, he's now married with a kid. Roy's boyfriend, Ray, had taken the photos for the first Lounge Lizards poster, and then again took a picture of me for a solo thing I did at Max's Kansas City.

These guys were the messiest people I ever met in my life. I thought that gay guys were supposed to be neat and have nice apartments. They had an awful, stinking dog, Garbo. Their apartment and their car were so unhygienic it went to a level that was scary.

Roy was always worried about his body. Sometimes his body was legitimately breaking down, but usually it was solely his obsession with himself.

His jalopy of a car, an orange Nova, smelled terribly of Garbo and was always strewn with fast food wrappers.

Roy, the hypochondriac, had a dream. A vision, really. He was about to make a bunch of money, $5,000, for acting in a Chantal Akerman film. This money was unexpected. What he wanted to do when he got the money was to pay a doctor $5,000 to drive his stinking orange Nova around Manhattan, while Roy sat in the backseat complaining to the doctor about all his ailments.

Roy brings in Curtis Fowlkes on trombone. Big, gentle black guy who is just as sweet and timid as can be. Curtis "Boner" Fowlkes could play that Fred Wesley/James Brown stuff if he wanted to, and that kind of soul is in his sound.

Tony leaves, to play with Bob Dylan, and now he's actually going to make a living. Dougie is playing in one of the rehearsal rooms at West-Beth Theatre. I stop by to practice because Evan has his piano in Paul Bley's room for a time. There's a kid down there with him playing, just the two of them, bass and drums. They stop playing when I come in.

This kid, there is just something about him. He's wearing these weird shoes. He's shy and he is not going to play while I am there. He doesn't say anything.

I just have a feeling about him and I call Dougie later to ask him.

"Who was that kid?"

"Who, Erik?"

"The bass player, the kid, whatever his name is. With the elf shoes."

"Yeah, Erik. Erik Sanko."

"Can he play?"

Dougie is a little hesitant. He's worried that if he recommends this guy and it doesn't work out, I will blame him.

But he steps up and says, "Yeah, he can play."

"How old is he?"

"Nineteen."

Without ever hearing Erik play, I hire him for the tour.

Roy also brings in Marc Ribot. Marc used to say about Ralph Carney, who played in Tom Waits's band when Marc did, that Ralph had the left brain of the smartest man in the world. It was true about Ralph, but in a large sense this was also true about Ribot.

Marc is a musical genius. So many ideas are coming out of that guy that it is actually often a problem. It takes him a while to figure out his spot in The Lounge Lizards. It is hard to know, especially for the guitar in the Lizards, how dissonant to be. Where to play with the music and when to go against it. I am constantly giving Marc instructions, at rehearsal, before the gig, after the gig, but it just never seems to sink in.

But really, Marc is right about this. He has to find the place for the guitar in this music himself, and no amount of advice from me is going to do it.

By design, the guitar often is used to foil the music when it gets too jazzlike. When Arto was in the band it was perfect, because he has a great textural sense. It was just that Arto legitimately never knew anything about music.

But Marc puts a good deal of time into just figuring out the color the guitar should have in the band. The role of that chair.

So it's Roy, Curtis, Ribot, Erik, Dougie, me, and Evan. Soon Dougie brings in E. J. Rodriguez on percussion. That is a crazy good band.

Each one of these guys is aware of all different kinds of music. I am drawing from everywhere, from James Brown to Balinese music, from Varèse to Coltrane, and they are helping me do it. And they all have that special thing where they can play their instrument as though they just found it on the street. They all have a certain naïve thing that allows them to play broken. This is an enormous problem with well-trained musicians: No matter what they play, you can hear the school in it. It can never get to that place of mayhem that we used to create, or to the other end of that spectrum, the place of the childlike dream.

Jim's friend Louis Sarno lived with the pygmies. Married a pygmy woman. He would record them. Their music. And Jim had lots of tapes. This music was so organically part of the pygmy life, and it was immensely complicated rhythmically in a way I am sure they were not aware of. This is what I wanted from my band. This organic rhythm. The idea that this song is in 11/8 or 4/4 is thrown out the window. "We are just all talking here, we are aware of Stravinsky and can play Stravinsky, but this is where we live."

In rehearsal the band got good really fast. I would come in with a melody and snippets of bass lines or horn parts, and we would work it out vocally in rehearsal.

These guys were all smart, funny, and musical. We loved one another. It was just like it is supposed to be.

I suppose this is why I resent the movies in a way, as the music was starting to become this really beautiful, powerful thing that was like nothing that had come before, and people only wanted to know about the movies.

There is a problem, though. Erik is a minor and it looks like he can't go on the tour. I have to sign all these official documents, like I am his legal guardian, saying that I will be responsible for him on the road.

Erik will say later that it was like giving an egg to a gorilla for safekeeping. But it's okay, because the gorilla signed for it.

Liz and I aren't getting along. I don't want to get high and she is committed. She is go-go dancing and disappearing all the time. She says she's going to the store and is gone for four hours. Her explanations are vague and distant. Not only is she disappearing, but my wad of hundred dollar bills, from the movie score, is dwindling. I cannot figure out how we are spending it this fast. It seems so obvious now—you read this and you know what happened—but I just refused to allow it into my head.

We're on Third Street, sleeping on the foam pad on the floor, and an insane racket from the men's shelter wakes us. Bloodcurdling cries and leering laughter. This is what Hell sounds like.

Liz doesn't open her eyes. She turns her head to the wall and says, "This isn't what life is supposed to be."

She's right. It's no way to live.

I am really trying not to get high. I slip up but I am not on a mission with it. Liz, for sure, is getting high and keeping it from me. She is supposed to be home at eleven P.M. and doesn't show until four A.M. I am dying to have some of that amazing sex we would have. Sirone has started calling me "Johnny Cakes" and then just "Cakes," which is kind of an insult. But I like the sound of it. I'm waiting on Liz and I do a painting of a guy waiting by a door. I write under it, "Pain for Cakes." Then when she comes home I change it to "No Pain for Cakes." When we used that for the title of our fourth album, some clever journalist thought that it was a reference to Marie Antoinette. But it was really a love message to Liz.

I had that turquoise blue couch, the one that Klaus Nomi had spotted on the street and helped me carry home. (I know I mention this before, but the image of me and Klaus Nomi carrying this turquoise couch through the East Village war zone is something one should form an image of in one's mind.) I walked into my apartment with Frank the manager and Liz was just sitting there on the blue couch staring at the wall. I didn't think much about it, but Frank was flipping out about it later.

"John, this is not normal, I've never seen anything so depressing. I think this Lenny Bruce and Honey shit is just boring. She was just staring at the wall!"

This was not unusual. I realized that often I would come in and she'd just be staring at the wall.

But Liz, shit, you had to love Liz. She was fun and funny and smart and sexy as hell. Liz really was everything you could hope for in a woman. It's just that she was a junkie.

I'd be driving and she would unzip my fly and take it out and yell, "John's penis!" like she had just found the prize in the Cracker Jack box.

She had that thing that I would fall for again later, that thing where her pain, her wound, was just so poignant. When she had come out to L.A. and it was clear that María and I were finished, the thing that pissed María off the most was that I was taking care of this girl who was just hopeless. María had never asked for a thing, outside of trying to get me to get a driver's license. Now I've got a bit of money from the film score and I'm flying this girl to L.A. to help her kick dope. María was hurt and enraged. She was right, too, she got a raw deal, but the heart just goes like that.

Stranger Than Paradise and *Paris, Texas* are at the Telluride Film Festival. Finally, I am invited. The last part of the trip is in this bumpy little plane and I do not like it.

There is a softball game between *Paris, Texas* and *Stranger Than Paradise*. Really more between the Samuel Goldwyn Company and whoever released *Paris, Texas*, with me and Jim on the *Stranger* team and a bunch of businesspeople I didn't know on the other team.

I'm a good ballplayer. Even though I am in a fog, I insist that I am sure that I am the best guy to play center field. In the first inning someone hits a fly ball to left center. It's a bit of a run but I lope under it, casually stick out my glove. I see the ball sail six inches beyond my reach. I have to run to the fence and retrieve it. This is bad. It's on my list of the top fifty moments I would like to have a do-over for.

Wim Wenders arrives late. He has been on vacation and he looks incredibly handsome. He is wearing shorts and his legs look like a star soccer player's. He doesn't know a thing about baseball and is positioned in short right field, twenty feet behind second base, so as to stay out of harm's way. Someone hits a rifle shot and Wim leaps and makes an astounding, diving catch that Brooks Robinson would have been proud of.

There are not really any women at this festival. I thought there would be. I have a room in this ski lodge that I have to share with the publicist. They spring this on me at the last minute and I am a little pissed. The publicist, Reid Roosevelt, is a nice enough guy, it's just this isn't star treatment. It is assistant director treatment, but that is what I always seemed to get when Jim was in charge.

I am sitting next to Wim at the screening of *Paris, Texas*. The lights go down and he whispers to me, "We had to cut the harmonica scene."

There was a thing in the film where I played harmonica over the phone to Nastassja Kinski, right after Harry Dean Stanton left the booth. When the film played at Cannes it was still in there, and it has come back to me a few times that the scene is great. That it got applause. I'm disappointed that he cut it.

We take ski lifts to the top of a hill to do a press conference. There is no snow because it's August and I don't like being up in this thing with the hard ground twenty feet below my dangling feet.

I am starting to seem like a big deal. Stan Brakhage introduces himself to me. Then Athol Fugard starts saying something to me. I don't understand what this little man is talking about and make a wisecrack. Someone says, "John, that is Athol Fugard, you should be more respectful."

So there is a big press conference. I think it is all kinds of funny, the conceptual questions that they are asking Jim and that he is addressing with a straight face.

Werner Herzog stands up. He is wearing lederhosen. He starts ranting, "John Lurie is the most natural actor I have ever seen! When Hollywood sees John Lurie they will be terrified! They will be shamed by their phony actors. Paul Newman and Robert Redford will run for the hills!"

After the press conference, all the business and press people take the ski lift down, and every creative person—Wim, Werner, Athol Fugard, Jim, me, and whoever else—decides to walk. I don't know if it's all for the same reason—fear—but I suspect so.

I get the feeling that *Stranger* is taking on a life of its own. That whatever the movie was, it no longer is.

The press have anointed it and that is that.

23

All the Girls Want to See My Penis

This should have been a great time for me. But somehow it wasn't. To be thrown into that kind of fame is very unbalancing. It is worse for your chemistry than drugs, in a way. You want the attention and the adoration, it gives you a buoyancy, but it rarely leads to anything real. Fame comes at you in hideous ways, from all directions, and there is no way to protect yourself, especially if you don't have a penny.

But you get high from it and you absolutely want it to continue. "Someone at the airport didn't recognize me. I have to fix that."

And now my poverty is hard to wear. It is not cool to be famous and not have the means to insulate yourself. I am walking down the street, a bit hungover, in a shirt I didn't have time to clean, and everyone knows me. They look. And there I am on the cover of a magazine staring out from the rack outside the store. Who am I? Am I that person, all tough and confident in clean clothes, or am I this wretch trying to get down Second Avenue?

That summer, before *Stranger Than Paradise* came out, I was with Liz. I was really with Liz and I didn't think about other girls. That thing where you walk down the street and you just don't even look at attractive women because your mechanism just isn't set off by it. I've got what I want, no need to look. You can be sitting at an outside restaurant and a beautiful ass floats by inches from your face, so close you can smell it, and you don't even turn your head. This, of course, in months, sometimes years, eventually wears off. Liz and I also had an understanding that if I was on the road with the band, of course I would be with other women, and the same went for her while I was gone.

But now all the girls want to see my penis. Maybe it has something to do with seeing somebody on screen at ten times their normal size. No, it's not that, it's something else. I don't know what it is. I wonder which creepy celebrities have women throwing themselves at them. Maybe all of them. What an awful thought.

The first time I got that look, that glance, was outside a theater in Paris. The band was on tour in Europe that summer after Cannes. *Variety* was playing at a theater and Bette Gordon asked me to come and say a few words after the film at some kind of cultural place.

I take a cab and get out but can't figure out where the theater is. There is this pretty young woman outside wearing a button that says she is working for the place. I say excuse me. I see that flash of recognition across her face and then she opens. Just opens herself.

Not like she is attracted to me but some other thing. I ask for directions and she gives me that pheromone thing, where she is saying, *You can have me if you want to. I understand if you don't, but if you want me, I am available to you. Take me.*

She was beautiful, and more than that, she had that thing in her face where you just knew that she was not only intelligent but kind and seemed to have a grasp on the weirdness and toughness of life, no matter how young she was. I should have just married her immediately and skipped past the rest of the beautiful, sexy, hideous insanity that was to come.

I go into the side of the theater and the people who are running the thing make it very clear that the packed house is here not to see the movie, but because it has been announced that I will be there. But I don't really have much to say. I am going to just answer questions. I am really just going as a favor to Bette Gordon.

It is unbelievable. I start to talk and all the women in the crowd start swooning. Three days ago in New York, I was this same exact person. Looked and walked and talked exactly the same. Nobody was swooning.

They run out of questions and there is a funny pause. I am standing there and haven't done this sort of thing before. I feel a little silly. A couple of the guys in the band, who played on the score, are out in the audience. Dougie raises his hand. I see that it's Dougie and call on him like I am a schoolteacher.

"Yes, Dougie?"

"May I go to the bathroom?"

"Yes, Dougie."

He gets up and runs out of the room.

That fall *Stranger* is a big deal at the New York Film Festival. Eszter and I are perplexed as to how Jim "Um, um, I don't know" Jarmusch has been proclaimed an auteur and a coming force in film.

We are up in the balcony at Lincoln Center. The fancy seats. I'm sitting next to Liz, with Jim, Sara Driver, the producers, and people from the festival. These are the fancy people in the fancy seats.

Liz seems bored and uncomfortable in the midst of all this ritzy, phony culture stuff.

She whispers into my ear, "You want a blow job?"

I am the star of a movie opening the New York Film Festival, at Lincoln Center, but at that moment, the blow job sounds much more compelling and real. So we sneak out from the VIP seats in the balcony. Liz goes into the ladies' room to make sure the coast is clear and we spend most of the rest of the movie having sex in a toilet stall.

I got asked to do something at this little club in the Village. Too small for the band, but the guy thought that I could play solo there.

I didn't realize how small the place was when I said yes. There is only room for about forty people. Because the place is tiny, the guy doesn't advertise and there is hardly anyone there at all. I wrote three pieces, and for the third, I had Liz and Rebecca dancing in G-strings. Just for the hell of it. I didn't think much about it, just doing it to do something, and of course, for the money, because I didn't have any.

When I go to play, there are only about twenty people in the crowd. It feels very odd and naked. But it seems like everyone who is there is somebody. I can't remember now exactly who. I know Francesco and Alba Clemente were there, John Sayles and his producer, and a couple other people of note. So it's a small room already and it feels uncomfortably empty and intimate. I can usually pull this kind of thing off, but tonight the sound is shitty and I can't.

I haven't really prepared much and the people who are there are almost all heavyweights in one form or another. I don't even know how they could have found out about it, but it's embarrassing to have them witness this tawdry fiasco. Liz and Rebecca both have glitter all over themselves, which eventually gets all over me. Glitter is hard to get off, so I'm covered in glitter when I go onstage.

The Village Voice did an article on me and I shared the cover of the paper with Whoopi Goldberg. When the band first started, we used to go and wait to get the *Voice* the night before it came out at Astor Place. We wanted to see if we had been picked for "Voice Choice," a listing of which bands were best to see that week. It was exciting.

Once, when I called Robert Christgau, the editor of the section, I got his wife on the phone. Christgau gave us a Voice Choice pretty much every time we played. But I had to inform him that we were playing, and now I had his wife on the phone. I had to tell her to tell him before noon or it would miss the deadline. I'd just woken up and the words were coming out garbled and sideways.

Try saying "Lounge Lizards" right after you wake up. She couldn't understand me.

"Can you please tell Robert that The Lounge Lizards are playing this week, on Friday?"

"Excuse me, who?"

"The Lounge Lizards."

"The Lungers?"

"No, The Lounge Lizards."

"I'm sorry, I don't understand."

"The Lounge Lizards."

"The Lozenges?"

"Yes, that's right, The Lozenges."

I went to the newsstand to buy *The Village Voice* with the feature about me. I kind of skulked in and tucked it under my arm like I was buying porn. I felt so uncomfortable with the whole situation.

I took the paper and went onto the basketball court across from the police station on Fifth Street, where I used to make Jean-Michel play. It was cold, leaves were blowing out on the court, nobody was out. I sat back against the mesh fence to read the article. I didn't want anyone to see me reading it.

The guy who wrote it had hung out with me for a couple of days. I hadn't really done an article like this before. I hadn't hidden anything from the guy. I was naïve enough to think that he would have the good taste not to put in personal stuff that had nothing to do with my work. Or if he did put in this personal stuff, that he would get it right. It wasn't as bad as what *The New Yorker* did to my life years later, but it was bad. And sloppy and worthless. There seems to often be something deeply wrong with these people who pretend to be journalists but are really professional gossipers. Their articles tend to have more to do with the psychological deformities of the writer than anything else.

The article was a lot more personal than I had expected. There was stuff in there about Liz that just had no business being in there, and there was a line that said: "Liz, his girlfriend, there are always lots of girlfriends . . . ," or something to that effect. That must have made Liz feel awful.

I felt invaded. Defiled.

One thing that really struck me as awful and just wrong was how he treated my mom's death in conjunction with Werner Herzog going crazy over my acting at a Telluride press conference. When he asked me about how I felt about Werner's exorbitant declaration, I explained that Werner had made one of my mom's favorite movies, and so his outburst had really warmed me. I said, "I wish I could call her and tell her." But he has me quoted in the article as just saying, "Oh, well." Like "Okay, my mom is dead, means nothing, let's move on!"

If I am going to share with you something about my mom, who has just died, man, put a little something about it in the article, you little parasite.

He wrote all this stuff about my personal life and got it all wrong.

Frank the Manager calls.

"They want you on *Letterman*."

"Really? I guess, okay."

I had seen Letterman be snide to a couple of musicians before, so I didn't really want to do it.

"You have to go and tell three funny stories."

"Okay, I can tell three funny stories."

"No, you have to go and tell three funny stories to the producer first and then they will decide to have you on or not."

"I have to audition? Forget it, Frank, I'm not going to audition to be on a talk show."

"This will be good for your career. You have to do it. That's how it's done."

"I don't have a career and it's not how I'm going to 'done.' What's with the Bottom Line gig?"

Frank had been hired to handle The Lounge Lizards; he was supposed to get the band a record deal. The acting fame thing just sort of fell in his lap.

"I haven't called them yet."

"That's great, Frank. I'm not gonna go. Letterman is a snerb."

"What's a snerb?"

"I don't know, I think I just made it up, but I'm not going."

Frank books the audition anyway, thinking he can convince me when the time comes.

But I am with Rammellzee, Toxic, A1, a bunch of other graffiti painters, and Liz in Paul's loft on Broadway near Waverly Place. We are getting high and painting in a mad flurry. I've disappeared into a wonderful, exotic world for a couple of days. When I get it together to call my answering machine, there are frantic messages from Frank and a message from David Letterman's office asking if I plan to make it to my ten-thirty A.M. appointment, as it was now eleven A.M.

Years later, when I started my own label for the *Voice of Chunk* record, I tried to get on *Letterman* to promote it. But they said, "I'm sorry, but we have it in our records that you did not show up for your pre-interview in 1984."

"Wow, that was six years ago. You guys are like the FBI."

24

The Stick, to Whom All Praise Is Due

For the most part I've left heroin behind. I thought that I needed it to write music, but I don't. I've got things to do. The music is something special now. I can't disrespect it.

The band plays in New York and it is starting to be great. It's wild and soulful and pretty much a blast.

It is hell running a band this size, especially when there is so little money. But the music makes it worth it. Makes it way beyond worth it.

William Morris wants to take me to the Russian Tea Room to discuss being my acting agent. This seems big time, the royal treatment. My uncle Jerry used to talk about the Russian Tea Room like it was a place that indicated something special.

The strange thing is that no matter how clean I look in the mirror at my apartment, when I get to the William Morris offices, under those lights, I am somehow fetid and soiled.

William Morris, which has pursued me like mad, once they have signed me, convince me that nobody has a clue who I am. They manipulate me into auditioning for dozens of the worst movies ever made.

I am bad at auditioning. I don't have acting chops. I can act if I am in something and find the character's skin. But there is no way that for five minutes in an office, sitting across from a casting agent, I can possibly do that. I don't want to be good at that.

Years later, I learned that my subsequent agent, Kevin Huvane, hated my guts. Like I had done some horrible thing to him. And I cannot, for the life of me, understand what that can be about. I was really only interested in the music. My blood was in the music. Acting was something that would be nice if the right thing came along. If I got an awful script, I wouldn't go in. And they were usually awful. But apparently Kevin Huvane still actively hates me to this day. I tried to call his office a couple of years ago to find out what that was about, but he wouldn't take my call.

Sitting there waiting for three hours to meet John Landis is not how I want to spend my time. I just cannot do that.

I would never have said this out loud to anyone, but my life goal was to find and express God through music. I was living in a culture that would scoff at this idea, and with all the sex and drugs this probably seems suspicious, but that honestly was my goal.

I met with the Coen brothers for the lead in *Miller's Crossing* but didn't get the part. I have a lot of respect for the Coen brothers and would have liked to work with them.

I didn't bother to go in for the meeting for *Reservoir Dogs*. The dialogue in the script seemed so silly because of the characters' names. Mr. Pink says this. Mr. White replies this, Mr. Pink says this, and Mr. Black says this. The way it read was ludicrous.

Other than those two movies, there really was nothing I was sorry that I was not in.

I go out to L.A. to do press for *Stranger Than Paradise*. Say more too-open stuff to *The Hollywood Reporter,* am misquoted and embarrassed again.

While I'm out there, William Morris sets up a meeting with a casting agent for a western with a bunch of stars in it. It has been impressed on me that this woman is very, very important. I'm out standing in the hallway, waiting to see her, the producer, and the director.

My stomach is upset, from breakfast at Duke's. It's gurgling and it burns.

As they call me in, a memorably horrendous fart rises up inside of me.

I think that it's fine, I'll leave it in the hallway. But this molten horror fart stays in the cloth of my pants.

It enters the room with me. It wafts into every corner, burning chips of paint off of the ceiling. Scalding the eyes of the casting agent's assistant.

Nearly everyone dies. I begin to sweat.

I think that fart ended my acting career, right there.

I call Rudy but his phone has been disconnected. I call his job, but they are weird on the phone, say he's not there, but there is something hidden in what they are saying. Call the next day and get the same evasive treatment, odd pauses in their responses. Something is up. The third day, when it happens again, I ask to speak to the supervisor.

"I'm a good friend of Rudy's from New York and this is the only number I have for him. When I call here I get this weird feeling from the people I'm talking to. Can you tell me if something is wrong or can you give me his home address?"

He doesn't know what to say. Legally he probably should not give me the address, but the guy is very human.

"If you're really his friend, maybe you can help him. I think he needs help." He gives me Rudy's address.

At seven P.M. that night, I've finished my interviews and I'm getting ready to leave my room at the Chateau Marmont. The news comes on as I look for the car keys. They are talking about thirteen murders that have happened in the last week. Right where Rudy lives. This neighborhood has erupted in bloodshed and they don't know why.

I start to drive out there and it is freaky. A guy crosses the street looking straight ahead, he pays no attention to my car as it approaches. His left arm is down by his side and he is nonchalantly carrying a ridiculously large handgun. He is hiding it from no one.

At the next stoplight a prostitute is standing there waving at me. She's completely naked but for a white towel, half pulled around her waist and half falling to the ground. A purple high-heeled shoe on one foot. She has the grinning leer of complete madness. At every corner there is more mayhem. Illicit insanity is everywhere.

It is the first week of crack.

There should have been banners: "WELCOME, CRACK!"

I find Rudy's place and knock on the door. He answers it, and his smiling face is so gaunt that I just stare at him in disbelief. He has easily lost a hundred pounds. That Buddha countenance is still there, but he is skinny as a rail. He doesn't seem the least bit surprised to see me.

His apartment is tiny. People keep knocking on his door to see what is going on, if he has anything. They have seen this white man arrive.

Everyone refers to everyone else as "scandalous."

His phone's cut off, they've taken his car, and he is going to get evicted in a couple of days.

He seems fine with it all. He is still somehow in that Buddha light of acceptance, but his body is addicted to crack. "This is where I am right now. This is my path."

Instead of trying to talk him out of anything, because there is no point, I just got high with him. Even though I had interviews in the morning and had vowed to be sharp. It seemed the least I could do. We went to the liquor store to get some rum to use instead of water in the pipe. The guy in the liquor store, as he handed me my change, said, "Sometimes the pipe talks back to you." Wow, the whole neighborhood was like a crack ashram.

At around five A.M. I said good night to Rudy. I realized that I would probably never see him again. I was so fucked up that I had to drive right in the middle of the taillights of the truck in front of me. I was lucky, very lucky, that that truck had the same exit off the freeway or I would have had to drive all the way to the ocean, not having the ability to see, drive, and read the highway signs to pick an exit all at the same time.

I went back to New York and was about to go on tour. Jean-Michel decided that he wanted to give me a giant going away dinner at Mr. Chow's. It had something to do with the *Voice* article, which had touched on all of my various projects up to that time. He amazed me when he admitted that he was jealous of all the things that I had done. That was very much not his style.

He was so tough and so sensitive at the same time. He always shocked me like that. He would be competitive past the brink of cruelty when he was ahead and then show enormous warmth and vulnerability a day later.

His idea was that we should join forces and each invite ten of the most interesting people we knew. At the time it seemed contrived, but the dinner really was incredible when I look back on it: Wim Wenders, Francesco and Alba Clemente, Julian and Jacqueline Schnabel, Joe Ende, Boris Policeband, Steve Rubell, Bianca Jagger, Tony Garnier, Andy Warhol, Tom Waits and Kathleen Brennan, Jim Jarmusch and Sara Driver, me and Liz. This dinner is where Jim Jarmusch met Tom Waits for the first time.

Andy Warhol was so impressed that he later said in his diary that it was the best party he'd been to in ten years. That he was going to start hanging out with artists because they were so much more interesting than the kind of people he had been hanging out with.

Now, in a certain way this is a big deal. Your party is the best party Andy Warhol has been to in ten years.

But, of course, when Andy's tapes were transcribed into what later was released as *The Andy Warhol Diaries,* Tom Waits and I were mistakenly turned into John Waite, who had a hit song that year.

John Waite would send letters to my office saying thank you for turning him into one of the cool people.

On the plane to Europe the movie is *Sweet Dreams,* the film in which Jessica Lange plays Patsy Cline. The movie is going along and then abruptly ends. A completely unresolved, nonsensical ending. Ribot starts laughing and saying loudly, so anyone within five rows of him can hear, "Patsy Cline died in a plane crash! I guess they didn't want to show that part on the plane!" And then laughs really loudly some more.

The first night of the tour is in Berlin. There is a church in Berlin that stands from before the war. The outside walls are riddled with bullet holes from World War II. The first time I walked by it, picking up someone from the train station late at night, I was moved almost to tears. I didn't expect it, it just welled up in me, to feel what actually happened there.

We've arrived from New York that morning and we're trying to stay awake until a reasonable hour to try to slip past the jet lag. We go for dinner and then a bunch of us go for a blurry walk. By the train station, by the zoo, and then just as we get to the church, I see a tree branch lying on the ground. It is fairly straight and about the length and width of a long broomstick. There really is absolutely nothing special about it.

I rush and pick it up. I hold it over my head.

I yell, "The Stick!"

Dougie yells in response, "The Stick!"

I yell, "The Stick!"

Everybody yells, "The Stick!"

"Bless The Stick, to whom all praise is due!"

"The Stick!"

So I carry The Stick and bring it back to my room.

The next morning at breakfast, I come down in the elevator with The Stick. A bunch of the guys are sitting having breakfast in a large, crowded buffet room. I stand on a chair at their table. The faces of the dining Germans look almost ill.

I yell, "The Stick!"

Dougie yells, "The Stick!" and stands up and waves his spoon at it.

Roy shakes his head and smiles. Ribot laughs.

I storm off, stop halfway across the dining room, and turn to face them. "The Stick!"

They all stand, brandishing spoons and bowls of oatmeal.

"The Stick!"

Then I swing The Stick violently in the air, with the whooshing sound filling the buffet hall, which is now mostly people staring at their food and not speaking for fear of becoming involved in this horror the Ugly Americans have brought to their breakfast.

The Stick is entrusted to Pascale, the tour manager. She was there when The Stick was discovered. The Stick travels on the tour bus with the guitars and horns. It is given a place of honor at all times.

We bring The Stick out onstage before the show and lean it against the bass drum. Center stage. After the third song, which is the first break in the set, I pick it up over my head and proudly yell, "The Stick!"

The band yells, "The Stick!"

Dougie does it the best because he is five foot four and very cute, so when he does something rousing or macho, it's heartwarming.

I explain to the audience the nobility of The Stick. Some seem to understand.

After about ten days of this, The Stick actually begins to take on a certain aura. There really is something to this stick, because we have invested so much energy into it. It also somehow stands for the band, a ritual for the tribe. An icon without a religion.

When Pascale leaves it behind in Austria, we are all deeply upset. Me, most of all.

The press is relentless. We said in advance to the promoters that no journalists or photographers were to be allowed at sound check, but they are everywhere. It is explained that I will only do press about the band or the music. It doesn't matter.

It is hard to concentrate. The only safe place is playing music onstage.

The band is great. Getting better and better. We're finding things.

I finish my interviews in a side room and walk into the sound check at the Metropol in Berlin on the first night. Dougie and Erik have already checked. I say, "Listen to this," and play them a melody I wrote after finally getting past heroin. It has some heart in it. Dougie adds a kind of go-go beat behind me and Erik starts playing. Erik is perfect at conceiving the simplest, most elegant bass lines, and in about four minutes we've written "Big Heart." It will become our signature tune, the one we close with, for years. That night we play it at an overly packed Metropol, and the crowd goes insane.

I keep trying to call Liz at my place but get no answer and no answering machine. Call at all different hours and don't reach her.

Finally I call Seth, who is Rebecca's boyfriend. They are living in my building in Eric Mitchell's place upstairs. I ask Seth to knock on my door and see if Liz is there. Maybe there's something wrong with the phone. But I am getting really worried about her.

Seth tells me that my door is open and that there is no one there. I call Seth the next day and my door is still open with no sign of Liz.

I go to lunch with Evan somewhere in Germany. There is a German and English menu. One of the specialties of the house is loin, but they have written "Lion."

The waiter comes to take our order. Evan says, "The lion, is that a whole lion?"

The waiter stares at him blankly.

We love that. We collect stuff from the hotels, especially in Italy. Destroyed English-language instructions. I have a sign I took from a hotel in Milan that says:

IN CASE OF SMELLING OF FIRE.
LEAVE ROOM WITHOUT MUCH EXCITEMENT.
FROM LINE BY ADVISE OF HALL PORTER.
BID OTHERS HELLO.

The tour manager puts two bottles of Stoli on the floor of the stage every night. They are always finished by the end of the show. That's what we drink when we're thirsty. People in the audience ask if they are props, but they most certainly are not. I never, or at least rarely, get drunk during the show. Usually the adrenaline and concentration keep me sober and lucid. A half hour after the show, I am smashed. After all the equipment is packed up, we go to a restaurant, then back to the hotel.

I can never calm down. If I am with a girl, it helps. If there is no girl, I am frantic. Can barely stand it.

And then I get up after an hour or two of sleep, still drunk and smelling like an ashtray. Try to find everything and throw my stuff into the suitcase and take the train to the next gig, which could easily be a ten-hour trip.

It's all pretty much a blur. When I started writing this book, I called Erik Sanko to help remind me of stories I might want to add. Erik started recounting stories, all about himself, that had occurred in cities I am sure I have never been to.

After playing in Berlin, the first night of The Stick tour, we were on the train from Berlin to Hamburg. I only vaguely remember this, but Ribot told me about it months later. It was the morning train and it was all businessmen. Properly dressed and all reading their papers. Apparently, I stood in the aisle, swaying with my shirt wrapped around my neck, exposing my hairy stomach and singing at the top of my lungs:

MY STOMACH HAS A BEARD AND IT LIKES TO PLAY WITH
OINTMENT!

MY STOMACH IS THE PRINCE OF MANY TOWNS AND VILLAGES!

MY PENIS HAS A FACE AND IT LIKES TO BARK AT GERMANS!

MY STOMACH IS A MAN WHO SINGS THIS SAD SAD SONG.

I'm glad that Ribot wrote down the words and reminded me of this, because I used these lyrics for the *Marvin Pontiac* album years later.

But we were intolerable. I apologize to anyone who ever had to travel in proximity to us. While flying to Europe, we were trying to establish whether the plane would weigh any less if the whole band jumped in the air at the same time. If my theory was correct, the plane should have lurched forward.

One, two, three! We all jumped in the aisle, making the rest of the passengers very uneasy.

Flying to Brazil, we took turns running the water and observing the sink in the bathroom to see if it would suddenly go down the drain in the other direction as we went over the equator.

I finally get Liz, not a clue what she's been up to and don't even ask why my door has been open for five days. I know I won't get a straight answer. I fly her over to meet us, more to keep her safe than anything else.

I pick her up at the airport somewhere in the south of France. I am so happy to see her coming through the gate, and what is really sweet is that while I'm hugging her, I can see the band watching us; they know what I went through those days when it seemed Liz had been swallowed by an evil shadow, and they all just are kind of beaming back, especially Roy. Like they're happy for my happiness.

This is very rare in life, when people are genuinely happy for you when something good finally happens.

25

Cheese or Hats Are Preferable

Once I saw Bob Marley on TV, doing nothing but dancing behind some other people singing. It was so open and disarming. He was honestly dancing like no one was watching. It looked a bit ludicrous and spasmodic, which made it even more appealing. I thought the same thing as I did when I listened to Martin Luther King Jr. for the first time: "God is coming through that man." And oddly enough, Andy Warhol made the same impression on me.

I had expected not to like Andy, that he would be phony and a user of people's energy, like a little mean-spirited vampire, but that wasn't the case at all.

Andy exuded something that was truly beautiful and almost religious in a way. He could be subtly snide, but in general there was something genuinely spiritual about the man.

He and I and Jean-Michel went to the premiere of the Brian De Palma movie *Body Double*. I watched Jack Nicholson get out of the limousine in front of us and throw his arms out wide and his head back with a taunting smile, to greet the sea of loud, clamoring paparazzi. He made them love him. It was almost as if he was emanating more than they could possibly parasite off of him.

I was impressed. I could never do that. I could absolutely never do that, at least back then. I was shy. I hated fame.

Now, this was a terrible movie, the audience there that night knew it was a terrible movie, and I was quite positive that Andy knew it was a terrible movie. After the movie was over, people were filing out, clearly discontent with what they had seen. Andy turned to me, gently took my arm, and asked in the sweetest way, "Was that any good?"

I loved him. He was in tune with something so pure that I was actually a little nervous to be around him, and not because he was Andy Warhol, but because his perceptions, in their completely unassuming way, were so succinct.

Willie Mays was always with Andy around this time. There was clearly a lot of love between them, though Andy's reasons for being attracted to Willie and Willie's reasons for his attraction to Andy were wildly different and incompatible, and that made it feel a little off. But still, there was something quite beautiful about it. Stealing the Everlast boxing shorts photo idea bothered me for a long time, but I have officially let it go at this point. Or maybe I haven't quite.

One night, we were somewhere and I had to call my manager, Frank, to pick us up because there was a taxi strike. It felt like we were twelve and had wandered way off and someone had to call their dad to drive us home.

So Frank picks us up. He is really nervous to have Andy Warhol in his car. We are coming downtown on Seventh Avenue, which has been divided into a two way street because part of Sixth is closed off.

There are traffic cones dividing the street. We are stopped at a light when a guy in a fancy, low sports car comes bombing through from the other direction.

The car looks more like it should be on a racetrack than the streets of Manhattan. The guy, at high speed, is weaving in and out of the cones, like he is slaloming. Knocking each one over with a gentle, expert nudge. The naughtiness and the immense driving skill are something to see.

Jean-Michel is yelling with delight, "He's bad, man! He's really bad! Oh, he is bad, man!" And Andy is sitting there, quite calmly, going, "Oh my . . . ," like your grandmother at the end of a fireworks display.

* * *

Liz and I move out to Brooklyn, Fort Greene, way before it becomes gen-trified. There is a basement where I am supposed to work on music, and Liz has a spare room for herself. I will barely ever practice or write music in the musty basement, and Liz's room will serve to harbor a four-foot-high pile of clothing with a couple of childhood stuffed animals sticking their legs out and not much else.

On the day we move in, Roy and some people drive us out there with what little furniture I have. After we unload the stuff, I don't want them to leave. I am terrified to let them leave. What are we going to do out here in Brooklyn? We'll only have each other to talk to, and sometimes Liz just stops talking and stares at the wall for hours. I can't just walk outside and run into people I know.

This is in 1984, in Fort Greene. There are no restaurants. We will starve.

The next morning I go out of the house and it's kind of nice. Trees line the street. At one end of the block is a bunch of wild, young crimi-nals, but the other way there is a nice park and it feels okay. I haven't been out of the house in the daytime in months. It seems kind of optimistic.

I find an old desk with the upper-right drawer nailed closed. Hand-written in pen, on the drawer, it says, "Remember What's In There."

I get the desk home and manage to carefully pry the drawer open. "Remember What's In There" refers to three photographs that, from the color, look to be about twenty years old. The photos are of a white GI and two Vietnamese kids. They were taken at a picnic table in an area surrounded by concrete. I can only assume that these are his kids, and that he was forced to abandon them when he was shipped home. It just breaks my heart.

I also find a big piece of wood, which I bring home for no reason. It's the wood I'll later use for the *Uncle Wiggly as the Devil* painting that ends up being the cover for the *No Pain for Cakes* album.

Eric Goode and his brother had a big dinner at Mr. Chow. They had done something at their club, Area, with every artist you could think of: Andy

Warhol, Julian Schnabel, David Hockney, Keith Haring, Francesco Clemente, Robert Mapplethorpe, and on and on—even LeRoy Neiman, with
his pet mustache, was there. They were about to do a group photo of the
event, and Jean-Michel, who had arrived wearing a bird's nest on his
head, started demanding, yelling actually, "John Lurie can't be in the
photo! He's not an artist! John Lurie can't be in the photo!"

I just stared at him and laughed. Jean-Michel was the only person in
the room who knew I was a painter. We'd painted together for hundreds
and hundreds of hours.

So fine, I don't care if I'm in the photo or not. But then, just at the
last second, I decide, *Fuck it,* and go running in just as they are about to
snap the picture. If you see this photo, that explains why William Weg-
man, who is standing next to me, is laughing so hard.

It doesn't work. Liz and I are not good. She's getting high and I'm fed up.
We said we'd stop and she just keeps hiding it from me.

We're out in Brooklyn and there are no restaurants anywhere
nearby. There is a tiny little place that has takeout food by a Jamaican
lady, but it's hardly ever open. The deal was that if we moved out there,
which I didn't really want to do, then Liz would cook. At least breakfast,
which she does on occasion, but with such seething irritation that it
doesn't seem safe to eat.

I suggest that she open a restaurant in the neighborhood. Oatmeal
could be her specialty. In fact, she could serve only oatmeal. When people come in to order, she could take her big spoon and slop it into their
bowl. She could spit, "Here!" at them like she does at me, while the customers cower in fear.

Liz laughs so cutely when I say that. It's strange, that thing where
you are with someone and it's over. It's cold and over. And you want it to
be over, but then she does this little something, a laugh, a quizzical turn
of the head. Something, just some little thing, and your heart melts to
her again.

Liz goes to her parents' place in New Hampshire to dry out. Women
are everywhere, constantly coming at me, but I don't want them.

Liz comes back and she's getting high immediately. Things aren't
good.

I stay out all night to give her a dose of her own medicine, and when I come home at like eight in the morning, she is in the kitchen with this creepy coke dealer guy that we both know. They both look at me, don't say anything. Something unseemly has happened. It's in the air. This is not a threat to me, this guy is a joke. I would have thought that if Liz was going to cheat on me she would have picked someone classier.

I just say, "Unbelievable," and they both leave without a word as they study the floor in front of them.

I also fire Frank. No Liz and no Frank. They hated each other. Always in some kind of competition, they each wanted the other one gone. The two people I talked to every day are now, suddenly, out of my life. My support system is gone. I get really depressed and just sit in the one chair in that apartment for a couple of days. I don't eat, don't leave the house. Don't move.

Then I watch Villanova, shockingly, upset Georgetown in the NCAA finals on my little black and white TV balanced on a chair, and it makes me come back to life. I hop in the shower, get dressed, and go out to a nightclub.

I give Liz the apartment on Third Street for the time being. I still see her once in a while. I said to her once, "If we break up, all I ask is that you don't sleep with Jean-Michel."

Of course, that is immediately what she does, and then she sleeps with Danny Rosen for good measure.

For a thousand dollars I bought this enormous gold Cadillac. It was the biggest car ever made. It was bigger than a van. Kind of had to steer it like a boat. I once drove all eight guys in the band comfortably to the airport.

I wanted to glue giant bull horns to the front of the car, but it died before I got around to it.

Since there was no food near my house, I had to come into Manhattan for every meal, because I didn't cook. I was lonely and never wanted to go home. I started sleeping with lots of women. A lot of them were beautiful, classy women, but just as many were women I would scarf up at a bar at three forty-five A.M. before it closed.

I went out with this wacko woman to Jackson Heights in Queens after the bar closed. She was the only woman left in the place, so she would have to do. Her name was Mona. She was talking and talking and then suddenly, out of nowhere, she would get really mean.

It turned out that Dougie had slept with her too. Dougie said, "Mona! She's crazy! When I fucked her, after I came, she yelled at me, 'Now get up and wash your hands!'"

If there was no girl, I'd drive back over the Manhattan Bridge with the sun coming up, so drunk that I would have to brace myself in order to drive. There is a part of the bridge where the road changes to grating, and there would be a sudden shift in the sound under the tires. Every night I forgot about it, and every night it scared me.

In the morning, while all the other cars were parked neatly, parallel to the curb, my big gold Cadillac would be parked almost perpendicular, blocking half the street.

I was at some gigantic fancy party at a club. Vince Gallo comes over and grabs me by the arm. He keeps saying, "You have to meet Val. You have to meet Val."

I let Vince Gallo drag me for a few feet and am in front of Val Kilmer. Vince yells, "John, this is Val Kilmer!"

Val Kilmer has not been in anything that I have seen. I have no idea who he is. But he looks at me as though I smell very badly. Sneers. And then walks away.

I say, "Thanks, Vince," and turn to go, when I bump into a woman holding a little placard. Apparently, the theme of this party is mystics. And this woman is a fortune teller.

Now she grabs me by the arm. I'm thinking, *I don't like this fame thing, people keep grabbing me by the arm.*

She says that I must go to St. Lucia. That I will have a spiritual experience that will change my life.

So a few months later, I book a trip to St. Lucia. I had discovered that disappearing to places like this really restores me, especially if I went alone and before the Internet made it impossible to get completely away from everything.

I'm on this deserted beach and swim out with my snorkel gear. I see a barracuda and follow it. It isn't big, two and a half feet or so. I'm sort of messing with it, diving down behind it. I look up and see a guy with dreadlocks sitting near my stuff on the abandoned beach, so I start to swim back.

To my surprise, the barracuda turns and is now following me. "You fucked with me, I will now fuck with you."

I get to the shore and say hello to the guy sitting near my stuff. He has a nice enough face. I have learned over time how to quickly read someone and am rarely wrong.

He tells me about a party in the neighboring town and says he will pick me up around nine. I say okay.

He picks me up on a motorcycle and I get on the back. He races through the narrow, dusty streets, darting in and out of traffic.

We get to the village and the party is the whole town. People are out and dancing everywhere. He buys me a beer and asks if I want to get some cocaine.

I say okay and he asks for $5, which I give him. He is back in a moment with this little ball of something between crack and coke. I taste it with my finger. It doesn't seem too strong or too cut with anything horrendous, so when he breaks it up and rolls it in a cigarette, I smoke it with him.

He sees some friends. We buy more coke. This is all pretty fun, really. We go back into an alley and smoke the cocaine cigarettes. It goes on for a while.

Around midnight the party starts to die down and he says we should go to another town. I get on the back of his bike and we go there.

It is basically the same thing. He and I and a few other guys are drinking beer and buying these little balls of cocaine.

This other guy, who doesn't seem to be part of their group, sits down next to me and asks, would I like to meet a woman.

I say, "I always want to meet a woman." And don't think much about it.

Around four in the morning I am getting ready to figure out how to get back to my place when this guy appears on a motorcycle with a woman on the back.

He tells me I can have sex with her for $30.

I say that there must have been a misunderstanding, I don't want to pay anyone to have sex.

He starts to insist that I have sex with her.

I tell him that this is nuts. And I am going home.

He says that I have to pay anyway because he has gone back to his village to get her.

It is starting to get heated. I walk away. He pulls out this gigantic knife, basically a small machete, and starts coming at me.

I run to the other side of a parked car. Now there is no one out. Just me and this guy brandishing the giant knife. He is on the other side of the car. Whichever way he goes, I go the other.

This is pretty frightening. Except this game of circling the car goes on for maybe ten minutes. It is beginning to seem ridiculous. I can avoid him all night if that is what he wants.

So I start to laugh.

His face swarms with something I can only call sadness. His head falls down in sorrow. If I am no longer scared, he has lost all the power in this situation. He walks away almost sulking.

Go to see Liz on Third Street. She is sinking. The phone keeps ringing and it is Mel Bernstein. Off of the answering machine speaker I hear message after message in Mel's angry, exasperated voice asking how she could have done this to him. Mel is a journalist and writer we used to get high with. He lives right down the block on the corner of Third Street. In one of Jean-Michel's paintings there is a map of Third Street with Mel's and my apartments. My place is listed as "Willie" or "Big Willie."

Mel is calling and calling, screaming for Liz to pick up. He is not someone you would think of as a tough guy, but on the answering machine he sounds ferocious and right. Liz is lying on the bed sucking her thumb and turns her face to the wall.

"What did you do to Mel?"

"Ah, nothing, he's a jerk," she says, not removing her thumb from her mouth.

A couple of hours later there is a knock at the door. It's Mel, and he seems like he's about to explode. He is standing over Liz, yelling. Liz is lying on the mattress and just looks off toward the wall, like Mel is an annoying bug. Mel gets so pissed that he starts to go at her. I grab his arms from behind—I'm stronger than him—and start to negotiate him out of the apartment. Whatever has happened, I am sure Mel is in the right, but I can't let him attack Liz like this. Right before I get him out the door, he grabs a beer bottle off the table and smashes it against the sink, so that it breaks perfectly into a weapon. I'm impressed, like, *Mel, I didn't know you had it in you.*

Mel holds the bottle up to my face.

"What are you going to do, Mel, cut me in my own apartment?"

Then Mel just looks really sad and leaves.

That is twice in two months that someone has come close to stabbing me and then walked away looking crestfallen.

I was still very poor. The money from the film score was gone in no time. I was invited to Francesco Clemente's house for dinner. Jean-Michel was there; Julian Schnabel; Bryan Ferry, who had been very sweet to me when I had dinner with him on the first Lounge Lizards tour; the art dealer Bruno Bischofberger; and Andy Warhol. When I walked in, Andy said, "Oh, it's the movie star!" I wasn't sure how to take it, thought it might have been Andy's version of an insult. He seemed to have a rule about never saying anything bad about anyone.

There was something in the level of congratulatory mutual admiration that rubbed me wrong. They were having dinner at this ostentatious table that Julian had made for Francesco. The table had sharp wire mesh hanging down underneath. Julian said it wasn't finished yet. Francesco and Alba had small kids. Were the kids to go running underneath this new kitchen table, they would surely have been decapitated. No one seemed to mind.

It was just too much. My poverty was making me bitter, so I got drunk and went sour on the lot of them. What on earth made every napkin they drooled on valuable?

I said too loudly, "How does it work? You drool on a napkin. Bruno decides that it is valuable. You sell it and then go out and buy this thousand dollar bottle of wine? I can appreciate that you guys are enjoying the fact that your work sells for a fortune, and for the most part I believe your work is good, but you must have some idea how many great artists there are taking quarters in tollbooths or living on the outskirts of Coney Island, who are as talented as you."

There was a hush. I had not actually offended anyone. They were unoffendable.

I had only shown myself to be uncouth. I was out of the club.

I was upstairs at Squat Theatre when the phone rang. Peter Halasz seemed very annoyed with whoever he was talking to.

I asked, "Who was that?"

He said, "They keep calling me to speak on new technology in the theater in Barcelona and I am not interested."

I said, "I would love to go to Barcelona."

Peter kind of tilted his head and smiled at me, almost a leer. He didn't even say it, I just knew what he was thinking: that I knew absolutely nothing about new technology in the theater and now he was daring me to go. So I went.

The only requirement was that I talk for forty-five minutes. I thought, *I can do that.*

I imagined a small group of depressed men with beards sitting in a circle in a musty room on the third floor, leather patches on the elbows of their worn tweed jackets.

They won't speak much English. They'll think that they haven't really understood. I'll ramble on for a while, see Barcelona, and collect my $500. Everything will be fine.

A sexy young lady meets me at the airport. She is to be my escort, as I am a distinguished visitor.

She spends a couple of days taking me to the Gaudí buildings, which really floor me.

She shows me an entranceway to a building with odd shapes of metal surrounding glass.

She tells me that Gaudí had had this very special, expensive glass brought from Paris. When it arrived he had them push it over so it would smash on the street. Then he took the broken pieces and built the metal frame around it.

That an artist, a real artist, could be supported by the financial and political powers of the time just blew my mind. Those powers usually are intent on stopping and disappearing the artist.

This conference is actually for some enormous and very stiff congress of international theater. There are thousands of people attending from all over the world and they take themselves very seriously. I get a little worried.

I try talking in my room for forty-five minutes. I find talking for forty-five minutes about nonsense very difficult.

On the day of my talk, I am brought to an enormous, elegant theater.

"This is where I am speaking?"

As I'm ushered down the aisle by my young, sexy friend, I begin to get really nervous. I see that there are at least seven hundred people there waiting for my lecture in the packed hall. Many of them had tweed jackets and beards, as I had expected, but these seven hundred men and women are from all over the world, and they do not look depressed at all. Their tweed jackets are not worn and they all carry an expression of sternness that is on the edge of angry.

And they are all wearing headphones! Which means that everything I say is going to be translated and actually understood.

I am in trouble.

I brought a little clock to make sure I go on for forty-five minutes. I place it on the podium.

"In theater," I begin, "and this happens often"—I paused and looked out at the sea of serious faces—"you will have several tangents that approach the stage and move slowly, even as far as the curtain. You can take these lines to mean one of countless things, but as they are spread out, and slowly you can do that so that even a child who is counting his fingers can read just how many times.

"Or you can fix it with glue. Or a piece of string. I like string myself. I've got no problem with that, but now, cowboys are all out singing in the desert, and they sing with these falsetto voices that are annoying the neighboring villages that meet solely on the same part we were talking about, before making it almost impossible to gauge where the sound is coming from. And you can have six of them, if you can afford that."

There is a slight grumble in the audience.

"Or fluidly. More fluidly than before, one can stretch it slowly back and forth to meet with just about any place that strikes your interest. Timing is of the essence, and particularly those who like that kind of thing, or cheese or hats. Cheese or hats are preferable because they are smaller and don't cause so much trouble when you try to put them in the case when you pack up."

The grumbling grows louder.

"You can take these vectors and measure them. But if you do I hope you have kept the string that I mentioned earlier. You might all want to make a note of this now."

Someone in the back yells something angrily. People around him tell him to be quiet.

"You can pile these vectors on top of each other. It really does depend a lot on what your budget is. The bell is ringing. Just like for dinner. In all forms of theater, and in most recording processes, a small barking dog or an accident on the highway can be measured, especially by someone who really cares about these things, and you have to have a large pot or some form of hamburger. Hamburger that you can see all over the highway."

The angry man yells again. Another angry man stands up and yells something from the other side of the hall. People tell them to be quiet. But what is odd to me, is that the people silencing the angry men sound angry as well, like they are defending me.

"Five, six, seven, red, green, blue. It really is all that it takes to have something really beautiful stretched out to the length of your arm. You can be sure of the result of pancakes."

There is more shouting. Back and forth. Some people are enjoying this immensely, they are beaming.

"Five, six, seven, red, green, blue. It really is all that it takes to have something really beautiful stretched out to the length of your arm. You can be sure of the result."

A fight breaks out.

I continue.

"We all take the measurements very seriously, and you can almost apply the same methods as you do when making pancakes at home with your children. God bless the children is what I always say, though they can be very messy."

As the ushers break up the first fight, another fight has started. And then a third fight starts, this one involving several people.

I go on like this for exactly forty-five minutes.

"Hamburger on the highway or other places can be gathered into large piles and then set on fire.

"Thank you!"

Several people stand up and applaud wildly. Several others are yelling in anger.

My escort says that she is in the back by the row of translation booths. When I finish, the doors fly open in a mad panic. The translators, those poor translators, mostly small balding men but a couple of plump women, race to get out of their little booths. They are gasping for air. They are drenched in sweat and mopping their brows.

One man is trembling.

I am on the cover of all the papers the next day. Most of the papers use a mad scientist photo of me, where I am holding a pair of headphones and my wind-up clock, staring at them like I have never seen more bizarre objects in my life.

26

Socks! Socks! Socks!

It really was a jail, where Liz went. She had decided to put herself in a rehab facility in New Hampshire. It wasn't one of these twenty-eight day places. It was for an indeterminate amount of time and they decided when you could leave. The people in this facility were mostly felons who'd had a choice between jail and this place and had made the horrible mistake of choosing the latter.

They weren't patients, they were inmates.

I talked to Chickie Lucas about it. Chickie had been a tough New York kid and had ended up in one of these places years before. And when I say "tough," I mean it in the best way. In order to be real, you almost have to be tough. Otherwise you are just a puff person with no real ability to stand up cleanly.

Chickie was a few years older than me, had mellowed a bit, but was still really solid. He told me, with his snaggly, rascal grin, that they had made him mop all the floors wearing diapers. That they just tried to break you, but that probably it was a good place for Liz.

A few years later Chickie died in a motorcycle accident. He died way too young. I loved Chickie Lucas, but I suppose this was the perfect way for him to go.

I always thought that if Liz could straighten up, we could make it work. But I didn't want her spirit broken. Her spirit was what I was in love with. I just didn't want her to be a lying junkie anymore.

At first, they let me write letters, but when I mentioned that I had gotten high once, they wouldn't let her see my letters anymore.

Months went by and they wouldn't let me communicate with her at all. I started to go nuts having these people blocking me from talking to her.

On her birthday, I looked into renting a helicopter so I could fly over the place with a megaphone but learned that that was illegal in numerous ways.

Liz's brother, John, came out to Brooklyn to inspect her giant pile of stuff, to see if there was anything she might want. He looked at the enormous heap and was dumbfounded.

"How does anyone live like this? What should I take?" He didn't really want to deal with it. Didn't want to take anything. I saved her little stuffed horse that she had had since she was a little girl and made John take it, at least, and her fur hat.

I was on the rebound and lost.

I had been dubbed the sexiest, coolest man in New York, which basically meant in the world, and I was a mess. While people on the outside saw my life as a wonderful, wonderful thing, I was a mess.

I devoured everything that was put in front of me. Girls, alcohol, cigarettes, drugs. I went to Area, the new club, every night. Every night I would leave as the club closed at four A.M., high on coke and drunk and with a new beautiful woman on my arm.

If I walked out without a beautiful woman on my arm, the bouncers would be shocked and comment on it in disappointment.

"You're leaving alone? Oh no! Not possible!"

There was an Italian American girl who worked as a bartender there named Mercedes. She was an exquisite beauty with dark hair, lips to write poems about, and a slight New Orleans accent. Jean-Michel said, "Mercedes was the hottest girl in town. All the boys were talking about her." And she was. Mercedes was the hottest girl in town.

I was shy to approach her. But then I was driving the Gold Cadillac Beast up First Avenue and this car swerved in front of me. I saw Mercedes scramble over the passenger seat into the back of the car. She was smiling and waving and yelling instructions to the driver, all at the same time.

But she was still too much. A girl like this just could not be interested in me. She was the best girl.

We played in New York, and the number of beautiful women available to me after the show was ridiculous. After that show, Mercedes's friend Karen came backstage and gave me Mercedes's phone number on a crumpled piece of paper, like we were in high school.

After the show someone gave me a bag of brown dope. I had pretty much cleaned myself up but snorted it. This was headache dope.

I spent the night at Mercedes's place. She was asking me questions and I was going on and on about myself. "Aren't I great?"

My head was just killing me. I was sitting on her bed holding my temples, groaning a bit.

"What do you want to do?" I asked.

"I just want you to feel better."

What a nice answer. It sounded like she meant it.

In the morning, we went in my Gold Cadillac Beast out to Brooklyn, but first I had to stop at the magazine stand and pick up an article about me that had just come out. Mercedes read the article out loud to me while I was driving over the bridge. She had that New Orleans accent, that lilt in her voice that eased out of her exquisite lips. But I was horrified. All my answers were the exact same things that I had said to her the night before. I was really becoming something exceptionally cheap.

We go out to Brooklyn and sleep. When we wake up, I pick her up off the floor, with my arms under the backs of her knees, and throttle her quite properly. I have my elbows under her knees and am holding her up against the wall. I am thinking, *Damn, this is how they fuck in the movies. Look at you.*

But this is the first and last time.

Next time I see her, something is up with my body, maybe due to my recent two week dip into heroin, I'm not sure why, but I can't get a proper hard-on. It just lies there like a squishy little thing. It gets a little life and flops around, but basically it's useless. I can't do it.

Then it happens again! Next time I see her it happens again! I can't fucking believe it. She is not sympathetic, whatsoever, and makes no attempt to put some life into the poor fallen warrior. She looks at me with disgust, then my cock withers a bit more and tries to hide up inside my stomach.

The whole thing with Mercedes only lasts a couple of weeks. I get hung up on her very quickly. While I'm sitting in the car out by my place in Brooklyn, I have this image of her walking down the street carrying our kid.

You have to be careful where the heart takes you when you are on the rebound.

She says she can't see me one night and won't say why. I park a block away from her apartment and watch her window. Pathetic. Stupid too, because you could see my giant Gold Cadillac Beast from space.

I know I don't have a chance. If you can't really fuck somebody, and all you can produce is Mr. Flaccid, you cannot hope to be taken seriously.

We have a gig at some city-sponsored outdoor event on the river, downtown. It's in the afternoon, and no one is going to see the band because everyone is going to see the Jean-Michel Basquiat–Andy Warhol show. At least no one I care about outside of my sister, Liz, who is down from Boston.

On top of that, this is the show where the poster is the two of them in Everlast boxing shorts with gloves on. My idea. And I am furious that Jean-Michel is doing our idea with Andy instead of me, and then Mercedes goes to the gallery opening instead of coming to see the band play. I am hurt and I am angry.

The show is over by the Hudson River, and afterward, I drive my giant Gold Cadillac Beast in circles at sixty miles an hour in an empty lot next door, bringing up a giant dust cloud. My sister, Liz, watches and is a little worried. Liz once had a dream that I was angry and going from room to room. After I left each room, it exploded.

Mercedes gets immediately fed up with me. She keeps doing things that upset me and I keep getting inordinately angry every time. Mercedes is used to being the terror in her relationships and isn't having it from me.

I am also becoming massively insecure from kicking heroin for the nine thousandth time. Early on, cocaine and heroin allow you to have an erection for four hours without coming. You have to piss standing on your head. But now I can't get a hard-on and I am so insecure that no one could possibly want to have anything to do with me.

I see her at Area about a week later. I tell her we need to talk. I am doing better. I'm thinking that I need a chance to show her how fantastically my penis is finally working now that I have kicked. She says she's leaving soon. We can talk outside.

I wait outside. Twenty minutes go by. I'm just standing outside waiting amid the stragglers vying to be let into the club. Finally, she comes out.

"What are you doing? I've been out here half an hour."

"I didn't tell you to wait," she says.

I want to scream that my cock is working now and she has to check it out. But I can't do that in front of the bouncers. I am their hero.

I am about to get furious, but she just walks off. I guess any chance that I had with this girl is through.

I wonder if I invented Mercedes, if, outside of her extraordinary beauty, she is not remotely the person that I created in my head. In actual fact, I am in love with Liz and just have nowhere to go with it. Or maybe that is bullshit. I have no idea why I couldn't get a hard-on. I had no problem on that first day. It only happened twice with Mercedes, but all that week my cock wasn't behaving properly, even when I was alone and tried to jerk off. Jerking off is something that I am very good at. Who the fuck knows? Because Mercedes, in her way, is very, very special.

In any case, after that night at Area, I am pretty morbid about all of this and go back out to Brooklyn. Can't sleep. I get up to drive into Manhattan to get something to eat, as the sun is coming up. The car won't start. It's completely dead.

I go to take the bike out of the trunk. I had bought this beautiful expensive bike that I would bring into Manhattan in the trunk, then find parking I didn't have to pay for and use my bike. Kind of loved this bike. Just so smooth, how it rode.

That bike could go so fast. I would always be weaving in and out of traffic, going much faster than the cars. Once I was racing down Seventh Avenue ahead of the cars as the light at Fourteenth Street turned yellow. I raced to make the light but saw this giant divot in the pavement. I was going too fast to avoid it. I went down into the divot and then the bike catapulted up, high, into the air. I managed to let go of the bike and land on my feet, running to keep up with my momentum. The bike smashed around between my legs, cutting my pants and ripping up my legs. People who were standing on Fourteenth Street watching this, as the bike flew through the air, applauded wildly when I was able to stay upright without getting really hurt.

There is a little hole under the trunk lock that I never noticed before. Open the trunk and the bike is gone. Stolen.

The car is dead. I have to pay $60 to have it taken away.

The girl, the bike, the car, all gone. Comes in threes.

Jim has written a new script, *Down by Law*. He has actually written this one. A prison movie in New Orleans with Tom Waits, Roberto Benigni, and me.

I'm not sure I want to do it. I didn't like so many things about how *Stranger* went.

But this pays $50,000. Fuck, $50,000. I kind of have to do it. I am broke and it's not like I'm selling my soul to do it.

I have a big problem with the fact that this is basically the same character I played in the other movie, and the way things were presented, people seemed to believe that that character was me and I didn't like that at all.

When Jim says that I can write some scenes for the guy to give him a different twist, I agree to do it.

The band plays the night before I leave for New Orleans to do *Down by Law*. I am pretty down about Liz and Mercedes. I am down about pretty much everything. Just as the music is starting to become something really special, no one wants to know about it. The only thing people are interested in is the movies.

The jazz world cannot possibly give us credit for making breakthroughs in their field. We started off so irreverently, being basically a punk band, that many will not look at what we're doing now with an open mind. Plus, I'm in a movie that's getting all this attention, so at best, I must be a dilettante of some kind, and the jazz purists want nothing to do with me.

Years after I became unable to play because of Lyme disease, we released a record of the trio playing live. And all the jazz press were wildly praising my playing, and it pissed me off. Where were they when this could have helped?

Lester Bangs wrote that The Lounge Lizards were "staking out new territory that lies somewhere west of Charles Mingus and east of Bernard Herrmann." But he was the only one who gave us any legitimacy back at that time.

There is a party arranged for me after the show. I go to the party and it turns out that they are charging people to get in. This isn't really a party for me. They are getting people to pay to go to their party by telling people I will be there. No one I know is there.

Life feels corrupt and hollow. And remarkably lonely.

I get to New Orleans and can't believe it. This hotel, now called the Bayou Plaza, is the hotel my family lived in for a while when I was six. We had moved from Minneapolis to New Orleans before we moved into a house on Peggy Avenue. A house with banana trees lining the backyard, with lizards and tree frogs everywhere.

It's November and I'm happy to be in the warm, muggy South.

My character is a pimp, and I want to meet and hang out with a pimp, or pimps, to see how it works.

Actually, how does it work? Why do prostitutes have these guys they end up giving all their money to? It has never made any sense to me.

Through a bunch of clandestine maneuvers, I get hooked up with this guy Angelo. Angelo is five foot ten and built like a rock. He has black eyes and is very tough. His ethnicity is impossible to figure out. He takes me around to all these different bars on the outskirts of New Orleans. Everywhere we go, he tells me to wait at the bar, and then he goes off and huddles with some guy or other, whispering, and then comes back. I don't have a clue what's going on. He told me his name was Angelo, but at every single bar we enter, they call him something else: Gino, Stoney, Sonny, Ricky, but never Angelo. I don't learn much, except that however I approach being a pimp in the movie is going to be my own invention.

Ellen Barkin is in the beginning of the movie. This is impressive. Ellen Barkin is actually a real actor.

I've been working out for the first time in fifteen years. We're at a restaurant and I say that I have to go to the gym.

Barkin says, "Why you going to the gym? I thought you were too cool for that."

"I want to have some muscles in the movie, so I can be a movie star, like you."

She looks at my emaciated frame and says, "Where are you going to put them?"

Benigni is a ray of light, hardly speaks any English, but clearly has a remarkable mind.

He is also a rascal and an irritant. A school where I am a founding member.

I start teaching him wrong English, explaining that it's slang. One time, he gets up from the table and says he has to use the bathroom, and I explain, "The correct way to say that is, 'I am going to flam.'"

Later, the camera and lights are ready and they call for Roberto to do a scene.

He says, "One moment, I must to flam." The crew looks confused.

He catches on pretty quickly, and then I can't tell him anything, no matter how sincere my attempt is to help him with his English.

The line producer had an assistant who was exceptionally smart. I found her really attractive. I found out that her name was Lisa Krueger.

We had talked a couple of times and she seemed completely uninterested. When we were in the hotel bar after shooting, I watched her, and when our eyes met she looked away immediately. Seemed to me as though she was recoiling in horror.

A couple of days later she was at the bar. I went up to her and said, "Let's flirt." There was a pause, so I said, "You go first." She liked that. She later explained that she did not want to go on location and sleep with one of the lead actors, it was garish and just too cliché.

So I was sleeping with Lisa, but we didn't want anyone to know. She had to get up early and sneak back to her room before the rest of the crew got up. Once, when I slept in her room, I was cutting across the courtyard enclosed by the hotel to get back to my room. As the first crack of light moved across the lawn, I ran into Claire Denis.

I had emphatically told Jim that he had to use Claire as assistant director, after watching her work on *Paris, Texas*.

I said, "Claire, don't tell anybody."

She laughed. "John, I am the first one up and every morning I see ten different people sneaking across this courtyard."

I really had a strong respect for Claire. She had that roll up your sleeves thing when she was working on a movie that felt more like she was going to war. Which is good, because it can be war. There are people who overdo that kind of thing, but Claire was going to war and calm about it. However, should anything arise, Claire would be ready. You just knew it.

The Red Hot Chili Peppers are in New Orleans to do a gig. I sit in and play the whole show on alto. I don't know the material, but the grooves are great and it's easy and fun to play along with.

The show's over and we go back into the dressing room. They aren't so big yet, this is not an arena, but there are a thousand people screaming for an encore. In the dressing room the band all start frantically ripping off their clothes.

"Socks! Socks!"

"Socks!"

I don't know what's going on. No one says anything to me and they're in a mad dash to take off their clothes.

"Socks! Socks!"

Each of them pulls a sock over his cock and balls, so that they're naked except for the socks.

I'm not prepared for this.

They run back out onstage. The crowd roars!

I think to myself that I can't do the whole show and not do this, and I take off my clothes as fast as I can. I've got these long, almost knee-high socks from Barneys that I'm wearing. When I put one on over my cock it hangs down almost to my knees. There's a guy standing by the side of the stage wearing sunglasses, and I grab them off his head as I pass.

The sunglasses help.

They start the song and I come running out and join in. It's impressive how energetically one can play when standing naked in front of a crowd.

Rockets Redglare is at the concert. He's doing a part in *Down by Law*. Rockets is gigantically overweight, maybe four hundred pounds, at the time.

I don't know this then, but Rockets sees me and my sock hanging prodigiously low and laughs so hard that he can't breathe. He collapses, but he's too heavy to be moved outside and they spread a circle around him on the floor so he can get some air, as the concert goes on around him.

The song ends and Flea comes over to me and says, "There's a vocal breakdown in the next song where you should lay out. I'll cue you."

I nod. They start and I'm playing, everything is fine, it's exhilarating. Flea cues me and they break down. *Bump ba bump . . . bump ba bump . . . bump ba bump.*

I'm not playing. What am I supposed to do? Dance? That's out of the question. I'm not going to stand up here and dance naked. Nope.

So I run off the stage.

It's uncanny how humans have this animal sense to know when they are being watched. One can feel a glance or a stare. Like when you're driving on the highway and passing another car, if you look at the other driver, even before you have pulled alongside them, they will turn and look at you defensively. Before you are even in their eye line. This is, inevitably, true. How do they know you're there? They don't look at every car that passes them, only if you're staring. It really is some animal thing.

I feel a thousand pairs of eyes burning on my ass as I dash from the stage.

Hillel Slovak is immensely proud of me because I'm the only person who has ever sat in with the band and then done the sock thing.

Down by Law seemed really stiff early on. The dialogue just seemed like a ton of exposition and not much else, though Robby Müller was certainly making it look astounding. Then Roberto walked into it and just freed it up completely. Some people just know their way around a camera. He knew how to do that, but he also could light up a room somehow.

When I saw *Paris, Texas*, I was astounded by what Robby Müller had done. I had never seen anything like it.

When I saw the dailies on *Down by Law*, I was astounded all over again. He was doing something incredible, but now in a completely different way.

Early on in the movie, he had flown a young woman in from L.A. She was not his girlfriend or wife or anything like that. On Thanksgiving, after watching the Knicks beat the Celtics at the bar, I went back to my room. There was a knock on the door and this woman Robby had flown in from L.A. walked past me into the room.

She walked drunkenly past me into the room, smiled, and sat on the chair.

I didn't know what the hell to do. This wasn't right. I was with Lisa Krueger and this woman was with Robby. What was she doing?

I couldn't throw her out. It just felt awkward as hell.

Then there was a loud smashing on my door. It was Robby. He dragged the woman, forcibly, out of my room.

The next day we were filming out in the woods after Tom and Roberto and I had escaped from jail.

The shot was ready to go, but Robby insisted that we wait until he set up a branch on a stand. It took twenty minutes.

I saw later that the purpose of this branch was to cast a mottled shadow over my face. So that I looked kind of like a diseased monster.

He never forgave me for what happened. And I don't know how else I could have handled it.

Robby was a true artist. But we never got along and it all goes back to that day. Even years later when we were both on the jury at a film festival.

But damn, I have met a lot of artists in my life, and I don't think anyone was as impeccable as Robby Müller.

It was nice with Lisa Krueger. She was sane and really smart and thoughtful. And she knew music. Lisa was someone you could marry, but I was too stupid to see that then. I was in a tornado of lasciviousness. The fame threw my whole thing off balance. Beautiful women wanting to be with you, everywhere you go, is something every man thinks he would want. But it all felt cheap in the end. I lost my balance. The cocaine and alcohol probably didn't help. And what the hell was I doing acting? I should have been playing music.

My favorite part of making *Down by Law* was at the end of the movie when we were shooting in the swamps in Slidell. Tom, Roberto, and I would be driven out to the set in a little motorboat early every morning. The boat would putter out, and we would sing together as we watched the wildlife and the sun came up.

We were always looking for alligators, which we never saw. Roberto would jump up and point at a stick and then say, "There an alli . . ." Then his voice would fall and he'd say, "No." Over and over again. He knew that he hadn't seen an alligator, he was just being silly and he should consider himself lucky that I didn't throw him out of the boat after the seventh time.

Once when I flew to L.A. with him, he was really tired on the plane. Couldn't get him to talk to me, no matter how much I bugged him. Right before the plane landed he drank a double espresso. We were in the cab and I was tired, but now, Roberto was zooming. He was reading every sign in loud—very loud—very bad English.

"La Cienega Boulevard!!"

"No Left Turn!!"

"Dry Cleaning!! One Hour!!"

"Pizza!"

I said, "Stop it!"

"Harry's Heroes!! 431-9007!!"

"Basta!!"

"We deliver!!"

"Basta!"

We're out in Slidell shooting and this local guy stops by. Tom Waits and I are talking to him for a while. Seems okay. Tom asks him about a restaurant we've heard of for catfish, just down the road.

"Nah, you don't want to go there. Niggers go there."

I'm shocked. I've never heard that before, just used casually in a sentence like that. Violence rises up inside me.

Tom just looks down at the ground and then walks away.

I'm really disappointed in Tom, thinking, *No, Tom. We have to fix this.*

I look at the guy and angrily say, "Listen . . ."

The guy is tilting his head and looking at me, waiting to hear what I am going to say. He has no idea why I am upset.

But then what? I say, "We don't use that word, we find it vile"? Nah, that isn't going to get through to him. It will be like trying to teach Mandarin to a squirrel.

"I'm offended by what you said and that is why I am going to hit you in the head with this rock"?

No, that wouldn't quite work.

So I do what Tom did. I look at the ground and walk away.

I thought about it for years afterward, what I could have done to make some kind of an impression on this guy, but never figured it out.

27

What Do You Know About Music?
You're Not a Lawyer

I n Thailand, one can hear laughter floating through the air, like a bird-call. Like life.

In Africa, one hears rich laughs that burst from the depths of soulful humans.

In Wales, the laughs have an up and down, singsong affect.

In Cuba and much of the Caribbean, it is much the same but different. There is music in it.

In expensive restaurants in New York, it is the tight-lipped sound of people who laugh from the neck up. There is no solar plexus in the laugh. It is only what they believe to be laughter.

One can learn pretty much everything about a person's soul from the openness of their laugh.

Naná Vasconcelos had the best laugh.

I got them to hire Lisa Krueger to be my assistant when I was doing the music for *Down by Law*, which was great because she was smart and knew music. Late one afternoon, I was hanging out with Naná Vascon-celos, the great Brazilian percussionist, and Arto Lindsay at my place. We were fooling around, recording numerous outgoing messages on my answering machine with me talking and Arto and Naná singing my phone number. Arto suggested that we go into the studio that night and record the score for *Down by Law*.

It was kind of a naïve suggestion. There is so much red tape involved in scoring a movie, even on this level. The music is timed carefully to the scene in the movie. But then I thought, *What the hell, we could go and play and probably get something.* It would hardly cost anything; we could just try some stuff and maybe it would work for the scenes in the swamp.

I was pretty sure that the producers would never say yes, but Lisa got them to okay it, and we went out to Martin Bisi's studio in Brooklyn, where we had recorded "Hammerhead." It went great. Arto and Naná had a real thing together. Got three or four of the twenty cues done in a way that never would have happened otherwise.

I knew roughly what the money was and went to Naná and asked if $250 would be okay.

Naná, who normally got real money to record anything, didn't complain, didn't say anything. He just laughed. He laughed like it was the funniest thing that he'd ever heard in his life. Kept laughing and laughing. He hadn't done it for the money in the first place, but now that it was mentioned, that was something else.

"Three hundred and fifty?"

He threw back his head and laughed harder.

This is the absolute best negotiating tool I have ever encountered, and I got Lisa to get him five hundred, which probably still wasn't enough to make him stop laughing.

The rest of the music I did a week or so later. We only had enough money for one day of rehearsal and I was trying to race through it.

We were trying to figure out how to segue from a sort of a blues into a more atmospheric piece of music. I wanted the blues to splinter apart gently, which might have been best if left to chance, with these great musicians, but I wanted to figure it out now to be safe, for the timing against the movie, which is always the tricky thing.

During this rehearsal time, at that exact moment, was when Jim's lawyers said the negotiations had to take place. They'd had months to prepare for this, but it absolutely had to happen right now. They were asking for all kinds of things that they hadn't asked for on *Stranger Than Paradise*. Said my deal on that movie "wasn't standard." They actually said, "We're not going to let John get away with what he got away with on *Stranger Than Paradise*."

What did I get away with on *Stranger Than Paradise*? I was paid a thousand dollars to do the score.

These same people who insisted that Jim, the "auteur," must be kept in a sanitized ivory bubble, because he might be in the midst of the creative process—I had been around the guy quite a bit and had not seen this "creative process" in action—were now ruining the only rehearsal that I could afford.

It looked like the deal was going to fall apart and I had to stop rehearsal and get on the phone with my lawyer. It's obvious how far something like this can take you away from the music, and it seems to inevitably happen. I have gotten better and better at dealing with this kind of shit, but I am sure that I have lost something because of it. Something beautiful.

I'm on the phone with my lawyer telling him that I can compromise on X, but no way on Y and Z. Jarmusch's lawyers are playing hardball, it looks like the whole deal is going to fall through, and as much as my head wants to get back to the music, it doesn't really seem to make any sense to do this because there isn't going to be any music. And if this does fall apart, someone has to pay all these musicians for their time, and for the rehearsal studio, and Bisi's studio, and Arto and Naná, and I am afraid it's going to be me. It's always me. My lawyer says he'll call me back in a minute.

My head is lost in the negotiations. We only have an hour and a half of rehearsal time left and ten cues to work out before the recording.

All the musicians are sitting around waiting.

Dougie suggests that we could transition from that blues to the other piece by doing—

And I snap at him: "What do you know about music? You're not a lawyer!"

Tony laughed his great little chuckle laugh.

* * *

The lawyer calls back and I just give in. I'm so anxious to get back to working on the music because it's just hovering there, close but unfinished. I would have taken no money and no publishing to just have the music recorded and completed. So that it had a life and became an actual thing that existed instead of something I felt bouncing around in my head. I just say, "Give them whatever they want. I think it's obscene, but I don't want to deal with this anymore."

I owe a lot to the musicians on a lot of music that I've done. Tony Garnier, Dougie Bowne, E. J. Rodriguez, Naná Vasconcelos, Marc Ribot, and Curtis Fowlkes all added a lot to the *Down by Law* score. And Evan, of course, who helped me orchestrate one blues thing that really made it more elegant. On a lot of it I gave the musicians the idea and they just played. It was also easier because there wasn't the thing that you have with Hollywood films where the music had to be timed out exactly. It was possible to play musically, with soft ins and outs, so that the music could be shifted a little when they put it to picture. This way you can avoid using a click track, which can stultify the feel.

Jim and I were always creatively close and on the same page. I didn't realize how lucky I was to be working with him like this. He trusted me completely. He never asked to hear sketches and never even made any suggestions, and only once, in all the film scores I did for him, did he ever cut a piece of music out. This was daring of him, because who knows what he might have gotten. Often by the time we were doing the music we were not getting along. I had thought more than once of giving him a score with twenty-five kazoos. But it was actually smart of him to leave me alone because he knew that, left to my own devices, I would give it my absolute best because I cared more about the music and the project than anything else.

For the most part, which is pretty incredible, Jim let me decide where the music should go in the movie. This is unheard of in Hollywood, where there are eighteen musically illiterate people making all kinds of decisions about where the music should go and what the tempo should be and whether bongos might be nice here and, most important, what's going to be on the soundtrack album. This way they can figure out what hit song will replace something the composer has already written and recorded and how they can line each other's pockets with shekels.

What I might have been best at in this life was doing film scores for movies, but it was almost always made so unpleasant that I had to give it up. The big movies in one way, the smaller movies in another.

I suppose they might put on my report card: *Doesn't play well with others.*

But I swear that is just not true. I just cared about what we were putting out into the world.

I was always shocked at how little people seemed to care about making the movie good. If you see something that is good, mad struggles went into it. Without exception. Some things roll out in an easy and nice way, but there are always bumps. I think about the look of determination on Claire Denis's face during *Paris, Texas* and *Down by Law*, like she was going to war. That really is what it takes to make something good.

The last Hollywood film score I did was for a movie called *The Crew*, directed by Michael Dinner. This was way later. Must have been in 1999.

Barry Sonnenfeld and Barry Josephson were the producers. I had had an extremely unpleasant time working with Sonnenfeld on *Get Shorty* and was nervous to be doing this score where he was involved.

He really felt like a guy intent on making a career for himself where he was above people because of how he had been mistreated in grade school. And with me in particular; from things I gathered that he said about Jarmusch when he was at NYU at the same time, Jarmusch was the cool kid, and I was clearly cooler than Jarmusch, so I would be forced to suffer for the traumas Sonnenfeld had gone through as Mr. Not Cool Whatsoever of NYU.

Once I heard Barry Sonnenfeld's voice, I should have run away.

Anyone who allows his voice to sound like Barry Sonnenfeld does cannot be someone who comes anywhere near music. His voice sounds like a duck wearing underwear that is too tight. He was at my place when I was working on the music for *Get Shorty*. As he spoke I watched the fruit, in a bowl on the counter, commit suicide and wither into a pile of rotted nothing.

I had gotten to the point where I decided I would do these film scores to have enough money to keep my music, the band, and the record label afloat, but that I would not get attached to the film score music, no matter how they butchered it, no matter how rude they were, no matter what they put me through. I would take the money and not care and make my own music with it. Of course, I could never actually get to that level of detachment.

In the contract for *The Crew* it said that I would be paid the second half of the money when the music was approved by their representative, though it wasn't clear who their representative was. I turned to my lawyer, Peter Shukat, and said that I didn't trust these people and the contract should specify who their representative was. Peter said that was ridiculous, that the director, Michael Dinner, was coming to New York and once he approved it, I was finished with the project.

This was one of those all-in deals where they give you a certain amount of money, a lot of money, and out of that money, you pay for the musicians, the studios, the orchestrator, the copyist, the video hookup, the engineer, etc., etc. If the thing stays in line, you can make money. If it goes all askew, it can be a disaster and you can lose a lot of money.

With composing a Hollywood movie, the timing of the scenes is what is so important. You have a scene that needs music for one minute and nineteen seconds and eleven frames. So you time it out exactly to the scene. When Hollywood sends you these scenes, they are what is called "locked," meaning they will not be edited again. This is a sacred rule. Then you can begin your work, because there is no point in starting to map out the music against the edit until it is absolutely finished.

I have rehearsals with the musicians before we go into the studio. It makes it more organic. It makes it like actual music rather than notes placed against a click track to the frames from a computer to another computer. Apparently this is no longer how it is done, which I hear over and over again from Tom Drescher, the music editor they saddled me with. The music editor's function is to fit the music into the movie. I'm fairly sure Tom Drescher is the man from the DMV who escorted my mother out thirty years earlier.

He keeps scoffing at the idea that I want to have a rehearsal. He has worked with James Newton Howard. No matter what I do, he says that that is not how James Newton Howard did it.

So I have forty of the best musicians in the world in the studio. We start to work on a cue and Michael Dinner says, "Oh, I think this scene may have been edited since we sent it to you."

This is really like the air traffic controller saying to the pilot, "Oh, you are all the way over there? That's a problem. Sorry, I was eating my sandwich. It's a really nice roast beef with honey mustard!"

So forty of the best musicians in the world wait for Michael Dinner to call the editors and find out the actual timing of the scene.

Turns out it has been edited. Bernstein and I will have to go to my place, that night, to work on this cue before we go into the studio in the morning.

We start to work on the next cue. Michael Dinner is on his cell talking to someone about his new car. He looks up and says, "Oh, I think this may have been edited."

Forty of the best musicians in the world sit and wait another twenty minutes while Michael Dinner calls his editing room.

Almost every scene is a different timing from the scene they sent me. The scenes I have been working on for two months.

Bernstein and I go to my house and do what I am pretty sure no other human beings could possibly do: rewrite each music cue to fit the timing that is happening now, without ruining the feel. We could just edit out bits or play things faster, but that would suck. That's what the people do to make all the movies you see suck—though you can't really figure out why they suck.

We get to the studio the next morning. We have not slept.

Michael Dinner is making phone call after phone call about his new car and about how to meet some attractive young actress.

There is one cue where there is a click track to count it off and then the click disappears. Calvin Weston, the genius drummer, is supposed to do a two-bar fill before the rest of the music comes in, but when we do it, Calvin botches it because he can't hear the click.

So we're going to just punch in Calvin's two bars at the top. It is kind of a confusing thing to do. The click suddenly appears in your headphones and if you are not ready it is hard to catch and then play naturally as something to be punched in. Experienced studio musicians have no problem doing that, but Calvin is not that, and experienced studio musicians are certainly not Calvin.

Calvin comes from and lives in a poor black neighborhood in Philadelphia, and he talks like that.

Tom, the music editor, and Michael Dinner are sitting, shoulder to shoulder, with their heads down. Every time Calvin talks back to us from the drum booth, Dinner and Tom lean in and whisper to each other and start to giggle.

When Calvin messes up the intro, they giggle again.

When I talk to Calvin about the best way to approach it and Calvin responds, they whisper again and giggle.

They are having a big laugh because of how Calvin talks. But these fools are devoid of rhythm and do not have any idea what a rare talent Calvin Weston is.

I get pissed.

"Tom, do you know why black people hate the music of James Newton Howard?"

"No, why?"

"Because he sucks."

The look on Drescher's face is so sour, I think he's going to have to rush off to the men's room.

But that also puts any hope of things' being civil with Dinner to bed. I have basically just told them they are racists, because they are acting like racists.

The thing is plodding along. Michael Dinner is spending most of his time on the phone talking about his new car. We finish a cue that he has not been listening to and when I ask if it is okay, he wants us to play it back for him because he has been on the phone talking about his car.

Every second in the studio with all these people and things being paid for by the hour is costing me money.

We play him the cue. He is not sure.

We play it again. He is not sure. He is not sure why he is not sure but he is not sure.

I rewrite it. We rerecord it. He is on the phone talking about his car.

We finish. Play it for him. He is not sure.

I am paying for all this indecision and he should have been paying attention from the top.

One of the musicians starts talking about this wild composer named Manolo, who punched a director while they were recording and knocked him out.

I say, "Oh thanks! That had never occurred to me as an option."

Michael Dinner now looks like a seven-year-old at his first day of school.

There is a cue that is a flashback to one of the lead actors' thinking about his estranged daughter. It is Super 8 footage of a little girl playing. I think what I wrote is quite nice and simple.

Michael Dinner is not sure.

"What are you not sure about?"

"I think that chord at the end."

So I set up a keyboard and play him every single possibility that that chord can be in the middle of this musical progression.

He has the look of someone who has eaten some bad Mexican food. He doesn't answer.

I play another chord.

Same face.

Then another.

Same face.

And I am sorry, but then I start to laugh. The musicians start to laugh. And Michael Dinner runs from the studio, I presume to his mother, as first grade has been rough for him.

The next day, he comes back and apologizes. Says he flashed back to being in the first grade. Which I guess I already knew. Danny Hedaya, an actor I kind of admire, stops by the studio. I hold out my hand, and he refuses to shake it and walks by me. I guess Michael Dinner has tattled on me.

The last day goes kind of okay. Michael Dinner approves every single cue and I think it is over.

Three days later, my new film score agent calls me and says that they do not like the score.

"Who doesn't like it?"

"The producers."

"Which one?"

"Barry Josephson."

"I can rewrite and rerecord some of the pieces, but I need to know what the problems are and what they want."

"I will have him call you."

"No, I should get this in writing. So I do not have to rewrite and rerecord up to the point that I am losing money on this project. I can't then have the next producer say they don't like it for other reasons."

I suppose this all gets colored for me in an even worse way because of Jon Ende.

Jon Ende is my dear friend. He named The Lounge Lizards. He is now dying of AIDS. He is on his last legs and is in hospice. I insisted to his friends that it was better that he be taken home. So that we could all be around him. I would help.

Jon was moved home. There is a nurse. But the place is a shambles. I always believed the stereotype that gay men were neat. But Jon Ende's friends, Roy among them, are the messiest gay men, or men of any kind, I have ever met, and I was cleaning up the apartment while they ate Twinkies and dropped the wrappers on the floor. I am exaggerating a bit, but it was kind of like that.

I go to Bed, Bath & Beyond and buy him new sheets and pillows. I wash the dishes.

I am supposed to go back the next day.

But then, I get a nine-page handwritten fax from Barry Josephson sent to my office. It barely makes any sense.

There are sentences like, "When the guys approach the boat, I don't like part of that music."

But in the movie, the guys approach the boat about ten times and there is music in several of those scenes.

Which scene? Which part don't you like?

I call my agent. She has already made it quite clear that she would prefer to be in the good graces of Barry Josephson and Barry Sonnenfeld and that she will not protect me, no matter what comes next.

She says, "You should call Barry Josephson at home. Here is the number. He is expecting your call."

So I call.

The woman who answers the phone pauses that weird pause of a liar and then says he is not there. But you can tell in a moment that he is there. And in my experience with someone who responds like she did, he is sitting right next to her.

I call the agent back and say that he is not there, though I suspect he is there but won't come to the phone.

She says that I should call in the morning, but do not leave my place until I hear back from them. They have threatened to not pay me the second half until I have fixed this. And I have to do it by Monday, meaning I will have to book the studio and musicians once I know what the hell I am rewriting.

This is a problem for two enormous reasons. I have to go to Jon Ende's house first thing tomorrow to make sure he is okay. And they have advanced me half of the money for the score, and this money has already been well overspent on the studio and musicians, etc. If they withhold the second half, I will be out of pocket about $100,000 for my last two months' work after I pay everyone.

I call Barry Josephson's house several times. Each time he is said to not be there but will call me when he gets back.

He doesn't call.

I am getting furious. I call my lawyer, who is little help, and my agent, who is clearly not going to back me.

Then at about ten o'clock on Friday night, I get a call. It is another one of the producers, but I have never heard of this guy.

He explains that he is one of the producers and that I have to stop being so difficult.

I ask how I am being difficult.

I explain that I have written the music per Michael Dinner's instructions and rewrote it on the spot to his tastes, and now I am finding out that people I have never spoken to don't like it. But I don't know what is wrong with the music or what cues they want changed, and no one will tell me. I also don't know who I am answering to on this.

Then he says, "I'm from Philadelphia, if you know what that means."

I explain, again, that I am willing to work on three or four of the cues, if I understand the problems and if he and the other producers are all on the same page about what the problems are, so I don't have to record the music into infinity.

He says with the voice of an actor in a bad Mafia movie, "John, I am from Philadelphia. Do you understand what that means? It means I am not one of these lightweight L.A. guys. We handle things very differently in Philadelphia."

"Are you threatening me?"

"I am telling you that I am from Philadelphia and you do not mess around with people like us."

"All I want is for you and the other producers to be happy with the music and be done with this, but someone has to tell me what is wrong."

"We don't like it. Listen, I am from Philadelphia, if you know what that means."

"Holy shit, I am from New York City, motherfucker. You want to try to fix this problem like this, then bring it. Asshole."

And I hang up the phone.

The report card says: *Doesn't play well with others.*

Oh, okay, I suppose that is true, and I am certain there isn't another film score composer in the world who would have handled it like this. But fuck these people, calling my home to threaten me. Makes me fucking furious just to write this. And how was I being difficult?

Monday morning comes. I have not heard back from Barry Josephson, though I have called several times. I have not been to look after Jon Ende and I have not booked a studio.

My agent calls and asks if I have spoken to Josephson. I explain that I have called several times and a woman keeps telling me that he is not there and he will call me, but he never does.

The agent says that he is home now, she just spoke to him. I have to call right away.

So I do.

I get the same woman on the phone, and though every bit of intuition in my being says that he is sitting right there, she tells me that he is not home.

I say, "Do you mind telling me who I am speaking to?"

She says, "I am his fiancée."

I say in mock excitement, "Well! You know, he is really dishonest. You should get out of there immediately!"

That wisecrack ends up costing me $170,000, and do you know what? I am not sorry I said it.

Ten seconds after I hang up, the phone rings and it's my agent.

She screams, "What did you do? He says that you threatened his family."

Fuck these people. All the way around. They aren't in this world for the same reason I am. I guess it is as simple as that.

That was my last film score.

* * *

The band is on the plane to Japan. Fourteen hours. I drink five of those miniature bottles of Jack Daniel's. The stewardess's jacket is hanging on a peg near the cockpit, unattended. I sneak out of my seat and go up and take it down without being seen. I put it on. The sleeves hardly go past my elbows. Then I take one small Jack Daniel's bottle in each hand and walk down the aisle, toward the band, yelling, "I'm a giant! I'm a giant!"

We are playing three nights at a club called Cay Bar, then in two different spaces that are in giant conglomerate buildings. These places have completely different functions during the day.

I didn't realize that Cay Bar was actually a posh restaurant. I tell Hiroshi, the tour promoter, that there is no way that we are going to play for people while they are eating, that we don't do that.

No problem, the owner is such a fan that food service is shut down while we are onstage.

After sound check, there is an English guy who wants to film us in Super 8. I wouldn't ever ordinarily allow this, but behind him, staring at me, is this very tall, exotic Japanese girl. This is his assistant, and if I say no, I might not ever see her again. She is wearing an absurd Audrey Hepburn hat with an enormous brim, and her gaze is otherworldly. Her name is Kazu.

All through the show, she is crawling around in her skintight outfit, down on the floor, right in front of the stage. Lying on her stomach, shooting upside down, and her unconscious gyrations are almost obscene. I play with my eyes closed, but I know the straight guys in the band can't take their eyes off her. She is exquisitely ethereal.

After the show, I invite her to Ink Stick, which is a bar/restaurant that we always go to.

She comes but won't come back to my room with me.

Dougie walks into Ink Stick just as I am saying to her, "I'm really mad at you."

Dougie knows I tend to go too far and says, "John, how can you be mad at this really beautiful girl? She seems so sweet."

"She won't come back to my room and I'm really mad at her."

Dougie does his little Dougie laugh and hugs me. Dougie is always hugging people. It is one of the great advantages of his size and cuteness. He can hug anyone at any time.

The guys go out sightseeing and shopping and come back with plastic samurai wigs. They're hysterical. You put it on and it looks so ridiculous. I wish I had a photo, because there is no way to explain how hilarious The Lounge Lizards looked wearing these wigs.

Before Roberto Benigni and Nicoletta Braschi left New York, I wrote a Nino Rota–like song for them called "Bob and Nico." Much slower and more quaint than our normal stuff. It had a nice, lopsided cadence. Wrote it for them and to record it, but we never did it live, it wasn't fierce enough. We play it that night at the Cay Bar, and at a point in the song where it breaks down to just the piano, we all put on the plastic samurai wigs, which are hidden around the stage. Roy looks over at me, sees me in the wig, and slumps to the floor laughing. We can't continue without Roy playing his part, so the band just hovers there for a second waiting for Roy to compose himself and play his part. He stands up, plays two notes, and looks out of the corner of his eye at me and just slumps back onto the floor. We can't finish the song.

After the encore we do this one-chord blues thing. Like an up-tempo New Orleans funeral march. Dougie wears the snare drum secured around his waist, by Marc's guitar strap. *Ba da, da da dat, ba da, dattle dat dat.* E.J. plays shakers; Marc plays trumpet, which he can really play but doesn't often do; Curtis is on trombone; and Roy and I are on sopranos. Erik was supposed to get a tuba but never did, and Evan just walks around yelling. We'll later record it and call it "Carry Me Out," but at this point we just walk through the crowd playing at the end of the night.

The Japanese girls are so cute and so shy. They cover their mouths when they laugh and they bow when they talk to you. But this is somewhat contrary to the notion of shyness: When we are walking out in the crowd, we're swarmed by them. They're screaming. I must have had my ass pinched thirty times.

Every time we're in Japan we drink enormous amounts. E.J. has never had so much fun in his life, he can't believe it. I walk out of a club, pass out, and fall flat on my face. Then get up, proclaim myself a genius, and get into a cab. Kazu tells me later—but I do not remember it like this—that I was vomiting all the time.

We are so out of control that the hotel moves the band all to one floor and puts no Japanese guests on the floor with us. The hallway is strewn with stuff.

When the Neville Brothers come to Tokyo, they are put on the same floor.

Someone knocks on my door. I go to answer it and no one is there. I'm sure it's Dougie who did it. I step out into the hallway and yell, "Dougie!" The door slams behind me.

And I'm not wearing any clothes.

I go down the hall and knock on Dougie's door. I am sure he's in there, but he won't answer. So I sit down in the hallway, naked, outside his room.

The elevator opens, and I am not so worried because the only people on the floor are us. And oh, I forgot, the Neville Brothers. At worst it would be a maid. I could cover myself up and she would let me back in my room.

Out of the elevator come several of the guys from the Neville Brothers. I am sitting on the floor naked.

One of them says, "Hey." Like this is nothing unusual.

I say, "Hey," back, as they walk on down the hall.

I have lunch with Hiroshi. He wants me to do interviews, and I don't want to do them but agree to a few. The Japanese photographers really seem like they want to turn you into Godzilla. They want to shoot you while you're talking, and at that moment that your face gets scrunched up or overly animated they start shooting like mad, or they invite you to eat and as soon as a little piece of sushi is hanging from the corner of your mouth, they start clicking away. Anything, as long as your face is contorted and you look like a monster. I am already hungover, so trying to make me look beastly is not really a problem.

There is also so much money there that the guys are all making a fortune. It seems like every time you open the door to the hotel room, you have to shut it really fast because so much money is blowing in. They are recording on records and all kinds of things.

Hiroshi wants me to wear these suits for a magazine article and they will pay me $10,000.

"What about a live record? Could we make a live record?"

"How much do you want?"

"For us? I don't know. Ten thousand for the band."

It is all set up immediately. Day after tomorrow we will record when we play at Space Harajuku. Easy as that. This is 1986, when America and New York are marvelous places and anyone from there is fascinating and wonderful to people in other parts of the world.

Space Harajuku is actually a car showroom on the first floor of a mall-like area. We soundcheck early. There is a recording truck parked out on the street. The engineer is Seigen Ono.

We do sound check and go into the dressing room to eat. We're in there maybe fifteen minutes eating, and when we come back out onto the stage, everything is gone. Where the audience will be is now a car showroom, with shiny, fancy automobiles lined up for sale. The Japanese are amazing like this, and what is even more amazing is that there was a cigarette butt on the top of Ribot's amp during sound check. When we go out to play the gig, he calls me over to his amp and shows me that they have saved the cigarette butt and placed it back in the exact same place as it was this morning, thinking that perhaps there was a reason for it. Ribot doesn't even smoke.

We do two shows and record both. First one is a little stiff, but the second one goes great and we use most of the songs from the second set for the album.

We have two days to mix. Seigen Ono is unbelievable and mixes the whole thing on the fly, and it comes out better than I ever would have expected. I walk back to the hotel listening to "Big Heart" blaring in my headphones.

It is one of the happiest moments of my life.

It becomes a soundtrack for the bustling insanity of Tokyo that turns it into something else entirely. Tokyo is re-created for "Big Heart": The man pushing a vegetable cart, the cab door opening, and the giant neon signs are all a real-life video engulfed in the song. Everything has a new life.

The band goes back before me and I stay to do the album cover. I am trying to learn Japanese. I go out with Kazu to buy art supplies for the cover. There are stink pockets in Tokyo, a spot on the street where it just suddenly smells of egg farts.

"How do you say *stink*?"

"*Kusai.*"

"Kusai koko des. Kazu kusai."

We go to the art store and then back to the room. I am trying to write "Big Heart" in Japanese characters. Kazu informs me that "Big Heart" doesn't translate to the same meaning exactly.

"It is like saying big liver or big spleen."

"Great!"

I am working like mad on the cover. Almost get it and then fuck it up. There is paper everywhere. I can't quite get it. Hiroshi comes by my room and asks about the cover. I say that I will get it eventually. On his way out, he reaches down into the trash and pulls out two different drawings that I have torn in half. He puts them together, side by side, on the table.

"How about this?"

"Can they put them together?"

"Sure."

Cover is beautiful.

I go back to New York. Lisa Krueger seems to be in love with me. I am going out every night and she is disappointed in me. I am very excited about the record but she says it's sloppy. Maybe it is sloppy.

Lisa Krueger is the kind of girl one should marry. I think I said that before. She is smart, kind, and pretty, and no bullshit, no games. She is wonderful. But I am burning myself up much too fast to even notice.

She sees clearly that I am not the boy for her, it will only lead to heartache. She wants a chance to get over me. I am just not ready for the kind of relationship Lisa wants. It isn't like she even complained about it, she just wanted something serious.

I certainly do not want to lose Lisa Krueger, so for her birthday I take her to the Cayman Islands. We have a fairly nice time, except I can't sleep at night, because I never sleep at night and spend most of my time reading a book about Zelda Fitzgerald.

I'm back living at my place on Third Street, and when we get back to New York, we go there. I turn on the answering machine as I am unpacking my bag. The last message is from Kazu. She is at the airport in New York and coming to my house. Right now. She says it like this has been the plan all along. But it wasn't the plan. Lisa doesn't believe me and gets up and leaves.

I watched Kazu in Japan. She would show her emotions so openly that it freaked out the Japanese. She would see someone she liked and fly across the room, arms waving, and hug them. This is just not done in Japan. Plus, she was a giant compared to other Japanese women. I was at a bar with her and saw her throw her head back and roar with laughter. The other Japanese people around her at the bar looked horrified. When Kazu realized that what she had done was meeting such strong disapproval, I saw her shrink into herself. All that beauty squashed by misguided public opinion.

I saw it and said, "You have to move to New York."

It was the only place for her, they would devour her soul there in Japan. I guess Kazu decided to take this as an invitation, so two weeks later she is about to arrive at my doorstep.

She arrives and looks all wild-eyed and frightened. My friend Boris Policeband says that she has the face of a five-year-old child who knows too much about death. And it is kind of like that, that look in her face that is lost and wise at the same time, and beautiful.

I think that this is bizarrely presumptuous of her and I am upset about Lisa.

I'm not going to throw Kazu out, but I did not sign on for this at all. I tell her she can sleep on the foam pad and go out to Area.

I don't think that Third Street is going to be safe for Kazu, and we move into Ian Schrager and Steve Rubell's new hotel, Morgans, on Thirty-seventh and Madison. I have been living there on and off for a while.

I go to see the Red Hot Chili Peppers at a club called the Saint. It was the Fillmore in the sixties, then a bank, then a gay club. Now it is hardly ever open, but the Chili Peppers are playing there. I'm backstage and Chris Blackwell comes into the dressing room. Chris Blackwell's company, Island Records, produced or is distributing *Down by Law* in the States. He sees me and says, "You're going to be a movie star."

"Fuck that. Are you Chris Blackwell?"

"Yes."

"Why don't you sign my band? You can put out the record we just made in Japan."

Blackwell gives me his number and tells me to come by tomorrow.

I go to meet Blackwell, and in the middle of the meeting, he gets a call. Gets off the phone and says, "Do you know Joel Webber?"

Joel Webber was supposed to manage The Lounge Lizards, or at least we talked about it. He was supposed to find the Lizards a deal, which of course he has never done. I haven't talked to him in months. Joel is very tall and very skinny. The only time he has been to a Lounge Lizards show was at Irving Plaza, the gig we did right before I went down to do *Down by Law*. Joel, who is easily six foot six, got into an argument with a short Puerto Rican guy from the club, who had reached up as high as he could and popped Joel Webber in the nose. Joel went home before the show started, holding his head backward to try to stop the blood from his nose from getting on his shirt. That's pretty much the extent of my involvement with Joel Webber.

"Is he your manager?"

"No! Why?"

"That was him on the phone, he says he's your manager."

Joel Webber runs the New Music Seminar. At this time it's a fairly important thing in the music business. For that reason, Blackwell says, "This might be awkward for me."

"He is not my manager, there is no contract. We never came to any understanding that he was my manager. We only thought that maybe he could find the band a deal, which he did not, and now I am here. I negotiated the Japan deal myself. He is absolutely not my manager."

"Well, you understand that I cannot offend this guy. Do you have a problem with him negotiating your deal? I can't do it otherwise."

I don't want to lose the deal, which would be that Island releases the *Big Heart: Live in Tokyo* record in the rest of the world outside of Japan. I acquiesce.

Blackwell and Webber start to negotiate my deal. I hear a few things back from Webber about the contract. The next thing I hear is they have gone to Toronto together. This seems a little strange. No matter how much negotiating this is going to take, it is odd that Webber would go to Toronto with Chris Blackwell on some junket.

When they come back, Joel Webber has been hired to be the new vice president of A&R at Island Records. Now his new job is to negotiate my deal with me.

He tells me that everything that he has negotiated so far will stand and that I should get a lawyer to finish the deal. This is amazingly dishonest. He also says that I have to have a manager. The band can't not have a manager.

He recommends this French woman named Valerie Goodman. Valerie works at a company called Time Capsule. I'm not exactly sure how it works, but Time Capsule sets up bands with studio space, handles the rentals, and does other odds and ends to make sure recording goes smoothly. Time Capsule was somehow involved with the *Down by Law* recording. I met Valerie then and thought she was pretty sharp.

I call Uncle Jerry to try to salvage the rest of the negotiations. But this shit that Joel Webber pulled is unbelievable. Dougie says, "Do you know why snakes don't bite A&R guys?"

"No, why, Dougie?"

"Professional courtesy."

The first thing that happens is that we have to do a new album cover. They don't like the Japanese version. They try to make me use one of their guys, but his work is ridiculous and I refuse. Evan does it with Keith Davis, and James Nares does a little drawing in the corner. Perry Ogden has shot me before and I sublet his loft on Fifth Avenue for a while. I like Perry and think he is talented and get him to shoot the cover.

Then the song "Blow Job" has to be changed to another title. I call it "It Could Have Been Very Very Beautiful" for Liz. Then I get an idea and put on the back of the album: "Dedicated to Miss Liz."

A message, eventually, she will see. When Liz finally does get privileges at Marathon House and is able to leave the compound, she is in a record store. Sees the dedication on the album but assumes that it must be for someone else named Liz.

28

The Handsomest Man in the World

Sydney Pollack was heading the jury at the Cannes Film Festival. Roberto walked around waving a ten dollar bill, announcing, loudly, to the sea of reporters and photographers engulfing us everywhere we went, that he was going to use it to bribe Sydney Pollack.

At the Cannes Film Festival, *Down by Law* got a standing ovation. This shocked me. Except for Tom, we were all there, sitting in the front row of the biggest theater I have ever seen. When the film ended they went mad. We had to turn awkwardly and face them and take our bow as they roared their approval.

Cannes is very disconcerting. No matter who you are talking to, they are looking over your shoulder for someone a little more important. The photographers can be sitting outside your hotel en masse but not take your photo until one person takes your photo. Suddenly there'll be a feeding frenzy of photographers, forty of them. Yelling, "John! John! Over here, John!"

I couldn't stand it.

I was relegated to the third-tier level of interviews. The ones nobody would ever see. *The Bulgarian Film Reader*. Stephen Torton said, "Jim and Sara are saying, 'Let's show John that he isn't all that important.' You are being punished."

I said, "Nah, they wouldn't do that."

But it turned out they had done exactly that. I found out, years later, from the publicist that she was instructed not to give any of the more important interviews to me. That Jim wanted to phase me out.

I had been accused of slagging Jim off on *Stranger Than Paradise*. But honestly, I really didn't. All I had done was say that the premise for *Stranger* was my idea. But apparently this is not how it is done in show business.

Thank God that Stephen Torton was there. He talked me into skipping out on the interviews. It never occurred to me that I could just not show up. Getting all the lower-level stuff meant that I was stuck being interviewed by people who didn't speak English, so they'd ask you, "Jim Jarmusch, how he is?"

"How he is?"

"Yes, thank you."

"What do you mean?"

"Yes."

Great, that's great.

I am sitting on the folding chair in the interview room when the door flies open with a bang. It's an Italian writer with loud clothes and even louder red hair. He storms into the room and before he even sits down, he booms out, "John Lurie! The music! Why?!"

I was repeatedly asked how Jim Jarmusch had discovered me, how he had coaxed such amazing performances out of a hopeless dolt like myself. It was kind of like asking a Native American what it was like being discovered by Columbus.

Somehow Torton found a basketball and we went bouncing it down the boardwalk, in search of a court, to the horror of the French. It really was strange how appalled the French were by two guys bouncing a basketball. Mouths were hanging open in terror. We never found a hoop, scared a lot of people, and went back.

I met this fantastically beautiful Egyptian model named Fadwa. She was a very bad girl, you could see it from a mile away.

Fadwa wanted to get some heroin. I hadn't been high in months and thought, *Why not?* So I gave her a couple hundred francs and she disappeared. I thought that I probably wouldn't ever see her again, but later that afternoon, there was a knock on my hotel room door and there she was. She had a package of white powder folded into a quarter page of a magazine.

I put a tiny bit of the powder on my tongue with my little finger. It didn't taste much like heroin. Didn't taste much like anything. I was sure she had been ripped off. I snorted a small line and didn't feel anything at all.

I had been invited to a dinner at the president of the festival's mansion. I didn't want to go but I was told that this was a big honor and I absolutely had to go.

There were these long, fancy tables with very famous and very rich people, dressed formally, getting ready to eat. I have never played so well with the rich in the first place, but now I was beginning to feel a little odd. I suspected that the thing I had snorted was ground-up sleeping pills.

When *Stranger Than Paradise* came out, Roger Ebert played a clip of it on his show and exclaimed, "That's John Lurie! I think we're going to be seeing a lot of him in the future! He's very talented!"

I was seated next to Roger Ebert at the dinner.

Then I fell asleep on Roger Ebert's shoulder.

I had a wild time with Fadwa that went on round the clock and didn't leave my room very often. I got a call that I was supposed to go to the awards presentation and I was a mess. Stephen had gotten me to buy this beautiful silk tuxedo that I had worn once, to the dinner. I found it crumpled up in a corner of my room. My room that looked like it had been vandalized by monkeys.

Spike Lee stopped by because he wanted to meet me, took a look around my room, and left immediately.

I picked the tuxedo up off the floor. It uncrumpled itself and looked gorgeous. Like some miracle fabric of elegance. Ten years later, Stephen wore that same tuxedo at his wedding.

My hair was going in several directions and my face was all swollen and puffy. We had to walk up this big, open stairway to get to the theater. It was kind of like the red carpet, and there were TV cameras everywhere. I must have looked like an ashtray with a bloated face, in a tuxedo, and I wonder how famous people do it, always in front of the camera looking fresh and clean and presentable. They probably don't take that much heroin and have never spent the night with Fadwa.

I wasn't doing this movie star thing very well at all.

I remember being home, dope sick or hungover, and watching my little black and white TV from my mattress on the floor, getting up only to use the bathroom, and I'd see someone sprightly talking into the camera, looking all clean and together. I'd think: *How does she do it?* Of course, there were times that I'd look out the window at people on the street and think: *How do those people have the energy to walk down the street? When do they have the strength to buy clothes?*

Sue Jacobs is Chris Blackwell's top assistant. The negotiations with Island are not going well. I do not want to accept any of the stuff that Joel Webber has negotiated for me, and I do not want to have to deal with this sleazeball Webber further, but he will now be my A&R guy. I meet with Sue for lunch and she tells me that if I do not accept the deal as it stands, it is not going to happen. But she does seem to be legitimately on my side on this.

Back in New York, I hire Valerie Goodman to run my business. She is always pleasant and very energetic. I give her a weekly salary.

I get a call from Joel Webber. He tells me the *Big Heart* record has sold seventeen thousand copies in the first week.

"Is that a lot?"

"Yes, that's a lot!"

We're about to go on tour for a month in Europe. Webber gets in the middle of it and somehow Island books us at the Institute of Contemporary Arts in London—ICA.

Philippe de Visscher, who is booking our tours at the time, is furious. He has booked one big gig in London at the Hammersmith. We're supposed to fly in, do the gig, and then leave the next day. Because the ICA is a small venue, we will play there five days. This means five days of hotels to pay for, the musicians get paid by the week, and everything else. It means there will be a lot of money lost. Philippe isn't going to take the loss himself, so now he is paying me five thousand less for the tour. I can't go back on what I promised the band, so the money is going to come out of my pocket.

I very much prefer to play one place for five nights. There is no travel, no packing, no sound checks. You can sleep late and maybe even meet some people from that town. But I can't afford to lose the $5,000.

I go back to Joel Webber and say we can't do the gig, that I'm going to lose too much money. He insists. Says that Island in London had to pull a lot of strings to get us a week at the ICA. This is a prestigious gig. It will be very bad for my relationship with them. I know the ICA from when I lived in London; it is kind of a cool place, on par with the Kitchen in New York, but it is not what I would call a "prestigious gig."

Joel makes a deal with me. He will get Island to put up money toward making a music video for the band. I like the idea and say okay to the gig.

A couple of weeks later, when I go back to Island about the budget for the video, they say they will put up $500. Five hundred dollars is absolutely, ridiculously, ridiculously nothing to make a video, but I think I can shoot it in Super 8. Get Stephen to help me and Robert Burden to edit it, and maybe we can pull it off. It might be fun, and even though I'm losing about $4,000 because of his interference in the tour and now they're offering $500 to make up for it, I think that if they pay for the video, then they might feel involved and will try to get it played.

I liked touring the most. I loved it. Even though I was always stressed out about getting paid, or the travel, which was always worse than necessary because the people planning it had never really looked at how to make it easier, or because the hotel always seemed to be under construction, or because the monitors sucked 70 percent of the time and we couldn't hear ourselves, or any of a list of horrors one can imagine if they have ever traveled anywhere.

But I loved it. A floating circus, and often—usually—the music was great. Frequently we would arrive and it was a disaster, usually with equipment. Dougie one night ended up playing on a child's drum set, which he destroyed by playing it with a hammer. Another time he played on a set called Jolly Drums. I knew they were called Jolly Drums because in big, animated, colorful letters on the bass drum was printed "Jolly Drums." How can someone bring you to their town to play music when they have signed a contract saying that they will have specified equipment, and then when you arrive it is nothing like what it is supposed to be? It is insulting to us and insulting to the music. Our only recourse would be to cancel, but the only reason we were doing the whole horrific thing was to play music.

But the duress often made us play better. It created an us against them situation: The worse the situation, the stronger we grouped together. We played with absolute rage. We would unify and fight, like men at war, until we had conquered the sound of the room. No gig was ever allowed to end before we had found that thing, before we had somehow conquered the sound of the room.

The first gig is at a jazz festival and there are a lot of famous older jazz musicians on the plane from the United States. Roy is completely thrilled. Most of the flight he sits and talks with Reggie Workman, who used to play bass with Coltrane. I will admit that for almost any horn player, getting a chance to talk with someone who actually knew and played with Coltrane is an enormous and exciting opportunity.

But there is something about the way Roy, who is one of the most truly obsessive people I've met in my life, is hunched and twitching in the seat next to Reggie Workman and just prying into him for information that makes me uneasy. Roy can be beautiful, soulful, and completely genuine, but right now he's giving me the creeps.

Well, Reggie has really done it. He told Roy that Coltrane used to play eighteen hours a day. That, while reading a book, he would also practice at the same time. He went offstage and practiced while other people were soloing. This is fairly common knowledge, but I guess that hearing it firsthand really set Roy off.

Not only is Roy one of the most obsessive people on the planet, he is in many ways one of the most unconscious. When he is practicing, he seems to pay no notice at all to what he is playing—the same line played over and over again, out of tune. It is not pleasant. But now he's trying to follow in Coltrane's footsteps and play eighteen hours a day. As soon as we check into a hotel, after traveling ten hours by bus, after sleeping two hours the night before, and with sound check in an hour, Roy begins his ritual squelching.

Dougie, who sleeps all the time, calls down to the front desk, in a fake foreign accent, and says, "Horrible noise coming from room two oh two. It must stop."

* * *

On tour it's difficult to eat. I've been on tour with the Red Hot Chili Peppers after they became gigantic, and it is not difficult for them to eat. But for a band on the level of The Lounge Lizards, it can be impossible. You have the hotel buffet breakfast, which in Germany is ham, cheese, and bread. On the train you can have a ham or cheese sandwich. When you get to the dressing room there is a display of ham, cheese, and bread.

Ribot said, "Which ham sandwich killed him?"

In Germany, a paper ran a huge photo of me on the back page with an article about the band and me as an actor. The title of the article was "The Handsomest Man in the World."

After that I was unbearable. I'd get into the elevator with the band and say, "Now the handsomest man in the world is getting into the elevator."

"Now the handsomest man in the world is getting out of the elevator."

"Now the handsomest man in the world is in the lobby and about to argue with the front desk about his long-distance phone bill."

I was absolutely making fun of the idea that they had proclaimed this of me, but the band couldn't stand it, especially Evan. And I don't blame them. So I cut it out after a day. But it's nice to be called the handsomest man in the world, particularly when you have a pimple on your forehead and your legs are hideously skinny.

Marc is sleeping with Pascal, the tour manager. This is a very bad idea. The tour manager's job is to book you into hotels, make travel arrangements, make sure you get paid by the venue, etc., etc.

But why it's a bad idea is that the tour manager is not on your side. The way it was set up, she was the employee of the promoter. She is his emissary. So she is the one who whispers to you at midnight, after the show, that at four A.M. you have to check out because the bus driver quit and you have to take the train to Nice. She is also the one to pay us and we have not gotten a penny yet.

Philippe de Visscher, the promoter, shows up somewhere in France and comes out to dinner with us after. It is a tiny stone restaurant and it is only the band eating there this late. I am getting very nervous about the money. We were supposed to get a deposit before we left, which we didn't get, then paid weekly at the end of each week. So far we've gotten nothing and it's two and a half weeks into the tour. When the guys need spending money, I have been fronting it to them out of my own pocket. Marc is sitting at the table strumming a guitar; the food is taking forever. I ask Philippe a second time about when we are getting paid and he makes an offhand joke about my learning to relax. I lose it. I smash my wineglass down on the table. It shatters, flies everywhere, and severs three of the guitar strings. I jump over the table and pull Philippe out of his chair. But then I stop because I am afraid maybe I have actually hurt somebody with the shattering glass.

I think on this same tour, we're somewhere in the south of France, very excited to be near the ocean. We're on the highway and there is this structure up ahead that looks like a bomb shelter, an unpleasant, heavy block of a building, made of concrete with no windows.

Someone says, "Look, the hotel!" This is a joke. This building is so awful that it has to be pointed out and ridiculed.

But the driver pulls into the driveway. This is the hotel.

"Drive away! Drive away!"

"Nooooo!!"

"No fair!!"

We check in and most of us decide to walk to the beach. We are white. White as paper. Most of us haven't been out in the daytime in months.

The people on the beach are all perfectly coiffed and perfectly bronzed. They are wearing perfect bathing suits.

Roy doesn't have a bathing suit, so he's wearing his white BVDs. Every molecule on him is white. He is more than pale. He shines pale. Roy is a hundred yards away on a massively crowded beach and I can easily identify him as the ultra-white speck amid all the perfect bronze specks.

There is something that we call the Toronto Trick. This happens a lot in small towns in Germany or Austria: Bremen, Ravensburg, and Saarbrücken come to mind. The audience, not wanting to seem like a bunch of rubes, sit with their arms folded and scowl at us while we play. I don't know what they're thinking . . . this way we won't get over on them? I don't know, maybe they're just living like that, sour.

We finish a song and there is a smattering of applause. You get nothing back, just nothing. Show ends and you leave the stage. They go berserk, demanding encore after encore. The weirdest thing is that it felt like they hated you while you were playing, and then you stop and they go crazy. Maybe they just want to make sure they get their money's worth. But it really seems like all of a sudden they love you.

Next we play Paris. We're playing on a double bill with Wayne Shorter, at this enormous place called La Villette. I have a lot of interviews to do, so they put me up in a big fancy hotel near the Louvre. They put the band in some stinking place with broken windows and no phones in the rooms.

I don't have a girlfriend anymore. Every night, after the concert I am engulfed in beautiful women. It is like they are having a social for us night after night, town after town. This is fairly consistent, except for in Italy and for some reason in London, but Paris, well, that is just nuts.

Check into the room and the phone rings.

"Miss Petra is downstairs."

Petra is a young woman I met in Berlin on the tour before. Spend a couple of hours with her, have room service, and then she has to go to some modeling thing. She's not gone ten minutes when the phone rings again.

"Miss Isabelle is here."

"Okay, send her up."

So then that happens.

That night, we haven't made plans, but Petra is waiting outside the dressing room. That's too bad, because Cecelia shows up. Cecelia is a Swedish model I know from New York. When she doesn't understand what you have said, she says "Pern?" instead of "Pardon?" She is pretty much the dirtiest girl I have ever been with, in a very wonderful way, and quite beautiful.

Cecelia wants to go to Les Bains Douches. This is the last place I want to go, but we go long enough for her to score some coke. Go back to my room and it lasts way into the morning. At nine A.M. I have her over my knee and am spanking her with her hairbrush out on the balcony. The front desk calls and asks us to please take our activities inside the room. They are getting complaints from the passing motorists.

Starting at noon, I have to do the British press. I have done articles for the *New Musical Express* before with this guy—I think his name was Roy Carr—who was smart and respectful. But these guys they send over from the two leading music papers are creepy, self-important poseurs. Makes you afraid to say anything in the interview, because you know the article is going to be about them and not you, and certainly not the music.

We get to London and are playing the ICA. It's not much fun. We're getting used to playing these really nice halls in Europe for a thousand to two thousand people. This place holds five hundred or so and the audience is sitting on bleachers. They look most uncomfortable. It isn't nice and it isn't wild. The crowd can't drink or smoke. If it isn't a beautiful theater with plush chairs and an exquisite sound system, they should be able to drink and smoke. I don't know why on earth Island has insisted we play here. It's not horrible, but it just doesn't make any sense.

I go into the big record store in Piccadilly Circus. I am in line to pay and the guy in front of me asks if they have the new Lounge Lizards record. The clerk tells him that they don't have it.

I step up to the counter and ask, "You don't have the new Lounge Lizards record here?"

"You're John Lurie, aren't you?"

"Yes, why don't you have my record?"

"You tell me. We keep trying to order it, everyone is asking for it, but we can't get it."

"You mean it's not out here yet?"

"No, no one in London can get it."

So why the fuck are we here, losing $5,000, to play the ICA to promote a record that is not available?

We fly to Sardinia. We are looking forward to this. Four days in Sardinia. The ocean. Stephen Torton is going to meet us there. I have brought a Super 8 camera and we are going to try to make the music video.

We arrive at the airport in Sardinia and they have one van for the nine of us.

"Well, it's a small island, can't be that far."

We spend four hours hunched in this tiny van with no air conditioning. It is 104 degrees. Knees, elbows, and irritation are everywhere. And sweat. We're tired and hungry as the van swerves and lurches around hairpin curves.

We finally arrive and our legs can hardly unfold out onto the pavement.

A truck with a loudspeaker drives around blaring, "*STASERA*, JAN LOOREEE! JAN LOORREE!"

The promoter comes up all smiles.

"Chow, John Lurie!! Chow, John Lurie!!"

Ribot declares that I am dog food and finds it funny for a little too long. It is amazing how the Italians greet you like everything is wonderful when it is anything but wonderful. Two of the guys in the band are vomiting in the parking lot, next to the van, because of the drive. Wonderful.

Before we left New York, I called the guys in the band and said that if they had stolen the cotton kimono robes from their hotel rooms in Japan, they should bring them with them on the tour for the video. They all swore they had not stolen the robes. I brought a couple of extra robes just in case, but of course every one of them had stolen his robe.

We shoot the video for the song "Big Heart" mostly on our one day off in Sardinia. Torton is wonderful.

We find a steep hill, overlooking the sea. A steep, rocky incline that is really more a mountain than a hill. The band all wear the Japanese robes and venture down a twisting, dusty path that goes all the way to the water. Torton stays at the top with the camera. I say, "Go!" and we march up the steep incline, legs high, muscles straining toward Torton, who is some two hundred meters above us. Get halfway to him and I say, "Okay, let's do it again."

There are grumbles. It is over one hundred degrees.

"Come on! This is fun!"

We do it again, this time walking all the way up to Torton.

"How was it?"

"Okay. I want to get it from that other cliff as well."

"Okay, everybody back down!"

More grumbling.

"Come on! This is fun! It's going to be on TV!!"

We go back down.

The basic idea behind the video is that we are insane monks, with Roy carrying a boombox on his shoulder like it is a sacred item. Everyone's face is really solemn. We come up the hill, through some ruins, and reverently place the boombox down, then wait, erect and unmoving. At a certain phrase that happens twice in the song, we all dance wildly. A kind of Muhammad Ali shuffle that we do facing one another in two squares for four bars, turn right for four bars, and then back.

It is the silliest thing ever made and I love it.

29

When Life Punches You in the Face, You Have to Get Back Up. How Else Can Life Punch You in the Face Again?

For years, I never left the island of Manhattan, unless I was on tour. And on tour you only see the inside of the plane, the airport, the van to the hotel, the hotel room, the venue, and the tour bus.

The only time you ever get any fresh air is when you step out of the tour bus onto the tar parking lot when you stop at a restaurant on the highway.

Otherwise, for years there had been no fresh air.

But fresh air is very good for you. You tend to forget that if you never get it.

Green things are good for you.

Evan and I rented a nice house in Killington, Vermont, to write the music for the next Lounge Lizards record. Val hooked the house up and got a piano moved in. She was amazingly good at getting stuff like that done.

For some reason I couldn't write a note of music.

I fell into a sort of coma. I suppose I needed to do this. I had been going at full speed, round the clock, for years, without ever stopping. Or maybe fresh air is actually bad for you.

Evan had discovered Astor Piazzolla and it had hit him really hard. He began working on his tango stuff for *bandoneón* all day long.

I don't know how Piazzolla came into Evan's view. I had not heard of him. Now, to me, that anyone who cares about music at all has not heard the music of Piazzolla is just wrong. Particularly a record called *Tango: Zero Hour.*

I feel similarly about Nusrat Fateh Ali Khan, who Evan also introduced me to. He took me to see him at the Brooklyn Academy of Music. It started out with harmonium and a bunch of guys with mustaches sitting on the stage, singing almost like they were not really interested, more like they were mumbling.

This went on for quite a while. I turned to Evan and said, "What the fuck, Evan? Why am I here?" as the men with mustaches sat on the stage sort of singing.

But it built and built. And then it built more. Over a long period of time, it just slowly built, and somehow you were inside it. Hypnotized by it. And then Nusrat started hitting these lines that ripped into my soul. It was like I had been transfigured.

As the proper, polite people sat there in their seats at BAM, absorbing their culture as people of their class are supposed to do, it hit me so hard that I jumped up and started screaming in approval, "Fuck you! Fuck you!! Motherfucker!! Oh!!"

Anyway, we were in Vermont and I could not write a note.

I went fishing, shot baskets, and slept a lot. Ev cooked and there was one restaurant nearby. Uncle Jerry and my sister, Liz, came up to visit for a couple of days, but nothing much else happened. I slowed to a halt, which I needed way more than I had realized. I was hoping that they would let me see Liz at Marathon House, which was close by in New Hampshire. In a way, that is why we went up there, but that didn't happen.

I drove down to New York to direct a music video for this Japanese singer I liked named Sion.

Then I went back up to Vermont and tried to write music. Nothing happened and then I just stopped. Evan was getting a potbelly. Evan, who had always been as thin as a rail, was putting on weight around the middle and seemed proud of it. The only physical activity that he would do with me was canoeing, which we did every day at sunset. Evan said he could go canoeing because it wouldn't affect his paunch. So we would rent a canoe and paddle around the outskirts of a lake. It was quite pleasant. We would say the kind of things to each other that brothers do and find incredibly funny. Things that would be lost on the rest of the world.

When I got back to New York, I moved into a big prewar brownstone. A garden duplex apartment on West Eleventh Street that would have cost a fortune, but they charged me about half the normal rate because they were selling the place and had the right to ask me to leave on short notice. Also, they had the right to show the apartment while I lived there, which led to constant wars with real estate agents who would show up with no warning, which was not supposed to be the deal.

Real estate agents in Manhattan can be a tough lot. If they came unannounced, I got pretty good at scaring them away. Or if I was too tired to scare them, I would come downstairs in my underwear, eating a cracker.

I gave Kazu the apartment on Third Street and moved to Eleventh Street by myself.

The band was playing at the Bottom Line one night and I was practicing in my apartment, in the afternoon, before the gig. Someone in my posh new neighborhood was yelling out the window from the next building, complaining about the noise. Then he threw a bag of trash into my backyard. I went out and yelled up. Saw someone duck back behind their window, so I knew which apartment had done this. I picked up a grapefruit from the trash that had spilled out all over my garden and threw it right through the glass of his window. It made a nice hole, exactly the size of the grapefruit.

I bought an eight-foot toy basketball hoop and put it upstairs in the spare room that was painted bright pink. For a while that was the only thing in the pink room. I would play one on one with Rammellzee with a little orange basketball.

Down by Law opens the New York Film Festival. It is a big deal. There are all these events and dinners.

There is this guy who calls himself Doc. He thinks that we should be friends. Kind of like the inevitable ex-drummer who comes into the dressing room and announces that because he once played drums, you must now be friends.

The guy is creepy, and every night that I go to a party for the New York Film Festival, there he is. And he wants to talk. On the third night, at Cafe Un Deux Trois, my friend Lori Singer is sitting next to me. When she gets up to use the restroom, he rushes to plop himself down in Lori's seat like he is playing musical chairs against invisible people.

He seems angry. Like, not angry about something specific but as if this is pretty much the essence of the guy. Doc says, "Look, I knew Tom Waits back when he was this nerdy, alienated guy that nobody liked. I knew him before he decided to change himself into the Bukowski persona that you think is Tom Waits. But that is not who he really is."

Well, this is somehow worse than the guy who comes into the dressing room and announces that he used to play the drums. This guy is trying to become my friend by exposing something about Tom that Tom would clearly rather not have known. And I want to get away from this guy.

Then he says, "The Tom Waits that you think is your friend does not exist."

Damn, another left turn.

Years later, I had a series of devastating problems, one after the other. In order to try to get my work back or to protect it, I had to go to war with forces far more powerful than myself. It completely disrupted, and almost destroyed, my path as an artist. It almost destroyed my desire to continue living on this planet.

These nightmares were going to be the bulk of this book and are the reason the title, for a long time, was *What Do You Know About Music? You're Not a Lawyer.* I wanted to hold people accountable by shining a light on what had happened.

But in the end, they are just such unpleasant stories, I didn't want to write them and can't imagine who would want to read them. Who wants to watch me turn over a rock to show all the little bugs crawling around? My hope is, as with all my work, that this book will be something that people find uplifting.

I have decided wherever possible to not even name people.

I will try to tell these stories here, as quickly and concisely as possible, without going too deeply into the ugly minutiae of each one. But I feel I really do have to tell these stories in order to be as honest as I've tried to be throughout the book.

Warning—if this shit bugs you, you may skip to the next chapter.

The first disasters were the making of *Fishing with John* and *Live in Berlin*.

Fishing with John was a TV show I shot in 1991 and 1992, where I would go ice fishing with Willem Dafoe or fishing in Thailand with Dennis Hopper.

I knew nothing about fishing, or next to nothing, so everything would go wrong.

It was intended that everything go wrong.

We had a narrator, Robb Webb, who sounded like the voice of God, sharing absolutely wrong and ludicrous information about nature.

He would say how brave my guest and I were to be embarking on an adventure of this sort. Because Robb's voice was so solid and so serious, it sounded like everything he said was absolutely, perfectly true.

Live in Berlin started out as a live Lounge Lizards record that we'd make in Berlin at the end of an upcoming 1991 tour, but then the idea came up of filming it and releasing the film worldwide with the album.

The concert film was to be paid for by the Japanese company that was producing *Fishing with John*, which was run by Mr. Okabe, who is a wonderful and honorable man, along with his equally wonderful and honorable assistant Fumiko Horiuchi. I loved these people then and still love them now.

However, their representative in New York was not of the same character. Like, at all.

* * *

Everything was going along fine.

It was my assistant's idea to make a concert film along with the live album and get the Japanese company to invest in it.

She brought in this young film director to make the movie. She told me that Robert Burden had approved the young director. Robert Burden was someone I trusted implicitly. He had edited, and saved, the first *Fishing with John* episode, as well as The Lounge Lizards' "Big Heart" video.

If Robert, who had very little respect for almost anyone, trusted this guy's ability as a director, then this guy was okay with me. But Robert was dying of AIDS. He was very ill, and I wasn't about to call him and find out if he'd really vouched for this young director who had been brought in.

The band was on fire throughout the entire tour. We were getting better and better each night.

We were well oiled and it sounded amazing.

We had four nights to play in Berlin at the Quartier Latin.

Nothing could possibly go wrong.

On the way to the first concert, I looked up to the sky and said, "Thank you. Thank you for this opportunity."

But the equipment was a disaster. We'd had decent equipment every night previously on the tour, but now, because the record company was arranging and paying for it, of course it sucked.

The marimba was tuned to 440 hertz and the vibes to 444. The horns and guitar and cello could decide to be in tune with one or the other, but not both, and thus we were all struggling to stay in tune with one another the entire night.

During the first song, the two-hundred-year-old timpani collapsed. Rolled off its stand toward the audience and then died.

During the next song, I noticed that Bryan Carrott, the vibes player, was not playing in a place he really needed to be playing. I looked over and Bryan was standing there holding the metal strand of silver vibe keys in his hands with a puzzled look on his face about how to put this thing back together. What he was wrestling with was so unwieldy, it looked like a baby metal boa constrictor.

This was all in the first ten minutes of the concert.

We kind of lost our balance after that.

Often, actually pretty much always, when a concert started badly, usually because of the sound of the room or the shitty equipment or some horror the promoter had put us through, we would rally, as one, as warriors, and overcome whatever was holding us back. We would conquer the sound of the room. But on the first of these four nights of concerts, we became discombobulated and did not recover.

But we had three more nights to get this right.

After the show, Michael Blake, the other saxophone player, came to me and complained about the hotel the band was in. Michael could be staying in the fanciest hotel in Berlin and still come to me and whine that the toilet made a squeaking noise when it was flushed and I would have to fix it. But in this case, it was fair.

They had the band two people to a room, and it was already in the contract that this could not be done. For years this could not be done. But they had me, the movie star, in a suite in a different, very beautiful hotel and had the musicians in a shitty hotel, two to a room, and the bathroom was a communal bathroom in the hallway. The bathroom had a smashed window, inviting cold fresh air in during your shower.

So after finishing the concert at two A.M., getting something to eat, and getting back to the room around four, I got up at seven A.M., hopped into a cab, and started looking for a hotel to move the band to. The reason I had to go out into Berlin to look for the hotel was that I sort of remembered the whereabouts of the last hotel we'd stayed in in Berlin but couldn't remember the name. I found the hotel and put my credit card down for eleven rooms for all the musicians and sound people.

Then I had to find instruments that worked. I went back to my room to call the promoters in Zurich and Munich to see if we could get the timpani, vibes, marimba, and drums from their gigs and have them brought in by that night. Their equipment had been fine.

I had been told by the German record company woman that the terrible instruments we had played the first night were the only possibilities in all of Berlin. Though, as I write this, I realize it cannot possibly have been true. And you'd think I would have known enough by this stage in my life not to trust what the record company was telling me.

I get the band moved over to the new hotel. And when the equipment arrives from Munich, I have to set up another, unplanned sound check, to work things out with the new equipment.

The woman from the record company stops by and sees that I am in a frenzy setting up things in the sound check and says that she has just the thing for me. She will set up a massage to make sure I am relaxed before the concert that night.

An hour before leaving for the club, there is a knock on my hotel room door.

It is this overly muscled guy with long hair down to his waist, wearing a bright, maroon-colored robe garment.

He does that bizarre eye contact thing, which I suppose he thinks makes him seem sincere, but it seems more like he is attempting to emit radiation from his skull and into mine.

He smells.

He has that horrible, hippie-smelling oil stuff that is supposed to mask his body odor, but it does not, and that hippie smell—what is that called? Patchouli? Whatever it is, I can't stand it.

He puts a mat down on the floor and tells me to undress. I strip down to my underwear, but he says, "No, no, you must take off everything!"

I hesitate for a moment but then go ahead and take off my boxers.

He takes off his shirt and he is repulsively hairy.

Then he takes off his pants, leaving only this loincloth underwear garment.

And this is just really fucking weird.

I go along with it. I do not have any idea why I go along with it. I think I am just too exhausted to fight against his insistence.

But when he starts to dig his knuckles into the small of my back, I feel his hair, his creepy fucking hair, on my back.

I say in a voice that would stop a bull in its tracks, "Stop. Stop right now and get out."

Now I fucking smell like patchouli. I take another shower. I still smell like patchouli. I throw on my suit.

When I am out in the hallway of the hotel, Tom Lazarus, the engineer who has been brought over to do the recording, looks at my body, which is being contorted by nerves, with my shoulders creeping up around my ears, and says, "Wow, John. What the hell happened to you?"

Damn, I am doing it. Getting into the minutiae of this. I will try to put it down more simply.

The overall story of this segment of the nightmare is that the woman from the German record company already owes me money on royalties for distributing *Voice of Chunk* in some territories in Europe.

There has been some confusion about whether or not *Live in Berlin* will be one or two records. I send her the first record when it is done but hold back the second record until she has paid me what I'm owed, which turns out to be a substantial amount of money.

For reasons I will get to shortly, I am forced to fire, with extreme prejudice, both my assistant and my lawyer. So I am in the dark about a lot of what has transpired.

But I have not been reimbursed for the flights bringing nine musicians and two sound engineers to Europe. I have not been reimbursed for the eleven hotel rooms in Berlin. I have not been paid the advance for close to the entirety of the first live record, and I have been paid nothing for the second.

When we finish the four nights, the German record company woman suggests that I go to her friend's studio in Málaga, Spain. She says it's beautiful there. It's a brand new, state-of-the-art studio. There is a special apartment for the artist.

I am picked up, at the airport, by a young man named Harley. He explains in great detail how his name is Harley because he loves Harley-Davidson motorcycles.

He hands me a key and drops me at the apartment.

It is no wonder that he did not want to come in. It is filthy. A level of filthy I have never really seen before, and if you have made it this far in the book, you must realize that I have encountered a great deal of filthy.

The worst part is that the mattress on the floor stinks and is covered in this long hair that seems to have been pressed into the sheets.

There is no one to call and nowhere to walk. No food.

The next day, Harley stops by, all smiles.

I am not any amount of smiles.

About an hour later, Harley and another guy arrive with a new mattress, still wrapped in plastic. They make it very clear that delivering this mattress is below their station in life.

I tell Harley that I must speak to whoever is in charge here.

Harley explains that they will be ready for me late that afternoon.

Two young men on the verge of devilment

86 5 19

Actor, Cannes, 1986

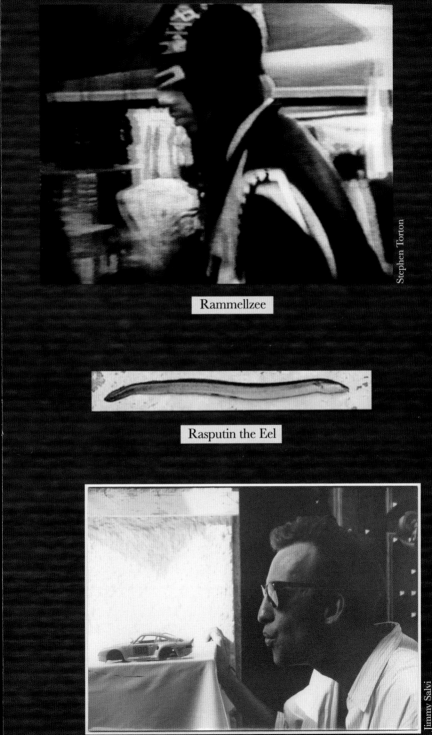

Rammellzee

Rasputin the Eel

Big Heart video

Evan—hallway dancing

Big Heart video

Franck Vidal

Rehearsal

Evan and I try to duplicate the photo of a very strange couple displayed outside the booth

Boris Policeband

Sometimes I wasn't liking Marty so much

Rebecca in Voice of Chunk commercial

With Natalia

Another glamorous dressing room

Guitar with Ribot

Pitching to Willem in Long Island after fishing; Kazu plays a bored center field

Kissing Miss Liz

The Lounge Lizards

Modeling Kazu's dress

With Lisa Krueger

I quit acting when Werner tried to convince me to be in his movie where I would be eaten by a bear

With Rockets Redglare

Elba, 1989

Calvin and me and hats

Torton and Willie Mays

Christian Lepanto

Christian Lepanto '89

Birthday dinner with Willem Dafoe and Steve Buscemi

James Nares

With Kazu in St. Barts

I ask where the studio is and he points up the hill but says that I cannot go there now.

"Why can't I go there now?"

Harley shrugs. "You can't."

So I walk up the hill and walk into the studio, which is nowhere near a finished studio. The consoles are on the floor. There are unconnected wires everywhere. But the thing that makes it most suspicious is that when I surprise them as I walk in, the owner and engineer and studio manager try to hide whatever machinery they have been working on behind their backs with an *Oh no, we've been caught* look on their faces.

Now I am freaking out. I try to reach my assistant, who is in Paris. I finally get hold of her, but she clearly doesn't want to speak to me or want to help me get out of this mess.

When I call back the next day, I hear the voice of the young weasel who directed the concert film. What is he doing there? Are they sleeping together? Has she been hiding this all along?

Has she brought in this kid, who, it already has been made clear, doesn't know what he is doing, to direct the concert film because they are secretly together?

And did she say he was approved by Robert Burden because she knew I wouldn't call Robert Burden about this while he was so sick?

So I go to mix the first record in Paris. Go back to New York and find out that there are all kinds of problems with The Lounge Lizards movie, and my assistant and, I assume, her secret boyfriend have to go to Paris again to fix some technical film problems that can only be fixed at a lab in Paris.

Sometime later, I learn that my money has been used to fly them to Paris and pay for their hotel.

I find out all kinds of things like that. And when I meet with the district attorney of New York, a year and a half later, I will find out really a lot of things like that.

The Japanese company who is paying for the concert film and *Fishing with John* is going bankrupt. They owe me a lot of money on *Fishing with John* for directing, producing, doing the music, etc.

When I go to collect it, their New York representative produces a one-page contract that says that I will be responsible for all overspending on the concert film. I know nothing about this paper. It is from my lawyer and signed by my assistant, who is listed on the contract as my manager. But because the concert film is being made by this guy who doesn't know what he's doing, it has gone more than double over budget.

So now instead of their owing me quite a bit of money, what was going to be my first really big payday in this life, they believe that I owe them something like $200,000.

And now they are bankrupt and have no money to finish *Fishing with John*.

They agree to funnel more money into the concert film because they have just saved the money they would have paid me, and on top of that, I, theoretically, am responsible for the overspending on the film.

People start telling me that they have seen my lawyer and my assistant around town together, late at night. This is just weird.

And it turns out that they, along with the Japanese representative in New York, have sold *Fishing with John* to distributors in Europe, without my knowledge or consent. And there is no money to finish it.

This is such a complicated story, to explain it in its entirety simply isn't worth it.

How it all lines up is, it's a perfect storm of disaster for me.

There is nothing in the contract with the German record company that says I owe them a second record. But they claim I owe them one. There is certainly enough material, but I don't want to give them anything else until they pay the owed royalties on *Voice of Chunk*, reimburse me for the several thousand dollars that I am out of pocket on the live record, and give me some kind of advance on the second record. We are at an impasse.

Next thing I learn is that my lawyer, my assistant, and the New York rep for the Japanese company, without my knowledge, have negotiated a deal for the concert film, as well, to be released in Europe with a German distributor.

In the contract, it says that I, John Lurie, who have no idea that any of this is happening, am responsible for any claims against the distributor by third parties.

Also in the addendum to the contract for the concert film between me and the Japanese company, which I was also unaware of, it says that I indemnify the Japanese company against third-party claims.

What this means is that there will most likely be a legal battle between the German record company and myself. They want their second record and I want the money that they owe me.

Because I do not own the copyright for the recordings, the German film distributor, who is releasing the movie in a few months, has no right to use the music without the record company's permission.

In the worst case scenario, and I can see all this happening a mile away, I will be sued by the German distributor when the record company gets an injunction on the film. In the contract that I knew nothing about, it says that I have indemnified them against third-party claims and they will lose a fortune on theater rentals and advertising. Isn't this fun?

So I fly over and talk to the head of the distribution company and ask him to please hold off until I can fix this legal mess before releasing the movie. He says of course, they can wait.

But then two months later, with no warning, the film is coming out in Germany, Austria, and Switzerland.

The record company gets an injunction against the film, so not only will I be sued by the film distributor and the record company, I will also be sued by the Japanese company, because my representatives have signed an addendum, again without my knowledge, indemnifying them against third-party claims.

Baskets of fun!

For the first time in my life, I have some money, and I am now headed to complete financial disaster.

On top of this, *Fishing with John*, which I think is going to be pretty great, will never be seen.

And! This beautiful, powerful, unique music was finally going to be heard outside of a couple thousand people a night in concert halls.

This was as good as it could have gotten and nothing could go wrong. I did the work. It was all there.

And now, I am out close to a million dollars. And I am about to be sued by three companies. It is a mess. I fight like mad.

I hire lawyers. I lose thirty pounds.

The lawyers end up bilking me for my remaining money without getting any resolution whatsoever.

I do finally, in the end, after almost two years of legal battles and doing almost nothing else but fight legal battles, get my royalties from the record company. Which come close to covering only my legal fees.

Also, I learn that I am broke. My assistant could sign checks on my corporate account, but I discover that she made friends with people at the bank, then moved money from my personal account to my corporate account by forging checks. She did this to the tune of $110,000.

I learn that one has only ninety days to challenge this with the bank.

After ages, I finally got to meet with the assistant district attorney in New York and learned that my assistant had $460,000 in the bank the week I fired her, when she was making $600 a week working for me.

On top of that, I had the $110,000 worth of canceled forged checks with a report from a signature expert claiming it was the assistant who had made these forgeries.

The ADA said, "We can see that she is doing incredibly fishy, dishonest things, but it is not a good case for us." And said he would turn down the case.

I was baffled. How was that not a good case? They had it all there on paper, but the district attorney would not budge and I walked out of his office wondering what kind of a world this was.

Whew . . . that is one. I'm afraid there is more.

Ideas come to you in different ways. Something stirs your brain, you let it sit there, another piece of the puzzle comes in. But with some ideas, they come as gifts. With music in particular, there will be an idea, usually something quite simple, that floats in, and you really have to pay attention to it. You have to protect it when you build things around it.

In 1989, I was staying in Grottaglie with Antonio, who had done the set design for *Il Piccolo Diavolo*, when the idea for *You Stink Mister* came to me.

I was napping in the afternoon for an hour and woke up with this image just stuck in my head. It was one of those gifts. The stone bedroom and living in Antonio's monk world added to the sanctity of the idea.

It was a movie with Roberto Benigni playing a cowboy who travels across a surreal landscape with a Native American.

A few weeks later I was staying with Sandro Veronesi in Grosseto, Italy, who told me a true story about an Italian cowboy who had challenged Buffalo Bill Cody to a cowboy contest and won. This certainly seemed like a piece to the puzzle.

I wrote it so that Roberto was a championship-caliber cowboy, but everything he had learned and mastered he had done in his mother's home, either in his bedroom or in the backyard, where he had built a makeshift horse out of broken furniture.

After he wins a ranch in America by beating Buffalo Bill in a cowboy contest, he travels to this bizarre new country. Inexplicably, frogs with fur fly around all the time. I wanted to shoot it in Kenya, which would make it much more expensive, but I was determined to do this. It needed that landscape.

Probably the best idea that came up for the movie was Juno's Flu.

Juno's Flu was an illness that lasted three days to a week. The symptoms were close to those of Tourette's syndrome but a little more dramatic and much sillier.

It was highly contagious, so that throughout the movie, all the characters came down with it.

So there are scenes where Roberto and his Native American friend, Coney, are staying with a group of extremely austere monks.

They are having dinner and the second-highest-ranked monk starts to suddenly interrupt the master with absolute nonsense. Everyone is shocked and horrified.

Until the master of the monastery exclaims, "Chickens! They are nimble! Woot!"

I went to the Florida Keys and lived in a hotel room that looked like a concrete bunker for several months and wrote the script.

Kazu came down and stayed with me for a while, and it was kind of great.

When I finished it, I sent it to Jim Jarmusch with a note asking for his comments. I was pretty pleased with what I had done but it was a little clunky. I had written one other script before but really didn't know what I was doing other than it was supposed to be 110 pages long.

I never heard back from Jim. It bothered me. I send him my script and he never responds? I didn't know what to make of it.

Two years later, I flew over to Rome to meet with Roberto, with a producer who wanted to back the movie.

It looked like this was all going to fall into place.

But the morning we were going over to see Benigni, the producer came to me with a very long face and said there was a problem. The money might not happen now.

I asked what it was, and he said, "Jarmusch is making a western about a white guy and a Native American traveling across a surreal landscape, and the money is now going to be hard to get."

When I got back to New York, I couldn't get Jim on the phone. I left messages but he wouldn't call me back.

Why on earth is he not calling me back? Did he really steal my idea?

So finally I wrote him a letter: "Dear Jim, Word is that the film you plan on making next fall is remarkably similar to my script 'You Stink Mister,' which you read in 1991.

"Is this true? What's going on?"

I get a letter back from Jim's office saying Jim's script contains no element or aspect of my script. And if I wish to go into this further I can send a copy of my script to Jim's attorney.

I never saw *Dead Man* and don't know how many similarities there are. Probably not many. But the basic premise of a white guy and a Native American traveling a surreal landscape is exactly the same.

I don't think there are a lot of movies made about a white guy and a Native American traveling across surreal landscapes. Perhaps this is a genre I have missed.

You Stink Mister never happened.

All the time you spend tryin to get back what's been took from you there's more goin out the door. After a while you just try and get a tourniquet on it.
—Cormac McCarthy, *No Country for Old Men*

Except for about a week, years later, when he suspiciously became my new best friend when he wanted me to do the commentary for the

Down by Law DVD (I had refused to do the one for *Stranger Than Paradise*), I didn't hear from Jim.

A couple weeks after this brief encounter was when my symptoms from advanced Lyme started to get violent. Jim called me because to just disappear after I had done what he wanted would have been odd. I told him what was happening to my body, that doctors couldn't figure out what was wrong and that I was terrified. I literally couldn't function or do the simplest of tasks. And that I kept having these overwhelming neurological attacks and I imagined that I was going to end up a quivering, drooling mess on the floor. I asked him, practically begged him, to please check in on me once in a while, because he lived just a few blocks away.

I never heard from Jim again.

As I said, if this stuff is getting to you, you can just skip past it to the end of the chapter. I certainly wouldn't mind doing that myself.

In, I guess, 1994, The Lounge Lizards were playing at Tramps. It must have been Directors' Night Out, because Wayne Wang was there, with Paul Auster and Peter Newman, and the Coen brothers were there as well. Love the Coen brothers. I think Prince was there too that night, or I might be getting the nights mixed up.

After the show, Wayne Wang, Paul Auster, and Peter Newman came into the grim dressing room and said they were doing a movie in Brooklyn, a spin-off of *Smoke*, a film they had just finished, and did I want to perform music in it?

They didn't think the whole band would work, but some smaller version of it.

First words out of my mouth were, "Fine, but the only thing that's important to me is that the sound is good. You can't just record it with a Nagra and think that that is going to be fine."

"Oh no, of course not. It will all be done really well."

I've played saxophone in movies, and you can't use a Nagra because a Nagra is for recording vocals. With music, and particularly with the saxophone, it loses all of the overtones. It takes the richness out of the sound, makes it sound like a shredded, irritating piece of string.

Saxophone players are nuts about their sound in general. I heard even Coltrane was nuts about his sound.

Sometimes, you record something and it sounds perfect and you can't figure out why. The variables are the mic, the reed, the mouthpiece, your horn and whether or not it has a leak, the room, and what you're recording on. But try as you might to repeat the thing that worked before, it usually does not work the next time.

But one thing I know now and knew then, for certain, is that you cannot record a saxophone with a Nagra and hope for good results.

I call Newman to find out how they're going to record the music. But he doesn't have an answer. I make it very clear that unless this is figured out, we shouldn't do it. Perhaps we can record it before and then play along to what's already been recorded. Or we can play and then match it in the studio later.

"Don't worry, John, it's going to be fine."

But I am worried. For many, many years I have worked hours a day to make my tone what it is. I have to try to make sure that this is done properly.

I call him again a week later and explain that music is a very precious and fragile thing. I want to do the movie but this has got to be done right.

"Look, John, there are professional people who are taking care of this. There is really nothing to worry about. I promise that the music will sound great and if it doesn't meet your satisfaction, we won't use it."

Okay, maybe I'm being a pain in the ass. Newman certainly thinks I am being a pain in the ass.

The Lounge Lizards are about to go on tour, and we're going to shoot *Blue in the Face* the day after we get back. We'll do the trio, the John Lurie National Orchestra, which is me on saxophones, Calvin Weston on drums, and Billy Martin on percussion.

I actually would prefer this, as it had become much more musically rewarding for me than the whole band.

Except, for a week or so before we leave on tour, I have a terrible flu. Shaking with a high fever. There are all these reports on TV about Lyme disease, which is becoming an epidemic. And I had been in North Haven, Long Island. There were constantly deer in the yard and I found ticks on my body.

On the plane to Paris, it starts to go really bad. There is a burning itch on my back. I go into the bathroom and lift up my shirt to look. There is a huge classic Lyme bullseye.

My fever shoots up to 105. My teeth are chattering. I have hallucinations that make me laugh. A stabbing pain in the top of my head that makes me yelp. I'm sitting next to this poor woman and suddenly going, "Ahhhh!" in pain and then laughing again.

I hear through the speakers, "Is there a doctor on the plane?"

Go straight to the hospital in Paris. They know immediately what it is and the doctor is great.

Why couldn't they have told me this at New York Hospital, where I went a week before the tour, sick as a dog?

I told the New York Hospital doctor that I found a tick on me, that I was in North Haven, Long Island.

"Would you please tell me if I have Lyme disease, because I have to buy $30,000 worth of plane tickets on Monday to take my band to Europe for three weeks. If I have Lyme, I have to cancel."

I got one of these doctors—everybody knows this guy, this arrogant, incompetent doctor guy. Doesn't listen to a word I'm saying when I'm explaining my symptoms. He waves for me to be quiet with his hand.

So, he doesn't listen. He knows better. They take some blood. Doctor says it's just the flu, I'll be fine. When the doctor in Paris calls New York Hospital for my blood work, turns out that they haven't even done a Lyme test with the blood they drew, though he told me they were going to.

Bible was wrong. Assholes have inherited the earth.

I do the tour. Play every night. The antibiotics work pretty fast. But still, I'm green. Room is spinning. Fever 102. My bones are being crushed. But I finish the tour.

I'm a hero.

So we get back to New York. Next day we're doing the Wayne Wang movie. Sick, exhausted, jet lag. I don't want to go, but I said I would, so I go.

My tone on the saxophone somehow is my salvation. When I'm

really playing, a prayer is being funneled through me, and in return, at the same time, the horn is my path to God.

I certainly don't expect a movie producer to understand this, but I was very clear about how important recording this properly is to me.

"Don't worry, John. There will be people there who have recorded music in movies countless times. I *promise* that you'll be satisfied with the way it sounds."

We arrive on the set in Brooklyn. Wayne Wang has a cold. Maybe he'll stop by later.

Wait a minute, I've got Lyme disease and he's staying home because he has a cold?! Maybe he'll come later?!

Paul Auster is excited to direct. A little too excited. And he is determined to be creative in his directing.

"Does he know what he's doing?" I ask.

People shrug.

I later find out or hear the rumor that Wayne Wang has one more picture to do with the company that's produced *Smoke* and he wants out. So he's going to whip off this little movie. The script is just a bunch of sketches that Auster has written. The plan is to do this thing mostly improvised and at some points Paul Auster will try his hand at directing.

Fantastic!

Drew Kunin is doing the sound. Drew did the sound for *Stranger Than Paradise* and *Down by Law*. I know Drew and not only do I like him, very much, as a person, I also know that he's an excellent soundman. If I did a movie, I'd ask Drew to do the sound.

But no one has told Drew anything about recording music today. He says that we should have recorded the music in advance and then played along to it, which is what I suggested. He'll do his best but this isn't the way to do music in a movie. And he apologizes to me before I even ask and says, "Sorry, John, but I can't be the guy who says this isn't going to work."

No shit. Where are the experts?

Calvin and Billy seem nervous.

There are two little scenes. One where Lily Tomlin is dressed up as a homeless man, trying to get enough money for Belgian waffles. Lily Tomlin really looks like a man. I tell Calvin that that's Lily Tomlin. He says, "No it ain't, that's a man."

The first scene is with Harvey Keitel and this woman Mel Gorham, who asks if we can play a rumba.

We are playing this nice little thing that I wrote for the movie and this woman starts yelling and singing and improvising.

Paul Auster thinks it's great.

Why am I the only person on this set, besides Drew, who understands that she can't be doing this? In order to rerecord the sound, she's going to have to loop every yelp exactly as she's doing it now. It'll never work. It will look very artificial and not have the same feel as the rest of the movie.

I take Paul aside and try to explain this to him. But he really doesn't understand. And it isn't that hard to understand. I had heard that this guy is a genius. Welp, um, no, apparently not.

I say we're going to have to quit. If they use this music like this, it's going to sound like I'm playing a rabid duck.

"Please let us go home and you don't have to pay us."

But Paul Auster is directing for the first time and my music is important to him. He has seen me play many times and loves it deeply. And apparently this woman's yelping is part of his creative vision.

I take Drew Kunin aside again. He tells me again, it is going to sound absolutely horrible.

They break for lunch and I meet with Peter Newman and Paul Auster, who implore me to stay. That if Miramax goes for this movie, they'll sink a lot of money into it and can fix everything.

I try to explain that no amount of money thrown at this will fix it. We cannot rerecord the music because the yelping will no longer be part of the sound.

But Paul Auster wants to direct and be creative in his directing debut, and yelping is his first contribution to the art of filmmaking.

I'm so sick with the Lyme disease that I don't have the strength to object. We just stay because I don't have the strength to leave.

We do the scene with Lily Tomlin, who, not surprisingly, turns out to be a wonderful human being. Then we go home.

About a week later I call Peter Newman, to ask him how we're going to redo the music. He says that Wayne Wang has seen the scene and he likes the way it sounds.

"Well, it's not up to him."

"Wayne thinks that to rerecord the music will give it a different flavor than the rest of the movie. He really thinks that it sounds fine and we're just going to use what we've already got."

"Yes! It is what I tried to explain to Paul Auster. It will be a completely different tone and not fit. But this is my music. You can't do this."

So there's a meeting at some editing place. They play me the scene. I hate it. The music sounds horrible. This can't be happening. I won't sign the contract.

"Peter, this is not what we agreed on. You gave me your word."

No response.

Wayne Wang, who seems very sweet, suddenly is showing an iron-willed tenacity that I should have realized was lurking back in there somewhere.

He actually goes into this routine about how I'm very talented but behavior like this will ruin my career. Is he threatening me?

I can't believe this. I mean, I want them to like me. I want them to appreciate the stuff I wrote for their movie, that we rehearsed on the road during sound checks while I should have been in bed. How is it going like this? The only thing I want is for it to sound okay. I have not asked for anything else since the beginning.

Their reasoning is this: Roseanne Barr doesn't like her scenes and wants to reshoot them. Now, they can't do that, and this would be basically the same thing. They just can't allow an actor to dictate how they will make their movie.

"But this is my music. I'm not acting. This is what I do. It is not the same thing. I'm passionate about this in a way that you'll never understand and you think you're going to use it sounding like that. You can't."

So I leave. On the way out Wayne Wang tells me about his next movie, which is going to have a jazz score. He must think I'm stupid, or so ambitious that I'm stupid. I think that's also when he tells me that I'm very talented but if I make a problem here, I won't work again.

I agonize over this. Do I sign their contract or not? Literally lose sleep. I don't want a battle. But how can I let that music go out like that? It is disrespectful to the music.

This guy Peter Newman seemed like an honorable guy. He gave me his word. And I really don't understand Paul Auster, who seems to be an enormous fan of the music but now is going to ruin it, at least for people who have ears. This was a fairly simple, commonsense thing that just could not be explained to him.

Then Peter Newman calls me and says that Harvey Weinstein is going to sue me unless I sign the contract. I have appeared in the movie, which indicates my intent. I cannot now say I do not want to participate.

I give up and sign the contract.

I send them a tape of some music with the trio playing in the studio, which isn't mixed but should give them some idea of what it should sound like. And perhaps they could use some of this music so that people can hear what it is supposed to sound like compared to this disaster that is in there.

They say no, they don't like it.

When the movie comes out, there are three of the pieces of music from the tape I sent them, the music they didn't like, placed in the movie. There is no deal, no discussion, no money, no nothing. Only thing I heard was that they didn't like it. But then they put it in the movie without asking me.

Well, now I pretty much have them. If nothing else I can demand a big payday.

They have used my music without my permission—copyright infringement. Except, a friend of mine is the music supervisor and it's going to cause her problems because she didn't clear this music. Not only will she be fired for this, she will probably not work again. Even though it appears that this is someone else's fault, it is going to get blamed on her. I let it go for next to nothing, because they have no money left and I really like my friend and don't want her to not work anymore.

This is where my reputation for being difficult comes from. I don't know how I could have handled it better. How I could have been more clear on what was necessary for the music to be in the movie or how I could have resolved it without giving up any more. But now I am "difficult." I start hearing it all the time.

Only one more, and this is going to upset some people. It is not pleasant. But it is true and it is what happened. It is what happens.

This one involves the beloved David Byrne. And I just put down the beloved Paul Auster, who is less beloved than David Byrne but still beloved. This is the first time *beloved* has been used three times in a sentence.

When The Lounge Lizards would play, you could look out at the crowd and anyone you could think of could be there. John Lennon, Bob Dylan, and David Bowie all have come to see the band play, Bowie several times. That should give you the sense that this was music worthy of a record deal.

I was heading toward going broke. I was holding it all together with string.

We couldn't get a record deal.

We were playing in New York, maybe at the Knitting Factory or the Bottom Line, not sure, but it wasn't a big place. And it was mobbed. This was 1995 or '96.

The band had just gotten back from a tour and we were hovering off the ground.

We finished a song to ear-shattering applause and when it died down, I said, "And this from a band that cannot get a record deal."

We would easily sell out two shows a night for a week at the Knitting Factory, but Europe was where the real fan base was. We had played a big theater in Milan with lines of people outside who couldn't get in, and a block away on the same night, Wynton Marsalis was playing to a half-full house. Patti Smith, too, was playing that night and not sold out.

But for years we couldn't get a record company to record us. I spoke to one guy from a record label who said that they very much wanted to sign us but couldn't figure out where in the store we should go. Under what category. So that posed a big problem for their marketing department. Isn't that kind of the idea? To make something original?

The next day there is a message at my office from Yale Evelev, who runs David Byrne's label, saying David was at the concert last night and wants to sign The Lounge Lizards to do a record.

When I call him back, he explains that Byrne's label is doing the CD for *Blue in the Face* and then, almost immediately, turns the conversation to the fact that they want to do a record deal but he has spoken to the *Blue in the Face* people and understands that I am a difficult person to deal with.

If someone is a difficult person, this is perhaps not the best way to begin a conversation. If someone is not a difficult person, this is perhaps not the best way to begin a conversation.

I ask where they got this, that I am difficult.

He says, "Oh, everybody knows this."

"Yes, but specifically, what have you heard?"

I never really get an answer but after pressuring Yale Evelev a bit, he tells me that it has something to do with *Blue in the Face* and they have been warned about me.

We start to do the record, with Yale Evelev giving helpful advice like, "The piano solo is too long and boring."

"The cello solo is too long and boring."

"You should consider covering a song. Maybe 'Riders on the Storm' by the Doors."

I love helpful advice about my music. It is very helpful.

Amid this helpful advice I am also told that their label, Luaka Bop, is having a cash flow problem. If we want to make the record, I have to put up the money myself and they will reimburse me.

I am so anxious to get this done and out, and I know David Byrne well enough to know he isn't the kind of person who is going to screw me on this, so I agree.

But it gets to the point where—I can't remember the exact figures, but I think the overall budget for the record was $110,000 and I put up $85,000 of that.

Yale Evelev keeps telling me that I am only known for my acting. But now, finally, I will be known for my music, which is how it should be. That the label will get behind this record in such a way that everyone will know about it.

We finally get the record done. It is called *Queen of All Ears*.

I am having trouble with the mastering and making the CDs sound anywhere near as good as the DAT recordings I have, but the record is good. It may even be a masterpiece.

This is around the same time as the movie *Get Shorty*, which I did the music for. The head of the marketing department in L.A. for Warner Bros. is . . . I forget her name. What I do remember about her is that she had blue hair and was twenty-three years old.

It turns out David Byrne's label doesn't get to decide how many records they are going to print. It's up to Warner Bros., because Luaka Bop is their subsidiary. That Warner Bros. will be deciding the print run is something nobody told me about. In fact, it was implied that it was completely up to Luaka Bop.

The blue-haired twenty-three-year-old goes to see *Get Shorty*, and when my name comes up on the screen, she says to her friend that they are doing an album with me.

Her friend—I don't know what color her hair is—doesn't know who I am. On the basis of this in-depth marketing research, it is decided that Warner Bros. will only let Luaka Bop print three thousand CDs.

Three thousand CDs is nothing. If they were actually getting behind the record, they would be sending out three thousand CDs for free, for promotion. We are about to go on tour to support the record and there aren't going to be any CDs anywhere.

I call my lawyer, Peter Shukat, to tell him what is going on.

Peter is a tough, smart guy, and I really like him, but he doesn't excel in tact. He gets David Byrne on the phone and screams at him.

David hates conflict.

I imagine him, after Peter yells at him, going to hide under the couch.

But what happens next is that they pull the plug on the record.

I get a letter from David saying, "Oh well, at least we tried."

But as it stands, I am out $85,000, the very last of the money I made from *Get Shorty*, and they have *Queen of All Ears* and won't release it or give it back.

This goes on for months and months. I don't know what to do. My lawyer and Luaka Bop's lawyers argue back and forth about how to resolve this, me paying my lawyer all the while.

Finally, against my lawyer's advice, I write David a letter myself, laying out the whole thing and showing how shitty this story makes his label look. The thing finally gets resolved, like a year later. I was really worried that the record would never see the light of day.

I have lost a shitload of money. The $85,000 I invested, plus I paid Luaka Bop whatever they had put in. But at least I got the record back.

And here, I suppose, is as good a place as any to apologize to David Tronzo for not giving him a solo on the record *Queen of All Ears*.

Tronzo is a phenomenal slide guitar player. I actually think his level of playing—his soulfulness on his instrument and his level of innovation—surpasses Marc Ribot, but Tronzo never gets credit.

He was supposed to have an enormous solo on the song "Happy Old Yoy," which was supposed to be the featured song on the album, but we never got the tempo right and I had to scrap the song, leaving Tronzo without a solo on the record. And I feel bad about it to this day.

So this shit happens to me. One after the other. Also somewhere in that time is the debacle with the film score for *The Crew* and Michael Dinner and the Amazing Barrys but I put that in another chapter to show mercy on the reader, as well as myself.

I look at it and think, *It has to be you, John. You are the common denominator here. It has to be you. You are doing something wrong that leads to these disasters. You think your heart and your motives are so pure, but maybe they aren't. Maybe there is some fucked up thing about you that is making these things happen.*

Of course, after a couple of these horror stories, most people would have given up. Especially if they could just act in some terrible Hollywood movie and go home with a suitcase full of money.

When life punches you in the face, you have to stand back up.

How else can life punch you in the face again?

So I decide to see a therapist and find out what I am doing that makes this shit happen to me over and over again.

I will be as honest as I possibly can be. I will hide nothing, no matter how embarrassing. I will tell the therapist everything in the hope of fixing this problem that I must be creating.

My friend Sheryl is all about therapists and constantly telling me I should see one. So I call her for a recommendation. She suggests Dr. Robert Valentine.

So I go see him and it is kind of helping in a way. I see a couple of things that I would not have seen otherwise, particularly about my father's being ill most of my childhood and the effect that had on me.

But it is a little strange. The guy wants to go and have a beer after one of the sessions and a couple other things like that that I find odd.

He comes back from vacation, somewhere in the jungle, and is adamant that it was more wild and dangerous than any trip I have ever taken. And I have taken some wild trips but never thought about its being an area of competition.

But he keeps bringing up this idea that there's no reason we can't be personal friends and hang out outside of our sessions.

About two months in, I am telling him about the fight that Tom Waits and I had during *Fishing with John*, and he is sitting on the edge of his chair.

I stop and say, "You seem inordinately interested in this."

He says, "That is because you are talking about a conflict you had with an equal. It isn't you fighting with someone you hire to be in your band or you fighting with the immensely powerful Warner Bros. or Harvey Weinstein. It is an equal."

I think, *Okay, that makes sense,* but then a moment later it dawns on me in a horrifying pulling back of the veil.

I ask—almost exclaim—"Have we ever met before?"

He goes, "Unh-huh."

"Are you Doc?"

"Unh-huh."

"And you didn't tell me that we had met before?"

I really can't believe this. This is the guy who tried to become my friend by telling me Tom Waits's deepest psychic secret, and I have spent two months revealing myself to the bone.

He says, "I thought if I told you, you would have discontinued treatment."

I just get up and walk out. I am in shock. My mouth has fallen so far open that I have to carry my lower jaw in my hands.

I get home and call Tom Waits.

"Do you know Dr. Robert Valentine?"

Imagine Tom Waits's voice in complete and utter disbelief: "Robert Valentine? He's a doctor now? Did he get his license in Mexico?"

Then a long pause, and Tom shrieks, "He's a stalker!"

30

Splobs

I go to L.A. to do promotion for *Down by Law*. This is when Roberto was driving me nuts, in the cab, reading all the signs, in a yell, coming in from the airport.

"Stop!"

"Pooch Pawler! Dog Grooming!"

"Carpet Cleaning! Benny's!"

"Bail Bondsman!"

"Coffee!"

"Speed Limit Thirty-five!"

I get to my room and can't get my horn and little keyboard out fast enough.

I almost always travel with this little keyboard that I bought in the Tokyo airport when I went to Bali by myself, right after Liz and I broke up. This keyboard cost me $88, this little Casio thing. I still have this little Casio and have written an awful lot of music on this little thing.

So I get to my room in L.A. and I am writing music like mad. Write almost all of the song "No Pain for Cakes" and some other stuff. It's odd that I spent a month in the country with Evan not writing a note and now it is coming out of me like a tsunami, faster than I can get a handle on it.

We go out to a studio in Astoria, Queens, and record our second album for Island Records. I have the engineer Seigen Ono flown over to record it. Every time he writes the word *album* he writes *almub* instead. I love it and want to call the record *Almub* but then decide on *No Pain for Cakes*. They use my *Uncle Wiggly as the Devil* painting for the front and Kazu does the photos for the back.

I've got a budget for three days of recording and it's a mad dash to get everything done. The last night I am there until ten A.M. and then Val, Seigen, and I go out to breakfast. We're giddy—not Seigen so much, but me and Val are loopy from lack of sleep.

Val tells me that I have to name all of the cues for *Down by Law* because they need them, immediately, for the record. Val is writing them on a napkin. I'm yelling out non sequiturs:

" 'A Hundred Miles from Harry.' "

" 'Are You Warm Enough?' "

" 'The King of Thailand,' 'The Queen of Stairs.' "

And for Naná Vasconcelos, who said this to every attractive woman who passed him on the street, " 'Please Come to My House.' "

Naná was funny like that. There was a very long period where, when he was on the streets of Manhattan, he refused to talk and would walk only looking up at the sky. After that period of silence, every time he saw a woman who was even remotely attractive, he would gloriously smile, bow, and then look in her eyes and say with his most elegant Brazilian accent, "Please come to my house." It was fucking adorable.

I think that those men who tell random women on the street that they should smile more or that they are prettier when they smile should get a mandatory jail sentence of six months or beaten up fairly badly. But this was not that. At least from where I stand, this was not that at all.

Later that night I go to this debauched club called Milk Bar. There is coke everywhere at this place, always. This guy with a magician's beard, who I have never seen before, says, "Here, John," and gives me a gram of great coke.

I am walking through the club drinking vodka and cranberry juices, one after the other. I just finished the recording and have a few days off before the mix. This is my night off.

This girl cuts me off in the crowd and bumps her award-winning butt up into my crotch. I think it's an accident and move through the crowd, but she finds me and does it twice more, boomba boomba. This is an interesting way to say hello.

So we go back to my place at around four A.M. and the door to the pink room comes slamming shut. I think, *Wow, Val is sleeping with Seigen.* Something about the way the door slammed just told me it was Val. There was no way that Seigen would ever slam a door like that. He would have done it quickly, but it wouldn't have made a sound.

This girl is from Kansas. We have sex two or three times. I am wired from the coke. She keeps saying, "You have really good energy." But when I turn her over to go at it a fourth time, she looks at me and says, "You're scaring me!" and grabs her stuff and runs out.

Kazu is not doing so great over on Third Street. She sounds very stressed. It is dangerous there and I don't think she is really safe being there by herself.

We have started to become friends.

After she lived on Third Street for a while, she got a place for free in the East Village, but when that came to an end, she went back to Third Street. Because Val's apartment has now become my office, I agree to give Val the Third Street apartment, where she can make phone calls and my mail can go, but she has to wait until Kazu moves out. But then Val splits from her husband, and she forces Kazu out so her ex can live there. I didn't find out until years later that Val had forced her out.

There is the big pink bedroom with only the basketball hoop on Eleventh Street, so I let Kazu move in with me.

Kazu and I become best friends.

It is wonderful living with Kazu. She takes care of me and we play like kids. We hide from each other in the enormous apartment and then jump out and smash each other with a little orange ball. Kazu's laugh is like a little kid's. It opens my heart the way a kid's laugh does. I do anything to make her laugh.

There is love in the house.

One of the oddest moments in my life was watching Naná Vasconcelos and Calvin Klein standing elbow to elbow in my apartment, both looking up at the ceiling, but for different reasons. Calvin Klein because he was bored, and Naná because he always did, as though he was expecting God to swoop down through the sky or the ceiling and say, "Hello, Naná!"

They were both standing next to the counter, looking up and oblivious to each other. I thought, *How odd. They each have no idea who the other is and they are both in my apartment staring at the ceiling.*

I had had a party to show off my new place. Calvin Klein had come in with Bianca Jagger. I must have met her at the Jean-Michel dinner at Mr. Chow. Bianca came in and displayed her fur coat to me. I said, "The coats go upstairs on the bed." She said, "Oh," like, *How gauche,* and dropped her fur coat on the dirty floor.

There was a woman named Miki that I liked. Mostly because she looked a lot like Liz. I had used her in the Sion video to get to know her. Gy could tell I liked her, and hated her immediately. At around four A.M., when the party was dying down, Miki hurried upstairs and hopped into my bed. Gy, thinking she would be spending the night, went upstairs and saw Miki as she was just getting into the bed and said, "Well, I didn't know it was a race."

Kazu would get a little jealous and tease me after a girl had spent the night. Miki had brought this very sweet smelling body oil. After Miki left, Kazu came into my room and said, "You smell like a bee. Buzzy bee." She kept running around my bedroom, shuffling the big alligator-head slippers that I'd bought her, singing, "Buzzy bee, buzzy bee, buzzy bee."

Kazu would call me "Dude" because I hated it. "Stinky Dude" when I farted. The morning after I had brought home a very young Uma Thurman, who must have been twenty then, Kazu came into my room and kept calling me "Illegal Dude."

"Want some breakfast, Illegal Dude?"

Island is not being nice about anything. They won't do anything to promote the album. It is like *No Pain for Cakes* never existed. Chris Blackwell won't take my calls. He seems to be a very charming rich kid who kind of plays with people's lives, work, and careers, like it is some kind of hobby. Once something is not new and exciting to him, he just gets bored and finds a new toy to play with for a moment, then that toy will be found broken in the yard later in the day. Except these aren't toys, these are people's lives.

Also, my acting agent is making me audition for these movies that I do not want to do. I don't know how they manipulate me into auditioning, but they are geniuses at it. They have managed to convince me that no one knows who I am. I do not audition well and it is constantly embarrassing.

I am on my way uptown in a cab. I have been bummed out for a few days. Then I see from the cab window *DOWN BY LAW Tom Waits John Lurie Roberto Benigni* on the movie marquee. What an odd thing it is, just when it feels like you are disappearing into psychic oblivion, to see your name up in lights, like it means something. Later that day, *The New Yorker* dubs me the "Humphrey Bogart of the Eighties."

I have to go to England and France to do press for *Down by Law* and the new album.

After that I have to go to Japan to do an advertisement. I decide to go back via Hawaii and take a few days off by myself.

I fly to Honolulu and book an expensive hotel. This is a mistake. The beach is horrible and the people staying there are horrible. I wake up feeling awful. At first I think that it's jet lag but I remember looking in the mirror in the room and thinking, *This isn't jet lag, this is something else.*

I can't face going through the expensive, shiny lobby, so I head outside via the back entrance. I come out onto a dusty alley with garbage from the hotel overflowing from trash cans, flies everywhere.

I start to walk down the alley to see where it leads and there is this guy up ahead coming toward me. He is limping really badly and his hair is all patchy and stringy. It looks like he must have mange.

Just as I get close enough to this guy to see that he has unbelievably bad acne, painful-looking boils all over his face, he smiles a rotten-toothed grin and says, "Have a nice day in paradise."

* * *

If the fire department asks for your address, don't tell them. They will only show up with axes to break everything and spray water on all your worldly possessions.

I get back to New York, and that bad feeling I had in Hawaii keeps coming back on me. I think that maybe it's the apartment. It seems like every time somebody comes over, they fall asleep, and Kazu and I are always feeling achy and tired.

We think that maybe it's carbon monoxide and start calling different people from the phone book. I try the EPA, and they say, "If you think there is carbon monoxide in your apartment, call the fire department."

I think, *That's weird, the fire department?*

I call the fire department and tell them that I think maybe there is carbon monoxide in my apartment.

"What's your address, sir?"

I tell them.

"We'll report it."

I presume that they are going to call me back and don't think about it further.

Kazu is cooking in the enormous kitchen. I am on the phone with Val, and there's a lot of activity outside of the first floor window, but it doesn't really register. Out of the corner of my eye I notice a large red blur and then another. And there are sirens, but when you live in New York City, there are sirens all the time and one just doesn't notice them. They become part of your day. But when the big red machines start stopping outside my house, the flashing lights make me go to the window to see what's happening.

"Oh no."

Fire trucks line the block.

Firemen bang on the door. They all have hatchets. They want to come in and start smashing stuff up. They really like to come into people's apartments and start smashing stuff. Almost as much as they like their sirens and flashing lights.

I never found out if there was a carbon monoxide leak or not.

I am not feeling great and spend a couple of months mostly in bed. Kazu looks after me. Cooks wonderful things.

"What do you want for dinner?"

"Splobs."

"What's sprobs?"

"Bob."

I have started calling her "Kabuki Bob" for no reason. The song "Bob the Bob" on the *Voice of Chunk* record is for her. I love Kazu. I really love her. In the purest way.

"Bob, say 'All the Puerto Ricans are parading at the Palladium.' "

"No, what are sprobs?"

"They are fried, fried, fried pieces of potato, then you boil them and then fry them again."

"What are sprobs, rearly?"

"Say 'All the Puerto Ricans are cabbing to the Palladium.' "

"No."

The amazing thing to me about the Japanese is that the pronunciations of "L" and "R" and "B" and "V" is not an oral problem, like how Americans can't roll their R's. It is an aural problem. They do not hear the difference. If I say "John Lurie" and then "John Roolie," it sounds exactly the same to them. I believe this to be true. At least that's how it was explained to me by more than one Japanese person.

I call her from my bed but she doesn't answer. I get up to go downstairs and I see her huddled over, next to the speakers of the stereo.

"What are you doing?"

"Nothing."

I can just faintly hear Billie Holiday floating past her.

Kazu has been hiding it from me, but she is practicing singing. Round the clock, she is listening to Billie Holiday and practicing. Two months later she can sing exactly like Billie Holiday, but with a slight Japanese accent. It is absolutely remarkable. No one can sing like Billie Holiday. Kazu can sing, exactly, like Billie Holiday with a Japanese accent.

What an extraordinary thing she is.

We went back to Japan. Kazu came with us to translate and to be generally fun to be around. She had a bottle of expensive moisturizer that I bought her. After the long flight, we were waiting for our ton of luggage to come off the conveyor belt. Every particle of hydration had been taken out of me from the flight. I asked Kazu for the moisturizer but she said that I had to wash my face first, otherwise I'd be wasting it. She was hoarding the moisturizer and we actually had a fight about it.

I wasn't well at all. I collapsed after the first show. At the end of the tour, I decided to stay in Japan with Kazu, to try to recover before flying to Europe to meet the band. She took me to this beautifully exotic hotel in Kyoto. The bathtub was made of wood.

Let me repeat until you grasp the beauty of this: The bathtub was made of wood.

The food was otherworldly. The woman who ran the place had an elegant, strong face. She would bring in the amazing food for dinner and bow. I bowed back to her and she bowed so low that she almost scrunched to the floor. Kazu told me later not to bow to her because she was in a position of service and was compelled to bow lower than me. The idea that this lady, with so much class, had to bow lower than me made me feel all confused. Clearly, in the pecking order of the universe, I should not have been allowed to grovel in the mud this woman walked on.

Then we went to a place where the whole town was dedicated to *onsen,* Japanese baths. The water has curative powers. You take these hot baths in all kinds of different waters. It completely wipes you out and then you sleep. Everyone who was there was there for the baths. The whole town was walking around in robes. Seemed like some low rent sci-fi movie. I asked Kazu where the town was where everyone brushed their teeth.

We went to some marine show and they had the dolphins in such tiny cages in the water that they couldn't even turn around. Kazu and I were horrified. We tried to free them. There was only a tiny padlock with a thin chain that held them in their prison. The ocean was right behind the cages. But we couldn't do it. We couldn't get the thing open.

When I had met her the first time, a year earlier, Kazu and a lot of really lovely new friends that we had met had come to the hotel to see the band off before we went to the airport. They all stood outside the hotel waving. Kazu was standing next to this wonderful, soulful woman named Kimea. As the van pulled off I could see Kimea hugging Kazu because Kazu was going to cry.

I ordered harshly, from the window, "Don't you cry." I was trying to make a joke.

Dougie said, "You really have a way with women."

This time, one year later, saying goodbye to Kazu at the airport, tears welled up in my eyes.

As I went down the escalator, she stood on the level above, smiling down at me. I could barely hold it together.

When I got to New York, I called her. Kazu said with glee, "I didn't cry! You cried! I didn't cry! Ha ha!"

31

I've Run Out of Madeleines

It is impossible to remember what happened on which tour. Two incidents I think are connected by a week could actually be years apart. A lot of the book I've figured out what happened when by using dwellings, projects, or girlfriends as demarcations of time. But on tour it is a blur of mayhem. Sound checks, sex, fire extinguisher battles, trains, double-decker sleeper buses, a glimpse of ecstasy on a musician's face during a heightened moment, more trains, more sex, trying to pack everything after two hours of sleep—it really is just a blur and I can't remember and I've run out of madeleines.

The first time we played in Sicily, it was an outdoor concert on a hill, in the middle of nowhere. We played for eight people and six sheep.

Joe Zawinul was scheduled to play solo before us, but things he needed for his elaborate setup had not arrived. He stood onstage holding a confusing mess of cables.

The smattering of people sat out there in the nice summer night air, waiting. They didn't seem to mind. There was nowhere better to be.

We went for a walk and came back just as Joe had given up trying to make anything work and played "Everything Happens to Me" on the piano. And then walked off.

The next time we played Sicily, it was a free concert in Catania, in a big dusty field. The Sicilians were there for the free concert and mostly had no idea who we were. This is the night the promoter rented us the Jolly Drums. A toy drum set with "JOLLY DRUMS" written in big letters across the bass drum.

When we arrive at sound check and the equipment is wrong, the band is all always calling me over.

I see Dougie with a wrench trying to fix his snare drum and he calls me over. "John." But I see the big *JOLLY* written on the front of his bass drum and shake my head. "Dougie, there's nothing I can do."

We wrote different tunes for the end of the show, when I would introduce the band. Usually some kind of blues or one-chord vamp. I never, or rarely, introduced the guys by their real names. I would make them the 1961 New York Yankees:

"On drums—Tony Kubek!! On bass—Bobby Richardson!! On piano—Elston Howard!! I'm your center fielder—Mickey Mantle!! Thank you very much! Thank you very much! Thank you very much!"

Because Ribot would look so insane when he played, and because he really looked a bit like him, I sometimes introduced him: "On guitar, the man who shot Robert Kennedy, Sirhan Sirhan!!"

Usually I was yelling so hard that the audience didn't have a clue what I was saying.

That night in Catania I introduce Marc as Sirhan Sirhan and don't think much about it. I introduce Marc fourth, and then move on to the horns, as usual. I'm introducing Curtis on the trombone and I see these Neanderthal guys pushing their way to the front of the crowd. They are all wearing white T-shirts with muscles built on top of other muscles. And they are all frothing at the mouth and pointing at me. About ten of them. They are trying to get over the chain-link fence that separates us from the crowd. They try to tear it down. They are pointing at me and screaming and what is even stranger is that they appear to be yelling in English.

After the show I ask the people backstage what was going on. I find out that they are drunk U.S. Marines and they want to kill me because of the Sirhan Sirhan comment, and I have to be hidden in the basement and snuck out, hours after the concert is finished.

We play in London, and I remember that we were great that night. After the show two well-dressed Arab men come up to me and say that the ambassador to Beirut would like to speak to me, and lead me out of the dressing room to meet him.

The ambassador loved the show and wants us to come to Beirut to play. I think it is a fantastic idea and we are exchanging addresses. Roy is standing behind him, wringing his hands and shaking his head no, no, no, no.

When I am talking to the ambassador, we speak eye to eye. He appears to be my height. When the conversation is over, he suddenly drops down and is a foot and a half shorter than he had been a moment ago. Then the two well-dressed bodyguards pick up the fancy box the ambassador had been standing on. The three of them walk off, with Roy still wringing his hands like I am about to force him onto a plane to Beirut that night.

We play these towns and at the beginning of the show, there is often a sea of local photographers standing at the front of the stage. All shooting upwards. This is the least flattering angle possible, straight up, underneath the face, shooting up the nose. It is worse if you are playing the saxophone and your neck and cheeks are puffed out with air or contorted in a straining exhale. When we arrive in a town there are usually two or three photos of me in the local daily paper, by their in-house photographer, from last year, that make me look something like an angry giant hamster with a double goiter.

We are playing in Poland and they have allowed fifty photographers to shoot the first few minutes of the show. They're right in front of the stage, fighting each other for position. They are actually fighting to be in position to get an even worse shot, right in the middle to shoot right up my nose.

I try to explain to them that if they went all the way stage left or stage right, it might make a better shot. They don't seem to understand. They don't seem to want to understand, since they are all fighting to get closer, no matter how ridiculous the shot. "Closer! Closer better!"

I hop down off the stage and try to get one or two of the photographers to get up on the stage so I can take their picture from below. When they develop the film they will see and stop this horrible practice of turning me into Mr. Goiter Hamster. I am not sure if they understand me or not but no one will give up their camera and now I am surrounded by photographers taking my picture while the band plays up on the stage.

The stage is actually kind of high, about five feet off the ground. The audience watches my initial awkward failure to climb back up onto the stage. I am thinking that the show is only five minutes old and this is going very badly, when someone grabs me from behind.

It is a girl who has rushed forward to show her love for me by frenetically throwing her arms around my neck. But I don't know that.

I have my horn, I have a deeply innate sense about protecting my horn at all costs. I protect it as one would protect one's child. The girl has come at me from behind, so I don't see her or know her intentions. I feel someone assailing me, and I put my elbow out, hard, to ward off an attack, but mostly the reflex was to protect my horn.

This poor girl goes flying. She lands askew on top of the people in the front row. So for the audience, it looks as though a fan has come running up to hug me and I've decked her.

In 2015, I had a show of my paintings at the Zachęta National Gallery in Warsaw. Several journalists asked why I had hit the woman during The Lounge Lizards concert years earlier.

Even though it said in the contract that my name could not be singled out on posters, that the band was called "The Lounge Lizards" and not "John Lurie and The Lounge Lizards," every time we arrived anywhere, the posters were huge pictures of me and said things like, "From *Down by Law* and *Stranger Than Paradise*, John Lurie with his band The Lounge Lizards." I couldn't control it. The band understood what was happening, but still, it created a wedge between me and them. It was harder and harder to hold it together like it was a tribe performing a shamanic ritual, which was the only thing that mattered to me. Somehow show business, just like the Catholic Church, was taking something magical and making it earthbound and creepy.

When the band was finally great, we would be on tour, and after we ripped the roof off the place somewhere in Europe, the press would come into the dressing room after the show and just want to talk about *Stranger Than Paradise* and *Down by Law*. It was exasperating.

Actually, it was heartbreaking. How could they not understand what they had just witnessed?

"Why did you shoot *Stranger Than Paradise* in black and white?"

"Jim was given the film by Wim Wenders, so that is what we used and it worked."

"Are you going to make another movie with Jim Jarmusch?"

"I don't know. Did you see the concert?"

"Yes, I was there. Very nice. What is Jim Jarmusch doing now? Is he writing?"

"Look, motherfucker, Jim Jarmusch had one good idea and it was mine. Now get the fuck out."

Poor Jim. I have a lot of warmth toward him in a way.

I have written this book over a few years and have left notes to myself saying, "Don't slag Jim off." But in the end, he made it impossible.

There are a lot of great things about Jim. And in some ways he is a fellow traveler.

We are all flawed. We are all flawed. We are all flawed. In a way, that is the point of the whole thing, how we are all individually, uniquely flawed.

32

Flies Swarm All Around Me

I was the forlorn Saint James with the tangled wig in Martin Scorsese's *The Last Temptation of Christ*. It was difficult for me to stand there for two months, looking amazed, while Willem Dafoe performed miracles in the desert.

The movie was shot in Morocco, which is a wonderful and horrible world. Marrakech was the strangest place I'd been. They have what they call the souks, basically marketplaces, set in an enormous labyrinth of confusion. There are snake charmers with cobras, people loudly selling rugs and silver, children begging amid the mayhem, forty-year-old cars going in all directions. And there is dust. Lots of dust that sinks into the back of your nose and throat and lives there. There's a man in an elaborate metal outfit who pours water on the ground from an ornate kettle. He points at you and expects, for some reason, that you are going to pay him for this service.

Turn a corner to find myself on a narrow path that is about two yards wide and forty yards long, with nothing but severed goats' heads. They are displayed on hooks and stacked eight high, all dripping blood and ravaged by flies.

There is a whirlwind of different music, live and recorded, that all meshes together. But the strongest thing is the smell. The smell of incense, orange peels, donkey shit, cheap motor oil, all blended into one. The first time I saw the movie, someone asked me what I thought and I had no idea, because every scene brought back such a vivid memory of what it smelled like there.

As one of the apostles, I was lumped together with a bunch of guys who all seemed quite lost. Each one of them had endearing qualities on his own. I particularly loved Vic Argo, who I wanted to take home and have him wander around my apartment in a comfy bathrobe and slippers, smoke cigars, and complain about everything in his wonderfully cute, grumpy way.

Despite their endearing qualities individually, my fellow apostles as a group somehow transformed into a bunch of louts. Most of them played the acoustic guitar. Louts with guitars, just what I needed. I couldn't walk by the hotel bar without hearing "Knockin' on Heaven's Door" and somebody yelling, "Hey, John, why don't you get your saxophone?" The answer to that question would have confused them, so I would just cringe and go on my way.

Most of these guys, being very American, after a short time, hated Morocco. Nobody but me left the hotel.

There was a great deal of hostility toward the hotel waiters. No matter what language you ordered in, what you got was not what you ordered. If, for example, you ordered scrambled eggs, they would bring you a cup of coffee. You then would wait to see if they brought you the eggs afterward because they had assumed you wanted coffee with your eggs. No eggs would come. You'd then point to another person eating scrambled eggs at another table, and the waiter would anxiously nod and hurry off, never to be seen again. You'd ask a second waiter another twenty minutes later what had happened to your scrambled eggs. He'd say, "Yes!" and also disappear. Perhaps they just got scared and quit. You'd ask a third waiter, who'd bring you your second cup of coffee.

Willem, Harry Dean Stanton, and I went outside the hotel to eat one night. We couldn't find the restaurant or it was closed, and we found ourselves on a very dark, deserted stone street that had been built three thousand years ago. There were no lights and no people. Harry was terrified, and I don't think he ever left the hotel again after that.

There were very few women on the set. There was a theory that Marty had planned it that way so that the apostles would be stuck in enforced celibacy, thus enhancing our acting by making the experience similar to the real apostles', but I don't think so.

Having a small part in a movie is often awkward. All anyone else cares about is that you don't screw anything up, but the actors want to somehow do something exceptional. So if you have a line like "Pass the blankets," and that is your only line for three days, you tend to overdo it and screw up your face in a ridiculous contortion and say from some odd place in the back of your throat, "Pass the blankets," in a way that would only really make sense if your line was, "There are many Hitlers but I am the best of them!" Or "I will sodomize the monkey! Tuesday I will do it!"

Whenever they were setting up the shot, there would be this massive surge by the apostles to get in the spot between Willem (Jesus) and Harvey Keitel (Judas), or between Jesus and Mary Magdalene (Barbara Hershey). The idea being that once you'd established your mark, you'd be guaranteed some screen time. It was something like getting in position against Charles Barkley for a rebound.

I didn't want to go to this extent to be in the movie. Marty was pissed at me for what he thought to be my lack of interest in participating, but I wasn't going to run and fight to get in the shot. I would have done it when I was eleven, but I was too tired now.

There is a scene in the movie where Jesus is walking across the desert with his followers behind him. It's done in a series of dissolves so that after each dissolve there are more and more people behind Willem. We do the shot by starting about two hundred yards from the camera. We walk about twenty feet, cut, then more people would be added. The very first shot of this sequence is just Willem followed by a horde of Moroccan extras. These are the blind and the crippled. These people really are blind and crippled.

Scorsese asks the cinematographer, Michael Ballhaus, "How was that?"

Michael says, "Well, the blind and the crippled weren't keeping a straight line."

By the time we get about fifteen feet from the camera, the whole enormous crowd is there behind Willem, but Paul Herman, zealous to get as much screen time as possible, is now five feet in front of Willem and Harvey, his jaw jutting forward.

Marty, who is Paul's friend, says, "Pauly, I can't use that. You can't be in front of Willem." To which Paul says, "Keep the shot, change the name of the movie."

Paul Herman is a real character. You can see him in tons of movies as a gangster, but in a way it is hard to think of him as an actor.

There's a scene where we're waiting for Jesus to come back from the desert and all the apostles are doing this improvised whining, questioning our resolve and wondering whether Jesus is really coming back. Pauly, with his heavy New York accent, says, "How can we be a hundred percent sure that he'll come back?"

Before the next take I say, "Pauly, you can't say a hundred percent." And he just throws back at me: "Why not, they only had ninety percent in those days?"

My first scene is near a quiet lake, surrounded by flat stone, stretching out far into the distance. Everything pressed low under the Moroccan sky.

Vic Argo and I are taking these very old fish, supplied by the prop department, out of a net when Willem arrives with the beginning of his entourage. These fish really stink but I'm trying to be a good actor and get into the part. I'm moving the fish from one spot to another and the oil from the fish is getting all over my robe. Vic is being more careful and daintily picking them up between two fingers.

To my understanding the story takes place over a five-year period. I wish I could have convinced the wardrobe department of that, because they refused to wash my robe for the entire length of the shoot. They said it might mess up the continuity. So now, for the rest of the movie, any time I stand in one place for more than a few minutes, flies swarm all around me.

I was impressed by Willem. He had a stamina that I admired. He never complained, which is something that's completely beyond me, especially when I'm acting. He worked long hours and he had tons of dialogue to learn every night.

He carried the whole thing well. As the lead in a film in the middle of nowhere and playing Jesus, no less, he had to set an example for everyone, cast and crew. There was nothing else around to draw on.

We were shooting at night. Willem and I were fooling around by a campfire and he was giggling like a little kid. Someone came to tell us that we were shooting in five minutes, and this transformation took place in his face. I swear that even his eyes changed colors.

Normally, I can't tell if my friends are good when they act, and in this case I certainly can't say. All I can see when I watch that movie is how unhappy I was doing it, that my wig is tangled, and what it smelled like there, but I know for sure that Willem's behavior doing that movie was immense.

Harvey Keitel had asked me to get him a cup of coffee. He felt that any actor who had a smaller part than him should treat him with the appropriate decorum. I liked Harvey but thought this was bullshit. Harvey had no idea who I was, but someone on the crew later told me that they had seen Harvey reading *Actuel*, a French magazine, by the pool a few days later. In this issue of *Actuel*, I was on the list of the one hundred most influential people of the last ten years. This apparently perplexed and concerned Harvey.

There was a group of very sweet Moroccan extras on the film. None of them spoke English and they were anxious to learn. They spoke a little French and so did I. I taught them that a popular slang greeting in America was, "Harvey, get me a cup of coffee." They sat on the ground in a circle, dressed as apostles, as I slowly pronounced the words, "Harvee, get me a cup of cof-fee." They would all say it back.

When they arrived on the set the next morning, they flashed big Moroccan grins and waved as they said over and over, "Harvey, get me a cup of coffee! Harvey, get me a cup of coffee!"

I was so pleased with the idea that I also taught them, "Marty, what is Michael Jackson really like?" Marty had just finished the "Bad" video for Michael Jackson. For Joe Reidy, the very good and very lovely assistant director: "Joe Reidy, my people will kill you." But the Moroccans were getting suspicious and these didn't work.

* * *

Willem has an enormous cock.

We were walking around late one night, going from bar to bar, vaguely looking for trouble. We took a piss in an alley, and I looked over to see this giant schlong hanging there and said to Willem, "What is that? A trout?"

Two guys came out from the other end of the alley. One pointed at Willem and yelled, "Klaus Kinski!," then pointed at me and said, "Mick Jagger!" The really odd thing about this is that one of them looked exactly like Dustin Hoffman.

They started walking with us. Every ten feet or so they would point at Willem and yell, "Klaus Kinski!" We would point and scream back at them, "Dustin Hoffman!" Then we would all laugh.

They took us down an alley to a bar filled with Moroccans. Lots of men and women dancing and a live band. Within five minutes every woman in the place had come over to sit at our table and all the Moroccan men had been left alone. It was uncomfortable. The music was typical Moroccan, except they had an accordion in the band.

Willem said, "Who the fuck brought the accordion to Morocco?"

I loved Marrakech. I had met a tribe of Gnawa musicians and was playing with them almost every night. And it is just so weird and colorful and exotic there.

Toward the end of the production, we moved to Meknes, which was nowhere near as interesting.

The only exciting thing that happened to me in Meknes was a group of kids, about fourteen years old, decided to throw rocks at me when I had gone for a long walk.

So I threw rocks back. They then encountered my throwing arm, which was still rocketlike at that time. They were shocked and scared and scurried away down the alley.

Everyone was excited because David Bowie was coming to play Pontius Pilate. Bowie is very far outside of my musical taste and I wasn't so interested, though I did think his acting was great in a couple of things and thought he was a brilliant choice to play Pilate.

That night everyone was in the bar. The apostles were playing their mind-breaking repertoire. "Knock knock knockin' . . ." People were demanding that I go and get my horn. I suppose because it was toward the end of the shoot and because Bowie was there.

So I went to my room and got my soprano.

I had drifted further from the cast and crew than earlier. After leaving my Gnawa friends in Marrakech, I really didn't want to be in Morocco anymore. I suppose really that I had fallen into a bit of a depression.

I had my soprano standing up on a table, where I was sitting alone. I noticed a hand reaching in to pick up my horn.

I have explained this before, but when you have a rare musical instrument, which my soprano was, one where you love the sound and it cannot be replaced, you protect it like it is your one-year-old child.

It was an extension of my soul, and no one on the planet had any right to reach in and pick it up without asking.

I saw this hand coming in and jumped up. I grabbed the person really hard by the wrist and pretty much yelled, "Who the fuck do you think you are?"

The man in front of me was David Bowie. Funny how the mind works. I noticed that he had two distinctly different-colored eyes. I had never seen that before and wondered if one eye was a colored contact lens.

Everyone stopped and looked over at the exchange in shock. Like, *Oh no, what has Lurie done now? Now he is yelling at our guest David Bowie?*

Bowie looked at me and smiled, then nodded in a way that seemed to mean that he knew where I was coming from and my behavior was justified. Everyone else looked like they wanted to hang me on the spot.

The odd thing was that years later, Bowie showed me exactly who he was in a generous and wonderful way. Harvey Keitel had brought David to see The Lounge Lizards at the Village Gate. They came backstage and David seemed to really have been moved by it. It wasn't that standard show business thing of the perfunctory "That was great." Then he came another time to see us a year or so later.

When I did the Marvin Pontiac record, I was trying to create a hoax around Marvin. Mostly because I was uncomfortable with my singing, I had created a character to do it, which was Marvin Pontiac. Then, because I really cannot stand writing a bio, which it seems one has to do every time one puts a project out into the world, I invented the Marvin Pontiac history for it.

Then I decided to make it look more like it might be a real thing. I got quotes from people like Flea and Iggy Pop saying how important Marvin had been as a musical influence when they were young.

Bowie's office was right up the block from mine on Broadway, so I had someone drop off the tape with a note from me explaining what we were doing and asking him to write a little something to concretize the hoax of Marvin Pontiac.

Not even five hours later, a nine-page fax came into the office. David had written this elaborate story of hearing Marvin when he was young and then playing with Marvin's son some years later.

I don't have that fax anymore. I wish I did. Things like that just go missing somehow. That and a letter from Paul Bowles are two things I had like that that I really wish had not disappeared.

Martin Scorsese was my absolute hero as a director. *Taxi Driver* and *Raging Bull* are perfect movies. I have watched both of them hundreds of times. Studied them. This was why I took the part in *Last Temptation*, to watch him work. I felt he was surely the best American director.

You know what they say about not getting to know your heroes, that it will lead to disappointment, but I am not sure that is it. Though it did go strangely with Marty and me.

Willem said something like, "You are both extraordinarily innovative introverts but from opposite ends of the spectrum."

I had always been impressed with just the extra work in the street scenes in *Taxi Driver.* They felt so real. I wondered how they did it. I would study those scenes.

But in Morocco it was mayhem. There was a scene where a crowd is heckling Willem. This young guy, an American who seems to be a college student on vacation, awkwardly throws garbage at Willem. This martial arts guy, who it has been explained to that Willem is the Son of God, jumps out of the crowd and decks the college kid. Then stands over him in some karate pose.

When we went to disrupt the money lenders, a crowd of Moroccan extras rush toward us, trying to get at Willem. They don't really understand the concept of it being a movie and they are really trying to get at Willem. It gets pretty rough trying to hold them back.

Vic Argo was in a particularly sulky mood that day and stood in the circle we had created to protect Willem, with his arms folded. He is not going to join in and help. He was going to sulk.

I don't know what the fuck came over me, I have only done something like this one other time, when I broke a doctor's nose with my forehead, semi intentionally, while playing basketball. But I saw Vic standing in the circle sulking, while we held off the violent extras charging in on us, and it pissed me off.

I stamped on Vic's foot. We wore these poorly made sandals that didn't protect the feet at all.

For the rest of the day, Vic sat there examining his foot saying over and over, "You broke my toe you fuck. You broke my toe you fuck."

This production had a certain mean-spirited air about it. The Moroccans were treated horribly. If a Moroccan was sick for a day, they were fired and replaced. There was an incident where one of the Moroccan extras had taken coffee from the cast and crew table, which they were forbidden to do. I heard he was beaten, though I am not sure this is true.

Basically, the Moroccans were not allowed to eat off the white people's table. The whole thing didn't seem very Christian to me, and Marty had claimed he was making the movie to get closer to Jesus.

The ones who enforced these rules were Moroccans, the ones with the higher-up jobs who spoke perfect English. They treated the other Moroccans like shit, so it was sanitized and never addressed. But to some extent I blamed Marty for this. Everyone could see what was happening, and there was no way a lot of this, which in the end was racism, should have been allowed to stand.

If you watch me carefully, you will see the scene where I lift up the sleeve of my robe over and over again to expose the Band-Aid on my arm. Or there is my brilliant acting moment where Willem cures a blind man and you can see me laughing over his shoulder.

I think they were having a lot of money trouble on the movie, and the way they were shooting this was ridiculous. The blind man has some gook on his eyes that looks like Play-Doh, and as the camera passes around the man's back, Willem peels off the gook and drops it on the ground. He is cured! I honestly couldn't keep a straight face.

On another scene, somebody was talking nine miles away from where they were shooting and Marty had a panic attack.

"This is very complicated! I have to concentrate!"

Everybody was doing the movie for what it cost them to pay their secretaries back home. I was sharing a cigarette with Willem a hundred yards away, outside, and Scorsese, who has asthma, screamed through a megaphone, "If anybody smokes, I'm going home!"

I said to Willem, "Then go home, you little creep," but I said it in a whisper, because if he could smell the smoke from that far away, then maybe he could hear me.

Early on, I told Marty that I wanted to watch him work. He didn't seem enthralled with the idea but said I could come to the set the next day and hang out behind him. I wasn't in the scene.

It's out in the desert and it's beautiful. I mean, insanely beautiful. I watch for a while. Ask him some idiotic, nervous question and he doesn't respond. I can't blame him. So I go for a walk in the giant hills of floating sand for about an hour. It is so beautiful. I get a little turned around and have to guess where they are on my way back. I come over a sand dune and I'm right smack in the middle of the shot that they are about to shoot. It's bad, I haven't ruined the shot as they haven't started, but they have to wait until I run down to where they are. I'm definitely not good. This is not cool. Don't you just love when you're with a group of new people in the middle of nowhere and you want to make a good impression, and suddenly you've done something this stupid? Don't you love it?

The next day on the call sheet, it states that only those people in the scene will be allowed on the set. It should have said "John Lurie" after it. And this is fair, I'd fucked up. But this was not what made me turn into an acting vandal. Well, this was partly it, but Scorsese kept dropping these little insults on me, all the time, and he hurt my feelings.

I was practicing the soprano outside, quietly and far away from anyone, during a lunch break. Scorsese and a few others were heading out to the location before everyone else and they walked by me. A donkey started to bray in the distance, which sounded sort of like a response to what I was playing. Scorsese laughed, but way too hard, and it wasn't a real laugh. Actually, his laugh never seemed quite right.

Once he turned to me during lunch and out of the blue said, "You make music for alienated people," then got up and left the table.

It is my last day on the set. I am going home tomorrow and it is also my thirty-eighth birthday. I thought that I was done for the day but they're making me wait around for hours.

"Why? I'm done."

I'm told they might need my reaction shot on something, that I have to wait.

"This is nonsense. I'm done. Michael Been's already gone and you can't shoot the shot because he's standing right next to me. And it's my fucking birthday!"

So I wait and wait and at the end of the day, I'm led around the corner and everyone's looking at me. Someone says, "Look, John."

There is a wheelbarrow in a dusty lot. I say, "Oh, a wheelbarrow." Harvey thinks that is hysterically funny, but then I see that there is a table with champagne and a giant cake on it. *Is this for me? Oh fuck.*

The cake says, "Happy Birthday, John." I get a little choked up and everybody's scrambling around. Everybody's lining up behind the table, me in the middle next to Marty. Someone says we should take the group picture now and others start to argue that, no, this isn't good, everyone's not here.

"But this is the most people we will have together from now on, people are going home." The sentiment is divided in half and people are getting pretty angry arguing about it.

I say "Thank you!" as loudly as I can, but my voice cracks. And as everyone is arguing and I'm about to cry from this really sweet thing that they've done, Marty leans in to me and says, "Okay, John, direct this."

Maybe I'm completely wrong, but I thought it sounded mean.

Went back to my room and painfully hacked off my beard. Saw my lascivious face for the first time in months.

33

The Last Time I Saw Willie Mays

I gave up the apartment on Eleventh Street before the band went to Japan. I started staying in hotels, mostly at Morgans on Madison Avenue. Steve Rubell was astounding to me. He and Ian Schrager used to do Studio 54 in the old days and now they owned Morgans Hotel and Palladium, a giant club on Fourteenth Street.

I would be out all night and at five A.M. get a lift from the Palladium back to Morgans Hotel with Rubell in his limo. He lived there as well.

Once I had to get up at nine A.M. to do an interview and was a complete wreck. I could barely see, and when I stumbled into the elevator, I hoped no poor soul would be in there to have to encounter the mess of a disaster that was me.

But there was Steve Rubell. All fresh and clean. Sparkling. And talking with four businessmen, sharp as a tack. Conducting business in the elevator with a big white smile on his face. I just had to hand it to him. Did he do this every day? Stay out partying all night and then get up, three hours later, first thing in the morning and conduct business as though he were one of them?

When he died, some magazine said something like, "Steve Rubell has gone to a club that, finally, one day, we can all get into." It was easy, certainly from the outside, to hate him and what he stood for. And in a way it was fair. But the guy sure as hell had something.

I lived in hotels in New York for a long time. I liked it. But it was crazy expensive. So finally, I reluctantly got an apartment on West Eighteenth Street. The people who owned the building, Tojili Partners, were a very sweet couple who ran a business designing ship parts. They worked on the top floor, in the place above mine.

The deal was that they gave me a key to their office so after eleven P.M., when playing the saxophone would disturb the neighbors, I could go up there to practice and not bother anyone.

Kazu had gotten her five-year visa and moved back to New York. She stayed on Eighteenth Street with me. We got her a futon, which she called "the Stingy Bed."

Ribot said I had the perfect life. Kazu was my companion, took care of me and the apartment. There was a lot of love between us and we had immense amounts of fun. Valerie took care of the business and sorted out whatever my mayhem had broken. And I was going out every night and sleeping with the most beautiful women in the world. I suppose he was right. But if he was right, why was I so fucking unhappy?

I was about to go to Taormina, Sicily, to shoot my part in Roberto Benigni's movie *The Little Devil*. The script was brilliant. Benigni is a little rascal of a devil who escapes from Hell and comes into this world to wreak havoc. Walter Matthau plays a priest, and I am the big devil who comes into this world to bring Roberto back.

The movie was going to be shot in English and Italian. They shot two whole separate movies. I wanted, very badly, to do my part in Italian so that I wouldn't be dubbed. Jon Ende hooked me up with an Italian teacher named Rosella.

Rosella was soft and smart and pretty. Kazu said that I should marry her. She was right, but Rosella was already married.

She would come to my apartment for three hours at noon every day, and we would work on my Italian—both learning regular Italian and then studying my lines.

It was February when I went over to Taormina to do the movie with Roberto. It was colder than I had hoped. You look on the map and it is right near North Africa. But you study the map a little further and Sicily is barely any farther south than New Jersey.

There was no schedule.

I thought that I had my part down in Italian, or at least I was close. There was a language instructor on the set who was supposed to help me with the dialogue. We had five different meetings set up and he never showed up for any of them. He was an American guy, very clean and snotty. It looked like he brushed his hair a hundred strokes per day . . . suddenly, my memory is telling me that maybe he was the original yuppie who overcharged me for the ride back from the West Coast when I was seventeen. But, of course, he wasn't. He was just an archetype for that irritating creature whose mission it is to block people from a happy and decent path. There seem to be more and more of him lately.

There was some kind of feud going on in the movie. The producers were undermining all the heads of the departments. They would go to the underlings and tell them not to do the set the way the set designer wanted it but the way that they wanted it, and if they did, they would be guaranteed a job on the producers' next feature. I don't know exactly what it was, but there was very uncomfortable shit going on, and when I became friendly with Antonio, the set designer, somehow this language guy and his tiny band of cohorts decided that I was their enemy.

It really made little sense. But people in a large group, off somewhere on location, head into some very uncomfortable patterns. *Last Temptation* was awkward, but there was some warmth on that set. This was different. There was some Machiavellian shit going on. People really seemed to not like one another and wanted to do harm.

There was a buffoon of a man who was the line producer. He would go out of his way to lie to you when the truth would not have been a problem for either him or you. He just lied first, no matter what, as though from habit.

I asked Roberto how to say *buffoon* in Italian.

"Is the same, *buffone*. Why?"

I pointed to the line producer with a tilt of my head.

Roberto said, "I see, yes, very good."

I don't know when I am shooting. I can't get an answer. There is no schedule. I can never leave because they might need me, but I am never needed. I am there for weeks.

I have one scene that is a couple of pages of straight dialogue. A little speech. I work on it over and over and over again. It is still stuck somewhere in the recesses of my brain. "*Una razza senza mutandine!*" It is like touching a memory part of the brain with a pin and it comes flying out.

I am close to getting this dialogue, I just need a little help. But then after lunch the buffoon says that they are shooting that scene right now. Like, *Surprise!*

No warning, no meeting with the language guy. Today is your day.

I try. I try so hard.

First off, I am nervous. Not out of control nervous, but it is my first day acting in this movie, in front of this crew, and there is a lot of inexplicable hostility floating around.

I run a couple of lines, and they are moving some lights when I hear loud laughing coming from my left. I look just in time to see the assistant director pursing his lips into what is clearly an exaggerated John Lurie face, and the crew is laughing. At me.

This makes no sense. Like, at all. I have never spoken a word to this guy. We have had no interaction and now, before my first scene, he is mocking me. I really don't get it and never get to the bottom of what is going on on this film set.

I have the words down in Italian. I am pretty sure I have the pronunciation down, but I am also sure my phrasing is weird as hell. Probably like an animated robot spouting off this speech.

I am delivering all this dialogue in front of a crew of seventy Italians and I know that I haven't pulled it off.

I'm furious. Had we done a couple of the smaller scenes first, I could have gotten it. Had anyone helped me with it, I would have gotten it.

I'm angry and the crew is just, "Well, he can't speak Italian. Why is he angry?" Which I can understand. I can't imagine being in a movie with a foreign actor who is barking out nonsensical English and then he gets angry because he can't do it.

But I have worked for months on this.

Roberto is working so hard and looks so frail that I am worried about him. He is in the hallway of the hotel waiting for Nicoletta. I call to him but he is lost in thought and doesn't hear me. I watch him move and gesture and then turn the other way like he is rehearsing and figuring out the camera angles for the next scene, all at the same time. Then he slumps, exhausted, against the wall.

It's beautiful in Taormina, but I am getting stir-crazy. I only have four scenes in the movie and I am there well over a couple of months. The hotel is a very old monastery. They work it out so that I can practice in the cathedral. I go there to practice and it sounds beautiful. I write the song "Voice of Chunk" in there but only go twice because something about it feels haunted and scares me.

I don't know why I say "feels haunted." It was fucking haunted.

As the grand devil, I want my voice to sound like John Huston's in *Chinatown*. Deep and rich. And I am doing the part like that.

In my scene with Walter Matthau, he says this is a terrible idea. That even when he won the Oscar, he didn't change the sound of his voice.

He calls me Baskets. He says it's because I walk like a basketball player. Someone once said that even in *Last Temptation*, in my robe and sandals, I walked around like a basketball player, all lanky.

Matthau seems to have no idea who I am. Which doesn't matter to me, but then I learn from his wife, Carol, whom I really love and who was married previously to William Saroyan twice, that she and Walter saw both *Stranger Than Paradise* and *Down by Law*, the latter right before leaving the United States.

Why on earth would he pretend to not know me?

That night, after he told me that all my acting decisions were wrong, we have a game of poker, where Walter tells me that everything I do in the first few hands is wrong.

Then I take all the cash he has.

* * *

Back in New York, I ran into Jean-Michel at the video store on Lafayette Street. I went, "Willie Mays!" He grinned at me but wouldn't talk. Just kept grinning at me without speaking.

Not an easy thing to do, actually. Just stand there and grin at someone without speaking. But he just stood there, staring at me and grinning.

In the last year of Willie's life, I only saw him a handful of times.

The time before the video store was particularly eerie and wrong.

A few months before, we had gone to the Odeon to eat. He hardly touched his food, just played with it. He loved to flaunt his money by wasting things. He'd order the most expensive thing on the menu and then smash it up with his fork, uneaten. He'd buy a four thousand dollar suit at Comme des Garçons and then paint in it the same day. I was jealous of that one, I have to admit.

After dinner he directs the cab to go way into the East Village to cop. It's odd, because he used to ridicule me for taking heroin, but now he's way into it, and I have stopped, this time maybe for real.

He bought ten bags, which seemed like a shitload of heroin to be buying at midnight on a Sunday. There was no way this could be good dope, the reliable dealers were only out during daylight hours. At night it was always a gamble. But around midnight on a Sunday, forget it. There was almost no chance you were getting actual heroin.

I am kind of shocked by the idea that he is going to do ten bags of street dope by himself in one night. But Willie was always like that with drugs, his pot was always the strongest and he could always snort more coke than anyone without wigging out.

We go back to his place and he wants me to snort a bag to see if it is any good. But I've kicked heroin and don't want to do it. Granted, this is the fortieth time that I have quit, but I may have really quit this time, it seems to be holding. Has been several months.

But, for certain, if I were to get high, I would be very particular about what dope I would take, and it isn't going to be this late Sunday night East Village shit.

I pour some on the mirror, take a speck with my finger, and taste it with my tongue. The allure is still always there.

"It tastes weird."

"Can I shoot it?"

"I wouldn't."

"Tastes weird how?"

"Just tastes like chemicals. Like you might be better off unclogging your kitchen drain with this product."

"Snort it."

"I don't want to."

"John Lurie is turning down free dope?"

"Fuck you. I'm not your fucking guinea pig."

This went on forever. I couldn't believe he was even contemplating shooting this stuff.

After that night I decided to avoid him for a while. It seemed I had really quit heroin and I couldn't be in a situation where it was around.

I hesitated putting this story in the book. That is not who he was, but it is who he was that night.

Andy Warhol's death had really destroyed him. I think hardly anyone saw him after that.

He fell into heroin pretty hard, but then I heard he had kicked in Hawaii.

He had called me from there. He was freaking out, crying and crying. He was going to quit the art world. This same exact thing had happened once before when he was in Italy.

He begged me to come to Hawaii. He'd send me a ticket. I couldn't decide whether or not to go. Sounded like he really needed me to come, but it was bad timing for me. I had rehearsals with the band coming up that I would have to cancel and all this music to sort out.

He called again and begged me to come. I was leaning toward going. Okay, he would call me tomorrow.

I talked to Torton about it: "What should I do? It sounds like he really needs me to come." Finally I decided to go, but then Jean-Michel never called back and I had no way to reach him.

His talent was gigantic. More than anyone knows. And he had an amazing motor, would just paint all the time. Even when he was a kid, staying at my place. He would pick up my oil pastels and start painting on the side of a cardboard box or a napkin.

I was poor and yelled at him for using up all my oil pastels. Too bad these art vultures weren't around then. They would have bought him ten million dollars' worth of oil pastels, enough to cover all of Third Street in oil pastels.

Man, it is so ridiculous, what is happening now with Jean-Michel. Do you think a fraction of this idolatry, of this obscenity in the prices for his paintings, would be happening if he were still alive?

America only loves its true artists when they are safely dead. When they are alive, they are much too dangerous.

And what really is the shame of it all is that he died so young. That fame thing is really hard to adjust to. Takes a while before you can find yourself after it is on you. Even though many people think they want fame, it is not usually a good thing. If he had had time to sink back into who he was, if he had been allowed to mature a little, I'm sure he would have become something truly amazing. As cruel as he could be, he had a kind and beautiful heart, and I think the cruelty was just partly because of his youth.

I'd go by his place on Third Street, the building that Andy Warhol set him up in, and he would have these paintings everywhere. Some just incredible. There was one, a skeleton with a halo, that just rocked me, and an elephant with a bunch of writing. I went home and worked on music for a while. When I came back, I asked where they were. I wanted to see them again. I had never done that before, asked him to pull out a painting I had seen earlier. Gives you an idea of how special they were.

He had painted over them. I couldn't believe it. Was almost angry at him about it.

But he was never precious about his work. In a way, that kind of impressed me. Around that time, we had smoked some of his ridiculously strong weed and were boxing in slow motion, making the sound effects as we went.

Whamp!

He delivered an uppercut to my jaw and I went backward from the imaginary slow motion blow.

Kapow!

He delivered another slow motion blow to my midsection. As I stepped back, my foot landed in a tray of paint. Then he caught me with another solid punch to the body and I went back again, and stepped onto an almost finished canvas that was lying on the floor. Leaving a big paint footprint.

I was horrified. "Oh, Willie! I am so sorry, man!"

But he just laughed. He didn't say, "No, John, it's okay." He just laughed.

Then we both laughed and went back to our slow motion boxing.

Years later, after he was gone, I went up to the Guggenheim to see this enormous show of his. There was a painting with a footprint in it. Pretty sure it had to be the same painting.

I stepped forward to show someone where my footprint was but was not even past the velvet rope thing. I just leaned in a bit and pointed. Guards swooped in from all directions.

"Sir! Sir! Stay back from the painting!"

"I—"

"Sir! Back away from the painting!"

I swear, if they equipped these guys with guns, they would have shot me.

They didn't believe me when I explained that I had already stepped on this valuable thing they were now protecting.

I was jealous about that too, I suppose. He was living in his muse, twenty-four hours a day—if a painting got ruined, fuck it, another would flow out—while I was having to run the band, trying to collect money owed from the last tour, trying to get the right drums for Zurich, making sure everyone had their passport, or explaining to a musician how a calendar works. I resented it, and he was living in his muse.

It was devouring my soul and I was losing my magic. I wasn't living in it. I was suffering, and he seemed to take pleasure in that, which I hated. Like that fate could never have befallen him.

We always fought. Then we would go around and badmouth each other, and it was just stupid.

I was talking shit about him one day when Torton turned to me and said, "Jean-Michel tells people that you are the only artist equal to him."

I suppose that was why we always fought. We were competitive. I never really had that with anyone else, not like that.

The guy was amazing. I loved him. With all the assholes in the world, especially leeching around that scene, why fight with him?

Another time, after another falling out, I wrote him a long letter saying that I loved him. That I would not badmouth him, not ever again. With all these creeps out there, why would I attack someone as beautiful as him?

He didn't write back. The next time I saw him, which was a long time later, he didn't say anything about the letter. I didn't want to, but I finally asked him, "Did you get the letter I sent you six months ago?"

"Yeah."

For a moment, he looked at the floor and didn't say anything. Then he said, "I cried," then walked away.

In the video store where he refused to speak, just grinned but wouldn't talk, that was the last time I saw him.

34

My Friends Cover Their Faces

When I was in Morocco doing *The Last Temptation of Christ*, this French guy recognized me in the marketplace and said that I had to hear the Gnawa music. I never open up to situations like this, when someone tells me there is music I "have to hear," unless it's Evan. The amount of times people have been correct in the past is next to zero.

But there was something about the French guy, who looked more Gypsy than French. It seemed like maybe I should pay attention. A spark behind the eyes and a worldly understanding that seemed to go beyond his years. One of those people who learn how to enjoy life by paying attention to it.

He said he knew two of the best Gnawa musicians, who happened to be in Marrakech at this time. He could bring them to my hotel room if I wanted. I could play with them, or they could just come and smoke kif with me and play on their own.

Gnawa musicians are part of a nomadic tribe that lives in tents and travels around North Africa performing rituals of dance and music. The

dance is something where they whip themselves into a frenzy of possession and is amazing to witness.

These two Gnawa guys came to my room and they were just beautiful. So sweet and respectful that it broke my heart. One of them played
this homemade half-bass, half-guitar instrument that had no frets, and
the other one had little metal maraca-like things and sang.

They both sat on the floor and we got stoned on kif. I took out my
soprano and turned on my tape recorder. The little guy with the metal
clacky things sang like he had a hole in his throat. It had the warmth of
your father singing you to sleep. Sometimes the other would sing a
response or repeat his phrase.

What a gift this was.

The music is fairly simple and modal. But it has an imploring tone
that is beautiful. It is like the music is just gently asking, "Why, God?
Why?," acknowledging suffering but without complaining.

I played with them and something happened for me. I had one of
those moments. An epiphany. It was not my being influenced by what
they were playing. It was the freedom and the very sweet and open vibe
that they had brought that freed me up. Something changed in my playing that night and stayed changed.

It was the purity in their reason for playing that really had hit me.
That was what I wanted, more than anything: to be part of a tribe that
played music for the right reason.

Back in New York, I was writing a lot of music—bass parts, piano
parts, guitar parts—to go with the melodies I was creating on the horn,
but it somehow didn't fit together rhythmically. Actually, it fit too well. I
was working a lot in odd time signatures, and somehow if the tune or
part of it was in 11/8, putting all the parts in 11/8 made it feel stilted.

Dougie helped me make an enormous leap by saying if something
was in 5/4, it wasn't necessary for everything to be in 5/4. Dougie and
Erik and I, and then later Marc and Evan, started working out stuff in
multilayered rhythms. So part of the band would be in 6/8 and then
maybe part of it would be in 5/4, and it created this kind of ocean of
floating rhythm that gave the music life. It was really exciting. It was the
first time, ever, that I felt, *Yes! This is it! This is what I want it to sound like,*
and the ideas were flying out of me. And something else was happening:
The music was getting pure. It was still crashing and irreverent, but at

the same time it was becoming somehow spiritual. This was beautiful and unified the band in a nice way.

We had a week booked at the hideous Knitting Factory, when it was still on Houston Street. The place was always filthy and seemed low-rent to me. I didn't want to play there. Sound system was no good. Your place can have ripped upholstery and pieces of plaster falling off the ceiling, fine, as long as it sounds good there. But it didn't.

Yet, when the owner, Michael Dorf, said with such awe that if The Lounge Lizards ever played his club he could die after that, I fell for it and said okay. Dorf was a really miserable guy to deal with. His name entered the vocabulary of downtown musicians over the years as a replacement for *screwed:* "Oh, you got Dorfed."

So all nine of us crammed onto that tiny stage and played. There was no air. It was August, and so hot and crowded you couldn't breathe. The audience was right up on you. I bought a canary and placed it on the stage, in a cage, like coal miners do, to test the air. The only good thing I have to say about the Knitting Factory is that the canary didn't die.

I'm getting ready to go to the show. Have my suit on, have shaved, am sitting on my bed rushing to get on my shoes. There is never enough time before a show to find a good reed and then be warmed up. I also have a superstition about not leaving my apartment a complete mess, so like Spalding Gray, I will start to leave the house and then decide I can't leave the garbage tilting over and circle back to fix it.

My other superstitions are that I can't play onstage with money in my pocket, and my socks absolutely cannot have any holes in them. Pretty much the only thing Evan and I ever fought about on the road was socks.

The phone rings. I try not to answer the phone before a show in New York because everyone is calling to be on the guest list. When we are playing in town, I change my answering machine message to, "If you want to be on the guest list for tonight's show please leave your message BEFORE the beep."

This works. There are lots of exasperated gasps and then hang-ups but no one demanding free tickets to the show.

It's Gabrielle on the phone. That's odd. I haven't talked to Gabrielle in a really long time. Since she got straight and I was straight, we just fell out of touch, even though Gabrielle was one of the funniest people I'd ever met.

"I'm sure you already heard."

"What?"

"Jean-Michel Basquiat died."

"Really?"

It's just weird. Doesn't make any sense. I haven't seen him in a while. I heard that he'd kicked heroin in Hawaii.

"How'd he die?"

"They don't know."

I don't feel sad or anything. I just feel strangely off balance. I go and play the gig.

I do remember, to this day, being in the middle of the concert, and for a moment the reality of it hit me. *Jean-Michel is dead.* Then going back into the music. The perfect place to go.

A few years before, Jean-Michel had come to my house at four in the morning. He was in a horrible state. He was weeping and his nose was bleeding from taking too much coke. He was having his first big opening in New York. At first I thought it was anxiety about the show. But after some time it became clear it was that his father was coming.

He was terrified of his father.

Even so, when I heard that Jean-Michel's father didn't want his friends going to the funeral, I thought, *Okay, I can respect that he wants a private funeral for the family.* But then I heard that the big deals in the art world had been invited. This made me furious. For Jean-Michel's funeral, the first thought is *Best way to market his work?*

So I went, uninvited. I crashed the funeral. Fuck, he was my friend, perhaps my closest friend. I loved him.

Someone had to be there who loved him.

There were security guys outside of the funeral. They took one look at my face as I approached and moved out of my way. I guess it was clear it would be a mistake to try to stop me.

The funeral wasn't about Jean-Michel's infectious, impish grin or his vulnerable pigeon-toed walk, which we would never see again. It wasn't about how, except for the times when he appeared to be channeling Idi Amin, he could be the most beautifully warm thing ever on the planet. It was about something else altogether.

I don't know, maybe I am being unfair. I can't tell people how to grieve. Sometimes when someone I care about dies, I get angry in all directions, especially if things seem phony.

I felt the vibe on the way out.

There was the line of people offering condolences to Gerard, Jean-Michel's father, and I could just feel that heavy Basquiat vibe before I actually saw him seeing me.

Gerard Basquiat stared at me. *You are unwelcome here.* Damn, an entire family that can channel Idi Amin.

Why am I unwelcome here? I loved him. Fuck you and these pretentious art people on top of it. Fuck all of you.

I don't remember seeing any of the people who truly cared about Jean-Michel at the funeral, like Suzanne Mallouk or Jennifer Goode or Shenge or Torton, but I am not in the habit of taking inventory at funerals.

They were all going somewhere after the funeral, I suppose the cemetery, but I bolted. Had to get away from it.

I went outside, and as I turned the corner, I ran smack into the coffin as it was being taken out.

Damn, that is Willie Mays in there.

They placed the coffin down outside the hearse and I put my hand on it.

Just at that solemn moment, I heard a shrieking voice, very loudly, go, "Oh my God! Is that him!?"

It was Rene Ricard coming to the funeral an hour late. Rene, in his way, was an absolute genius. He also could be the most obnoxious person on the planet. At Bruce Balboni's birthday party, when Bruce had OD'd and was put in the bathtub and being shot full of saline to revive him, Rene was the one who went around the party singing, "It's my party and I'll die if I want to."

I was almost surprised Rene didn't scream out, "This is fabulous!" as he stood over the coffin.

I had a lot of affection for Rene, but I really did not want to see him at this moment and walked off, with a cold, ugly feeling inside me.

My uncle Jerry had been sick with lymphoma and was getting chemotherapy. I had been bad about going to see him. Kazu and I had gone up to his place on Central Park West about three weeks earlier, but I had only been up to see him once since he had been admitted to Roosevelt Hospital.

Halfway through the evening that Kazu and I visited, he'd started having violent pain in his back. I'd called his doctor on his instruction and was told to get him over to Roosevelt Hospital, take him in via the emergency room entrance.

Except, I was told at the emergency room that they had no rooms at the moment. He would have to wait. He was on a gurney, pushed against the hallway wall, with people rushing past us constantly, in all directions.

There was nowhere for us to stand. We were in the way, so after an hour, we left him, writhing in pain, on the hospital gurney in the hallway. And since then I had only been up to visit him one time. So I felt terrible about that and thought, as I walked with Jean-Michel's coffin behind me, I'd walk through Central Park and go visit my uncle Jerry.

When I got to Roosevelt, I saw Nina, a friend of my uncle's, through the glass entrance. Nina was crying. She was weeping in that really deep, uncontrollable way that can only mean one thing.

I realized that Jerry was gone.

I don't know what happened next. I found myself ten blocks away on Fifty-seventh Street. I had no idea how I had gotten there. I'd lost the jacket and tie that I had worn to Jean-Michel's funeral, and my white shirt was in complete disarray.

It was too much. My brain had diswired. I walked back to the hospital and someone handed me my jacket.

"I want to see him."

"No, you don't want to see him."

I just kept wondering if he was scared. I hoped he wasn't scared.

Jerry's answer, if you told him that you believed that there was something after this life, was, "Well, that's good for you. I don't, but if you believe it, then for you it is true."

He was such a sweet man. Just a good New York Jewish lawyer who did a lot of things for a lot of people. A breed that doesn't exist anymore. There is a line in that movie *The Pledge*, where Jack Nicholson says to Sam Shepard, "I give you my word. You're old enough to remember when that meant something." That was my uncle. He was like that. Old school.

I felt bad that I hadn't been up to see him in the hospital more often.

There was a memorial for my uncle at the Promenade Theatre. He had been a part owner. The place was packed. Eli Wallach headed the whole thing. Stella Adler was there.

Sarafina performed. Actors' Equity had said that it was time for Sarafina to return to South Africa, that they must now be replaced by local performers. That is just so incredibly wrong and Jerry saw that. He fought hard, pro bono, to keep them in the country. Now they were playing his memorial.

It was really all kinds of beautiful.

The band all agreed to lug their own equipment and play at ten-thirty in the morning for the memorial because they all liked Jerry that much. Was incredibly sweet of them.

We had a song that is on the *Voice of Chunk* album called "Uncle Jerry." I had written it quite a while before he died. It was important to me that it was understood that this was not written as a posthumous tribute. It was something written when he was healthy and alive. I try to explain that to the packed house of mostly older people and it just comes out all kinds of wrong. Sounds kind of wise guy–ish or something. I don't know why, but it's off.

We start to play and it's good. We're really playing. I go off into that mode. I am in the music and playing my heart out. When I go to that place, I basically forget everything else. I don't know where I am. I am just gone, I am just gone in the music.

When the band plays live we usually end with something powerful and uptempo that will lead the crowd into calling for an encore. We have a hard out and then I yell, "Thank you very much!!" and we leave the stage.

Well, we are playing at the memorial and we are in it, we're really playing. The song ends, I throw my arm over my head and scream, "Thank you very much!!"

And then I have the unsettling realization of where we were.

Most of the people there are in their seventies and have the look of a crowd that has just witnessed something deeply inappropriate. My eyes go up to the middle of the theater, where Kazu, Stephen Torton, and my sister, Liz, are sitting, just in time to see all three of them cover their faces with their hands, all at exactly the same time. Like *Oh, John, what did you do now?*

35

John Lurie: Pathetic and Ignorant

An outdoor shower in the tropics is one of those perfect things. It opens your pores to life. Wholesome and erotic all at once.

I rented a house on the beach in Ajuda, Brazil, for a week before the band came down to play in Rio de Janeiro. This was at the end of the summer in 1988. Stephen Torton was living in Belo Horizonte and met me.

The house only had an outdoor shower, which had a hot water heater that was oddly wired. You could take a shower but would get a shock when you turned the water on. Then during the shower, when you were wet, you'd get a much worse shock if you touched the taps. Then you were guaranteed your worst shock of the day when you turned the water off.

Stephen and I would hear each other in the shower going, "Ow!" and the one not in the shower would find it very amusing.

Two journalists sat in the sand on the beach in their suits looking for me. They didn't know what I looked like. They had a photo of me, which they held in their hand and referred to. We'd walk past them on the sand and they would look at their photo, squint at us, look back at the photo, and then decide that I wasn't me.

Another group of journalists showed up and asked me to do an interview. I said no.

They said, "Very good for you, very good for Brazil." They were very pushy. Since this sentence, "Very good for you, very good for Brazil," was repeated over and over again, and appeared to be the full extent of their English, I refused.

They published an interview without talking to me at all. They just filled in my answers like they wanted. A third group showed up. They seemed fairly bright and respectful, so I, finally, acquiesced. When the article came out, it said that Stephen was my boyfriend.

To get to our house on the beach, one had to take a ferry from the village. The ferry went from one rickety wooden dock over rushing water to another, all day long. Instead, Stephen and I rented two gigantic kayaks to go back and forth. Not normal kayaks, but clumsy, twelve-foot-long plastic boats. They were heavy and difficult to carry.

We find the easiest way is to each take an end of each kayak and try to negotiate our way through the narrow streets. The village is surrounded by a high concrete wall and we can't figure out how to get the kayaks into the water. The locals watch us straining with these monstrous, colorful things as we walk to where we think the water is. But when we get to the end of the street, there is the ten-foot-high concrete wall barring us from the water. We have to retrace our steps. The locals see us struggling and stare at us with the same lack of expression. It makes us start to laugh. For some reason whenever I am carrying something heavy with a friend, it makes me start to laugh, but we have to walk past these guys, again, drinking beer, leaning against the wall and it was just too silly. We go down another little street that leads to the sound of the rushing water, but although the water is right there, splashing on the other side of that wall, we are blocked.

We have to walk past them again. My arms are straining under the weight and the laughter from my chest is making it hard to breathe. We take another route, but there is still the wall. I tell Stephen that I cannot walk past those guys again and we decide to hoist the kayaks on top of the wall and push. They plop into the ocean, and we have to then climb the ten-foot wall quickly and swim after our kayaks that are being swept away by the estuary.

We row halfway across, but in these ridiculous kayaks, it makes it almost impossible to row in the whirlpool out in the center. There is a point where the ocean rushing in meets the estuary rushing out. We are stuck in one spot rowing as hard as we can and not moving. We go with the current and angle a bit down the shore to get across. Once we are out of the suctioning whirlpool, we can finally negotiate the kayaks to the house. A week later, when we return the kayaks, it is even more difficult. It takes an hour to go fifty yards. We are exhausted and can't go farther. But if you stop paddling for a moment, you are whisked out to sea. It requires superhuman concentration and effort to even get to the wall, which is still one hundred yards or so from the dock, to return the kayaks. We get to the wall and hang on for dear life. Regroup our strength and then pull the kayaks over the wall, Stephen doing most of the work. When we return the kayaks, we find out that fourteen people in boats, some experienced boatmen, have drowned in the whirlpool spot in the last year.

I don't know how this happened, because no one knew what flight I was on, coming from Ajuda back to Rio. I didn't know myself until right before I took it. The little plane struggled so hard against the wind that it seemed like the kayaks and everything else in Brazil went backward. When we land at the airport, there is a chaotic whirlwind of cameras on the tarmac, seventy photographers, all there to take my picture as I get off the plane. At least I have a tan.

Miles Davis, who is the biggest act booked at the festival we're playing, has canceled. By default, I have been proclaimed a star of enormous magnitude. My arrival is on the front page of all the papers. They have put my hotel and room number in one of the articles. I don't know what to make of any of this. The press in Brazil seems to have one goal, and that is to drive me insane.

On the front page of one of the papers, I think the *Folha de S. Paulo*, there is a huge photo of me getting off the plane. In large letters I am proclaimed a musical genius, a great actor, and the most charming and attractive man to come out of the United States in many years.

I am on the front page of most of the papers, and most of them have idiotic headlines saying, "THE SAX APPEAL HAS ARRIVED!" or some such nonsense, but always using the catchy phrase "Sax Appeal." Meanwhile at the same time in history, George H. W. Bush is accepting the GOP nomination, Iraq is celebrating a cease-fire with Iran, and Seoul is preparing for the opening of the Olympics. But what is important to the press of Brazil is that "the Sax Appeal has arrived to turn all the girls' heads!"

Another paper, maybe *O Estado de S. Paulo*, sees that *Folha de S. Paulo* loves me, and because they must disagree with everything their rival writes, they decide that I am an abomination. They write, "John Lurie is very temperamental. Skinny, his white skin burned by the Brazilian sun, he arrived telling everyone how tired he is. Poor baby. Behaving like a French person in front of cheese that wasn't very good."

What could I have possibly done to provoke that? I have not yet done an interview. We have not even played and I am despised.

They also hate the band and do things like run photos of Dougie Bowne, our drummer, on the back page, with the caption, "Erik Sanko, The Lounge Lizards' bass player, one of the festival's worst."

Meanwhile, because they have published my hotel and room number, I cannot leave the room without being mobbed by journalists and young women.

I have a terrifying press conference. I want to guide them to talk about the music, but all they seem interested in is who I am sleeping with and what I wear to bed. I make the mistake, during the press conference, of answering the question "Do you like Brazilian music?" by answering, "I hate all nationalities equally."

Stephen thinks that that is where it all went wrong, but I think it was brewing all on its own and anything I did would have been wrong.

I have been listening to tapes of the Bayaka pygmies. It is the most beautiful thing that I have ever heard. When they ask what music I'm listening to, I tell them about the pygmy tapes, but apparently they think that I am messing with them.

A guy stands up and says, "John Lurie, the musicians think you are a great actor and the actors think that you are a great musician." There is no question. He just stands up and says that.

This is the first time in my life that the music actually is sounding real to me. We are making breakthroughs and it has a lot of heart. That, and the fact that Jean-Michel and my uncle Jerry have just died, makes the music particularly precious to me at this time.

But nobody writes about the music. They write things like, "John Lurie has come to turn all the young girls' heads. He is a hunk." They keep calling me a hunk. *Zero Hora* proclaimed me "the Hunk of the Festival." A hunk? I am six foot two and at the time weigh no more than one hundred fifty-five pounds.

The whole thing is gaining a leeringly Machiavellian character. I am getting uncomfortable because photographers are pressing in on me everywhere I go and reporters are misquoting everything I say. If I refuse to say anything, they'll just make something up.

I am asked if I would like to see some great Brazilian music. There is a lot of Brazilian music that I love, and this thing they want to take me to is presented to me like it is exceptional.

We arrive at the club. I take one step in and realize that it's a setup. There are photographers everywhere. We are not there ten seconds when the tour manager asks if I would please have my photo taken with one of their most famous soap opera stars. I can't really say no. I am whisked over to stand next to this aging actress with too much makeup. The next day, in the paper is a photo of me and the soap opera star. The article says that I am pursuing her, but she has decided against it because international affairs are too exhausting. This happens with several other Brazilian actresses as well. Photos I don't even remember being taken, or I am sitting on a couch next to someone I have never talked to or even noticed and in the paper it states that we are having a torrid affair.

The tour manager ushers me over to a table that is reserved for me. The music is awful, but I can't leave because no one is watching the pedestrian jam session. They are all watching me, and the press has already complained that I haven't seen any Brazilian music since my arrival and that I must be an uncultured snob. A journalist asks how I like the saxophonist who is onstage. I say, "He sounds like Jackie McLean with some fingers missing." One can imagine how that translates.

I am at the table and I feel like they are going out of their way to drive me completely mad. I can't stand the music and I want to leave. Then a bright light is turned on and directed at my head. There is a film crew there to film me watching this horrific band. I ask them to stop. They just grin and continue to shoot, so of course I throw my drink at them and walk out. The drink was a vodka grapefruit, and what is typically ridiculous is that in every newspaper's account of the incident, the drink is reported to be a caipirinha, like it has to be a Brazilian drink. Of course, my little tirade is on the front page of all the papers.

Flying saucers have landed in Mexico City, but that story is on page 2.

We have met a lot of great people in Rio, but when you ask if they are going to the concert, they just look at you kind of funny. Turns out that the price of the ticket is about three weeks' wages to the average Brazilian.

The night we play in Rio, I am taken aback by the scariest, most opulent, jewelry encrusted crowd I have ever seen. So much money just sitting out there. And so little interest in the music.

It's the first bad concert we've had in ages.

I really wanted it to be amazing. I wanted it to be so good that there was no way the press or these wealthy zombies wouldn't have their world rocked a little bit. But that didn't happen.

I'm in Brazil and feel it requires that I take some cocaine, so I get some after the show.

On the way out, three young, very sexy women pretend to block my path, smiling coyly. They all speak a little English but not much.

We all go back to my suite. There is a fourth woman who is with them but doesn't want to go. But from what Portuguese I can understand, they are her ride and she has no choice but to tag along.

I am in the bedroom with the three. Two are sitting on the bed with the third over in the corner, sort of running through a series of sensual poses.

I don't know what to do. I don't know how to start this.

As I am standing there, in the awkward silence, one of them, Patricia, takes out my cock and sucks it for about thirty seconds. Quite well, I must add. She really is sucking my cock well.

Then she stops.

I think, *Oh good, it has started.*

Patricia has a proud look on her face, like, *I started it.*

Then Bea takes out my cock and sucks it for thirty seconds.

Eventually all three of us are naked and having various kinds of sex, but they aren't into one another. They don't even want to inadvertently touch one another. It is really more like, *John Lurie is in town and we must fuck him to add his name to our scorecard.*

It goes on for a while but is never really the kind of sex you can get into. And while this is going on, every time it seems to be going somewhere, the fourth one bursts into the room and starts screaming in Portuguese that she wants a ride home.

Finally, the posing one, whose name I don't think I ever got, and the fourth one leave. There is some normal sexual activity and a lot of cocaine.

I wake up in my enormous room, alone and very hungover. I call down for breakfast.

The room service guy arrives with a gigantic, shiny smile and a tray of food.

He goes over and rips open the curtains. Sunlight is not something I planned on dealing with for a number of hours.

But the room has a huge balcony that hangs over the ocean. He opens the door and I realize that he is on the right track when the sea air floats into my brain and cleans it up a bit.

The waiter insists that I go to the outside table to properly enjoy my breakfast.

I follow him out.

He looks over my shoulder, and something that can only be described as terror darkens his face.

He says we'd best go back inside and starts hurrying to pack the tray and move back into the room.

I turn to see what could have possibly frightened him like this.

There is Nina Simone, looking like a predatory gargoyle.

She has the most feral look on her face I have ever seen in a human being. I knew she was in the room next to mine and have always been a giant fan, was hoping to meet her.

But this is different. This is like we have come across a wounded lion and we have invaded her territory. The look in her eyes is filled with absolute rage and is screaming, *GO AWAY! GO AWAY BEFORE I HURT YOU!*

It is clear that it is not safe to be out there, and we both rush back into my room and close the curtains.

Not another word is spoken between the waiter and me, but as he leaves, our eyes meet. We know we have had a brush with death that no one will ever really understand.

The press madness went on. They went to Milt Jackson from the Modern Jazz Quartet and asked him how he felt playing at a festival with punk bands like The Lounge Lizards. He responded by saying that he didn't know our music, but The Lounge Lizards didn't sound like a jazz band to him.

They came to me and said, "Milt Jackson says that your band is not jazz and that it was embarrassing for him to play at a festival with you." I said, "I don't think that Milt Jackson has ever heard us, and it doesn't matter to me if the band is labeled jazz or not." They went back to Milt Jackson and said, "John Lurie doesn't care what you think because your band is old."

I don't know what Milt said to that, but they came to me and said, "Milt Jackson thinks that it is a disgrace that your band wears sneakers and dirty clothes when you play." This went back and forth in the papers every day.

They decided to have a screening of *Down by Law* and announced in the paper that I would be there to present the film and sign autographs. Of course, no one asked me until forty-five minutes before the screening. I told them that I had sound check and could not go. They said that I had to go. To which I responded that I didn't have to do anything but play. They kept people waiting for two hours in the lobby for my arrival, but I never showed. No wonder the whole country ended up hating me.

They continued to argue about me on the front page of the papers. Stephen spoke perfect Brazilian Portuguese, or as Erik called it, "the sexy language with all the beige in it."

Stephen translated an article to me that said, "The sax player/actor John Lurie was completely lost at the register trying to buy a beer. Like a monkey with a huge amount of Brazilian currency in his hand. He was confused by the money and the language. A Brazilian actress and her musician boyfriend took care of him so that he wouldn't feel so *Stranger Than Paradise*."

Val and Stephen started hiding the papers from me. Stephen later said, "We had to protect him, like Nixon."

Even the stuff they were writing that was supposed to be favorable was annoying. *O Globo* said, "John Lurie—Saxual Orgy!"

At the end of the week, *Estado* had a big photo of me on the front page. Underneath the photo was the caption "JOHN LURIE: PATHETIC AND IGNORANT."

The amazing thing was that there was no article to go with it. Just the photo and the caption.

Perhaps Tad Friend should move there.

36

Voice of Chunk
The Gregg Popovich of Music

There was love in it.

We wouldn't say it out loud, not then, but it was like that. There was love in it. It was strong and exciting and exotic and nothing remotely like it had ever existed before and there was love in it.

This music was amazing. Now I wanted to record it. There was a two-year period where I decided to just go on tour and play. No more acting. No more trying to get a record deal.

I wanted what the Gnawa musicians had: A tribe that traveled from town to town and played music. Music that worshipped and exclaimed the beautiful weirdness that is this life.

This music was ready to be recorded, and if I waited too long it would be in danger of going stale. Of course the last thing I wanted to do was start shopping the idea of a new Lounge Lizards album to record companies. Take something exquisite, alive, and precious, and lay it before soulless dolts in fancy office buildings and then wait for them to assess it, to tell us whether or not we are worthy of being recorded? Oh hell, no. It didn't make sense. I just couldn't do it.

So while Evan and Liz took the money that we'd inherited from Uncle Jerry and bought the homes that they still live in today, I took almost all of the money I had inherited and brought the Lizards into the studio.

We had a band meeting. We all sat on the floor of my place on Eighteenth Street and Kazu brought out beers, which added something nice in the air. Kazu always brought out something nice in the air.

I saw it as something I was doing for all of us. But I wanted to make sure, before I took a risk like this, that they felt the same way and at least we would have a band when the record came out. That they would commit to keeping the band together for a year or two. I mean, I was about to take ten times more money than I had ever seen before and invest it in the hopes of making something beautiful and special.

But that does make sense, doesn't it? What else are you supposed to do with money? For that matter, what else are you supposed to do with this life?

I would give them each a certain amount for the whole record—I think it was three thousand each for five days' work—and they would get a royalty in the event that it ever went into the black.

Everyone was there and into it. Completely into it. And of course, each of them would be a member of the band forever, if that was what I wanted.

Except Marc Ribot didn't show up for the meeting.

Being in the studio with nine musicians is expensive. A studio that is large enough to accommodate so many musicians playing live is expensive. You need separation in the sound, so that one player doesn't bleed onto another player's mic. You need a large room with many booths and baffling, which is expensive. A studio capable of providing that many separate headphone mixes is expensive. The engineer is expensive. Tape is expensive. Recording these days is not so expensive, but recording a large band, live, even now, with the ability to have overdubs is really expensive.

Expensive. Expensive.

Almost any time that I've been in the studio, I've been in the position of anxiously watching the clock because of the allotted budget. The music loses something because you are trying to play without making mistakes. You don't go all out. You are much more about playing it safe, to make sure that you have everything without some ghastly mistake in a cut that you cannot afford to rerecord.

This time there was no budget. We could do it until it was right. I had only the slightest trepidation that the money would get out of control and run out. God was on my side. It had to go well.

Making a record is a very artificial thing to do. You are trying to encapsulate, in sound, this thing that is a little moment of soul. This thing that, initially, has come to you like a child's prayer. Then it blossoms with the musicians in rehearsal and then explodes into life when you play it.

It has been beautiful in the past, and for the record you want it to be as exquisite as it has ever been. You want it to be perfect. The best time, ever, that that song is performed live, you want it recorded. That is really all that will do: the best this song is ever played.

That time the tempo picked up really slightly after the B section in Kyoto, you want that. But you also want the section after that to be played a bit slower, like that one time in Munich, where you nailed it a year ago.

You want it to be free and loose but concise and mistake-free.

You want all of that.

But now you are in an artificial environment. The drummer and the percussion player are in booths. You can't see them, just the tops of their little heads.

Everything comes to you through headphones. You can't feel the bass or the drums. You can't feel the guy standing next to you when he stomps on the floor in the middle of his solo. There is no muscle, no sweat. Just little ticks of information in your ears, coming through a machine, into wires, into your headphones.

People think that music is sound, but truth be told, music is vibration.

So many nights, we played in rooms with bad sound or where the sound onstage was untenable, but halfway through the show we had conquered the room and intuitively found a way to make it glow. It has nothing to do with science and everything to do with something else that cannot be defined. You never really learn anything for the next time. It is just about finding the vibration of the room. I was half-watching this thing about Quincy Jones on TV, but when he said that when he goes into the recording studio, he always takes a moment to let God in, then I sat up and paid more attention, because that is what it is.

Something that starts as a warm tickle in your brain. A little bubble of light. A gift. That is now being recorded and traveling through wires to other musicians and going through more wires into big machines and recorded onto plastic and sent through wires to more plastic, then mass produced by the tone deaf in a factory in New Jersey. And that little, pure bubble of a prayer is supposed to still be there and organic. But you want the thing to be heard; you want that inspiration to travel, to be a beacon. You want to send it out into the world, in the pure way that it came to you. And if you can accomplish that, you will make the world a better place.

I was getting ready to go to the studio. I was excited as hell to record this music. I was on a mission.

Kazu made me breakfast. She came marching through with her big floppy alligator-faced slippers that I got her as a present.

The phone rang and it was Ribot. He stated that he wasn't going into the studio to be paid one lump sum for the record. He had to get whatever the union requirement was. The union requirement was based on three-hour increments. I think that back then, it was $250 for every three hours.

Not only did he insist that he had to be paid union wages, the entire band had to be paid like that.

But I had calculated that money. What I had offered them would end up being more than the union session rate for the time they were going to put in. So it was ridiculous for him to be arguing for them to get less money.

But I wanted them all there. To all be into the making of this thing. And I didn't want to be recording with one eye constantly on the clock, calculating that if I let the horns go home in half an hour when we overdubbed the bass parts, I could save $1,200.

I just wanted to go in, allocate a certain amount of money to the project, which was a lot of fucking money, and then work on the music, all together, as a unit, until it was great.

It was really rubbing me the wrong way how ugly and aggressively

Ribot was standing up for his principle. He was angrily and steadfastly defending the sanctity of the union, as though Karl Marx were his uncle.

The whole thing pissed me off, because Marc had not made it to the meeting and had not even called to say he would not be there. He ambushed me on one of the most important days of my life. I thought it was an important day in all their lives.

Forget about movies. Forget about record companies. Just have a tribe that goes from town to town and performs this ritual.

Maybe somehow in a way that I don't and didn't see, I was not true to this. But if that was the case, I really do not see it. Even today. I know my heart and intention were in the right place.

Something not good was happening. There was this faint rumble of dissent. Slightly uncomfortable glances. We were supposed to be trying to document this thing of love that we had created, and now something was poisoning it.

The second day in the studio, Curtis was late. Several hours late.

He finally called. His place had been robbed.

I felt bad for Curt. I knew he was going to be a mess when he finally arrived. He didn't do well with this kind of thing. But then it occurred to me that now I was going to have to pay all the guys while we waited for Curtis. Two hundred fifty dollars per person, every three hours, if we did it Ribot's way, which still hadn't been resolved.

There was an uneasy feeling about the whole thing. A wedge was growing between me and the band. I knew that the whole movie star thing was difficult for them to take. No matter how hard I tried, no matter what it said in the contract about not using just my photo or not calling it "John Lurie and The Lounge Lizards," we would arrive in a town and there would be an enormous photo of me with "JOHN LURIE! FROM THE MOVIES!" and hardly a mention of anyone or anything else. And damn, Evan was in the band. How did that make him feel? Evan wasn't a sideman. None of them were.

I also knew that every time one of them met a woman on the road and would be in a hotel room in Berlin or Rome or Paris, just at the moment they were unhooking a brassiere, they inevitably would be asked the question, "What's John really like?"

Fuck, I would have hated me too.

But there was another thing going on as well.

On the tour before, Marc had discovered a piece of paper, in the tour manager's room, with a breakdown of who in the band was being paid what.

It looked to Marc like I was making more than the entire rest of the band. What was not taken into account was the enormous amount of expenses that I was being reimbursed for—airline tickets, rehearsal studios, salaries for sound people, hotels on days off, and just on and on.

But no one mentioned this piece of paper Marc had found to me. And it was just assumed that I was ripping off the band. And I had always taken great pride in treating the musicians as well as possible. And if we were struck by any of the infinite ways the tour could lose money instead of making any, like the biggest concert being canceled or a train strike or whatever, I paid them what was promised and took the loss myself.

Years later, I kept hearing about this piece of paper that Ribot had found that made it look like I was getting rich. Every musician in Manhattan seemed to have heard that I ripped off my musicians. Like it was Lower East Side musicians' lore. And I never got a chance to explain it. Bothers the fuck out of me. I lost a fortune on that band.

Despite all the tension, there was so much magic in that music that It, the Magic, kind of went: *You guys can act like a bunch of babies, but I am still here. I am Magic and cannot be denied.*

I recently had a conversation with Evan about musicians and how disappointing they can be as human beings. It was specifically about going through cancer treatment, and though people knew I had cancer, I only heard from three of the eighty or so musicians who had been in The Lounge Lizards at one time or another.

When you share that kind of love with people, it is something really disappointing and confusing when the love is needed and isn't there.

Evan said this amazing thing, and I wish I had written it down at the time to get the exact quote, but he said, "When you are playing music with people and it is really what music is supposed to be, that is their deepest essence that you are communicating with. This is not always who they are in their daily lives."

* * *

I was scarfing down some food, listening to the takes from the day before, trying to get all my shit together for the studio, and arguing with Ribot on the phone about union scale again, all at the same time.

Ribot hung up on me.

I was furious.

I was about to go out the door in a rage when I heard the tape that was playing behind me, in the living room.

And it hit me.

It was the song "One Big Yes." It got its title because someone had posted a personal ad in the back of *The Village Voice* that said, "John Lurie, your music falls on me like they say love should, with One. Big. Yes." The music on the tape was so beautiful. It hit me that it was so much more than this fight, and I slumped to the floor in the hallway and wept.

I could feel Kazu watching me cry, having no idea what to do.

Earlier that year the band had been in Brazil and had recorded a few of the songs because we had a lot of time off and the studio was incredibly cheap.

The studio was up on a hill above that enormous statue of Jesus. There was a Ping-Pong table outside, and while we played, Ribot would play a note on the guitar every time the ball hit the paddle or the table. *Pink pink ponk pink.* The band was always having moments like that. We were fun as a band.

The only thing that was usable from Brazil was the song "Uncle Jerry." I had had the engineer run a cable down the hall and into the bathroom, where I did my solo. When I was warming up, walking around the house/studio, I had noticed that there was a great naturally resonant sound in the bathroom.

After recording the song, with me in the bathroom and the guys in the studio, I came down the hall and into the big room with the rest of the musicians. Curtis smiled at me and pointed one finger toward the heavens. Like, *Yes, John, you nailed it.*

The song "Voice of Chunk" was conceived on that tiny electric keyboard in a fifteenth-century church in Sicily. Then Erik came by my place on Eighteenth Street and added the bass line. A simple six-note line that powerfully, exquisitely, held the whole thing together. We recorded it in Brazil, and though the band was solid and Ribot's solo ascended perfectly, the recording really wasn't good enough quality to use. So we redid it in New York.

But something was wrong. The groove had lost something. I couldn't figure out what was wrong, but Dougie had clearly changed his part. I kept asking Dougie and Erik to come by my house and compare the two versions, but they really didn't want to. They didn't want to bother.

Finally, Erik and Dougie begrudgingly came over to listen and see what I was complaining about.

They understood the problem immediately and agreed that the New York groove was not as good, but said that it was fine.

But it wasn't anywhere near as good as it could be. I had to cajole each musician to come back into the studio for a quick two-hour session to redo the song. With everyone complaining, "The tapes are fine. We don't want to go back into the studio."

I was baffled. Everyone agreed that the Brazilian takes had a much better groove, something that Dougie had changed in the couple of months in between the recordings but didn't want to bother to go in and do again. That they had done enough work on this album and it wasn't great, but it was fine. I couldn't understand their attitude. Why wouldn't they want to come back in for a few hours to make it better? It just didn't make sense to me. This was the version of the song that would last forever; it had to be done right. "It's fine." What the fuck is that?

I was determined to make this record as good as possible. I was amazed that they weren't. I pushed them really hard to get it how it was supposed to be, with everybody whining about this and that. I was at war against anything that stopped this album from reaching the thing. The world does not need another album. But the world can most certainly use something that, when heard, makes chills go up your spine.

Most of the stuff we got. In more than moments, it's there. The material and the memory we had of it, the love, carried over. Despite the squabbling and the whatever, mostly it is there.

I can almost listen to it today and enjoy it. But not really.

After the recording, I took a vacation with Kazu, Glenn O'Brien, and James Nares in St. Barts. That was a nice combination of people. Kazu and I slept in the same bed but weren't having sex.

Glenn thought I was a pervert to not be having sex with Kazu.

I have been afraid of flying for a long time now. I don't remember when it started, but I must not have been afraid then. To get to St. Barts back then you had to take this odd, skinny propeller plane, which sat about twenty people, from St. Maarten. Even before the propellers started, the woman behind me begins making this weird, high-pitched noise.

The plane sputters and lurches down the runway but does not get up enough juice to get off the ground and get up over the mountain directly in front of us, so the pilot slams on the brakes and we skid off the runway onto the grass.

The woman behind me had to be let off the plane. But I didn't think anything of it. And today I am scared shitless to fly.

The next morning I woke up really early, like four A.M., before it was light. I went and climbed up on top of this hill that was next to the house. Caribbean turquoise water. I felt pretty good. To get that recording in the can gave me something. I felt this at other times later in my life when I finished a project that meant something to me, but not like this.

It was like something had been added to my essence. My soul weighed a little more.

I just sat there and watched the water for a long time.

I had my best vacation ever in St. Barts. Snorkeled and fished and ate well, and St. Barts wasn't as creepy as it seems to have become now.

We had a jeep. Kazu and I would stand up in the backseat as Glenn drove. We'd sing at the top of our lungs, "Why can't the French people be like me? Happy and holy and living free." I have been cheerfully irritating people for a long time.

Val was worried about all the money that I had spent on the record, so she talked me into accepting this job composing the music for a TV show that Aaron Lipstadt had done, which I forget the name of, some horrid police thing, and then *Mystery Train* for Jarmusch. So when I got back from St. Barts, I had to write and record the music for both of these projects before going in to mix *Voice of Chunk*.

Mystery Train was the last work I did with Jim. He wanted the same instruments that they had used in Elvis's *Sun Sessions*, which was a nice, limited palette to work with. I bought a great Gibson, a hollow-body guitar, through the mail. I thoroughly expected that it would be a piece of shit, but when it arrived it was this beautiful guitar with a deep, throaty sound when you played it through an amp.

It was just me on lead guitar and harmonica, Dougie on drums, Tony Garnier on bass, and Marc Ribot on rhythm guitar. Marc was there mostly to help keep a glue on things in case my guitar playing went haywire. I had never played guitar in the studio before. I don't think that I had ever played guitar anywhere but on my couch before. So who knows what might have gone wrong. I didn't know how to sit or stand and be comfortable playing. I was so used to slumping down on my couch or playing in my bed, it seemed odd to actually be sitting up and playing.

Mixing *Voice of Chunk*, like any recording that I've cared about, was a nightmare. I had spent so much more money than the budgeted hundred thousand, but I wasn't getting the right sound in the mixing studio.

Mixing. I can't stand mixing. It's like taking the purity out of the music and then trying to cram it back in again.

You want the music to have the wild energy of the rough tapes, but you also want to refine it. Make the trombone louder in that part, fix the piano in this part. There is a long period of time while the engineer is doing stuff with the machines that I do not understand. Before beginning to mix each thing, there is a three or four hour period while the engineer is working furiously, and there is nothing for me to do, except do drawings on whatever paper is in the studio. I hear stuff a certain way and want to keep it like that, but the next time the song plays, it is gone. And there is no real language to explain what has to be different. "The attack on the snare doesn't have enough *boing* in it anymore."

On the record I want the horn to sound like it does to me when I play. This is, for some reason, hard to capture. I had one engineer tell me that my skull resonated when I played and that is why it sounded better to me. But in order to recapture the sound that I wanted to get, we had to add stuff from outboard equipment, which seems beyond unholy to me.

Maybe that is partly true, but I know for certain that with the saxophone, a whole series of overtones tend to get lost. With each note there is a series of overtones that give the note its fullness and warmth. To me it is one of the problems with digital music in general, these overtones are often missing. In the old days there was just one mic in the middle of the room, and I think that, besides the fact that they were wonderful players, this is the reason players like Ben Webster or Johnny Hodges or Lester Young sound so full and rich.

For some reason that I do not understand, in order to recapture the natural sound of a lot of the instruments, they have to be fed through all these machines. One tiny turn of the knob that got the sound right on the piano made the horns sound plastic. Add a little treble to the snare drum and suddenly the bass sounds like it was played on an old synthesizer.

The hundred thousand for the record was all used up. I wasn't getting the right sound in the mixing studio and was spending more and more money trying to get it right. In the meantime, all the unrest in the band was fermenting. I was in the mixing room on Broadway and Bleecker for fourteen to sixteen hours a day, had spent all my money, and felt very unappreciated and lonely working on it.

We were working on the song "A Paper Bag and the Sun," and I went outside to buy cigarettes at five in the morning. There wasn't a soul around, and the buzzing streetlights on Broadway were intoning the song back to me. For some reason it reminded me of a line from a Rimbaud poem, "rain soaked bread." And that was how the song got its title. It was very much like a message being sent to me through the streetlights, which made me want to go on.

We were finally getting the sound right when Dougie announced that he was leaving the band. He had signed a deal with his rock band, World at a Glance. He was going to be a rock star because Island Records was finally getting behind his band and he had to quit because he would have time commitments.

Hadn't we just had a meeting where all the musicians said that if I put up all this money to make the record, they were staying? That they were committed to this band's being a band?

And for fuck's sake, at one point Dougie had quit Iggy Pop's band to play with The Lounge Lizards. A huge and courageous leap.

World at a Glance lasted about six months. Torton called them Band at a Glance.

Then I got into a war with Erik on the writer's credit. I had given him a share of the publishing on songs in which I felt he had greatly enhanced the basic nature of the piece, like "Voice of Chunk." How it normally worked was that I would come up with a melody line and maybe a guitar part, and usually the bass part or something else. I would have three or four things mapped out before bringing the stuff into rehearsal for the band to kick around. We would try this and try that, with the musicians adding stuff—amazing stuff—as it went, and I would direct it: "Try that later, maybe up an octave, and wait till the horns finish their first line."

It was a really good way of working. It was a way of weaving their exceptional and idiosyncratic talents into the compositions. And I think perhaps my greatest talent is finding the beauty in a musician's idiosyncrasies. I am the Gregg Popovich of music.

It was a creative process that we were all part of, but I directed it, and the basic concept was always mine. When it came time to record, I would hand out credit to the guys for their participation, but it was difficult to really quantify. If someone had come up with something great, I would give them 20 or 25 percent of the writer's credit, but usually on the more open pieces I would just try to make sure that each of them got some credit and money to make them all feel like part of it. This was absolutely not something that I had to do. I had written the music, and if someone added a B flat on the end of a line, that was really not deserving of a writing credit.

Well, suddenly Erik thought that he had written everything. There were two songs that I only had the melody for, and he'd come by my house and added bass lines that made the whole piece come into shape, and for these I gave him a writer's share, a well-deserved writer's share. But there were songs now that had actually been finished pieces before there was any bass on there at all. They really did not need his part. Erik wanted credit for these, and I felt like I was getting robbed.

It made me really angry. I loved Erik, and I think that this was just part of that momentary insanity that bands go through, but it was at the perfectly wrong moment.

I was Captain Ahab chasing this mystical thing. And I caught it. That record is magic. If you can't hear that, I feel bad for you. But what I had to do to get there, that ferocious push, I don't know, I guess that is just what it costs.

I was shocked that the guys weren't going to rise up with me. There was a cheapness of spirit.

Why are you playing music if you have this opportunity and you are okay with its not being as good as it can be?

I guess it was some Matthew 26:41 shit.

I loved the guys in that band, but when it came down to making the music right or my relationship with them, well, the guys weren't going to win. That band could turn a room upside down. That is the shit. That is absolutely it.

I loved that band. I just loved the music more and had to protect it.

37

Rasputin the Eel

Nobody wanted it.

When *Voice of Chunk* was finally finished, I hired a lawyer to shop it to labels in the United States, but we couldn't get anyone to touch it. "Record sales are very slow right now. The industry is in trouble." Good! For the shit you're putting out, it should be in trouble.

Of course, it is hard to know if the lawyer I was paying was actually doing anything. They often don't. You pay them but have no idea if they have done anything. But it really did seem like nobody wanted it. I sent it out myself to a couple of places and got no response. I thought, *This isn't possible, it's so beautiful. Even an idiot can hear that. How can they not want it?*

We got some distribution deals in Europe and Japan, where the band was much more popular. But in the United States, nobody wanted it.

After recording the *Voice of Chunk* album, that band had broken up. I felt like it was time to push Ribot out of the nest. He was doing all these amazing things onstage but played his parts differently every night. The problem was, Evan's parts on the piano and Ribot's parts on the guitar had to lock into each other. But live, Ribot couldn't hear what Evan was doing because the piano was so quiet onstage. So every night, Evan would have to change what he was doing to hook into Ribot. I didn't like how Evan's genius was forced to be led around by the whims of Ribot's brilliant insanity. To me it seemed the only path for Ribot was to be a leader. That way he could go out there and do what he did and people would have to try to follow him.

So it seemed best to give him a friendly push to start his own thing. We met at a bar and I explained how I was feeling and he talked about where he was at and it seemed like an amicable separation. But I guess it wasn't taken like that.

A few months later Marc had a party, either for his birthday or an album release, and Val and I were conspicuously not invited. I was hurt and thought that it wasn't right, so Val and I were having breakfast outside at Café Orlin on a beautiful day and we decided that we would send a Strip-O-Gram to Marc's party. It was just supposed to be a joke. We didn't intend it as something mean.

Val called some number and among our various options was a stripper dressed as a policewoman. So we decided on that. We would send a policewoman to Marc's party. I wrote a little non sequitur poem for her to recite. I don't remember exactly what it said but was something like:

Who will wrestle the royal commander to his death? Oh I will!

And on Tuesdays, on Tuesdays.

Yes! Yes! It will be and flowers.

Holy divinity of snurks.

He used to be your boss. He used to be your boss.

Well, we thought it would be fun. A little mean, but mostly funny. We felt like it was really shitty of Marc not to invite us, but basically we understood. We just wanted to send a little message.

It really backfired.

The stripper dressed in a police uniform was a big woman and, from the reports that I got later, very aggressive. She was walking around with a nightstick and pushing people around a bit. Everyone at the party actually believed, for the first ten minutes or so, that she was a real policewoman, investigating a noise complaint. She asked who was responsible there. Marc said that he was, and after doing lascivious things with her nightstick, she pulled him toward her. When she started taking off her clothes and reciting the poem, Marc went along with it because he thought that his girlfriend, Pascale, as a surprise, had ordered it for his party. I guess it was really hideous. And the party was in the afternoon, so there were kids there. Oh fuck, that is really bad.

When she got to the part of the poem that went, "He used to be your boss. He used to be your boss," Roy Nathanson shrieked in accusatory horror, "John Lurie did this! John Lurie did this!"

I am sorry, Marc. I really am sorry. It wasn't supposed to go like that.

The *Voice of Chunk* album was scheduled to come out in Europe in the summer of 1989. I had to do something for the cover artwork and put a new band together.

I have often been accused of taking too much control over everything. So I thought that I would try not to get too involved in the artwork. I turned it over to a designer who was a friend of a friend; I won't mention his name. I did a photo shoot with Ari Marcopoulos of my face in profile, which we gave over to the friend of a friend to design the cover around. It was the first time that I'd ever used just my photo, alone, on the front, and I wasn't entirely comfortable with the idea. The band was a band. Period. Even though the band on this recording no longer existed, and probably to use my face was better for marketing reasons, because of the movies and my handsome-like-a-dog face, this wasn't really what the music was about. It was very much a group that brought out the beauty in this music.

When I go to see what this guy has done for the artwork, I really can't believe it. He has taken the photo of my face and blown it up over the entire cover. Just my face with "Lounge Lizards" and "*Voice of Chunk*" written in. This is a record, not a CD, so the size of my face is enormous. About 30 percent bigger than it is in real life.

"What's this? I can't use this!"

"No, it's good. It means that The Lounge Lizards are big now."

My brain spun on its axis.

This guy had been very busy watching and playing golf.

"This makes me look like I'm Donald Trump. The band is going to think I've lost my mind."

"No! It's good."

"The only way I can use that photo is if you write, in big letters: 'HEAD IS NOT ACTUAL SIZE.'"

I have to figure something out quickly because the album is scheduled to come out soon in Germany and then the rest of Europe.

I'm not sure what to do, but while I am getting a shiatsu massage from Ellen, the genius shiatsu person, some ideas float into my mind.

We will take three pictures of Kazu's mouth, and we will need an eel.

Ari is incredibly adept at helping me implement it. We take the pictures of Kazu's mouth outside of my house. These are to go, three times, along the bottom of the cover, and the eel is to underline the photo of my face.

The eel has to be pre–rigor mortis so we can put it in a straight line. Ari and I go to South Street Seaport to see if we can buy an eel that has just recently died. There aren't any. "Maybe tomorrow, probably not."

So we go to the docks where the fishing boats come in. No eels. Someone there suggests we go to Chinatown.

A friend of Ari's and mine was beaten up in Chinatown just days before. He was yelling at his girlfriend and suddenly these Chinese men appeared from everywhere and stomped him. Apparently the Chinese don't take kindly to anyone's being rude or boisterous on their turf.

We go to a fish market that doesn't have any eels. Then a restaurant, nothing. We both have to be somewhere else in an hour but the cover is overdue. We walk past a restaurant and see eels swimming in a tank in the window.

I go inside and ask to speak to the owner. He's a stocky Chinese guy in a classy old suit. I ask him if I can buy an eel. He says no.

I ask him again: a hundred dollars for one live eel.

He puts his arm behind my back and ushers me outside. He won't look at me.

We're out on the street and he starts to go back into the restaurant.

"Wait a minute, I want to buy an eel. How much do you want?"

He shakes his head, still won't acknowledge my existence. He won't look me in the eye. He thinks I'm a white ghost.

"I'll give you two hundred fifty for an eel."

No response. He shakes his head and walks in a circle. I'm getting pissed. I want him to at least look at me. I haven't forgotten about my friend who was beaten up here two weeks ago, but this guy is too rude and I am not having it. He has to at least look at me before I'm going to walk away. Ari looks very nervous as a crowd starts to gather.

I'm really about to lose it, when a little old lady comes up behind me and pulls at my sleeve. I think that she's going to tell me to be careful, but she whispers, "You want to buy eel? Follow me."

So we do. She has a little fish store down an alley. Inside a tank of moldy-looking carp, there are three live eels sticking to the bottom. It's difficult to catch an eel in the net, as the aerated bubbles gush up to the surface and block your vision. You can't really see their dark forms sliding along the bottom. It takes her forever but she finally gets one. I give her a hundred dollars and we race for the car with the eel in a bucket.

Ari and I are both late. We've got to do this quickly. We get to the Lower East Side and get out of the car. I dump the dying eel out onto the sidewalk. It slithers slowly. Ari tries to take its picture but it's wrapping around itself. Then it starts to rain.

I ask if we can do it at my house, and Ari says, "Yeah, we can shoot it on the windowsill."

We race over to my house, park illegally, and run up the stairs. The eel is covered with dirt from the sidewalk and I go into the bathroom to wash it off.

I'm holding the eel in the middle. It is completely dead and lifeless now, just a dead floppy thing, but when a single drop of water hits it, it springs to life!

Unless you've been through this, you cannot possibly have any idea how strong an eel is. It's trying to bite me. Its mouth full of razor teeth goes whizzing by my face. The water has also made the eel so slippery that I can barely keep my grip. But it's not the slipperiness that is so difficult, it's the eel's incredible strength. My arm is flailing around trying to hold it, and there is no way that I am going to let go of this live, slithering creature in my apartment. The slime is indestructible and will never be cleaned away. I will have to move out.

The eel snaps at my face as my back smashes against the corner of the bathroom door.

I am holding on for dear life.

Ari hears the crashing sounds coming from my bathroom and comes to the door just as I am grabbing the eel around the neck with both hands. I can see the whites all the way around Ari's irises as I strangle the eel to death. It takes a long time and I go on longer than necessary to make sure the thing is dead.

Afterward I feel awful.

"You think it's bad to strangle an eel?"

"Not if we don't tell anyone," Ari says.

We put the eel on the windowsill and snap five or six photos. It looks good. Ari splits and I go into the bathroom to wash my hands, but the slime won't come off and my bathroom is covered with eel gunk that seems to only get more potent when you apply water.

I can't get the stuff off my hands and I grab a towel and run out of the house, carrying the towel. When I get home that night the eel is gone. It's not on the windowsill where we left it.

Later, at about ten that night, when I walk to Seventh Avenue, I see it in the gutter, fifty yards from my house.

Rasputin the Eel was still alive on the windowsill. After falling four flights and climbing up six steps back to street level, it then slithered almost all the way to Seventh Avenue in the gutter before finally succumbing to its death.

38

It Never Hovered Above the Ground

The vibe with the shreds of the band that remained was awful.

Dougie had left. Ribot was gone. Erik and I had had so many arguments about the writing credit that I just couldn't take it anymore.

So it was Curt and Roy on trombone and saxophones, E. J. Rodriguez on percussion, and Evan on piano. We had to find people to play bass, drums, and guitar for the summer tours that would support the release of *Voice of Chunk* in Europe. I started asking around, getting lists of names.

We had auditions. Painful auditions.

There was a feeling of sadness and some amount of an anger underneath, because at one point, everybody in the old band had deeply loved each other and the new band didn't fit together so well.

Maybe I am not Gregg Popovich because his players, as tough as he was on them, loved him when they left or seemed to. And this was sadly not that.

* * *

This band is: Roy Nathanson on saxophones. Roy is Jewish, white, and gay. At least he was gay at the time but turned out not to be. Curtis Fowlkes on trombone. Curtis is a shy gentleman, black, and a beautiful musician. Of course, the kind and lovely Evan Lurie, my brother, who is also gay, on piano. Brandon Ross on guitar. Brandon is a thin black guy with a beautiful face. He has sort of an elegance about him, except his dreads smelled horrible. He also seems like he would really have preferred to be on the debate team than a guitar player. Al MacDowell on bass. Al is a kind of person I had never met before. He never, ever loses his confidence. He is never startled. I think this comes from martial arts training. He has a powerful body and the face of a black cherub. Al is an extremely talented wall of granite, with all the sensitivity of a wall of granite. E. J. Rodriguez, who is straight and Puerto Rican, is on percussion, and Calvin Weston, who screams like his body is on fire while he plays. Calvin could turn a room upside down.

Al and Brandon both were clearly well educated and came from the "good" side of the tracks. Calvin came from somewhere else entirely, where things were hard, very real, and the Devil lived right down the block.

Al MacDowell could control his instrument like no one I'd ever seen. We had this incredibly fast tune called "Sharks Can't Sleep." This song was really as fast a thing as I could play on the saxophone, sixteenth notes at a raging tempo. Incredibly, Al could play the melody on the bass, no mistakes, no problem. The bass part used to be a fast walk, which is what it should have been. But Al, because of his massively macho skills on the bass, insisted on playing the lead line in unison with me. But it didn't make musical sense. He was doing it for the same reason that a dog licks his balls. I told Al to play the line as it was and Brandon acted outraged: "You have Al MacDowell playing a walk. You are wasting his talents!" It was just stupid, and Brandon was just arguing to argue. But really, the clear, unsaid implication behind this was that I was white and Al was black, and thus I did not have the right to tell Al what to play. Brandon never had a problem when I explained to the white guys how I wanted something played. Never even noticed.

The first gig we did with that band was a warm-up at the 9:30 Club in Washington, D.C. Took the band out of New York to a gig that didn't matter that much. We had been the first band to play the 9:30 Club, twelve years earlier, when it opened.

The 9:30 Club is a small rock venue, holds maybe four hundred standing people. I had remembered it being nice back when we had first played there. Now that smell of stale beer and leftover cigarettes that hit you when you came in was a sign. That stale beer smell is pretty much a guarantee that the sound system in that club will suck and that the local sound guy is the owner of a fried and ugly brain, has bad hair and bad skin, and will hate you if you are pretentious enough to want the sound to actually be good.

It is a nice day, and I usually don't have to get to the sound check until a couple hours after load-in. Everything has to be set up, power lines have to be run. In the really good places, everything is done when you arrive as per the specs of the contract, but in a place like this, it is a war for our own soundman to get anything set up in time for us to have any sound check at all. Frankly, it was playing a number of these kinds of venues that led me away from touring in the United States. It just seemed disrespectful to the music. Unless we could get booked at actual concert halls, we wouldn't do it. And in the United States that just never happened. We were never seen as anything other than a punk band.

I step outside. It's beautiful out. But this neighborhood has gone to hell. Crack has moved in like a raging weed and completely taken over. The people walking around look nuts and dangerous. They look like they are either covered in bugs or have been transformed, Gregor-like, by cocaine, into actual giant bugs.

I don't think that it's safe to go any farther than the doorway of the club. Calvin comes out and stands next to me.

I said, "Sure is buggy out here."

Calvin just went, "Woooo," and went back inside. Which was interesting because Calvin's neighborhood in Philadelphia was intense, just with far fewer giant bugs.

Calvin has a nice brownstone on a beautiful tree-lined street. There are sweet older women sitting out on their porches. But one of the times I visited him, it turned out that the kid who lived three doors down from him had been shot to death by the kid ten doors down.

These kids were both about fourteen. But how the older women addressed it was that it was a shame but by no means not a regular occurrence.

We had played the 9:30 Club another time about five years earlier and the dressing room had gotten robbed. But there was something so caring and elegant in how it was done.

Every item of clothing that had been gone through was folded and put back. Forget folded; whoever had robbed us had folded the clothes in the dressing room more neatly than we had left them. All personal items were placed back, carefully, where they had been found. Only the cash was taken, not even the credit cards.

I can't imagine this. You have to think about what it is like to rob a dressing room in a crowded club. You have to be in a mad scramble to find money and get out. Your nerves must be jangling at you. But this guy had taken the time to leave the room neater than he had found it and to do no actual harm to the people he was robbing, other than taking a few dollars. I loved this guy.

Kind of an odd thing to have more affection for someone who has robbed you than for the people who haven't.

It reminds me of another thing that had happened on Third Street years before, when it was still the worst neighborhood in the world.

I saw it coming. Two Hispanic guys approached me, and I could tell immediately by how they looked at me so intensely and then looked off, as though trying to be nonchalant, that they were coming.

One went out into the street between the parked cars and the other kept coming down the sidewalk in my direction. It was done in a rhythm that felt like they had done it a hundred times before. Then I was even more sure it was coming. The one in the street, when he got to the sidewalk, circled back behind me. The one in front of me pulled out a knife the size of a small machete, as did the one behind me.

I was trapped. And honestly, though I saw it coming almost a full forty-five seconds before it happened, I am not sure what I could have done to avoid it.

I was completely calm.

They went through my pockets and found $10. The one who came from behind started motioning for me to take off my shoes, but the one who had come from the front was clearly the leader of the two. He looked into my eyes. And bizarrely, we had a moment. We somehow connected. Soul to soul.

He said something in Spanish to the other one, who stopped yelling at me and reluctantly gave me back my $10. I will never forget that front guy's eyes. Brown with a little speck of green. Brown with a little speck of green.

After the 9:30 gig, I had to fly to Chicago, and the rest of the band drove back to NYC, at night, after the gig. When I got back to New York, Evan called me and said the vibe was not good in the band.

I couldn't get him to be more specific. But Evan never complains about this stuff, so I knew it had to be something. I guess the ride back was horrific for some reason.

After the warm-up gig, we went on the first leg of the European tour.

Musically and spiritually, it was a bad period. The first gig in Paris, we blew the fucking roof off the place. Al and Calvin could play with such ferocious energy and power that it created an unconquerable roar.

But there was no nuance, no subtlety. There was nothing precious about it. There was no love in it. It just plowed through and was not about the reason that I wanted to make music.

I said somewhere that the band was macho, but macho like your baby's first steps. That was what I wanted.

That band did have a lot of power, though.

Veronica Webb came up to me after the show in New York and said, "It's like having your brains fucked out, over and over again," like that is somehow a good thing.

But then off somewhere was Brandon, playing with so many effects that it sounded like a fluffy *whoosh*. It was nice on its own, or in a quiet setting, but in this crashing onslaught we were making, it just sounded like someone was playing a hundred yards away, the day before. Nothing he played cut through the roar that we created, so the guitar melodies were lost. And the guitar melodies were written with the idea that it was the one instrument that was guaranteed to be heard on top. The one thing that would cut through.

I tried to get him to change his sound or anything he was playing was just going to disappear and be added to a sort of lost, mushy sound. But Brandon said that his sound was his domain and that I had no business asking him to change it.

Fair enough, but in the places where the written guitar parts were intrinsic to the essence of what I had written, the guitar couldn't be this little elf waving from a faraway hilltop.

There was something beautiful about Brandon. But it was really weird, because when I would try to get Al and Calvin to lighten up— partly to get them to take it down a peg to make some room for Brandon— then Brandon would be in my face about how I shouldn't be telling the great Al MacDowell how to play.

I could sense that there was an underlying feeling in the remaining musicians from the old band that this mess was all my fault. There was a lot of sadness and anger because of the firing of Marc, and Erik and Dougie's being gone.

I suppose as a leader, it was really my fault. Maybe there was a better way to deal with Marc and Erik. Marc was an unbelievable musician, and Erik was someone who I loved and who was all-around artistically brilliant. Maybe there was a way I could have kept that band together. *Downbeat* had said, "A band of characters playing music with character." And it was true.

I so wanted the music to work in a soulful way, but all the attention was going to the movies or how I looked or who I was sleeping with.

Maybe I had become an egomaniac. Privilege is hard to see when it is you being handed everything.

But fame is a very hard thing. It is almost worse than drugs. It gives one a false sense of buoyancy and you don't want to let it go. You want more of it. And everyone you encounter assumes that it is better for you to become more famous. Not just your agent or manager or whoever, but everyone.

It is moving counterclockwise to your soul.

If you know anyone who has suddenly gotten famous, have a little patience with them. Maybe treat them like they have just had a serious operation and will need some time to recuperate before becoming themselves again.

The tour was broken into two parts. A month in Europe, back to New York for a week, and then back out for another month.

Calvin and Al would stake out the back of the bus by themselves and smoke tons of pot. The smell would usually pull E.J. to the back for a hit, but he wouldn't hang with them. E.J. felt that Calvin was overplaying and not leaving any room for him on percussion, which was largely true. Curtis and Roy would huddle, whispering together, and Evan and Brandon did the same separately, off by themselves. The band was horribly ununited. From the back of the bus, you could hear loud, sophomoric snickering, followed by hyena laughs. I could tell from Evan's face that he felt it was directed not so much at him, but at gay men in general. You could hear bits of phrases like, "And then I ate all the way up to her kidneys," or over and over, "Hey, bitch, what's for dinner? I'd like to have a steak, but I'd rather slide it in ya." And then roars of ugly laughter.

Evan, repeatedly, was letting me know that there was a problem. I could see it was causing him pain. But he wouldn't be specific about what was happening. I have no idea what kind of shit went on when I wasn't around.

And there was no way to really deal with it.

When I got back, I called Ornette Coleman about Al and Calvin because he had worked with them. I just needed advice on how to deal with a band that had somehow gone off the rails.

Ornette was an angel. Literally an angel. I asked him about Calvin and Al: How did he get them to play what he wanted and were they out of control on the road?

"Are they smoking a lot of that stuff?"

"Yeah, all the time."

I didn't ever have a problem with musicians' smoking weed, as long as they didn't bring anything across borders or forget their instrument in the hotel room. But Ornette had a long theory about why marijuana was bad for the music.

I told him about their being out of control, how hard it was to lead a rehearsal, and that the general vibe was really insidious.

Ornette said, in that soft, lispy voice, "I don't know, man, they even make fun of me!"

And I could see it, too, Ornette up there like a mad scientist schoolteacher, with the odd way he talked, and Calvin and Al at the back of the class giggling and setting some girl's hair on fire.

I talked to Ornette for a long time about music and knowing exactly how it is supposed to sound and then trying to get the musicians to do it. And that thing of where the musician might know exactly how it was supposed to be played and that they were capable of doing it, and even if that musician, too, knew that to play it that way would be better for the music, they would *still* not want to do it because they didn't want to be told what to do.

And the more exceptional the musician, the more difficult it was to get them to do what was needed.

And I was thinking, *Shit, this happens to Ornette? When do you arrive? When do you not have problems like this?* It reminded me of Scorsese complaining about how hard it was to get the money to do *Last Temptation* and how he wished he could have done it this way or that way. And I was thinking, *What? Martin fucking Scorsese can't get the money he needs to do it properly? How is that possible?*

Ornette had been supportive of me right from the very beginning. He had come to see the band play our fourth gig back in 1979, when we were really finding our way. His only comment was that we "needed to play in different unisons."

But that he had enough respect for me now to take the time to talk—that was special to me. I had a ton of admiration for Ornette, and it was a gift to be able to pick up the phone and talk to him about music and running a band.

Later, I had a similar relationship with Elmore Leonard. When I was doing the music for *Get Shorty*, which Elmore had written the book for, my office got a call that Elmore Leonard wanted to talk to me.

So I called him and he just wanted to know the general direction of the music. But then after that, we talked on the phone regularly. Often about nothing. And it was so wild, how he was a creature from a whole different time. You called Elmore Leonard on the phone and he would just answer. There was no assistant screening the call. I don't think he even had an answering machine. Only one time did I call and a woman, I guess his wife, answered, and she said Dutch was at the baseball game.

I would call Elmore and it felt like he was always just sitting on the porch watching the sun go down. There was a relaxed warmth about him. And this book, if it is any good, owes something to Elmore for the two or three things that he suggested to me.

When I think of Ornette and Elmore, it makes me sad. It feels like they were almost too decent to live in a time like we have now. They didn't have the armor for it.

But why the fuck do you need armor?

When we got back to Europe, after the break, Christina, the sweet tour manager, was standing outside the hotel with everybody after we had checked in. She looked at Brandon and said, "Your skin looks lighter than before." I noticed Calvin was looking at me out of the corner of his eye to see if I caught it. Then we both grinned. Later that night, Calvin poured a glass of red wine on a girl's head at a restaurant, because Al had told him to do it.

Calvin was devilment incarnate. And it was not usually fun or remotely acceptable. It wasn't really Calvin so much, as it was Al pushing Calvin to do these things, and then Calvin did them. Oddly enough, over not so much time, as Calvin changed, he and I became deeply connected. I grew to love Calvin.

Toward the end of the second leg of that tour, I was getting further and further away from the band. Often I was flying to the next gig, while the band drove. I was doing it partially to get there earlier to do the mountain of scheduled interviews, but partly it was because I felt shitty all the time and needed to get whatever rest I could. And I didn't admit it to myself, but I think I wanted to get far away from the toxic band dynamic.

When the Lizards were on tour it was difficult to get clothes cleaned. We were rarely in one place for more than a day and the hotel would never be able to do dry cleaning in time. Getting your laundry back can be like gold. Clean socks! Hurray! But dry cleaning usually takes more than a day.

There is something very creepy about getting up in front of two thousand people wearing dirty socks. Or even if the suit I was wearing looked okay from the audience, somehow it felt phony as hell to get onstage wearing a smelly suit. It just seemed wrong, like I was lying to them.

More than once when I'd completely run out of clothes on a tour, I tried washing socks and underwear in the sink, but the stuff would never dry in time. So I'd be driving in a cab to the airport holding my boxers out the window trying to dry them before putting them in my suitcase.

I was nervous when I looked at the schedule for the second leg of this tour and saw the only place we could get cleaning done was in Ljubljana. I had just bought these three very elegant Armani suits for a lot of money. They were perfect. I have trouble finding clothes I like and these just hung perfectly. It was a lot of money to spend on clothes, but I'd decided, fuck it, they were going to be my Lounge Lizards uniforms for years to come.

I am not sure how the fashion thing happened. It was something I never gave much thought, something, in a lot of ways, I am opposed to because of the financial hierarchy.

When the band first started I would buy $5 suits at the used clothing stores in the East Village. I had one pair of shoes that were held together with gaffer tape. Which I liked just fine. But now it was expected that I was going to be some kind of fashion plate.

In 2000, British *Vogue* voted me one of the best dressed men of the last century. They would be pissed as hell if they saw what I have been wearing every day for the last ten years or so: sneakers; cargo pants or basketball shorts; T-shirts; and a Carhartt sweatshirt in colder weather. Every day. Basically, I dress exactly as I did when I was nine years old.

But I really wanted to protect my three new suits. They were something to me like no clothes had ever been before.

I didn't want them ruined, which had happened more than once before on tour, and I was particularly nervous about this kind of thing in Eastern Europe, so I had Val fax the promoters in advance, saying that it was important that I get my dry cleaning done in a decent place.

I fly to Ljubljana by myself. I'm trying to get through customs when a man with a machine gun comes up to me and starts screaming at me in Serbo-Croatian. I don't know what he's saying but interpret his gestures with the end of his gun barrel to mean that he wants me to stand in a certain spot, and I do. He goes off, leaving me there.

Moments later another guy with a machine gun comes and starts to scream and moves me to another spot.

I'm standing there waiting to understand how I am supposed to get out, when the first guy returns, his eyes bulging with surprise and rage to see that I have moved from the place where he left me. He screams and I try to point out the other guard, who has now disappeared, and I go back to the first spot.

When I finally clear customs, there are two people waiting for me: a very tall, very thin man with a black beard and a very pained and tortured face, and a plump woman who I believe is his wife. Probably to be a jazz promoter in Yugoslavia is not the easiest thing.

After nodding at me in recognition, the first words out of his mouth are, "Where are the suits?"

Maybe Val has gone a little overboard in expressing the importance of the suits, but this should ensure that they get cleaned without incident.

I explain that first I have to unpack. I don't know if they think they're in a special carrying case or what.

They drive me to the hotel in their tiny little car, my knees up around my ears, and follow me to my room. Which is weird. The whole hotel is weird.

There are five clothes dryers against the wall in the lobby.

My room, which is supposed to be a suite, is actually four adjoining office rooms with a bed and makeshift bathroom. There is industrial carpeting, and one room is filled with desks and office chairs stacked on top of one another. It is an office space that was quickly transformed into what is supposed to be a suite.

I give them my suits. I'm a little embarrassed by all the concern, but at least I am sure that with this much attention, they will be safe.

The next day Evan goes for a walk. He usually goes for walks when we arrive somewhere new or different. I like that about him but I never do it myself. Evan, all his life, has been curious about things. That is a great quality, especially when one gets older. Stay curious.

Lack of curiosity kills the human.

When he comes back, he notices that whatever is spinning around in the dryers in the lobby looks an awful lot like my suits. He looks away quickly and shakes his head. *Nope, that's not what's happening. Can't be.*

When I run into him he says, "I hate to tell you this, but I think that I just saw your new suits in the dryer in the lobby."

There is a pause as this information starts to settle in my brain.

Then, fearing how I am going to react and not knowing what else to say, Evan says, "Why are there dryers in the lobby?"

I don't find any humor in this at all, and Evan, being my younger brother, is rightfully worried that this is going to have bad consequences for him, because if my suits are ruined, my mood will go pretty dark.

I get my suits back in a folded stack. I see that the fabric is all bunched up. I unfold the top jacket in terror. Just from looking at them I can see they are now best suited for a boy just under the age of ten. There is no sane reason to try it on, but that is what one does in this situation. I have to arch my back in a sort of yoga pose to get it onto my shoulders. The sleeves come to my elbows.

Apparently what has happened is that the promoter has taken the suits and given them to the hotel, saying they must be very careful with them. The hotel has given them to the cleaning woman, who has thrown them in the washing machine in the basement and then dried them in the lobby. I have seen this cleaning woman and her angry face around the hotel. I imagine when she threw my three thousand dollar suits into a washing machine, it was the first time she had smiled in years.

The hotel is government owned, and four Yugoslavian officials come to the hotel to inspect the suits. This is now an international incident. They hold the suits in their hands and stare. They ask if I can put one on. I am in my underwear trying to get the suit on and they finally realize that with all but one of them, this is impossible.

They confer as government officials do.

It is decided that I will be driven to Italy, where I can purchase three suits. I have a concert that night, so I must leave immediately. They send a driver who takes me to Trieste. The driver is very smart and well educated. He quotes Pablo Neruda to me on the drive. He is an engineer but lost his job because some government enemy pushed him out. I don't fully understand the story. It is scary sometimes when you go to a place like this and you meet some really solid, bright person and their job is driving the American saxophone player to and from Italy to buy a fancy suit. One tends to remember that even though they have just shrunk all your clothes, you have been pretty much protected throughout this life.

The Italian men in Trieste must all be quite small, because nothing is close to fitting, and I come back empty-handed.

When I return, it is decided that the government will pay for my suits, but there is a lot of paperwork and they will have to give me a voucher and then mail me the money in the States.

The check didn't come, and soon after that, the war broke out. I didn't think some piddling thing like a war should cancel their debt, but I no longer knew who to write to.

We play in Ljubljana. I wear the one suit that I can still get on, my pant legs three inches above the tops of my shoes. No one seems to notice.

After that I have to drive to Vienna to do a press conference that is insisted on by Thomas Stöwsand, who is promoting the tour. Stöwsand at this time is pretty much the biggest independent jazz promoter in Europe. He always gets the highest-paying gigs. He is famous for sending bands willy-nilly across the continent: Berlin on Tuesday, Prague on Wednesday, London on Thursday. He goes for the highest price with no thought about the fact that these are actually human beings, and he is having them travel for sixteen hours by bus or train between all the gigs. The thing that is amazing about the people who promote tours for a living is that if they were shipping tomatoes or fish, they would have to be more careful about their travel arrangements, because the product would spoil.

I particularly don't like Stöwsand because years before, we traveled to Vienna from God knows where and then did a show, and were scheduled to take the train that night to arrive at the North Sea Jazz Festival the following afternoon and play. I saw Stöwsand after the show, and he came up to me and said, in a way that was begging for sympathy, that he was exhausted because he'd arrived from New York that morning.

Like, *Poor me. I am jet-lagged.* This guy was having musicians hop in a van after a concert, travel for thirteen hours across Europe, and then arrive somewhere, do sound check, play a great concert, and then do that again day after day, and he was going to complain about being jet-lagged from flying across the Atlantic?

So I don't like Stöwsand much in the first place. My suits are shrunk. The band has no love in it and I don't want to go to Vienna to do a press conference. And I don't feel well. I just feel like shit all the time.

I like press conferences better than doing ten interviews in a city. Obviously, it is faster, but it also seems like the other press there are your witnesses in a way. So when they write something you didn't say, at least the rest of the press in that town knows that you didn't say it, and maybe they will back you up. Also, if someone asks a really stupid question, you can make fun of the question, which you can't do one on one.

But this press conference is not a press conference. I expected to be at a podium or a desk, maybe on a stage. But this is a lunch, where everyone is just milling around. There are no questions. I am just being observed by the Austrian press as I am eating. It feels hideously uncomfortable. I am a panda that will hopefully mate.

I am depressed. The band is meeting me in Graz, where we play tomorrow, while I'm staying in Vienna that night in a fancy hotel. I feel ravaged by the "press conference." Felt like going to a dinner party with people you don't know and don't like, but they all know you. And you are being observed like you are some kind of beatnik experiment. The band is not soulful, there is no solace in the music right now. So it really isn't worth putting up with all this. I think, very seriously, about taking the tour money in my pocket, twenty thousand in U.S. cash, and walking out of the hotel without my stuff. I could go to the airport and catch a flight to Africa. And be gone.

But I can't do that to Evan. Still, I have the money in my pocket and I am pacing around the hotel room thinking, *Go, just fucking go, do yourself a favor, it's your life, go to Africa,* when the phone rings.

It's Evan. There is stress in his voice.

"There's a problem here. I think you have to come to Graz immediately. Things aren't good with the band."

There is a desperation in his voice, and Evan really never asks me for anything.

"What happened?"

I imagine that the trip from Yugoslavia to Graz was probably hideous, with Al putting Calvin up to all kinds of antics. There was just that ugly vibe. I had never heard Evan sound so shaken, and I wonder what happened that he isn't telling me about between him and Al.

I am sure that was most of it, just this uncomfortable vibe. But there has been an incident.

What happened is this: Calvin just had his first baby, the first of many. He called home to see how the baby was and his brother, who was his nemesis, answered the phone.

Calvin asked how the baby was doing and his brother said something mean and hung up the phone. So Calvin dialed his mother's number. His brother must have dashed out of the house and run down the street to his mother's, because he answered the phone there as well and hung up in Calvin's ear.

Well, Calvin went nuts. Really nuts. This explosive rage that he had made his playing something to behold with awe, but in daily life it was insurgent and dangerous. He destroyed his room. Everything in it. The police came and arrested him. If he paid for the damage, they would let him out of jail. Evan and Al, an unlikely duo, went to Calvin's destroyed room to look for his tour money. Calvin had told Al not to pay, that he would stay in jail. Evan had a pretty good idea that Al knew where Calvin had hidden his money but Al was making like he had no idea. I guess Evan got really mad and demanded that Al tell him where the money was and Al suddenly went, "Ooh, look, I found it." I would have liked to see Evan yelling at Al so hard that he confessed. They paid the hotel with Calvin's tour money and he was let out of jail.

I had fucked up. I had always prided myself on my intuition in putting a band together. Who would go with who. What number of alpha males versus whatever different kinds of energies and sounds might be fitting into the band. I was so good at this, and I had blown it.

For example, I had met these twins in Elba one summer. They were playing in a bar every night and I sat in with them sometimes. These twins had something really nice in their playing. They had great rhythm and they had this quiet sweetness about them.

I had an epiphany, and when I got back to New York, I told Kazu, who was desperate to get her music thing off the ground but couldn't find musicians to play with, that there were these twins, and that if it were ever possible, she should start a band with them. Soon after, the twins moved to New York and they started Blonde Redhead.

But I have that thing. I have it deeply. I can figure out who is best to play with who and how to find their deeper talents. But now the vibe was terrible and I knew that Evan was really unhappy. This was horrible for me; I didn't know exactly what had happened, and I still sensed that it had something to do with his being gay and Al's somehow fucking with him when I wasn't around, but I didn't know what to do.

Because of Calvin and Al's energy, that band was never bad. There was never a bad gig, but there was never a great one either. I never once got that thing. I never once got chills when the music just seemed to hover beautifully above the ground.

39

Giant Diving Bugs Bombing Our Faces

After the tour I went and stayed with Roberto Benigni and Nicoletta for a couple of weeks in Rome.

I bought them the ugliest ashtray that I have ever seen. It had an ugly stand to go with it.

It was magnificent in its ugliness.

I insisted that they never throw it away. That it was important to me.

There was a lot of pained laughter, but the next two times I went to see them, my ashtray was still there, in a place of honor on the veranda. I bet they talked about my ugly ashtray every time they had guests.

Both Roberto and Nicoletta can be hard to read, like if they want to hide something they can do that like world class poker players. I asked them, "Do you hide my ashtray in the basement and drag it out when I come to visit?"

They both said no in a way that I believed, but I am not certain.

When Roberto was not working, he slept for twenty hours straight. Never saw anything like it.

Then he would drink three very strong espressos and dash out to play poker until ten or so the next morning. Come back as white as a ghost. He would never tell me if he'd won or not, but he sure as fuck did not have the look of somebody who had won.

I wanted, badly, to go and play. But he absolutely could not be convinced to take me. It was out of the question. I almost had the feeling that this was how he got off, like a masochistic poker loser.

I hope not, but that did seem to be what it was.

Roberto is really something. I wish the United States had gotten the chance to see who he actually is. There is a great wisdom and beauty. But when *Life Is Beautiful* was getting all the attention and he was on TV all the time, he really didn't speak English. It wasn't an act.

I have been on TV shows in places where I don't speak the language. It is very difficult. You have no idea what is going on.

So he did that irritating clown act on all the TV shows, and people got fed up with him very quickly, and I don't blame them. It is just a shame it went like that. He has an important mind.

I loved the housekeeper, Pina. She did my laundry and cooked for me. She was like a mom.

One morning, while Roberto and Nicoletta were out of town, I spent a wild night with a sex beast named Barbara. We drank and snorted coke all night. She lived somewhere on the outskirts of Rome.

She fell asleep and I could not, so the next morning, I left. But had no idea where I was. I walked and walked on a road made of dust until I finally found civilization and a taxi.

I arrived at the house completely disheveled. I was ashamed for Pina to see me like this.

She smiled, said something in Italian about the life of a young man, and made me breakfast without my asking.

Roberto and Nicoletta thought I had come to visit them, but I really had come to visit Pina.

After that I went to Grottaglie, a small town near Bari on the coast of Italy, to see Antonio, the sweet set designer from *The Little Devil*. Antonio had converted an old church into his home and it was beautiful, always filled with flowers. The church was made of stone and cool inside on sweltering days. And flowers. There were always flowers.

I was supposed to meet Julie Caiozzi in Marseille after the tour, but I made the mistake of canceling on her.

Julie was pissed. There were a lot of women that perhaps I should have married in this life. Julie Caiozzi is at the very top of the list. She was sexy as hell and understood the weirdness of life.

I called her years later. She had the same number. I think she had had a kid—not sure how I knew that—but I just picked up the phone to call her. It was late at night in New York. I was in the middle of negotiating a film score deal, can't remember which one, but I was on Church Street, so I guess it was *Get Shorty*.

I mentioned the problems I was having and she just started to laugh. At me. And there was so much wisdom in her laugh. Like, *John, they are going to pay you a quarter of a million dollars to write music? You have a roof over your head? You have food? You don't have a child who is sick? What are you complaining about?*

She didn't actually say any of that. She didn't have to. It was in the kindness and the wisdom in her laugh.

I slept very well at Antonio's. The only place I have ever slept better was in a bedroom at Flea's old place that he called "The Secret Room." The room was like a little bunker of a womb and I slept perfectly there.

I woke up one morning at Antonio's with the idea firmly implanted in my mind of making a western, starring Roberto. I know I mentioned it earlier, but this is when it happened. I saw the whole thing—the outfits, the horses. No story, but everything else, the two of them walking horses across a landscape that looked like Africa.

This came to me so strongly that I had to do it. There are those moments in music or in painting, where a thing floats in and is somehow complete. And it is very much not really yours. It is a gift. And this was like that.

The idea of a surreal western bumped around in my head for a while. Something, also from the dream, demanded that the title had to be *You Stink Mister*. I don't know why, and had to figure out a way to work that in.

I spent a lot of summers in Italy after tours. Playing there was usually a disaster. Something, technically, was always horribly wrong. But I love Italy so much, to just be there.

We were playing in an outdoor place in Florence, in the middle of the summer. When we arrived for sound check, the row of floodlights was raised to only six and a half feet above the ground. They were hovering about two feet out in front of my and Curtis's heads when we stepped up to the mic to play.

The band does the sound check and I ask to have the lights raised so I can see what it's going to look like. There isn't usually time to check the lights, because sound check is always late and chaotic, and the most important thing is to get the sound right. But it is always best to check the lights with the local lighting technician to make sure he is not partial to mauve or fuchsia or strobe effects.

I'm told that the lights can't be moved.

"Well, they are going to have to move. They can't stay like that."

"Yes! Yes! Of course, the lights go up later!"

When we arrive to do the show, the lights are still in the same place. The arm that raises them is broken and has apparently been broken all summer.

So when we go out to play, there are spotlights inches from our faces. Feels like we are getting burned. But the worst thing is that, because it is outdoors on a hot summer night, some kind of giant diving bugs are bombing at our faces throughout the entire show.

The Italians could always go way out of their way to make a fool of you and then laugh, like, *John! You are taking yourself much too seriously!* After two-inch bugs have been denting your forehead for the last three hours.

But I liked vacationing there after the tours. It was in Grosseto that I discovered there was a *buttero,* an Italian cowboy, who was famous for beating Buffalo Bill in a cowboy contest. This was perfect for my western movie.

I spent some time there with the writer Sandro Veronesi. I don't know Sandro's writing but he was very smart and curious. He was also ridiculously handsome.

One night we were invited to this home that was basically a castle. A stone porch hung hundreds of yards over the sea below. It was the home of a famous producer and his aging movie star wife. The producer had a somewhat dubious reputation and was very involved in the porn world.

They bring out the most incredible cocaine. I haven't taken any in a while.

As we're about to leave, some harsh words are exchanged and then it turns into an ugly shouting match between Sandro and the producer.

The Italian is going too fast for me to understand. I'd missed the beginning and now I have no idea what is going on. But veins are bursting out of both of their necks.

We get in the car to drive off and I ask Sandro what the fuck that was about. He tells me that we were both supposed to have sex with the producer's wife so he could watch. That he had shoveled out all this cocaine and thousand dollar bottles of wine and expected something in return. But Sandro could be a rascal and I have no idea whether or not he just made that up on the spot.

The next morning, we get into Sandro's father's sailboat and he sails me over to Elba. I am so fucking hungover. I imagine I smell like a wet dog.

We arrive at the beach in Elba and there is Titti Santini, my music promoter, standing on the beach.

They really almost have to carry me up this very steep hill, and Titti plunks me down in this little apartment he has rented for me.

I went for a week to Elba, and then I had to get to Paris to do this thing for Comme des Garçons. I had agreed to be a runway model. This was in September of 1989. I don't know why I said yes to this.

I liked Comme des Garçons clothes at the time, and I think Rei Kawakubo is a real artist, but I am opposed to fashion.

When I think about important fashion statements, I think about when Dougie was playing drums with Iggy Pop, and the guitar player came into the dressing room with sandwiches taped all over his clothes and asked, "What do you think?"

They paid really well and put you in a nice hotel, and Don Cherry and John Malkovich were doing it, so I said, "What the fuck, why not?"

The insidious thing to me with fashion is that only really rich people can afford the stuff. And that is the real idea behind it. It has nothing to do with how the stuff looks, but it is a demarcation line between the rich and the poor. "I can afford this and thus I am better than you." It doesn't matter that the shirt looks like shit and has a toucan attached to the shoulder.

There is a similar thing with the art world. "This piece of shit plastic dog has no inherent value, it is not beautiful or moving or even particularly well crafted. Its value is that it costs one hundred million dollars and I can afford it. And you cannot."

Fashion makes everybody insecure, or at least 98 percent of people.

First, you are too poor to afford it. But more than that, it provokes inse-curity because you feel you are too fat or too skinny or too short or your ass is too big, and you are clearly, overall, not good enough.

You go into these stores and the salespeople look down their noses at you. It makes everyone nervous. I don't know why they do it, because I would imagine that customers who are actually comfortable buy more clothing. It is about the salespeople themselves' having to let you know that, for some unexplained reason, they are better than you.

I remember going into Barneys once and the sales guy looking me up and down in disgust.

And I started to feel insecure and uncomfortable. I didn't buy any-thing, and on the way out, there was a picture of me in the elevator, wear-ing some suit. Like, *Look at this elegant man, you too could look like him.*

Yet the sales guy made me so uncomfortable that I left. So if I am literally the model of what an elegant man looks like, how the fuck does Joe from next door or Sally from down the street deal with this shit? Because I, at least, have some ammunition to defend myself.

"Come here, you pretentious salesfart. Look! That is me in the photo! I can't be that disgusting."

But I am in Paris and I am a fashion model.

The hotel they put me in is gorgeous. There is a note in the bath-room about calling the chambermaid when you are ready to have her draw your bath. People live like this?

It is strange to walk out from behind a curtain onto a runway, where there are hundreds of Parisians sitting there examining your clothes with great discernment.

I can't stop laughing.

I try not to laugh because everyone else is taking it all so seriously, like they are getting ready to meet the Pope.

I also don't want to offend Rei Kawakubo, because I really do respect her. She is an artist. But she gets a kick out of my irreverence for the whole thing. I reach into a cooler full of beers and get my sleeve all wet, right before I am supposed to model this outfit.

She covers her mouth in that polite Japanese way so as not to let people see she was laughing.

Each time that you go out on the runway, there is a smattering of applause for the clothes you are wearing.

I bet Julian Sands and John Malkovich $500 that my clothes on the next trip out would get more applause. They agree. We shake on it.

They both go out to their normal smattering. I go out, take two steps, and stop. Then I thump really hard on my chest, point to the clothes, and then throw my hands out, as though I have just been enormously triumphant in something. The crowd goes nuts. Mad applause.

I get back behind the curtain and Sands and Malkovich both agree that I have won. They are a little shocked. They hadn't seen what I had done because they were rushing to change into outfit seven.

But that night, when they see the tape of the show, they refuse to pay because they say that what I had done wasn't right. I really hate people who don't pay their gambling debts. Because I won that bet and they knew I had done it quite fairly. They too had been free to thump their chests to advertise their outfits.

I got in a little trouble because I said in an interview that France was changing its slogan from "*Liberté, égalité, fraternité*" to "We wore these clothes and then we died." Then I left Paris.

After Paris, I had to fly out to L.A. to do a little thing in *Wild at Heart*. I had met David Lynch years before when he was casting *Blue Velvet*. He was considering me for the part that Dean Stockwell ended up doing, lip-synching "In Dreams."

Thank God I didn't get the part. Usually when I see an actor doing a thing that I have read or considered doing, I think, *Ahh, he fucked it up, I would have killed it.* But Dean Stockwell was so unbelievably great in that part, it would have been a true shame if the part had gone to me instead.

Earlier that year, I had been up in Maine with Willem Dafoe and Liz LeCompte. Willem had a copy of the script that Lynch was doing next, *Wild at Heart*. I read it and was floored by it. The script was filled with pathos and beauty. Unfortunately this pathos and beauty are missing from the film.

David Lynch is a very sweet, smart, and talented guy. A genuine human being. I preferred him immensely to other directors I had worked with.

But Lynch had recently, repeatedly, been declared a genius. The result of this was that any idea that popped into his head was then stuffed into the movie with not the slightest attempt at discernment. Almost like he was going, *Shit, I didn't know I was a genius, but who am I to question that? I better put this speck of an idea in the movie.*

"For the next scene let's have some naked fat ladies running through. And a fire eater!"

With Nic Cage's help, I thought they'd ruined one of the best scripts I'd ever read. I know there are people who love that movie, but that was what I thought.

Anyway, that was how I ended up in the movie. I liked the script so much that I told Willem to tell David that if there was a little part in there for me, I would be happy to do it.

Willem is staying at a hotel called L'Ermitage. It is expensive. They have the best lamb sausages on the breakfast menu.

I have heard this many times since at hotels, but this is the first time I hear this thing, where you call to be connected to another room and they say, "My pleasure!" before connecting you. Feels strangely kinky.

The hotel must have staff meetings where they discuss the guests and how to stroke their egos. Because I come in at four in the morning and the security guy is walking my floor. I feel a little like I don't belong in this fancy hotel as he eyes me coming down the corridor.

He gets closer to me and starts to hum a Lounge Lizards tune. First, this guy really doesn't look like a Lounge Lizards fan, but the thing he is humming is from a record that has only been purchased by eleven people, and he doesn't look like he could be one of the eleven.

Willem is fun. He has to have these fucked up teeth and gums for the movie and he is wearing this plastic teeth thing all the time. He loves his plastic teeth thing. Sleeps with it in.

My first day, they ask if I would mind driving out to the set myself, and also, would I mind picking up Pruitt Taylor Vince? A production assistant will come to my hotel and show me the way to Pruitt's and then direct us to the set.

I say okay to this because I like Pruitt. I did a scene with him in *Down by Law* that got cut out of the movie. Pruitt at that time was a local New Orleans actor and trying very hard to get a break. I thought the scene was fantastic, particularly Pruitt. Benigni was like this times a thousand, but Pruitt was really an actor. Had it down. My acting was so hit or miss; it was not really what I did, and I always appreciated people who had acted enough that there was something solid about it. That they knew their way around a camera.

We drive over to Pruitt's place and it takes forty-five fucking minutes to get there. The PA goes into the apartment building to get him. Then the PA comes back and we wait another forty-five minutes for Pruitt to get his fat ass ready to come out of his house.

We drive out into the desert to where they are shooting. I can't remember exactly what it was. The scene is no longer in the movie. There is a band playing in a garage behind us and we are supposed to be yelling over the sound of the band. The band isn't actually playing. They are miming playing and the sound will be added later. So there is no sound to yell over.

Nobody yells.

Nic Cage comes in and talks in his normal voice and the guy answers him in a normal voice. When it comes my turn to speak, I'll be damned if I am suddenly going to be the one who is yelling, so I talk in my normal voice.

Lynch gets pissed at everybody for not yelling. We do the scene again and nobody yells.

They'll have to cut the scene because nobody is yelling. But that poor band, just like Pruitt in *Down by Law*. I know they were really psyched to be in the movie.

And I kind of owe them something. The guy playing the harmonica gave me the one he was playing. It was just perfectly broken in. It lasted for years and had a deep, rich sound. It is the one I used when playing the harmonica solo in "I'm a Doggy" on the Marvin Pontiac record.

I really wish I knew how to break a harmonica in like that one was.

We finish early. I can leave. But I have no idea how to get back.

I'm asked if I would mind waiting for Willem and could I drive back with him. They will return my car to me in a couple of hours, but they don't have a PA right at that moment.

I don't see it coming. They bring my car back at nine-thirty that night and it is drained completely of gas. That is just disgusting. I don't need to be treated like a movie star, but don't rip me off.

I had two scenes in the movie that were supposed to be shot on concurrent days and then I was going to fly back to New York. Except the next day I got a call that said they were moving my second scene to three weeks later.

I assumed that they were covering my hotel, but after a few days, I inquired about it and was told that they were only paying for the one day that I worked.

"Well, I am in your movie, I don't live here. What am I supposed to do?"

"Well, you could fly back to New York."

"Are you paying for the flight?"

"I'll have to check."

They refused to pay for the flight. Lynch was not to blame. I later found out that this was all per the producer Monty Montgomery, who had done a movie, *The Loveless*, that I had scored in 1981.

Man, I don't understand why they couldn't just be normal. They didn't need to treat me like I was treated as a model in Paris, nothing close to that, but they were going out of their way to show me how unimportant I was to them. What kind of sickness makes people behave like that?

So I moved over to the Chateau Marmont, which was much less expensive. I really didn't want to pay for a place where they had staff meetings to figure out how to stroke the guest's ego. The juxtaposition of that compared to how they were treating me on the movie would have confused me.

Natalia came over from Germany and we immediately got scabies at the Chateau. Scabies are hell to get rid of. They itch like mad and cause these raised welts all over your skin.

To get rid of them you have to paint yourself with this poison and then wash every fucking thing that you own. I am pretty sure that this was before the Chateau got bought by someone else.

So I have two and a half weeks to wait to do my scene. Natalia is hanging out with Donald Cammell and his beautiful wife, China. I am mostly hanging out at the hotel, watching TV. I guess I have fallen into a depression.

* * *

My band has somehow lost its soul, they are treating me like less than a nobody on the movie, and I still cannot get *Voice of Chunk* released in the United States. Nobody wants it.

I am a giant in Europe and Japan, but that doesn't seem to mean anything to anybody.

I saw Keith McNally at the airport in Paris. He owns or owned a lot of the hipper bars and restaurants in New York: Balthazar, Pravda, Nell's, Cafe Luxembourg, Odeon, etc.

The week Balthazar opened, Keith insisted that I stop by. I was sitting there when Donald Trump walked in. He was with a friend of mine's beautiful ex-wife, and they had only been divorced about a month.

The way Trump was parading her around for everyone to see pissed me off. So I had the waiter bring a glass of their cheapest wine to his table as a sign of my loathing.

Trump refused the wine, but I look back on this as some of my finest work.

As we waited for our planes, Keith McNally asked what was going on, why I was in Paris, and I told him, "My record *Voice of Chunk* is number two in Germany this week." I was pretty proud that a record I had paid for myself, and a jazz record no less, was number two.

Keith said, "Oh, really? Mine was number one," and walked away.

Mostly my mind is not quiet. I had tasted fame and I was addicted to it. For a long time, I wanted fame back. It took a shovel to the head in my life for me to realize that I was much better off without it.

But then, like a junkie. It is so like being a junkie. I need your fix. Oh, it is just sick.

Really what I wanted was respect for the music, as I do now for the paintings.

But I couldn't even get a deal for the *Voice of Chunk* record. I really wanted that music heard, and without some big injection of fame, it seemed that that would not happen.

It's late. I can't sleep and get up and turn on the TV in the other room, while Natalia sleeps. They are selling some idiotic product, a cat's collar that says "Meow" when you push a button, which you can only purchase via TV through the mail.

And then it hits me. I know what I am going to do next.

40

Fifteen Minutes Outside of Nairobi, There Are Giraffes

I get back to New York and explain to Val how I am going to become the Boxcar Willie of jazz.

Back then there were only a handful of channels on TV. And late at night there would be ad after ad for Boxcar Willie, a fake hobo who sang country music and made train noises with his voice. I couldn't imagine that the ads could be that expensive, because who the fuck buys a Boxcar Willie album at four in the morning?

"We're going to make an ad, maybe two. And then we are going to sell *Voice of Chunk* ourselves by phone with an eight hundred number. Fuck the music business."

This is late '89. There was no internet. This was the only way that I could think of to get people the music without having the gatekeepers involved.

There are always gatekeepers. More and more gatekeepers. And they have invented jobs that are shoved into the music and art and movie businesses. And all they seem to do is keep people who love the artist's work away from the artist's work, throw in worthless opinions, and somehow get paid to do that. It is all part of the Conspiracy to Maintain Mediocrity.

We shoot the commercial where Robert Burden had worked, which is a special place for me, but really only because of Robert and that he is no longer with us.

I say into the camera, "Hello, I'm John Lurie. And I am here to tell you that now you can listen to the strange and beautiful music of The Lounge Lizards, here in America, just like people in other lands."

I stand in front of a large painted scrim and the camera floats by me, with the music starting, and we dissolve to reveal Kazu, sitting all beautiful amid a pile of boxes from Chinatown and exotic ornaments, wearing a hat I had brought back from Bali, looking just as open as a soul can be. Then Veronica Webb in Moroccan garb, Gy Mirano as an Incan princess, and Rebecca Wright, standing bolt upright holding a spear, with the look of an invading Hun, in front of an Astroturf mountain covered with plastic sheep.

It cuts to a card with the information on it and Mercedes, New Orleans accent afloat, saying, "To order call 1-800-44-CHUNK," and then cuts back to me, looking very bewildered and saying, "Hello?" into a plastic phone. The girls are all gorgeous and it works pretty well.

It might seem odd that these were all ex-girlfriends and everyone got along so well. But it wasn't really odd at all, so you are odd to think that if that is what you are thinking.

The second spot is me, in an elegant robe that wasn't mine, lying in a bed surrounded by stuff: a cake with "Voice of Chunk" written on it, some plastic fish, my alto, some toys, and I don't know what else. The camera comes down slowly from above. I say: "If you're like me, you like to get things through the mail. Maybe because it makes me feel less lonely. Everything you see here I got through the mail."

Then the music swells, and I look up and smile. "Listen! That's the new Lounge Lizards record, *Voice of Chunk*, and now you can receive that through the mail!" Cut to the card with the info and then to Mercedes holding a phone and yelling like I'm in the other room, "John, another order!"

They were exotic and stupid. I was sure it would work. Val set the whole thing up. We got the 800 number, a place to manufacture the CDs, and a fulfillment company somewhere in Tulsa or Omaha. She also got the ads placed on TV, which was not so easy, because we were not part of a giant corporation and it was difficult to purchase ad space directly.

Around that time, I was living on my own. Kazu and I had had a fight about raisins in a chicken sandwich and she had moved out.

We shot the ads in early winter and planned to release the thing around January, after all the business was together.

It was a disaster.

The ad, which had looked quite beautiful, when it is broadcast on TV looks and sounds terrible. My ad would play and then a Coke ad would come on and all the colors are bursting and the sound is pristine. I discovered that if you were not a giant corporate sponsor, your ad was duped and duped again and then shuffled in with the corporate ads and duped again. And there was nothing I could do to fix it. All the color was drained out. The sound was gurgly and far away.

People came by my house to watch the first ad on TV. All drinking and not paying attention.

And the ad is on and off in thirty seconds. It is nothing.

I am broken. It looks awful. And no one even seems to notice.

They just say, "Hey, you're on TV!" and then go back to talking too loud about something else.

So I scream at someone for having their shoes on my bed and throw them all out.

But it was a disaster financially as well.

Not that people didn't order it. We sold thirty thousand copies in the United States, which for a jazz record was enormous and for an independent label was enormous, but it was not a well-run business.

The fulfillment company would sometimes send out empty packages. They would send five CDs when someone had only ordered one.

Every time someone called the 800 number there was an eighty-cent charge, and ours was really close to other numbers, so we got a slew of wrong numbers that cost us with each call.

Every time the ad would run on MTV, thousands of kids would call asking what kind of music it was. Eighty cents for every kid who called.

They would reach an operator in Tulsa who would read a description that was snippets from some of the best reviews.

I call, myself, to see how they do.

I ask what kind of music it is.

The woman, with that accent from wherever they sound like that, says, "The music from North Africa . . . with Mr. Cultrane. Mr. John Cultrane, is that right?"

"What?! What are you saying?! No! That is not right!"

"Cultrane?"

"No! It isn't Cultrane! Jesus fucking Christ!"

"Sir, please—"

Click.

I call again, get another operator with an equally bizarre description.

I yell at her and hang up.

I remind myself that every time I call it costs me eighty cents to yell at the operator.

I call back and try to explain how the description of the music should be read. I think part of the problem was that we sent several descriptions of the music. We had the Lester Bangs quote "Staking out new territory that lies somewhere west of Charles Mingus and east of Bernard Herrmann." I was always proud of that one, partly because it was Lester and partly because of how much I admire Mingus and Bernard Herrmann.

And we had the *DownBeat* quote "Music with character played by a bunch of wild characters." And something I had written, and something by this wonderful woman from the *Christian Science Monitor,* of all places, who really grasped the music. I think it was her quote, anyway, something about taking the music of Hendrix and Coltrane and melding it together and taking it a step further.

So I am going to call and explain to the operator how it should go.

She answers, "1-800-44-CHUNK."

She answers, like the others, with complete disinterest, which was not what I'd expected. I'd expected someone with a delightful enthusiasm. Of course, it is two in the morning wherever she is, this is most likely her second job as she raises her two kids, and she is probably the only person awake in whatever place I am calling.

I say, "Hello, where am I calling?"

"This is 1-800-44-CHUNK."

"Yes, I know that, but where are you?"

"I am in Wichita."

"Oh, I thought you were in Tulsa."

I am thinking that they have the same accent in Tulsa as they do in Wichita.

She explains that they have several operator stations scattered across the country but she doesn't really know.

And she also, clearly, doesn't care.

And I don't blame her.

I just started to feel sad for her.

I tried to explain what it was supposed to say, but she didn't believe it was my product. I was just some nut calling in. Which is exactly what I was. I was some nut calling in.

There was other stuff too. But once I had the idea and got it up and running, I wasn't interested in running the company, and oh fuck, what a disaster it was.

I was just so bummed by the whole thing. I put all my money and soul into making that record. And it ended the band. I really felt that they had abandoned me, more than I had done something to make things go like they did. And then no record company would touch it, even though every time we played we drew enormous crowds. And it moved people. It clearly made a difference. And now I was doing this and had lost all the rest of my money and couldn't make it work.

Maybe it was too beautiful. Maybe the Devil was trying to stop it.

I just wanted to put something into the world that touched people like Coltrane and many others had touched me. Like Martin Luther King's voice had touched me. And please, I am not comparing myself to any of this, but that was what I was hoping to do.

I have always been so jealous of Gaudí. I don't even know his story. I would just see his buildings in Barcelona and think, *How the fuck did this happen? They paid to let him make these weird, beautiful, unusual structures? No one tried to stop him? They gave him the money to make this stuff? What lucky fucking true artist ever gets in that position?*

Most "artists" who get themselves into that kind of position are usually good at one thing only: getting themselves into that kind of position.

I have been slow to learn this lesson. For a while, I was friends with Danny Elfman. He is certainly talented and has done some great music for film. But after talking with him several times when I was having trouble dealing with a movie producer or the agents that we shared, I realized his true genius was dealing with these people.

He knew how to do it. And I just fucking do not.

At the end of the eighties, for New Year's Eve 1989, I played a saxophone solo concert in Stuttgart.

Some of my solo concerts had been perfect. About a third of them were perfect.

If I had a half-decent sound system and the kind of venue that led to the audience being respectful to the music, like a theater rather than a nightclub, and if I allowed the space and silence to work for me instead of rushing to pour sound into every moment, it really could be like a perfect thing. A poem.

But the venue was so important. A year before, I had done a concert in a giant disco in Milan. Right before I went out onstage to play solo saxophone to three thousand standing people, they were blaring Donna Summer. It just didn't work. Of course it didn't work. It had to be in a theater, where people were seated and there to listen to music. It was a concert, and if some promoter was just trying to make money using my name, it could be a disaster.

That concert in Milan, they kept yelling out intelligent things like, "Are you Jack or Zack?," a line from *Down by Law*. It was awful.

But then the next night, in Torino, it was magic. Maybe the Shroud guided me through it.

So, to play New Year's Eve is a risk. People are out to have fun on New Year's Eve and I thought it was a bad idea, but the promoter and Val talked me into it. Val because of the money, and the promoter promised it would be a serious music venue.

There was a kid named Larry Wright who used to play drums on a compound bucket in Times Square. This sixteen-year-old kid could play stuff that would make you positive that there must be reincarnation, because it was shit that he just could not know about. African stuff and jazz stuff that he clearly had never heard, as he only listened to hip-hop.

What was particularly interesting and inexplicably complicated were his segues from one beat to the other. Where he was finding his next beat, that was where this stuff would come out that would just make me do a double take. "How does this kid know that?"

Ari Marcopoulos had made a short sixteen-millimeter movie about him and suggested that I take him to Stuttgart to open for me on New Year's Eve. I thought it was a great idea and said yes, but then Ari ran into some obstacles. Larry's parents were estranged, and my understanding was that his mother was a crackhead and his father was a junkie. Even though I was going to pay him a thousand dollars to play one night, and even though they claimed that they wanted him to go, they really didn't want him to go, because if he went to Germany for three or four days, they would not be collecting the sixty or eighty bucks a night that he was bringing home in quarters and crumpled dollar bills, which he collected playing on his bucket, in Times Square. And they needed their money regularly.

They said that they wanted Larry to go, but every time that Ari went up to Harlem to bring them to the passport office, because they had to sign for him, as he was a minor, they came up with an excuse as to why today was no good. And these two were not really doing anything with their days, except for waiting for Larry to come home with $60.

So finally Ari went up to their place with this large martial arts, community-minded guy who basically threatened them into letting Larry get his passport right away.

I should have known that a saxophone solo show on New Year's Eve was a mistake. The thing with the solos is that if I have the audience, I can relax and stretch it. I can play with them, hold back, not give them just what they want when they expect it, leave big silent pauses, play one note with a perfect tone and let it sit for a moment, and then take a sudden left turn.

But if they are not with me, if they are restless or noisy, then I tend to push and I am lost. I play too hard and too much and am exhausted after fifteen minutes.

This, on New Year's Eve, where they have paid quite a bit of money for their ticket, is a guaranteed way to make people feel ripped off, when the concert is only forty minutes long.

Before the show, Ari, Larry, Natalia, and I go out for New Year's Eve dinner. Larry couldn't be much more than five feet tall and he has one eye that is horribly crossed. In general, his behavior is perfect, polite, and not rambunctious at all. But he is a tough kid from Harlem, and if a six-foot-four German guy looks at him the wrong way, Larry is in his face and ready. This happens a bunch. There is something about this tough little black kid with crossed eyes that the German men find very entertaining and want to poke at. I think that someone is going to get killed.

We are at the restaurant and Larry orders fish. The restaurant is really good. I have to hand it to Natalia because this is just about the best food that I have ever eaten in Germany. She is also great with Larry.

Larry's fish comes and he looks at it. Takes his fork and plays with it for a minute.

Natalia says, "What's wrong, Larry? Don't you like your fish?"

"This ain't fish."

"Yes, Larry, of course it's fish."

"No it ain't."

"Taste it."

Larry takes a little bite of this beautiful piece of fish and spits it out.

"That ain't fish. Let's go."

Ari explains to Natalia that Larry has only had McDonald's Filet-O-Fish sandwiches and this is very unfamiliar to him.

Larry gets out there and plays on his compound bucket, which we have brought from New York. He is great.

Natalia and I went out to every toy store in Frankfurt and bought up all the tiny noisemakers for children, little plastic saxophones and clickers and tiny whistles, which were thrown out to the audience before the concert.

I go on at midnight, and as I approach the mic, I hear champagne corks popping. At that moment I know the music and energy of what I am about to do is not going to match the expectation or energy of the crowd. I don't know what I was thinking, playing a saxophone solo on New Year's Eve. Clearly what I am about to do is not going to be festive enough for the occasion. As I've said, I remember every bad concert that I ever did and this was one of them.

There are bits of that concert in the Ulli Pfau film *John Lurie: A Lounge Lizard Alone*. There are moments that show what the solo concerts could be. There is also footage of Natalia and me going around and buying the toy noisemakers.

I was kind of bummed out, but only for a minute, because the next day, Natalia and I went to Africa. I had gotten all my shots. We were flying from Stuttgart to Frankfurt and then on to Nairobi.

When we switched planes in Frankfurt, everyone's bag was out on the tarmac. You pointed at your bag and then they loaded it onto the plane. Except my bag wasn't there.

The man from Lufthansa said that was fine, that it would be on the next flight. I was a little worried because my anti-malaria medicine was in my bag and I had no idea if it was a real danger or not to not take it.

Natalia and I had decided to stay one night in Nairobi and then drive east, to the ocean, ending up somewhere near Mombasa.

When we arrived in Nairobi, I called Lufthansa to find that there was no next flight, that in two days there was a flight and that I could arrange to have my bag sent on to Mombasa.

How shocking to find out the airline employee on the tarmac had lied to me to speed things along.

We didn't know what we were doing. I found out later that there were forty-three different ways we could have been killed traveling unguided through the African jungle from Nairobi to Mombasa. I had assumed that Natalia knew the ins and outs of Africa, and she had assumed the same about me.

Kenya is amazing. One isn't fifteen minutes outside of the city before being hit with the primordial landscape. The vegetation stretches out against plains under a low sky, and it creates an atmosphere that can only be described as Africa. There is that thing—you can feel that life started there. And everywhere you look, there are animals.

Fifteen minutes outside of Nairobi there are giraffes and zebras, off a hundred yards to my left.

When we are almost there, maybe five miles outside of Mombasa, we get a flat tire. Natalia is impressed that I know how to change a tire. Well, not really impressed. She is surprised.

But we are in this little village that the road runs through, and the sun is going down. It is in that perfectly relaxed moment of the day when the sky spreads a kind warmth over everything. I lived for years in Grenada at the top of a very steep hill, and at sunset, you could see people's walks, particularly women's walks, change into something different. A saunter.

I think the time of day saves us. Because the people who walk by stare at us with open hostility.

And I am thinking, *Fuck, these people used to live right on the ocean, where life was good and food was plentiful, and then the white people pushed them out. Of course they hate us.*

When we get to Mombasa, there is a message that I can pick up my suitcase at the Mombasa airport.

We go over to the airport the next morning.

It is chaos.

There are crazy looking guys in makeshift uniforms with machine guns. They walk around and point their guns at people and yell. Like they are keeping order. But they are doing the opposite of that.

There are all kinds of animals. Everywhere. And lots and lots of chickens.

It is packed to the gills and there is no one anywhere to ask where I might be able to get my suitcase.

There is no Lufthansa counter. There is no information booth.

People are screaming at each other in Swahili.

A Muslim guy in a robe is walking five goats on leashes and is blocked by a Kenyan guy in shorts with no shirt with three goats. They yell at each other.

I turn to Natalia and ask, "Why do people bring their goats to the airport?"

She laughs pretty hard but doesn't answer. Any woman who laughs with a deep openness at the absurdity of life makes me love her immediately.

We push our way through the crowd looking for an information booth, or even just an airline counter, but there is nothing, only mayhem. Then, unguarded, just leaning against a post, is my suitcase, all by itself in the middle of the airport.

* * *

On the way back from Mombasa we zigzagged through the game parks. We saw a ten-foot snake and Natalia wanted to get out to catch it. I had to explain to her that it was a cobra.

She decided to take a shortcut, but it didn't look like a shortcut on the map to me. Really it was because we hadn't seen an elephant yet and she thought that this might be the way to find one.

That drive was magical.

I had been depressed for a long, long time. I couldn't get out of it.

Africa saved me. You can feel that life started there.

ACKNOWLEDGMENTS

Ben Greenberg
Nesrin Wolf
Loring Kemp